Political Survival in Pakistan

Presenting a framework that incorporates macro forces into micro-level strategic calculations by key agents, this book explains key political choices by leaders and challengers in Pakistan through the political survival mechanism. It offers an explanation for continuing polity weakness in the country, and describes how political survival shapes the choices made by the leaders and challengers.

Using a unique analysis that synthesizes theories of weak states, quasi-states and political survival, the book extends beyond the rationalist accounts and the application of choice-theoretical approaches to developing countries. It challenges the focus on ideology and suggests that diverse, religiously and ethnically defined affinity groups have interests that are represented in particular ways in weak state circumstances. Extensive interviews with decision-makers and polity-participants, as well as narrative accounts, allow the author to examine leaders' decision-making in a state bureaucratic machinery context and the complex mechanisms by which dissident affinity groups may support 'quasi-state' options. This study can be used for comparisons in Islamic contexts, and presents an interesting contribution to studies on South Asia as well as Political Theory.

Anas Malik is a political scientist at Xavier University, USA. His research interests include the political economy of development and political Islam, with a focus on South Asia and the Middle East.

Routledge advances in South Asian studies
Edited by Subrata K. Mitra
South Asia Institute, University of Heidelberg, Germany

South Asia, with its burgeoning, ethnically diverse population, soaring economies, and nuclear weapons, is an increasingly important region in the global context. The series, which builds on this complex, dynamic and volatile area, features innovative and original research on the region as a whole or on the countries. Its scope extends to scholarly works drawing on history, politics, development studies, sociology and economics of individual countries from the region as well those that take an interdisciplinary and comparative approach to the area as a whole or to a comparison of two or more countries from this region. In terms of theory and method, rather than basing itself on any one orthodoxy, the series draws broadly on the insights germane to area studies, as well as the tool kit of the social sciences in general, emphasizing comparison, the analysis of the structure and processes, and the application of qualitative and quantitative methods. The series welcomes submissions from established authors in the field as well as from young authors who have recently completed their doctoral dissertations.

1. Perception, Politics and Security in South Asia
The Compound Crisis of 1990
P.R. Chari, Pervaiz Iqbal Cheema and Stephen Philip Cohen

2. Coalition Politics and Hindu Nationalism
Edited by Katharine Adeney and Lawrence Saez

3. The Puzzle of India's Governance
Culture, context and comparative theory
Subrata K. Mitra

4. India's Nuclear Bomb and National Security
Karsten Frey

5. Starvation and India's Democracy
Dan Banik

6. Parliamentary Control and Government Accountability in South Asia
A comparative analysis of Bangladesh, India and Sri Lanka
Taiabur Rahman

7. Political Mobilisation and Democracy in India
States of emergency
Vernon Hewitt

8. Military Control in Pakistan
The parallel state
Mazhar Aziz

9. Sikh Nationalism and Identity in a Global Age
Giorgio Shani

10. The Tibetan Government-in-Exile
Politics at large
Stephanie Roemer

11. Trade Policy, Inequality and Performance in Indian Manufacturing
Kunal Sen

12. Democracy and Party Systems in Developing Countries
A comparative study
Clemens Spiess

13. War and Nationalism in South Asia
The Indian state and the Nagas
Marcus Franke

14. The Politics of Social Exclusion in India
Democracy at the crossroads
Edited by Harihar Bhattacharyya, Partha Sarka and Angshuman Kar

15. Party System Change in South India
Political entrepreneurs, patterns and processes
Andrew Wyatt

16. Dispossession and Resistance in India
The river and the rage
Alf Gunvald Nilsen

17. The Construction of History and Nationalism in India
Textbooks, controversies and politics
Sylvie Guichard

18. Political Survival in Pakistan
Beyond ideology
Anas Malik

Political Survival in Pakistan
Beyond ideology

Anas Malik

LONDON AND NEW YORK

First published 2011
by Routledge
2 Park Square, Milton Park, Abingdon, Oxfordshire OX14 4RN

Simultaneously published in the USA and Canada
by Routledge
711 Third Avenue, New York, NY 10017

First issued in paperback 2015

Routledge is an imprint of the Taylor & Francis Group, an informa business

© 2011 Anas Malik

Typeset in Times New Roman by Integra Software Services Pvt. Ltd, Pondicherry, India

All rights reserved. No part of this book may be reprinted or reproduced or
utilised in any form or by any electronic, mechanical, or other means,
now known or hereafter invented, including photocopying and recording,
or in any information storage or retrieval system, without permission in
writing from the publishers.

British Library Cataloguing in Publication Data
A catalogue record for this book is available from the British Library

Library of Congress Cataloging in Publication Data
Malik, Anas.
Political survival in Pakistan : beyond ideology / Anas Malik.
p. cm. -- (Routledge advances in South Asian studies ; 18)
Includes bibliographical references and index.
1. Political culture--Pakistan. 2. Pakistan--Politics and government--1988
I. Title.
JQ629.A91M35 2010
306.2095491--dc22
2010012726

ISBN 13: 978-1-138-94812-9 (pbk)
ISBN 13: 978-0-415-77924-1 (hbk)

Contents

List of diagrams   viii
Acknowledgements   ix
Abbreviations   x

1   Political survival in a weak state   1

Rulership, extraction, and the fiscal sociology of the state 6
Perspectives on state strength 8
Financing government expenditures: a "text-book" approach to
   government finance 10
   Taxation/domestic extraction 10
   Money creation/accommodational policies 10
   Borrowing/financing abroad 11
Shocks and extraction 12
Warmaking and statemaking: how wars affect
   state power 13
Nonwar IPE shocks and consequences for
   state power 15
Regime type and fiscal policy 16
Political survival and challengers in a strong society
   and weak state 17
   Affinities 21
   Groups and "groupness" 22
   Assessing "interests" 25
Method and data 25
Overview 28

2   Weak state, strong society, negotiable polity   30

Constitutional instability 38
Pakistan and Islam 40
Political parties 43
Disputed borders 45

vi *Contents*

Internal jurisdictions 46
Selection institutions and winning coalitions in Pakistan 53
    State institutions vs. government institutions 53
    Military and civil bureaucracy 54
    Landlords 62
    The "feudalism" debate 65
    Business 65
The current context 67

3 Leadership and extraction   70

Extraction in Pakistan: the early years 74
    International financing 76
    Taxation 77
    Land reform 79
The Ayub Khan regime (1958–1969) 80
    International financing 84
    Taxation 86
    Land reform 87
The Zulfikar Ali Bhutto regime (1971–1977) 88
    International financing 91
    Taxation 93
    Land reform 95
The Zia ul-Haq regime (1977–1988) 97
    International financing 99
    Taxation 100
    Land reform 102
Overview of money creation 102
Conclusion 104

4 Challengers in a weak polity   108

Jinnah as challenger/leader 117
East Pakistan and Mujib ur-Rehman 119
Zulfikar Ali Bhutto as challenger/leader 122
G. M. Syed and Jeay Sindh 124
Mumtaz Ali Bhutto 130
Challengers in Balochistan 132
Altaf Hussain and the MQM 135
Pushtun ethnonationalism 139
Religio-autonomism 140
Insurgency in the tribal areas 142
The search for new provinces: de jure quasi-states? 144
    Saraiki ethno-nationalism 145
    Northern areas 147
Conclusion 148

Contents   vii

5 Quasi-states, extraction, and governance

150

National leadership after Zia ul-Haq 152
Alternating Prime Ministers: Benazir Bhutto, Nawaz Sharif 155
Musharraf's rulership strategies 160
Caretaker governments 162
Administrative capacity and political will 163
Corruption and private benefits 171
Policing 173
Informal land allocation 175
Underground and parallel economies 176
Sectarian religious quasi-states 177
Devolution 181
Conclusion 184

6 Conclusion

187

Leadership and extraction 188
Challengers and quasi-state strategies 190
Incumbent extraction choices, quasi-state strategies,
  and governance 191
Internal and external actors 192
Islam and ethnicity 193
Leadership, developmental outcomes, and distributional
  coalitions 196
Institutional fragility 199
Political survival and political capacity 200
Fiscal reform and devolution 201
Class-based affinity groups 205
Altering the fiscal path 207

Notes	209
Bibliography	213
Index	226

Diagrams

1.1	Overview of shocks, suggested relationships	13
1.2	Basic challenger strategies	19
1.3	Challenger strategies in weak polities with quasi-states	20
3.1	Summary diagram of suggested extraction relationships	72
3.2	Average price of crude oil	93
4.1	Office-holding possibilities	109
5.1	A three-sided relationship	151

Acknowledgements

In the course of this project, I have incurred numerous debts of gratitude for support graciously offered and given. These include but are not limited to:

W. Abbasi, A.- W. Khan, the Lodhis, Nawaz and family, M. Alam, A. Abdullah, and many others for their assistance with interviews, contacts, and logistics in Pakistan.

My colleagues at Xavier University: James Buchanan, John Ray, Janice Walker, and Kandi Stinson, for continued support; Trudelle Thomas and Brennan Hill, for guidance on writing; Lindsey Ritzert and other library staff, for help with holding materials; Andrea Altman, for research assistance; and the Xavier Jesuit Community for their generous funding through a Faculty Fellowship.

Bill Thompson, for insisting on a case study; Quinn Mecham and the Middlebury College Clifford Symposium, for providing an opportunity to air early ideas; Bruce Bueno de Mesquita and Ahmet Kuru, for providing valuable comments along the way.

Dorothea Schaefter, Suzanne Richardson, and David Joseph, for cheerful guidance through the publishing process.

Marilyn Grobschmidt, Michael Thomas, and Saif Syed, for their friendship and advice.

And my family, near and far, particularly Abdul Malik, Razia Sultana, Saad, Aisha, and Intisar, for inspiration, encouragement, and love.

Anas Malik

Abbreviations

APDM	All Parties Democratic Movement
APMSO	All Pakistan Muhajir Student Organization
ANP	Awami National Party
BNP	Balochi National Party
CCI	Council of Common Interests
CENTO	Central Treaty Organization
COAS	Chief of Army Staff
CSP	Civil Service of Pakistan
FATA	Federally Administered Tribal Areas
FR	Frontier Region
FSF	Federal Security Force
IB	Intelligence Bureau
ISI	Inter-Services Intelligence
IJI	Islami Jamhuri Ittehad
IJT	Islami Jamiat-e-Talaba
IPE	International Political Economy
JSQM	Jeay Sindh Qaumi Mahaz
JUI	Jamiat Ulema-e-Islam
JUP	Jamiat Ulema-e-Pakistan
LOPS	Logic of Political Survival
MMA	Muttahida Majlis-e-Amal
MQM	Muhajir Qaumi Mahaz; name later changed to Muttahida Qaumi Movement
MRD	Movement for the Restoration of Democracy
NAP	National Awami Party
NSC	National Security Council
NSF	National Student Federation
PIU	Produce Index Unit
PML	Pakistan Muslim League
PNA	Pakistan National Alliance
PPP	Pakistan Peoples Party
SAARC	South Asian Association for Regional Cooperation
SEATO	South East Asia Treaty Organization
SMP	Sipah-e-Muhammad Pakistan
SSP	Sipah-e-Sahaba Pakistan
UP	Uttar Pradesh

1 Political survival in a weak state

"Politics," wrote Harold Lasswell, is about "who gets what, when, and how" (Lasswell, 1936). The logic of political survival assumes that political leaders seek to retain office and challengers seek to obtain it. The winning coalition on which an incumbent leader's position depends has consequences for tenure and governance. The underlying theory is elegant and has been elaborated in an award-winning work, *The Logic of Political Survival* (Bueno de Mesquita et al., 2003), henceforth *LOPS*. One vexing phenomenon is that leaders who preside over peace and prosperity have short-lived careers, while those that are corrupt, and preside over misery, have longer tenures in office. *LOPS* has an explanation: the former rely on a broad but fickle winning coalition, while the latter rely on narrow winning coalitions that reap private benefits and are more loyal to the incumbent. Highly institutionalized contexts (such as stable democracies) have recurrent patterns that offer more information about outcomes associated with particular choices. Bueno de Mesquita et al. (2003) have developed their theory based mainly on such contexts. Some have included political survival considerations in examining Middle East politics (Barnett, 1992; Solingen, 2007), and in relation to foreign aid and institutional change (Bueno de Mesquita and Smith, 2009a, b).

Compared with well-ordered polities with accepted frameworks for obtaining and transferring political authority, institutional roles in Pakistan are more easily violated. There are repeated attempts to rewrite basic rules of the game. According to *LOPS*, the leader's extraction of resources from society varies by regime type: autocratic leaders impose higher tax rates on polity members than democratically elected leaders. In Pakistan, tax rates are only one contested element; tax breaks and special licenses are key private goods that both elected and unelected leaders have offered. In the standard *LOPS* depiction, challengers can seek to replace the existing leader through normal or revolutionary means; in Pakistan, some challengers can seek to replace the national political leader, but also seek autonomy or secession, thereby undercutting the state's monopoly on extraction and coercion, or creating a new polity altogether. The Pakistani experience contributes to existing theory by generating hypotheses regarding leader and challenger behavior in weak states with strong but fractured societies.

Additionally, political survival mechanisms describe processes whereby Pakistan remains a weak state. Domestic extraction is hampered by the demand

2 *Political survival in Pakistan*

for private goods from a narrow winning coalition. Poor governance and political exclusion resulting from a dysfunctional fiscal sociology provide opportunities for challengers to pursue quasi-states. Suboptimal extraction, emerging quasi-states, and poor governance are mutually reinforcing, contemporaneous processes. The analysis suggests paths whereby weakness is potentially exacerbated to ensure state collapse and failure, and conversely, how the low extraction/quasi-state emergence cycle may be stalled or altered.

Extraction is a key state activity, as noted in numerous formulations (Levi, 1988; Organski et al., 1984; Tilly, 1990). Extraction strategy refers to the means by which rulers appropriate the financial resources needed to fund their policies. These means are broadly divided into taxation, non-tax revenues (including borrowing and foreign aid), and money creation. The strategy that is actually followed is usually some combination of these three. According to the "fiscal sociology of the state," broad-based extraction is associated with better governance and delivers more public goods in comparison with narrow-based or external rents-based systems (Moore, 2004). This view was elucidated by Joseph Schumpeter and found explicitly or by implication in the "rentier state" literature (e.g. Beblawi and Luciani, 1987; Mahdavy, 1970). High non-tax revenues (such as income from oil or foreign aid) provide resources for social spending and contribute to regime stability (Morrison, 2009). By helping circumvent the politically more risky taxation route of generating needed funds, non-tax revenues help support political survival. This in turn may perpetuate a weak fiscal skeleton and associated poor governance outcomes.

Pakistan is distinguished by a relatively narrow tax base and low tax effort. Moreover, Pakistan has had opportunities to invest in its extractive capacity, enhance its domestic extraction, and improve its bureaucratic apparatus. While there have been some incremental changes, major steps such as effective agricultural taxation and reform have not been taken. Furthermore, Pakistanis and Pakistan-observers often express concerns that the state is near failure or collapse, that it is already a failed state, or that it has failed at specific historical moments (e.g. Qureshi, 2005). Existing explanations have emphasized macro level forces such as the extraordinary defense burden on Pakistan, its lack of a unified indigenous nationalism, and philosophical problems with the idea of Pakistan (Cohen, 2004; Jalal, 1990; Nasr, 2001a). Other studies with a more individual-level focus have emphasized idiosyncratic personalities and unique historical circumstances (Talbot, 2005; Ziring, 1997). This book offers a framework that incorporates macro forces into micro strategic calculations by key agents and generalizes these based on the logic of political survival.

In analyzing Pakistan and similar contexts, ideology is often emphasized over strategic and tactical decision-making. This study questions the causal primacy ascribed to ideology and suggests that incumbents and challengers seek to manipulate religious and ethnic affinity groups in strategic ways responsive to weak state circumstances. Ideology in such contexts is not best understood as a handbook or guide to actual policies. Rather, ideology serves as an idiom for rationalizing policies and articulating interests, and for signaling an affinity between

Political survival in a weak state 3

group members. Ideologically diverse actors exploit common political opportunities, such as space for creating quasi-states, in similar ways. Path dependence matters; Pakistan's history has signaled to challengers that quasi-state and secessionist strategies can achieve results. The theoretical framework and hypotheses generated by this study suggest a mechanism by which quasi-states can emerge: a continuing fiscal crisis of the state, a governance vacuum, para-institutional proliferation, and autonomous extractive and security entities, bolstered by prior examples.

"Political survival" as a behavioral assumption about political leaders has been used by Barbara Geddes, Barry Ames, and implicitly or explicitly by Margaret Levi and Douglass North. The research program and particular theory described by Bueno de Mesquita et al. (2003) have developed some elements further, and have generally attempted to present a grand analytical model positing leadership behavior, public/private goods provision, institutions, and institutional change. *The Logic of Political Survival* uses formal logic, case histories, and other data to explain leadership tenure and policies.

This book offers an important theoretical extension to understanding political survival, increasing its explanatory reach. *LOPS* is focused on national-level political leadership within a well-defined, stable polity. The *LOPS* authors acknowledge that understanding political survival in non-democracies is in its infancy, demanding further study. I argue that the logic of political survival can be extended to weak states and fluid institutional environments. This is particularly appropriate where the state is predatory, and where challengers and "strongmen" can behave in a quasi-state fashion. Some key definitions are needed at this juncture.

Leadership is defined as "one or more central individuals with the authority to raise revenue and allocate resources" (Bueno de Mesquita et al., 2003: 38). Strictly speaking, this has to do with the authority to raise taxes and allocate funds to pursue chosen policies (Bueno de Mesquita et al., 2003: 39). Leaders seek to survive as their "primordial political goal" (Walker, 2004: 486). Leaders "want to keep their positions of power and privilege" (Bueno de Mesquita et al., 2003: 24). In certain cases, one policy option may help ensure an incumbent leader's political survival yet be suboptimal for most citizens, while another option may provide more benefits to more citizens yet be risky for the incumbent's political survival. In such cases, the incumbent's policy choice is usually the latter.

Challenger refers to prospective substitute leaders (Bueno de Mesquita et al., 2003: 38). Leaders face three threat categories: challenge from an internal candidate for leadership; revolutionary overthrow (which may undo or alter institutional arrangements with respect to leader-society relations); and external challenge. Revolutionary change in *LOPS* is seen as not qualitatively different from other internal challenges, but as having a difference in degree. Leadership is a coveted, competitive position in all societies, and leaders are concerned about challenges to their position.

According to *LOPS*, "the infinite variety of real-world institutional arrangements can be distilled to just two critical dimensions: the selectorate and the winning

4 *Political survival in Pakistan*

coalition" (Bueno de Mesquita et al., 2003: 42). The *selectorate* is "the set of people with a say in choosing leaders and with a prospect of gaining access to special privileges doled out by leaders"; the *winning coalition* is "the subgroup of the selectorate who maintain incumbents in office and in exchange receive special privileges" (Bueno de Mesquita et al., 2003: xi). To survive, the leader must generate and maintain a "winning coalition" within the "selectorate." The *disenfranchised* are those polity residents who are not in the selectorate, and who do not receive private goods. In a weak state with changing and unclear selection institutions, the precise distinction between the disenfranchised and the selectorate may be blurred.

How large the winning coalition is relative to the selectorate affects leaders' political survival and behavior. Bigger winning coalitions produce more public goods, which ultimately empower and expand societies in ways that people value. Public goods, in their ideal-type definition, are nonrival and non-excludable. Social infrastructure, external and internal security, the rule of law, equitable and universally applied tax structures, and transparency and accountability can be described as public goods. Public goods often reduce transaction costs and lower barriers to social exchange, enhancing productivity and well-being. Public goods provision may require collective support, or may be provided when hegemonic entities shoulder the burdens in the expectation they will enjoy net gains in their private cost-benefit calculus.[1]

A mantra from *LOPS* is: "good policy is bad politics and good politics is bad policy for small-coalition leaders" (Bueno de Mesquita et al., 2003: 325). For an incumbent leader who relies on a small winning coalition, providing public or majority goods does not carry significant political survival payoffs. In comparison, providing private goods to a narrow winning coalition helps retain support and ensure survival in office. (The corollary is that the good policy is good politics and bad policy is bad politics for large-coalition leaders.) This has consequences: giving aid to small-coalition leaders will likely increase corruption and greed. Another troubling tendency is that the large-coalition countries tend to intervene and support small-coalition leaders. The fact that Pakistan's military governments received significant international and particularly American financial assistance fits this pattern.

Pursuing political survival makes rational leaders seek and adopt policies that reward their winning coalition in order to maintain support. Resources are needed to retain key supporters. In democracies, the required winning coalition is proportionately larger, and this affects resource allocation. Where the winning coalition is larger, the rewards distributed to followers become difficult to distinguish from public goods. Resource distribution in democracies tends to be more equitable. In contrast, autocratic leaders' policies reward fewer citizens because their winning coalition is smaller, and because there is a clearer difference between private and public goods.

Autocratic leaders tend to stay in office about twice as long as democratic leaders (Holcombe, 2005: 456–457). One issue is how easy it is to mobilize a competing winning coalition. In democracies this is relatively easy, and support for any given leader is fragile, producing risk-aversion among leaders in foreign-policy decisions such as war-making (Walker, 2004: 487). The "loyalty norm" does not mean a norm in the New Institutionalist or Constructivist sense (i.e. as formal or informal rules that structure social interactions) but rather refers to loyalty to the current leader among winning coalition members. In small winning coalition systems, there is a high risk that supporters will be excluded from a successful challenger's future winning coalition; as a result, loyalty to the incumbent leader among his winning coalition members is also high.

What follows below are the theoretical bases for the logic of political survival in a weak state, specifically exploring leader choices regarding extraction and quasi-state opportunities for challengers.

Max Weber defined the "ideal-type" of the state as "an organization, composed of numerous agencies led and coordinated by the state's leadership (executive authority) that has the ability or authority to make and implement the binding rules for all the people as well as the parameters of rule making for other social organizations in a given territory using force if necessary to have its way" (as worded in Migdal, 1988: 19). Real states fit this description to greater and lesser extents. Thus, the state is an organization with primary authority in a given territory. The regime of a state describes the style according to which national politics are organized. Examples of such styles are the traditional categories of democracy and autocracy.

A regime is administered by the government, or the managers of the affairs of the state. The administration of a regime is centered on the chief executive and named after him. One regime may see several administrations (for example, succeeding rulers in a monarchy). This regime-administration distinction was used by Barry Ames in his work on Latin American politics (Ames, 1987). Chief executives and state managers engage in mainly short-term estimations of costs, although there is reason to consider variation in discount rates for the future (Barnett, 1992; Levi, 1988). Chief executives and administrations react to threats to survival. Such threats can be domestic and/or international in origin.

Irrespective of ideology, regime leaders strive to obtain revenues. Levi (1981) argues that regardless of particular values they may hold, all leaders seek resources from society. Levi makes the assumption of the rational, revenue-seeking ruler robust for ideologically driven, ostensibly "altruistic" leadership. Such leadership stamps its own particular vision of the "social good" as the substantive goal toward which its activities are rationally directed. Despite this, the ruler still seeks the same maximization of revenue as a means justified in terms of the requirements of ideological goals (Levi, 1981).

The *LOPS* perspective suggests that society's constraints on leader behavior are based on perceived threats to political survival. International society refers to all groups and organizations outside a country's borders that may possibly be a source of finance. This includes donor governments, international lending institutions, and other international agencies that may provide grants. The degree to which a leader's political survival is tied to a particular donor's willingness to provide aid helps

6 *Political survival in Pakistan*

determine the donor's influence on a leader's policies. In cases where such donor dependence is high, it is arguable that the donor, although formally outside the polity, is nevertheless for practical purposes a member of the winning coalition.

Rulership, extraction, and the fiscal sociology of the state

Prominent perspectives on the state describe resource extraction as a primary state activity. These are exemplified by authors from diverse disciplinary backgrounds, such as Organski et al. (1984), Evans (1989), North (1981), and Tilly (1985). Although these approaches range from rational choice to "sociological" in analytic origin, they converge on extraction as a central state process. A "fiscal sociology" paradigm links the mode of extraction to political development, and finds an early statement in Joseph Schumpeter's essay, "The Crisis of the Tax State," which describes the fiscal skeleton as key to understanding how societies and states evolve politically (Moore, 2004).

According to Organski et al. "any state must perform three principal functions: maintain national security (i.e. external defense and the repression of internal rebellion or disorder), collect resources to meet collective needs, and mobilize the population for national purposes" (Organski et al., 1984: 45). Taxing constituents is a fundamental activity of the state. The rise in central political power is closely correlated to a rise in taxation. "Because whatever governments may wish to do will require resources, the amount of revenues they extract can be used as an indication of the level of political power attained by central authorities" (Organski et al., 1984: 45). People resist taxation whenever possible and "the growth of the state is punctuated by rebellions against taxation in all its various forms" (Organski et al., 1984: 50).

Charles Tilly (1985: 181) argues that states engage in four basic activities. These are defined as follows:

1   War-making: Eliminating or neutralizing their own rivals outside the territories in which they have clear and continuous priority as wielders of force.
2   State-making: Eliminating or neutralizing their rivals inside those territories.
3   Protection: Eliminating or neutralizing the enemies of their clients.
4   Extraction: Acquiring the means of carrying out the first three activities—war-making, state-making, and protection (taken from Table 1.1 in Rasler and Thompson, 1989: 7).

Extraction is therefore a central activity of the state, providing the resources necessary to carry out the other three activities.

Evans (1989) distinguishes between a "developmental" state, which engages in entrepreneurship and plays a needed role in economic transformation, and a "predatory" or "rent-seeking" state, which extracts rents from the population as private gains for the leader and state functionaries and their clients. Resource extraction and reallocation is an integral activity in both predatory and developmental states. Zaire is an "exemplary predatory state" (Evans, 1989: 569) while Taiwan, South Korea, and Japan may be described as "developmental states" (Evans, 1989: 572). From a political survival perspective, a narrow winning coalition leader is more inclined to predatory behavior while a leader whose support rests on a broad winning coalition is more likely to be developmentally inclined. Polities that consistently require broad winning coalition-based leaders will more likely be developmentally inclined. If necessary, state resources are obtained directly in taxes from most of the population, then many among those taxpayers will be included in a winning coalition. When the winning coalition includes a high proportion of the population, leaders will provide more public goods. This is the fiscal sociological basis for a developmental rather than a predatory state.

Economic historian and Nobel Prize winner Douglas North defines the state as an organization with a "comparative advantage in violence, whose boundaries are determined by its power to tax constituents" (1981: 21). Central to understanding North's model of the state is the notion of the "potential use of violence to gain control over resources" (1981: 21). North's model of the state assumes a single wealth- or utility-maximizing ruler (1981: 23). One characteristic of this model is the exchange process between the ruler and the constituents; the state trades a group of services in return for revenue (1981: 23). The basic services provided by the state to constituents are the "rules of the game." The objectives of these are first, to provide a structure of property rights for "maximizing rents accruing to the ruler," and second, to "reduce transaction costs in order to foster maximum output of the society and, therefore, increase tax revenues accruing to the state" (1981: 24). North argues that "[o]ne cannot gain a useful understanding of the state divorced from property rights" (1981: 21). Property rights are essentially the "right to exclude" (1981: 21). Efficient property rights are prerequisites for sustained economic growth (North, 1981: 23). Yet states sometimes produce inefficient property rights.

The terms of exchange between the ruler and constituents are conditioned by two factors. First, the state seeks to act as a "discriminating monopolist, separating each group of constituents and devising property rights for each so as to maximize state revenue" (North, 1981: 23). Second, there are always potential rivals to the leader for providing the same set of services to constituents (these rivals may be external, such as other states, or internal, i.e. competing individuals within the state aspiring to rulership) (1981: 23–24). An alternative way of conceptualizing these conditions is that the "degree of monopoly power of the ruler" is "a function of the closeness of substitutes … [available to] the various groups of constituents" (1981: 23–24). Throughout North's work, the fact that microeconomics nomenclature is seen in terms such as "opportunity cost" and "monopoly power" is no accident; North's explicit aim is to create a theory of the state analogous to Ronald Coase's theory of the firm (Coase, 1937). To summarize, in North's model of the state, the latitude of action available to the ruler rests on the ability of his constituency to replace him. Leaders that are easy to replace have less autonomy than those who are harder to replace.

8 *Political survival in Pakistan*

Fiscal sociology looks at the far-reaching consequences and implications that fiscal policies and patterns have for sociopolitical development (Moore, 2004). According to Joseph Schumpeter's "The Crisis of the Tax State," rulers in the *demesne* (domain) state funded themselves from their own estates. In the tax state, rulers obtained funds through tax levies on private incomes and properties (Moore, 2004: 298). Broadly, levied taxes are linked to binding constraints on government and the institutionalized political representation that underlie liberal democracy. This fiscal social contract proposition has variants. There are "synergies" between the degree to which rulers depend on tax revenues, whether representative government emerges, and how the state performs in competition with other states. Political problems in Southern states are due to high dependence on natural resource rents (especially from oil and minerals) and strategic rents (especially foreign aid) instead of taxes (Moore, 2004: 299). If rents are removed so that rulers are forced to depend on tax revenue, will a "democraticness-accountability-state effectiveness dividend" follow? (Moore, 2004: 299). The answer to this question has practical policy implications.

In an argument that parallels the fiscal sociology tradition, Bueno de Mesquita and Smith (2009a) assert that "governments with access to revenue sources that require few labor inputs by the citizens, such as natural resource rents or foreign aid, reduce the provision of public goods and increase the odds of increased authoritarianism in the face of revolutionary pressures" (Bueno de Mesquita and Smith, 2009b: 167). Governments without such "unearned revenues" respond to revolutionary pressures by providing more public goods and democratizing (Bueno de Mesquita and Smith, 2009b: 167). Governments that rely on only a small segment in the polity for their resources of rule have an easier time repressing revolutionary opposition; governments that rely on many must accommodate their supporters with political concessions.

Foreign aid is one form that such "unearned revenues" can take, although brings with it donor expectations for recipient behavior. Despite its ostensible purposes, aid can actually reduce the incentive political leaders have to provide public goods. Due to its political survival consequences, "aid benefits donor and recipient leaders, while harming the recipient's, but not the donor's, citizenry" (Bueno de Mesquita and Smith, 2009b: 309). A political leader who obtains necessary resources through foreign aid does not have the same accountability to the domestic population as one who obtains resources through taxation. According to this logic, aid given for "development" spending may be counterproductive.

How a regime extracts resources can simultaneously reflect and stimulate state strength. Before I explore the deeper meaning of this statement, it is helpful to survey some views on state strength.

Perspectives on state strength

Efforts to identify strong and weak states sometimes produce disagreements due to differences in how scholars define state strength with respect to society. Opposing images of strength and weakness in states may be due to scholars that

Political survival in a weak state 9

"are looking for strength in different realms" (Migdal, 1988: 8). One focus is on state capacity for extraction, particularly direct taxation (e.g. Organski et al. 1984; Snider, 1996). Other dimensions include the degree to which a state is centralized, and the degree to which the state bureaucracy is partisan (Kuru, 2009). Other approaches emphasize the state's monopoly on violence and the power to coerce. A focus on "capabilities involving state penetration of society and extraction of resources" has occupied "proponents of the strong state image" (Migdal, 1988: 8). These researchers have examined taxation and related issues.

Advocates of "the weak state image, meanwhile, have examined capabilities involving regulation of social relationships and appropriation of resources in determined ways" (Migdal, 1988: 8). These scholars have looked at the state's efforts to transform society and implement policies. A related dimension is the strength enjoyed by actors in society. Weak states are often further constrained in their policy goals by strong social actors who represent alternative channels for determining who gets what, when, and how. Weak state depictions include references to the policy instruments at the state's disposal (Katzenstein, 1977) and the state's ability to change social structure or private behavior in intended ways as well as to resist private pressure (Krasner, 1978).

The distinction between political "will" and political "capacity" is often used to understand extraction behaviors. On the surface, it would appear that "capacity" is a structural constraint while "will" involves choice by a political leader. This distinction can be accurate in the extreme short term, but is misleading in other contexts because political will is needed to build capacity. Relative political extraction captures how a state performs in tax/GDP ratio relative to what would be predicted for that state based on per capita income, economic sector sizes, and other factors. Relative political extraction has been used as a key indicator for measuring political capacity (e.g. Snider, 1996). Previous weakness in extraction may indeed cause present and future weakness, but political survival mechanisms produce, underlie, and sustain it.

The *LOPS* focus, based on an established polity, is simply on the "tax rate." Presuming that the capacity to tax is equivalent, *LOPS* predicts that autocrats are likely to pursue a higher tax rate. In weak states, however, tax collection is itself a problem, and a developmental challenge. All extraction strategies are not equal; some produce more public goods and others more private goods. There is also reason to think that most small winning coalition governments will pursue an extraction strategy that has more "public bad" than "public good" consequences, and will likely keep states weak. Large winning coalition governments may be better placed to pursue an expanded taxable capacity. Political survival considerations drive short-term choices that have long-term development impacts. Extending the *LOPS* approach offers a key mechanism for assessing why some states enjoy sounder fiscal policy, tax reform, and efficient property rights. Understanding these connections requires, first, an understanding of how fiscal policy works generally in developing countries.

10 *Political survival in Pakistan*

Financing government expenditures: a "text-book" approach to government finance

Although the political economy of public finance policies of developed countries has received substantive empirical attention, less empirical work has been done on the political determinants of fiscal policy in developing countries (Roubini, 1991). In a general textbook-style survey work, Richard Goode (1984) outlines issues of government budgeting, taxation, spending, money creation, and borrowing with special reference to developing countries. There are three major channels for financing government activities. These are taxation, borrowing, and money creation. The three are not mutually exclusive policy choices. Rather, they can be engaged in simultaneously.

Taxation/domestic extraction

A "tax" is defined as a "compulsory contribution to government made without reference to a particular benefit received by the taxpayer" (Goode, 1984: 75). The ratio of tax revenue to GNP or GDP is a customary measure of the level of taxation (Goode, 1984: 84). Determinants of tax ratio are the demand for government expenditures, the availability of non-tax sources of finance (such as borrowing and money creation) and the willingness to use these, and the taxable capacity of the country (Goode, 1984: 84). A useful distinction is that of "taxable capacity" and "tax effort." "Taxable capacity depends on the ability of the people to pay and the ability of the government to collect. Tax effort is the degree to which taxable capacity is used" (Goode, 1984: 84). All taxation is not equal: direct taxes usually require more bureaucratic wherewithal, and are associated with greater state strength, while indirect taxes are easier to collect but require a smaller proportion of the polity to interface directly with state agents.

Money creation/accommodational policies

Money creation occurs when a government finances its expenditures "by additional currency or bank deposits that are transferable and generally acceptable in domestic transactions" (Goode, 1984: 212). Seignorage in the form of printing money is a tangible act of money creation. Frequently, money creation takes the form of legal borrowing from the central bank. This results in net addition to the money stock (this may possibly also be the case in government borrowing from commercial banks, but this relationship is less clear) (Goode, 1984: 212–213). Central bank independence matters in shaping extraction, particularly in monetary policy (Eijffinger and de Haan, 1996). Autonomous central bank governors are less likely to be pressured to engage in money creation policies for the incumbent's political expediency.

In some ways, money creation is close to the "accommodationist" policy route suggested by Barnett (1992) as the first policy choice of all regimes. The accommodationist route is first chosen because it is easy to employ and uses existing monetary and fiscal instruments. Money creation fits this description. Furthermore, money creation has an element of disguise in it. It is possible that the public does not immediately catch on to this policy activity. Weak governments are especially attracted to this option. Goode (drawing on Keynes' *Tract on Monetary Reform* (1971)) describes policies of money creation in the following way:

> Financing by money creation appeals to a weak government. Unlike taxation, no administrative machinery is required and no administrative cost is incurred. The process is impersonal and at first usually unnoticed. Adverse incentive effects are not apparent.
>
> (Goode, 1984: 214)

Thus, the relatively unobtrusive nature of money creation and its ease of implementation make it appealing for weak governments in particular.

The main effect of "large and continuing" money creation is inflation (Goode, 1984: 213). (Balance of payments deficits are another effect, but these are constrained by the availability of foreign exchange reserves and international credit (Goode, 1984: 213)). (A substantial literature exists on the effects of inflation on deficits. Additionally, inflation has the potential to affect tax revenues and it has multiple effects on various parts of the economy. The net political consequences of inflation are ambiguous (Goode, 1984: 229)). Rapid increases in consumer prices without swift, corresponding wage increases will likely feed public discontent, particularly in countries where significant numbers live on the poverty line.

Borrowing/financing abroad

The public debt burden is widely considered to increase fiscal requirements (e.g. Snider, 1996). Few opportunities for non-bank domestic borrowing exist in developing countries. Goode (1984: 198) provides some reasons for this. Borrowing from abroad is different from domestic borrowing "in that it gives the borrowing country command over more goods than it is currently producing" (Goode, 1984: 203) and is more than a simple redistribution between public and private sectors (Interview with Ishrat Husain, former Governor of State Bank of Pakistan, 2009). (Repayment and debt-servicing requires a transfer of resources out of the country, which is not the case with domestic borrowing.) Domestic borrowing from the public raises interest rates, squeezes spending elsewhere, and is not sustainable as a strategy beyond the short term (Interview with a former finance official, 2001).

Goode suggests that borrowing may be "advisable to meet an emergency that would otherwise require a sharp increase in taxation" (Goode, 1984: 197). This lends support to the idea that in times of heightened fiscal requirements, governments face a choice of finance strategies. They can create money, increase taxes, or obtain resources from abroad, by borrowing or otherwise.

12 *Political survival in Pakistan*

Shocks and extraction

Shocks have the potential to become critical junctures and produce major changes in regime policy. Many scholars have pointed to war and international crises as promoters of domestic institutional change. These include Evans et al. (1985), Ikenberry (1988), North (1981), and Rasler and Thompson (1989). Barnett (1992) argues that wars and other international crises produce the potential for radical changes in policy by opening up the policy process and allowing the expression of different policy proposals by new groups. Both "state and domestic actors recognize that crisis politics demand a deviation from the routine to satisfactorily confront the exceptional challenge" (Barnett, 1992: 251). Furthermore, standard operating procedures and habitual ways of dealing with problems are not up to the task of dealing with a crisis. Therefore, decision-makers are more likely to find new alternatives as well as overcome social and bureaucratic opposition and inertia (Barnett, 1992: 251).

The definition of international shocks used here is those exogenous events that have the potential to result in radical increases in fiscal requirements. In certain cases these drive major changes in public finance government policy. A war, in particular, is significant because it presents an immediate external threat. As Barnett puts it, "where war is ongoing, intense, and life-threatening, governments may be [...] more willing to extract from their societies" (Barnett, 1992: 288, note 60).[2] Other international shocks include changes in international credit and other markets. By dramatically reducing the flow of capital into a state, these shocks also have the potential to produce radical changes in the fiscal requirements of states (Snider, 1996: 93).

A useful subclassification of shocks is to divide them into shocks to spending and shocks to revenues (Roubini, 1991). Shocks to spending occur when the spending needs of the state are suddenly increased. Shocks to revenues occur when some outside factor, frequently economic, cuts into the base from which government revenues are obtained. This produces a revenue shortfall. Wars can be classified as shocks to spending, and international economic shocks can be thought of as revenue shocks, but neither fit exclusively into these categories. In other words, it is conceivable that wars produce a national emergency in which the normal economic functioning of society is impaired so there is a shock to revenues. It is also conceivable that an international economic shock may produce a shock to spending, such as an oil price rise that necessitates higher payments or an expensive shift to a different energy source.

In certain conditions, external shocks drive state attempts to increase extractive capacity, which in turn has implications for state power with respect to society. The sources from which states derive the revenues they need to operate have a significant influence on state-society relations. State-society relations are based on an implicit bargain or contract under which the taxes and compliance from the citizenry have been traded for the security and order provided by the state. International political economic shocks sometimes spur states to alter their sources of revenue, and in particular to seek increases in extractive capacity. IPE shocks also have the potential to directly affect society. This implies a remaking of state-society relations.

Political survival in a weak state 13

In diagram form, this linkage may be outlined as follows:

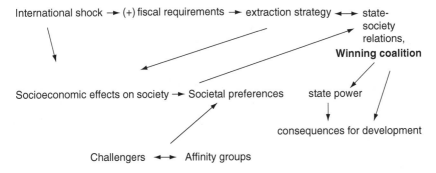

Diagram 1.1 Overview of shocks, suggested relationships

Warmaking and statemaking: how wars affect state power

The tendency for state-building results from the outside environment in which states are situated. In brief, "[a] prime motivation for state leaders to attempt to stretch the state's rule-making domain within its formal boundaries, even with all the risks that has entailed, has been to build sufficient clout to survive the dangers posed by those outside its boundaries, from the world of states" (Migdal, 1988: 21). War involvements are times when external dangers become especially prominent and have the potential to spark efforts to build state power.

Barnett summarizes the "warmaking-statemaking" argument as follows:

> A security threat forces the state, owing to its pivotal role as defender of the country's borders, to mobilize the required material and human resources, and to take extraordinary measures, both politically and economically, to confront these foreign challenges. The end of hostilities does not, however, signal the state's withdrawal to its prewar stance, as these new-found procedures became a permanent part of its policy arsenal and thereby contribute to the expansion of the state apparatus and its control over society.
>
> (Barnett, 1992: 258)

State power is thus "a beneficiary of war," a condition "best evaluated by examining [the state's] capacity to implement and extract from society" (Barnett, 1992: 258).

A key focus in Barnett's argument is his description of financial policy:

> The government's financial policy is shaped by both the underlying distribution of societal power and the state's institutional capacities that enable it to penetrate, extract from, and monitor society. [...] [A]ll state managers are attentive to and constrained by the flow of resources upon which the deployment of the state's means depends, and the ability either to develop alternative

14 *Political survival in Pakistan*

sources of financial means or to loosen its dependence on the capitalist class substantially increases its autonomy. This independence may come from either the acquisition of foreign loans, which might give the state an additional instrument of control over society, or a fiscal crisis of the state, which might compel the government to devise new fiscal strategies.

(Barnett, 1992: 27)

An important factor in the "underlying distribution of societal power" is how challenges to the incumbent arise, and the positions taken by challengers. In a weak state with low institutionalization, challengers have routes to ascendancy not considered in the political survival calculations of leaders in well-institutionalized, stable polities. These options are described in more detail below. Barnett suggests that when faced with the need to raise resources, states will try "to mobilize the required resources at a minimal level of political cost" (Barnett, 1992: 31). The shape of political challenge influences strategic calculations regarding political costs. Resources can be mobilized through accommodational, restructural, and international strategies.

The accommodational strategy relies on "already existing policy instruments" and modest changes in those instruments. This relatively routine action preserves the status quo and therefore carries few political costs. This strategy is "invariably" the state's initial approach (Barnett, 1992: 31). Money creation as described by Goode (1984) would be an accommodational strategy. Truly radical money creation (such as the printing of currency in the Weimar Republic) is not the relatively unobtrusive accommodational policy envisioned by Barnett (1992). Such drastic actions are too exceptional to warrant special treatment of money creation activities as non-accommodational or possibly even restructural policies. Instead, money creation will generally be treated as an "accommodational" policy.

In the restructural strategy, "state managers attempt to restructure the present state-society compact in order to increase the total amount of financial, productive, and manpower resources available to state officials" (Barnett, 1992: 32). Restructuring can follow a "centralization" scenario in which the state increases its direct control over societal resources, through such measures as introducing direct taxation (Barnett, 1992: 32). Alternatively, it can follow a "'liberalization' scenario, in which the state disengages from or withdraws control over society and economy to increase the societal contribution" (Barnett, 1992: 32). The objective of both tactics is to increase the proportion of social resources at the disposal of the state.

The international strategy involves "attempts to distribute the costs of war onto foreign actors" (Barnett, 1992: 33). The international strategy appears to be the most appealing from the standpoint of domestic political stability. The availability and sufficiency of external arrangements limit the implementation of this strategy (Barnett, 1992: 33).

Barnett (1992) suggests that leaders' extraction preferences are guided by two objectives. The first is war preparation. This involves mobilizing financial resources, the actual instruments of warfare, and personnel (Barnett, 1992: 21). The second objective is political stability, meaning protection from domestic

Political survival in a weak state 15

challenges to rule (Barnett, 1992: 22). When these two objectives conflict, one may have to be privileged. Political "Realists" (in the academic discipline of international relations) suggest that external security will take precedence. An alternative view, based on the observation that state survival has been "virtually guaranteed" by the sovereignty principle, suggests that state managers, concerned with their own survival, will privilege domestic stability over war preparation (Barnett, 1992: 24–5).

It is arguable that in the modern era, except under those very rare circumstances in which state survival is threatened, concerns for domestic stability will always take precedence. The incumbent regime's private interests may diverge from the "public interest," the "national interest," and the interests of future regimes. For example, if a regime feels that it is not negatively constrained domestically, or can avoid domestic repercussions, it will borrow hugely and mortgage its future in the knowledge that the costs of such borrowing will be borne by other, future regimes. In contrast, a regime that faces accountability for failing to be a more balanced fiscal performer will be more likely to pursue greater domestic taxation.

Regimes will subvert all other objectives to political survival when they are threatened and in danger of being replaced, because "[n]o agenda is worth anything if its sponsor has not lasted through the hazards of politics" (Migdal, 1988: 226). In other words, survival overwhelms other preferences as a value for incumbent leaders. During wars and other periods where fiscal requirements are heightened, leaders must undertake initiatives to meet costs. Extracting additional resources domestically is a politically sensitive act likely to generate opposition. As a result, regime leaders will try to export the costs of adjustment. International strategies will usually be preferred to domestic extraction.

Nonwar IPE shocks and consequences for state power

An IPE shock happens when flows of external capital are drastically reduced or cut off entirely (Snider, 1996: 10). External shocks can produce revenue crises of two kinds: liquidity crises and solvency crises. The revenue structure and level of political capacity determine whether an IPE shock becomes a liquidity crisis or a solvency crisis. Both liquidity and solvency crises are fiscal crises—government revenue falls far short of expenditures. Both are subcategories of Roubini's "revenue shocks," meaning a shortfall in revenues collected (Roubini, 1991). The crises differ qualitatively in the respective policy solutions demanded by each.

Regimes address a liquidity problem with a "short-term 'quick-fix' package of measures designed to remedy a foreign exchange shortage [...] [t]he standard set of instruments includes fiscal austerity, credit ceilings and raising domestic interest rates" (Snider, 1996: 11). Solutions to liquidity crises involve short-term macro-economic policies. Solvency problems need these measures as well as longer-term structural adjustment, including such measures as trade liberalization, deregulation of commerce, and tax reform (Snider, 1996: 12). Solutions to a solvency crisis are "medium term" and require deep structural changes.

Despite the differing demands on regime economic policies, both liquidity and solvency crises increase fiscal requirements and therefore have the potential to

16 *Political survival in Pakistan*

drive efforts by the regime to generate revenues and cover financial shortfall. When faced with an IPE shock-based revenue crisis and its associated fiscal requirements, regimes have at least three options, which may be implemented exclusively or in conjunction with each other. The first is to seek resources internationally, whether through foreign aid, IMF aid, or more external debt through other forms of international borrowing. The second is to restructure domestically and extract more from the population. The third is to engage in minor domestic changes using existing instruments of fiscal and monetary policy. The theoretically possible options for financing regime expenditures are thus identical to the options available in the case of a war crisis. To the extent that domestic restructuring is chosen as a policy activity, and given that domestic restructuring typically produces an increase in the power of the state, IPE shocks have the potential to produce an increase in state power.

Both IPE and war shocks have the potential to change the fiscal requirements of states and thereby affect regime extraction strategies. However, there are qualitative distinctions between the two. If a country has strategic value to capital-rich outsiders, the regime may be able to obtain international financing in the context of IPE shocks. Additionally, wars may run counter to the interests of foreign aid donors, who would then act to reduce the amount of international funds available to combatants. In other words, other nations could cut off regime financing to prevent wars from continuing, creating simultaneous war and IPE shocks.

Regime type and fiscal policy

The *LOPS* argument regarding winning coalition size and leaders' policies can be situated in literature on regime type and extraction. The *LOPS* authors carefully note that "large-coalition" systems are not automatically equated to democracy and small-coalition systems cannot be equated to autocracy. Some definitions, however, seem to fit *LOPS* rather well. For example, Levi's distinction between autocracy and democracy is that these political conditions are "a reflection of the proportion of the population who are part of the contract every ruler must make with the supporters on whom his power depends" (Levi, 1981: 4). Regime types are a continuum and are distinguished by the extent of this contract. A contract with a very narrow segment of society represents an autocracy while a contract with a broad segment of society is typical of democracies. A contract implies "buying off" a segment of the population instead of coercing it into acquiescence. Levi's approach is helpful in understanding Olson's perspective, detailed below.

Olson (1993) argues that taxation is generally likely to be higher in autocracies than in democracies. Autocrats depend on a small population segment, and therefore can retain office by buying off that group, and maximizing tax revenues for the autocrat's own uses. Democratically elected leaders depend on the majority of the population, and are constrained by the majority's wish for a lower tax rate. This reasoning does not work well in transitional and unstable polities, where there may never have been a successful second election in which the

Political survival in a weak state 17

taxation principle could be tested and learned at the polls. Nevertheless, there are some important insights that can be gained from looking at civilian regimes in comparison to military regimes; civilian regimes typically rest on a broader winning coalition, although one that may still be rather narrower than the majority of the population.

Organski (1997) suggests that more limits on the power of government elites mean higher political costs of taxation but lower economic costs of borrowing. Closer to the autocratic end of the political spectrum, it is relatively easy in terms of political costs for elites to extract resources in the form of taxes. Because of low limits on their power, state elites face difficulties in offering security against the possibility that they will arbitrarily renege on debts. The *LOPS* authors, however, point to an additional dimension that complicates this: small-coalition-based leaders tend to obtain greater international aid than large-coalition-based leaders (Bueno de Mesquita et al., 2003).

Thus, various possible linkages between regime type and extraction strategy have been articulated in the theoretical and empirical literature. The "tax rate" discussion in *LOPS* presumes an established tax system, where the distinguishing policy decisions between rivals for political office is their preferred tax rate. But in weak states, the question is not the tax rate per se, which may be unenforceable in most circumstances, due to poor policing and enforcement mechanisms. Instead, the key question is likely to be whether the state attempts to expand the tax base, bring more people in society into the tax net, and thereby build political capacity. This is usually politically risky, but there are junctures at which it becomes much easier—usually during a war emergency or another threat to national survival. If extractive capacity is not developed at those times, it is not likely to be developed at any time. Here, increasing the tax base, or expanding the tax net, is itself a public good, because it expands the state's reach, and forms the basis for what North would call "efficient property rights" (North, 1981). While *LOPS* presumes a lower tax rate is better for society in weak states, my argument is that an expanded, equitable tax base is better for society, development, and prosperity.

Extraction choices by leaders offer one dimension in political development. A corollary is the effort by challengers to obtain office and make changes. How this works in a weak state requires elaboration, which is offered below.

Political survival and challengers in a strong society and weak state

Migdal (1988) suggested that weak states often have strong societies. "Strongmen" are powerful political agents that exert influence and constrain the state's ability to extract and allocate resources. Local strongmen's activities represent alternative and sometimes rival governance mechanisms to the state. "Strong society" does not necessarily mean large, unified social groups; rather, linguistic, sectarian, or other ethnic divisions may fractionalize society. "Strongmen" may compete with both the state and with each other for influence and authority.

18 *Political survival in Pakistan*

A related theoretical problem for *LOPS* in weak states is that the polity's boundaries are often fluid and unclear. This makes political calculation more hazardous and uncertain. The lines between "internal" and "external" threats are blurred. This "boundary problem" is replicated in different iterations, and illustrates how "reality" is socially constructed. If enough participants agree to a certain border, the border exists. If the border is enforced, it exists. If challenges to the border are successfully repulsed or deterred, the border exists.

Traditionally, political scientists have used domestic hierarchy and international anarchy to distinguish politics *within* countries from politics *between* countries. This has been the basis for the subdisciplinary divide between comparative and international politics. These differences become meager in very weak states, where something approaching anarchy may reign. A country may have a flag, UN membership, an anthem, a sovereign investment risk rating, the ability to issue bonds and borrow on international markets, and a sovereign government without formal anarchy, but still experience effective anarchy within its territory. Anarchy is not a constant or a binary; there may be greater or lesser degrees of it in different areas, and this can change over time. Very weak or failed states may be functional anarchies and resemble miniature international systems. Because individuals are easier to eliminate than states, domestic anarchy may be more severe than international anarchy in terms of the security dilemmas that are generated (Kasfir, 2004: 61).

The Logic of Political Survival has been written for contexts where the rules of the game and actor roles and choices are relatively clear. There are other contexts where political survival is a key goal but the rules of the game are not clear. According to *LOPS*, challengers can pursue either a "normal" challenge, seeking to create a winning coalition within the existing rules, or a "revolutionary" challenge, seeking to reorder the polity in ways that favor the challenger, and includes new groups into the selectorate and winning coalition. Crucially, in a weakly institutionalized polity without well-established rules and selection mechanisms, the line between "normal" and "revolutionary" is hazy. Challengers and leaders routinely seek to reorder the polity in ways that favor their political survival.

According to *LOPS*, challengers can pursue numerous strategies. They can try to replace the national leader by creating an alternative winning coalition, and encouraging defections from the existing coalition. In a system that allows political parties, challengers may seek to lead an opposition party. They can try to pose a revolutionary challenge, an effort to unseat the existing political order so that the politically excluded become the included. Revolutionary struggles pit disenfranchised individuals seeking to change the system against selectorate members who seek to retain the system. Selectorate members are likely to defend the existing system, because they receive private benefits or believe that in the future they may receive private benefits (Bueno de Mesquita et al., 2003: 368).

A "quasi-state" refers to an entity that to varying degrees engages in war-making (eliminating external rivals), state-making (eliminating internal rivals), protection (protecting their clients' interests), and extraction (locating the means for these activities). These are key elements in what Charles Tilly (1985) counts as state activities. A quasi-state strategy significantly complicates and adds to the menu for choice that challengers have in weak polities. If the state is Hobbes' "Leviathan," then in a weak state, it coexists with what might be termed "levia*thins*"—state-like entities that sometimes directly clash with the Leviathan.

Leviathins represent political opportunities for challengers that are not captured in political survival theory in its present form. Furthermore, quasi-state Leviathins often pursue autonomy or secession, adding a strategy not identified in *LOPS* except under the broad "revolutionary change" rubric. "Leviathins" are typically less powerful than the Leviathan, but may be stronger in some battlegrounds and contexts. The Leviathan may fight the leviathins, coopt the leviathins as intermediaries in state-society relations, or be indifferent and allow leviathins to coexist. Leviathins have to survive, and might want to remove the Leviathan—or carve out a secure space where the Leviathan will have a hard time displacing them. Leviathin entities frequently gain legitimacy by providing state-like services to their constituents. They operate in environments of weak institutionalization, ineffective legal systems, and near-anarchy where the whims of the powerful easily overwhelm the appeals for justice or order made by the disempowered.

A challenger has political opportunities and options provided by a weak state context. Selection institutions are not well established, and it is easier to try to alter these. The bar to pursuing revolutionary options is lower. A local quasi-state might not be revolutionary if it preserves the existing "selectorate/winning coalition" at the national level. But quasi-states do generally erode state power, as they are parallel jurisdictions that may both rival and serve existing leaders. When a quasi-state leader pushes for secession, however, it does become revolutionary.

According to *LOPS*, a challenger may seek office within an existing polity, or seek to rewrite basic rules through revolutionary change. This may be represented as follows:

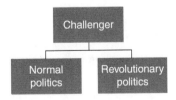

Diagram 1.2 Basic challenger strategies

In weak polities, the line between normal and revolutionary politics is fuzzy, and a third option is present. A challenger may be able to create a quasi-state and simultaneously pursue normal and revolutionary politics. This may be represented as follows:

20 Political survival in Pakistan

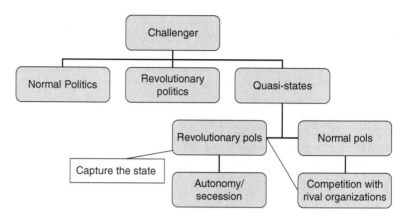

Diagram 1.3 Challenger strategies in weak polities with quasi-states

In Diagram 1.2, the challenger choice is to contest based on revolutionary or normal politics. In a weak state, a challenger has a third option—to build or control a quasi-state, and then to participate in revolutionary or normal politics; or to engage in normal or revolutionary politics without a quasi-state. These are not mutually exclusive options. Establishing a "quasi-state" might be a step to capturing the state, perhaps by precipitating a civil war in which the state loses and the quasi-state takes over and absorbs state offices. Or establishing a quasi-state might provide the resources needed to field candidates for leadership or other office in the state.

Some challengers have relatively little "war-making" and "state-making" activities. They nevertheless pursue autonomy or secession, and try to exert pressure that will redraw state borders or alter domestic jurisdictions. De jure quasi-states are challenger-led autonomist groups who press their claims through existing institutional channels in a polity. The weakest de jure quasi-states are little more than vocal secessionist postures by small groups. But they nevertheless exist, because challengers recognize that there is possible political opportunity—greater authority within a particular jurisdiction, and/or more benefits as the state coopts the challenger.

In contrast, de facto quasi-states are those that extract revenues, and engage in war-making, state-making, and protection behaviors but do not necessarily press their claims in an articulated fashion within the polity. Some de facto quasi-states are difficult to distinguish from criminal organizations. Tilly (1985) has argued that protection rackets resemble war-making/state-making activities. De facto quasi-states may or may not pursue de jure autonomism. In practise, both de jure and de facto elements may be found in quasi-states to different degrees. A successful de jure appeal may produce secession and formal sovereignty, or a new agreement on autonomy and devolution.

Challengers can pursue normal politics or revolutionary politics, and decide whether, how, and where to deploy quasi-state action. Choices are uncertain and may be reversible. Challengers will pursue the action that best meets their political survival goals. Quasi-state options are particularly attractive to those challengers that believe their prospects for leadership within the existing polity are blocked. In choosing quasi-state options, they must consider affinity groups, rivals, and the leader, as well as prospective alliances. The quasi-state presents a political opportunity for challengers that may be pursued when these other factors present a strategic calculus. Quasi-state leaders may not be "challengers" in the strict sense that they seek to replace an existing leader; they may be quite willing to forgo direct challenges to an incumbent in return for autonomy over their quasi-state arena.

Importantly, a clear territorial base is not always an absolute requirement for a quasi-state. Some religious groups act as powerful war-makers but are not identified with a specific territorial base. Once some state-like functions are performed, the challenger represents a "quasi-state." Defining this precisely is difficult but, nevertheless, interesting and important features can be seen. Among quasi-states, and between quasi-states and the state, there is potential competition for sovereign authority and governance. These may exist in parallel to each other, in open conflict, or persist in uneasy, unreconciled contradiction. Security dilemmas can spur quasi-state development.

There is strategic interdependence in decision-making by leaders and challengers. Actors' strategic choices are shaped in part by their expectations about others' behavior. "Challengers need supporters to come to power, and so leaders may use oppression to deter selectors from joining the nascent coalition supporting a challenger" (Bueno de Mesquita et al., 2003: 241). Challengers with quasi-states organizations face a second-order internal challenge problem—those who wish to challenge the leader for office can also create a splinter faction and split off from the main party, group, or movement. In quasi-states, the rules and enforcement are typically even more fluid and uncertain than in the national state. Challengers must contend with incumbent leaders who seek to divide and rule, among other tactics.

Affinities

Affinity refers to the "bonds between leaders and followers that both can use to anticipate each other's future loyalty" (Bueno de Mesquita et al., 2003: 60). Affinity may be drawn from ethnicity or religion, or result from personality, ideology, party identification, family ties, and other factors; affinity may also be a simple preference for one individual over another (Bueno de Mesquita et al., 2003: 61). A critical suggestion from *LOPS* is that for analytic purposes, the nature of the affinity does not matter. Affinities reflect tastes, which in turn shape coalitions. In the *LOPS* ordering, affinity is presented as a way to represent the "commitment" problem and the relative advantage that incumbents have. *LOPS* suggests that due to "affinity between leaders and followers, not all members of the selectorate are equally attractive as members of the winning coalition" (Bueno de Mesquita et al., 2003: 37).

A question arises regarding causal and sequential relationships between ideas and material interests. It is problematic to presume that material interests fully drive ideological choices, and that public rhetoric is merely deceptive propaganda offered as a fig leaf. This is tantamount to the analyst claiming omniscient insight

22 *Political survival in Pakistan*

into a political actor's "true" motives. Taking stated ideological positions at face value risks missing strategic communication and representation by political actors. Motives are notoriously difficult to get at: actors might misrepresent true interests for strategic purposes such as bargaining, and there are tendencies to represent things in ways that serve an individual's personal cognitive needs. Spruyt (1994) follows Max Weber and suggests a useful way to proceed: an "elective affinity" between material interests and ideas:

> Individuals who engage in particular activities such as warfare or the pursuit of monetary gain will be predisposed to ideologies that explain and justify the activity to the agent. Elective affinity is a predisposition to certain ideas, not the instrumental construction of values or ideas solely to serve one's material interests. Weber does not deny the independent status of ideas. There are always charismatic individuals who can determine the limits of the possible and redefine the contours of the permissible. But whether such ideas become routinized will depend on their material support. The carriers of such ideas will often depend on economic power or coercive means to spread and develop these ideas. Social groups will look for political allies who can advance their preferred order. Conversely, political elites have an incentive to propagate and foster new ideas to gain support from social groups. They manipulate cultural symbols for their own instrumental reasons. It is thus the correspondence of interests and ideas that brings actors together in a coalition and thereby empowers new sets of ideas in political practice.
>
> (Spruyt, 1994: 69)

The "elective affinity" approach allows for a role to be played by flexible leaders, and a predisposition toward certain ideas, as well as the possibility that some ideas become entrenched. New ideas can be a way to generate new support, and the potential for deliberate manipulation is accepted.

Groups and "groupness"

Challengers claim to represent and lead a broader community, presupposing a coherent, pre-existing group. Yet groups may be evanescent. What constitutes a "group," where does group identity come from, and how do we identify a "real" group? Where do groups come from? How do their demarcators of difference emerge and evolve? When do boundaries gain political salience? How can they be identified in a cross-sectional snapshot? Moreover, groups and movements may be fragmented rather than unitary. Who speaks for the group in such contexts? Is it the leader, constituents, or movement ideologues? These questions are difficult to resolve in fluid settings where institutions and organizations are changeable and informal. To Pierre Bourdieu, "real groupness," depended on a group's "capacity to be *represented*, and to be identified by its leadership" (Bayat, 2005: 892). An affinity community represented and lead by a challenger would be considered a real group by this definition.

Political survival in a weak state   23

A vast, diverse literature explores how groups are organized and mobilized. To Max Weber, groups' activities derive primarily from their belief systems. Accordingly, ideas and symbols play fundamental roles in social change and, in an elitist view, "groups are activated principally by charismatic leaders who are able to galvanise people committed to a particular idea." Weber's concept of charisma "implies a notion of an anonymous crowd vulnerable to irrational impulse instigated by the emotional guidance of leaders" (Bayat, 2005: 896). Materialist perspectives may point to shared class interests as the basis for coalitions. Mancur Olson (1982) pointed to the role "distributional coalitions" (groups that seek to retain or increase their share of national resources) play as a key factor in determining public policy. Because smaller groups have a relatively easy time engaging in collective action, societies tend to see powerful interest groups representing relatively small social segments. Encompassing coalitions pursue majority goods rather than private goods but are usually larger and have a more difficult time overcoming collective action barriers. Dahrendorf (1959) argues that "conflict groups" are mobilized when three factors are in place—communication, leadership, and legitimacy in the eyes of the broader community. Relative deprivation is a prominent explanation for rebellion (Gurr, 1970). Collective action problems present a key obstacle to successful mobilization; an entire research program can be centered on overcoming such barriers (Lichbach, 1995).

Some group efforts fit into the social movement category, and may be considered social movement organizations. Charles Tilly defines a "social movement" as "a sustained, organized public effort making collective claims on target authorities" that uses "a well-hewn contentious repertoire on the part of people who proclaim themselves to be worthy, unified, numerous, and committed," while other analysts would add "a durable network structure" and "at least the rudiments of a collective identity" as necessary ingredients (cited and summarized in Tarrow, 2005: 6–7).

Social movement theory focused attention on:

> *political opportunities*, sometimes crystallized as static opportunity structures, sometimes as changing political environments; *mobilizing structures*, both formal movement organizations and the social networks of everyday life; *collective action frames*, both the cultural constants that orient participants and those they themselves construct; and established *repertoires of contention*, particularly how these repertoires evolve in response to changes in capitalism, state building, and other, less monumental processes.
>
> (Tarrow, 2005: 23)

Although the social movements literature emerged from European and American cases, a growing literature has examined Muslim societies (e.g. Wickham 2002; Wiktorowicz, 2004). While the present study does not concentrate explicitly on social movements, political opportunities and collective action frames provide helpful categories within which mechanisms underlying quasi-state emergence may be described. Moreover, the quasi-state strategy suggests a parsimonious

24 *Political survival in Pakistan*

way for the social movements literature to capture the constraints and opportunities affecting challenger choices in ethnically fractured societies.

The purpose here is not to explain all group formation and mobilization. It is to describe how a weak state and a heterogeneous, "strong" society in a polity with low institutionalization yield political opportunities for challengers to pursue quasi-states. Social affinities and groups can provide the support base for quasi-state builders. Social movement organizations can seek to build social movements and also perform quasi-state functions.

Ethnicity and religion can provide (sometimes overlapping) bases for affinity and group identity. Ethnicity and religion can both be considered "affinities" around which groups may form and coalesce. Membership in an ethnic group usually comes from the "descent rule" (Fearon, 2004). Religious and sectarian affiliation can be more easily adopted and changed in some circumstances. Both can provide "imagined solidarities" and help motivate individual participation and group mobilization. Conflict can itself spur and reinforce group identity, a possibility that can be strategically exploited. As Varshney succinctly put it: "If ethnic violence is to be explained, it is assumed that ethnic identity has already been formed, whereas it can be shown that conflict itself is identity-shaping and may have been created for that reason by ethnic partisans" (Varshney, 2002: 38–39). A similar process can apply to religious affinity groups.

Ethnicity can become politicized and produce ethnonationalism, which is defined as "a movement within an established state to change the power distribution among different ethnic groups, privileged or underprivileged, sometimes leading to search and demand for the creation of a separate state" (Inayatullah, 2002: 65). In other words, ethnonationalist groups mobilize politically and may seek to secede from a state. Political inclusion can moderate such demands: "It is frequently seen that parties seeking secession, when permitted participation in politics, de-emphasize or de-escalate their demand of secession to less extreme demands" (Inayatullah, 2002: 66). In assessing ethnic mobilization, Hechter and Levi distinguish between interactive groups, who become distinct due to their greater internal interaction, and reactive groups, who respond to changes in other groups (cited in Inayatullah, 2002: 65).

Ethnicity and religion may provide dense social networks that can be an appealing basis for coalition formation (Fearon, 2004: 9). It makes "economic sense" to organize a coalition along ethnic lines sometimes—where "economic" is understood in a broad sense as obtaining valued objects and realizing preferences, whether they are "material" or "moral" interests. One issue is whether "constituents" or "leaders" drive the process, or whether there is an interdependent causal simultaneity rather than a unidirectional cause and effect. Whatever the answer, challengers can appeal to ethnic groups as political coalitions in certain circumstances. In a weak state context, this may translate into the "economic" calculation that greater autonomy is a realistic possibility with net benefits and bearable costs. This remains closest to an instrumentalist understanding, in which ethnicity is a concept deployed and manipulated strategically by elites for political and economic power (Varshney, 2002).[3] At an extreme in such circumstances, secession may be pursued.

Political survival in a weak state 25

Assessing "interests"

Political conflict arises in part because actors' interests diverge and clash. Challengers and the groups they purportedly represent have "interests." Interests may be defined as "having a 'stake' in something, or 'being affected' by something" (Bayat, 2005: 901, following Balbus, 1973). From this perspective, "ideologies" only represent another interest constellation. While some ideologies privilege material interests above "moral" interests, all represent "being affected by something." Interests can be material, economic, political, social, and moral. Some interests exist whether or not people perceive them as such: clean air is such an objective interest, but "'interests' attached to social, political and economic realms often have 'subjective' bases in that they are socially or culturally constructed" (Bayat, 2005: 901). Reconciling "objective" and "subjective" interests remains theoretically problematic.

"Official transcripts"—what leaders and their mouthpieces claim as the true doctrinal position taken by a social movement or quasi-state organization—may not fit exactly with what others in the group or constituency narrate. Where the focus is on political survival constraints facing leaders, it is not necessary to detail all the hidden transcripts and subnarratives that go into mass agitation. In reality, hidden transcripts may be inconsistent with each other and represent many different behaviors engaged in opportunistically by multifarious actors seeking to express their interests and values. In other words, while challenger coalitions in weak polities need not be like the US model—business-like highly organized ventures— they nevertheless need to have an identifiable leader or contending leaders. And, internally, challengers face their own political survival constraints.

The state and national leaders also seek to legitimize their rule and to mobilize support through appeals to affinities, as well as active efforts to inculcate political allegiance, sometimes through nationalism. State leaders in religious Muslim societies typically seek to maintain Islamic legitimacy, but employ frames that "do not call for broad societal or state transformations, but rather emphasize individual piety and concern for personal salvation, thus supporting a politically quiescent variant of Islam" (Wiktorowicz, 2004: 18). Pakistan has been exceptional in this regard, partly because "official Islam" is bound up in the country's very creation. Religious leaders have often sought to outflank others in their religious credentials, and in so doing made moves toward Islamization in society. Moreover, official Islam has been used to try to enhance the state's power with respect to specific societal actors.

Method and data

This study combines process-tracing and analytic narrative to produce a political survival interpretation of leader decisions regarding extraction and challenger pursuit of quasi-states. The goal is to generate hypotheses based on the Pakistani experience. These hypotheses extend the logic of political survival in ways appropriate to weak states with strong, fractured societies. Quantitative data from

26 *Political survival in Pakistan*

developing countries have been characterized as "poetry"; Pakistani data are no exception, and have been termed "notoriously poor, inadequate, of dubious quality, and often fabricated to suit the needs of the government in power" (Zaidi, 1999: xvii). Statistical sources often disagree. Government statistical surveyors in Pakistan have found reporting discrepancies that cast doubt on basic economic figures. In this context, it is helpful to consider different historical accounts and obtain informed polity participants' perspectives from in-depth interviews.

Empirical information for this study comes primarily from in-depth interviews and secondary accounts. The investigation is based on several field research trips to Pakistan between 2000 and 2009. Interviews with bureaucrats, military officials, legislators, journalists, and other informed government observers offer evidence for mechanisms by which state extraction remains weak. Interviews with challengers' official representatives, affinity group members, journalists, government administrators, and other polity residents illustrate and suggest mechanisms by which quasi-states emerge and are sustained. Conversations with skilled and unskilled workers, merchants, corporate executives, and various others from Karachi and elsewhere offer perspectives on poor governance. Interviews also shed light on perceptions and expectations, providing insights into factors that may influence decision-making.

Leaders make extraction decisions in a bureaucratic machine context. My interviews were with former government officials, military officials, legislators, observers, and activists from the Ayub Khan/Yahya Khan, Z. A. Bhutto, Zia ul-Haq, and later periods. Together with historical accounts, these guided interviews outline mechanisms by which extractive capacity remained hobbled, thereby exacerbating state weakness. They offer insights into the complexities and decision points affecting what resources were extracted from whom. The winning coalition helps determine extraction decisions, and these build or undermine state strength at later points. Leaders with different political survival pressures—or those who had simply not yet perceived the threat—ventured radical change in domestic extraction. Interviews with informed observers and participants indicate what choices were made, and how the costs and benefits of different choices were perceived.

"Vice-regalism," under which the military and civil service are dominant in governance, is usually described as a colonial legacy. Although the upper level civil service recruited some able technocrats, the Pakistani state was rather weak and did not have the apparatus for effective management. In that condition, bureaucratic decision-makers were often overwhelmed, and more so as national political leaders intervened for political patronage purposes. Over time, bureaucratic positions were more commonly assigned as private goods to incumbents' supporters, as a way to retain a winning coalition, and to ward off challengers. These changes became apparent through greater roles played by retired military officers, selective corruption cases filed under various regimes, failure to get cases heard on merit, and evidence of demoralization. Less insulated from the incumbent political leader's wishes and vagaries, high-level bureaucrats were no longer as secure in their positions, and decreased their expected length of tenure. These and other

Political survival in a weak state 27

decisions by leaders help explain Pakistan's failure to develop more effective bureaucratic machinery. When combined with pressures for private goods from the winning coalition as well as threats from challengers, these factors provide insights into the failure to extract more broadly and effectively.

Interviews, secondary accounts, and official statements describe mechanisms by which political entrepreneurs and affinity groups may support "quasi-state" options. These interviews were with functionaries, activists, sympathizers, and those without strong affinities to particular ethnic and religious organizations and groups. The interview subjects included illiterates, lower-middle class peddlers, clerks, rural-to-urban migrants, middle class business owners and workers, and upper-middle class figures. Challengers and their active and potential supporters may be depicted as a pyramid with leaders at the apex and constituents towards the base. At the widest area in the base, there is overlap with other constituencies. Examining the base can trace the outer limits of what is possible: what leaders can do with their followers, without alienating them. Moreover, individuals at the base offer "hidden transcripts": insightful views that often differ from the "official transcript" public statements offered by leaders, and which thus illustrate underlying complexity (Bayat, 2005). Secessionist posturing has become a learned political tool, used recently by those expressing aspirations for a Saraiki province, or autonomy for Gilgit-Baltistan, for example.

My interviews describe perceived state vacuum, breakdown, and predatory behavior, and reveal the degree to which patronage ties and quasi-state networks are important. Perceptions matter because polity members who believe that the state is broken or severely dysfunctional are more likely to support quasi-state entities. This was repeatedly apparent during discussions with various activists and social movement sympathizers. In addition, evidence that interviewees felt deep insecurity as well as attachment to pre-existing networks was overwhelming. To varying degrees, quasi-state aspects such as an armed militia, an extraction mechanism, mobilization network, and some leadership structure, were present.

The interview data reveal an apparently contradictory dual consciousness that sometimes prevails; activists, sympathizers, and observers could simultaneously accept that the state existed as well as the quasi-state, and that both had authority in practical terms as extractor/protector/allocators and also in symbolic terms as legitimate claimants to high authority. This may be partly because people hedge their bets against future possible winners and losers, but the sheer prevalence and persistence of this phenomenon suggests that it has become entrenched in the Pakistani polity. Interviews (primarily from Karachi) relating to the Muttahida Qaumi Movement and Jeay Sindh are significant sources; other interviews offer perspectives on different groups. How these relate to political Islam is intriguing; for example, my fieldwork shows that the Jamaat-e-Islami and the MQM are often competing for an overlapping constituency, producing both alliances and conflicts. Attempts to reach the religiously inclined among one's co-ethnic community may take a sectarian tack: for example, Jeay Sindh activists have developed an affinity for Barelvi-oriented Sunni Tahrik and an opposition to Deobandi-influenced Tablighi Jamaat. These alignments suggest increasingly exclusive and unbridgeable group

28 *Political survival in Pakistan*

boundaries. In turn, that might be the basis for more legitimate, resilient quasi-states that cannot be easily dislodged. The current insurrections in the Frontier, and ongoing clashes in Balochistan, are stark reminders that overt challenges to state authority persist.

The above empirical contributions add to existing theories. They also offer new data on perceptions by people who face daily interactions with not only the Pakistani state's official representatives, but also with quasi-state organizations. This study combines interview material with existing narratives and accounts to examine leadership and challenge in Pakistani politics. In the contemporary Islamic world, where many Muslim-majority countries are low on indices of state strength, this project suggests a generalizable way to think about leader and challenger strategies. There are implications for other countries with weak polities, difficulties with extraction, and challengers that may be on a quasi-state trajectory.

Overview

Government can be understood as the means by which communities pursue collective goals and adjudicate conflicts. "Government" can happen in the central governments charged with administering sovereign territorial states, and at various other levels and contexts, not necessarily all territorially based. There is a normative element in comparing governments: they can be good or bad. As described by Margaret Levi, "good government" is effective (able to protect the population from violence, ensure property rights, and supply desired public goods), representative, and accountable to the population it is meant to serve (Levi, 2006: 5).

One reason good government is normatively desirable is because it is more likely to improve more people's quality of life. A key conclusion is drawn from the "Hobbes Index," the authors' measure of welfare, from which they conclude: "The political transition from a society ruled by an exclusive group to one with a broad, inclusive coalition structure appears to be fundamental for sustained improvement in the quality of life for the world's economically, socially, or politically oppressed peoples" (Bueno de Mesquita et al., 2003: 485).

If political survival considerations are a key driving mechanism in policy choice, then there is a guideline for identifying prospects for positive change with incumbents and challengers. This carries implications for how and when normatively good government might emerge, as well as why bad government has staying power despite ideological declarations or ostensible office-holding functions.

Political survival has promise as a vital mechanism explaining the strategic constraints under which critical policy decisions are made. Extraction is a central, defining state activity, but not all extraction choices are equal. Some bring more public goods, and others bring more private goods. Challengers—whether contenders for existing office, revolutionaries, secessionists, social movement builders, quasi-state leaders, or in additional guises—have their own significant choices. Furthermore, looking at one context in detail allows for diachronic comparisons that offer some control for other factors, and this offers one route for evaluating hypotheses.

To proceed, Chapter 2 introduces Pakistan as a weak state with a strong but fractured society, wherein incumbents and challengers seek to manipulate key rules for political survival. Chapter 3 examines extraction strategies in Pakistan, comparing "good" policy choices with those driven by political survival needs, up through Zia ul-Haq's regime. Chapter 4 examines key political choices by challengers in Pakistan, and focuses on quasi-state strategies. Chapter 5 considers governance, extraction, and quasi-state challenges after the Zia ul-Haq period and posits a persistent three-way relationship. Chapter 6 concludes with implications for theory and case, and broader questions for further investigation.

2 Weak state, strong society, negotiable polity

Cynical Pakistanis believe that politicians seek "kursi"—to obtain and retain office—above all else. This matches the political survival approach. Yet the logic of political survival is more elaborate, and this exploration informs both theory and practice. There is a role for miscalculation and bad political advice. Ayub Khan was advised that India would not attack if he initiated the military actions that led to the 1965 war; dissatisfaction with the war fueled anti-Ayub sentiment. Yahya Khan was advised that holding free elections in 1970 would not produce a dominant party but weak groupings that he could divide and rule; instead, a dominant party emerged in East Pakistan and another sizeable party in West Pakistan, which eventually undid both Yahya Khan and the state of Pakistan. Z.A. Bhutto was encouraged to promote Zia ul-Haq, the officer who eventually detained and then executed him. Nawaz Sharif was advised to secure his position by moving against Musharraf, which precipitated Musharraf's "countercoup." In each case, bad political advice may have contributed to poor decision-making. But this also speaks to uncertainty in the polity and the apparent risk-taking that political leaders are inclined toward, if only because things are so opaque that it is like playing chess in the dark. In such a context, perceptions are all the more important to explore.

Pakistan has what may be termed a "strong society" (Migdal, 1988), but one that is fractionalized and ethnically diverse, with historical tensions over language rights and religious sectarian identity. Approximately half the country's population was lost when Bangladesh was created from East Pakistan in 1971. Pakistan is, nevertheless, the second most populous Muslim-majority country. It is a declared nuclear power, has an enduring rivalry with India, and has irregular forces that have often traversed official boundaries. Pakistan remains a low-income, largely agricultural country, with low literacy rates and many people on or below the poverty line. Pakistan's stability is a global concern, and it is not a well-institutionalized polity.

Formal selection institutions for leadership have been frequently violated or altered for political expediency. Virtually every incumbent leader has sought to change or suspend basic constitutional rules in an effort to further political survival. Key questions on borders and jurisdiction remain indeterminate or are subject to renegotiation. Interviews reveal that polity members believe key formal rules to be blatantly manipulable or violable. Uncertainty and information asymmetries come with low institutionalization. Yet polity members' perceptions tend to converge on

Weak state, strong society, negotiable polity   31

who key veto-holders and selectorate members are: the military, the civil bureaucracy, great landlords disparagingly called "feudals," industrialists/business groups, religious leaders, and possibly, new media. The judiciary may be entering a more powerful position in the selectorate; the jury remains out on this question.

Influence wielded by vested interests and distributional coalitions have repeatedly diverted governance away from producing public goods and toward providing private goods. Collusion, principal-agent shirking and defections, and rent-seeking activities undermine and complicate the formal rules according to which both state and market are expected to operate. Pakistan has not experienced extensive land reform, nor successful agricultural taxation. Economist Ishrat Husain, a former Pakistan State Bank governor, has described Pakistan as an "elitist state" in which "the market is rigged and the state is hijacked in order to deliver most of the benefits of economic growth to this small group." In contrast, successful East Asian economies have seen rapid growth, rapid poverty reduction, and more equitably distributed development benefits (Husain, 2000: xii–xiii).

Scholarly works on Pakistan's political history and governance emphasize specific themes. To Jalal (1990), the elephant in the national policy-making room is the disproportionate national income share that has been devoted to defense and the military, a path begun due to the perceived threat to survival immediately after Pakistan was founded. In Jalal (1995), the key issue is broadened to the struggle between unelected and elected institutions. To Siddiqua (2007), the overriding distributional coalition is what she has termed "Milbus," the increasingly autonomous military class that dominates the economy and polity, and has done so through business foundations, land grants, special privileges and licenses, soft loans and loan forgiveness, and other preferential treatment, in addition to the vast budgetary resources devoted to the military. To Ziring (1997) a key legacy is the "vice-regal" tradition, rule that depended on a local ruler supported by formidable administrative and military apparatus.

In debates about trade-offs between development outcomes and defense burdens (what in some variants are termed "investment squeeze"), Cohen (2004) and Jalal (1990) both suggest that security priorities have undermined development in Pakistan, in generating accountable institutions and in allocating resources to education, health care, nutrition, water, sanitation, and other human development needs. Jalal's focus in *The State of Martial Rule* is "the dialectic between state construction and political processes while weaving in the related economic, strategic and ideological dimensions" (Jalal, 1990: 3). State survival was the overriding concern in Pakistan, according to Jalal. Cohen suggests that this will continue to be the case, with continuing detrimental effects: "Pakistan will likely remain a national security state, driven by security objectives to the neglect of development and accountability and unable to change direction because of a lack of imagination and legitimacy" (Cohen, 2004: 299). National medal-winning civil servant Tasneem Siddiqui believes that the 1965 war was a "turning point" from which Pakistan "lost all momentum for development" (Siddiqui, 2001).

These views treat "Pakistan" as a unit. While attention is paid to individual leaders and particular groups, they are typically not based on a systematic

32 *Political survival in Pakistan*

theoretical premise about agency. The political survival based approach has the advantage that it incorporates insights and tendencies noted within the literature explicitly into a strategic calculus based on perceived constraints and opportunities. Agents include incumbents seeking to retain office, entrepreneurial challengers, and more widely, polity members pursuing membership in winning coalitions. In the process, some may risk or accept state failure as long as they can secure leadership in a truncated political entity. State survival is central to the extent that individual political survival is served by state survival. When the two diverge, leaders and challengers may accept "state failure" or facilitate it. The incumbent leader is a presumed agent of an abstract principal, "the state." That agent pursues political survival and in so doing may work at cross-purposes to the principal.

It is useful to contrast Pakistan with India, given their historical origin and enduring rivalry, while recognizing that "the base from which each started and significant differences in political, economic, and social circumstances make direct comparisons difficult" (Harrison et al., 1999: 1). The two share a common heritage of British colonialism. The Indian subcontinent had been under the Mughal Empire before the British East India Company's advent. By the mid-1700s Mughal rule had ceased to be effective. The lack of a strong central government in the Indian subcontinent provided the British East India Company with an opportunity to expand (Razi, 1997: xiv). In one narrative, the 1857 "Indian Mutiny" was partly a Muslim attempt to curtail British power in India, which failed (Siddiqui, 1972: 1); an Indian nationalist narrative describes this as a "War of Independence."

Partition in 1947 was accompanied by bloody communal rioting and what later would be termed ethnic cleansing. The rushed British departure and inadequately transferred and apportioned political authority likely contributed to the violence that ensued (Ganguly, 1994: 39; Wolpert, 2006). Casualty estimates range from hundreds of thousands to one million. Many more became refugees (one claim is that 8 million refugees entered Pakistan). Pakistan inherited what was "Northwest India" and East Bengal due to their heavily Muslim populations; subsequently known as West and East Pakistan, the two halves were separated by hundreds of miles of Indian territory. Partition also divided the populous Punjab province. A war soon broke out over Kashmir.

Kashmir, a princely state, could choose to accede to India or Pakistan. Although it was a majority Muslim state, its Maharajah (ruler) was a Hindu, and he delayed deciding accession before leaning toward India in a controversial action. Fighting between India and Pakistan erupted, without a formal declaration of war. On October 22, 1947, Pukhtun tribesmen from Pakistan crossed into Kashmir. Within three days the Kashmiri Maharaja agreed to join the new Indian state (over joining Pakistan). Indian troops were flown in to Srinagar, the Jammu-Kashmir capital, and the conflict became a war as Pakistan committed itself to the Kashmiri cause. The Indian army suffered setbacks in fighting the raiders, then made some advances after the spring of 1948. The official Pakistan army joined the conflict. Finally, a UN-brokered mediation brought an end to the war on January 1, 1949. It is estimated that there were a total of 1500 battle deaths, although limited firepower prevented more costly material and human destruction. India lost approximately

Weak state, strong society, negotiable polity 33

5000 square miles (Ganguly, 1994: 13–14). India agreed to a UN-resolved plebiscite in Kashmir that would allow Kashmiris to vote about whether to join India or Pakistan. This plebiscite was not implemented and, 15 years later, another war broke out.

Indian apprehension had grown since the 1963 Sino-Pakistan border agreement. As 1964 ended, Indian officials incorporated Kashmir fully into the Indian state, removing its special or undetermined status (Brines, 1968: 238). Pakistan claimed this as the precipitating factor for military hostilities, as it removed the possibility of a legal resolution of the Kashmir issue and threatened to remove it from international attention (Brines, 1968: 239). The conflict began early in 1965 in the Rann of Kutch, a marshy wasteland bordering West Pakistan (Brines, 1968: 9). Non-military fighters from Pakistan entered Kashmir in early August 1965. The first major engagement of the official Pakistani and Indian militaries took place on August 14, 1965. Attacks and counter-attacks escalated to the point that, in early September, both sides started using air power to support ground forces. India reacted to Pakistani gains by moving to attack the Pakistani cities of Lahore and Sialkot (outside the Kashmir region). The Pakistanis counter-attacked into the Indian Punjab region. Destructive tank battles took place. A stalemate was reached and a UN Security Council ceasefire resolution was accepted by both sides by September 22. The material and human costs were higher than the 1947–48 war for both sides: Pakistan lost 20 planes, 200 tanks, and 3800 personnel, and India lost up to 70 planes, 190 tanks, and 3000 personnel (Ganguly, 1994: 47–48).

Kashmir has continued to be a heavily contested region. Indo-Pak relations have been peppered with border clashes, wars, and brinkmanship over Kashmir, as witnessed in the 2000 Kargil crisis. It is widely believed that India and Pakistan have been and continue to be threatening to each other's security (Tellis, 1997; Thomas, 1986; Rizvi, 2000; Kukreja and Singh, 2005). India's security thinking has been dominated by concerns about Pakistan and to some extent China (Subrahamanyam, 1982: I). Pakistan's security thinking has been dominated by concerns about threats to national interests and survival from India.

Prior to independence and Partition, tax farmers and revenue collectors had been converted into landlords for the convenience of British revenue collection (Brown, 1963: 53). Central government resources in British India were obtained through a combination of taxation, borrowing, and manipulation of the money supply (Tomlinson, 1992: 277).[1] The British did not impose many direct taxes, which might have caused instability and rebellion, and even ran deficits:

> The British earned very little taxation in India. In fact, the low taxation accounts for the success of the British Raj in governing India. The British earnings in India came for the most part from managing credit and currency flows that were used by Indian and British entrepreneurs. It also benefited from trade, and from taxing British manufacturers and merchants that made money though trade with India [...] As was also the case in Malaya, absence of taxation made direct control of labor, crops, and the vast territory of India

34 *Political survival in Pakistan*

> unnecessary. What mattered was stability, which could be achieved through indirect rule.
>
> (Nasr, 2001a: 41)

Thus, a weak fiscal skeleton was in part a colonial legacy. In the lead-up to Partition, the British colonists' revenue-raising apparatus was largely left in place in central government and financial institutions such as the Inland Revenue and Customs and Excise offices (Joshi and Little, 1994: 8). The Reserve Bank had been created in 1935 and was retained by India post-independence. The British had created the Indian Civil Service for higher-level civil bureaucrats, and produced the institution and model on which the subsequent Indian Administrative Service and Civil Service of Pakistan were based. Implementation of Partition agreements on government revenue divisions were not resolved immediately but continued to be negotiated and disputed as late as 1960 (Talbot, 1998: 101).

The Pakistani state inherited not only the colonial pattern but also the intermediaries the British relied upon. As with India, British rule was "shaped by trade rather than revenue extraction" (Nasr, 2001a: 41). British rule was not focused on building extractive power and political capacity; it instead "relied on intermediaries to establish control" (Nasr, 2001a: 41). These "intermediaries" later on become the local "strongmen": powerful figures and entities distinct from the national government and not necessarily holding formal office, but nevertheless acting as veto-holders, gatekeepers, and enablers (Migdal, 1988). National policies may succeed or fail depending in part whether strongmen acquiesce. Examples might be the landed elites in Sind and Punjab and tribal leaders in NWFP and Balochistan, who help maintain control.

The British feared the Russian threat to North-West India, and accordingly sought consent to rule through patronage. "Stability" mattered more than trade and revenue here (Nasr, 2001a: 42). The Pakistani government's current troubles in enforcing central state authority in this region may be partly because the people here have never been "subdued," and only been fought or wooed. This perceived geopolitical threat from Russia was echoed by the security analysts in the later twentieth century who suggested that when the Soviet Union invaded Afghanistan, their real design was on Pakistan, and ultimately to a warm-water port on the Arabian Sea.

Both countries also inherited military resources from British India. The existing pre-Partition army was divided on a "roughly 2:1 basis, with the larger share going to the India Union" (Kavic, 1967: 82). Air power was similarly divided, with approximately two thirds going to India (Kavic, 1967: 102), and likewise, with a small navy (Kavic, 1967: 116). Significantly, all functioning plants for the production of defense ordnance after Partition were located in India (Kavic, 1967: 126). Furthermore, Pakistan may have been short-changed in the military resources it received. When the army in India was divided, Pakistan received only six armored regiments (compared to 40 received by India) and eight artillery and infantry regiments compared to India's 40 and 21 respectively (Talbot, 1998: 99–100). This meant that any "startup" costs of war preparation were likely to be higher in Pakistan.

Thus, common historical origin did not mean that the two states started on a level footing. India inherited more British colonial resources on the whole, and was several times larger than Pakistan in population.[2] Nevertheless, both India and Pakistan are usually characterized as low-income countries, and have health, literacy, and educational indicators that are typical for these. Agriculture has dominated both economies, although India experienced land reform and its industrial base is proportionately larger. Export earnings from a few key commodities were important revenue sources. Ninety-nine percent of export earnings in Pakistan in 1948–49 were based on five commodities: raw jute, raw cotton, raw wool, hides and skins, and tea (Husain, 2000: 281). High population growth rates in both countries have been associated with a low national savings rate, and consequently low domestic resources allocated for investment.

Poverty and low living standards have occupied development planners in both countries. Despite relatively little analysis of poverty in Pakistan, economist Ishrat Husain argues that over the early growth period, "the extent of poverty in Pakistan increased, verifying Kutznets hypothesis of an inverse relationship between economic development" (Husain, 2000: 184). Although income inequality data from the 1970s and 1980s pointed to a possible reversal of this trend, Husain finds that adjusted income inequality measures describe "a widening gap between the top and bottom quintiles" (Husain, 2000: 184). Kuznets curve hypothesis suggests that in its early phases, development brings increased income inequality, and as development proceeds further, income inequality will eventually be reduced. This has not yet taken place in Pakistan.

India is usually identified as a democracy, while Pakistan has undergone military rule in large periods. Although it underwent a notorious "Emergency" period under Indira Gandhi, India is generally perceived as having more viable, solid, and continuing political institutions and constitutional framework than Pakistan; due in part to the lack of a military threat to civilian rule (Harrison et al., 1999: 3–5). Pakistan, in contrast, is not as far along in finding an effective and stable government, and has seen repeated military intervention and martial law (Harrison et al., 1999: 3–4; Siddiqua, 2007). There have been shifts back and forth in executive authority from the president to the prime minister; army chiefs have filled a quasi-presidential or presidential role at times (Raza, 1997: 26–27; Rehman, 2008a). Martial law regimes have appeared with regularity, including Ayub Khan's rule starting in 1958, Zia ul-Haq's regime beginning in 1977, and General Pervez Musharraf's takeover in 1999.

Nasr argues that Pakistan was similar to Malaysia; both were "weak states," because (1) the initial bargain leading to their creation involved "intricate negotiations over power between future state leaders, colonial powers, and various ethnic and social groups" (Nasr, 2001a: 25), resulting in states that were "greatly constricted as the scope of their powers was decided by those negotiations and was from the outset controlled by checks and balances that obviated the possibility of formulating effective economic and social policy," and because (2) both also "lacked effective machinery of government" (Nasr, 2001a: 26). Pakistan was created not through a broad, unified, and sustained struggle against colonialism, but as powerful elites

36 *Political survival in Pakistan*

collaborated with the British against Hindu hegemony (Nasr, 2001a: 25). In the lead-up to independence, significant "state-building" through mobilizing people and resources did not happen. State weakness at Pakistan's inception also arose because the British Raj machinery was left behind in Delhi; Pakistan's new administration "had to govern out of a hotel in Karachi without the rudiments of a national government over provinces that had no natural grid among them, and some of which were reluctant participants in the Pakistan movement" (Nasr, 2001a: 26).

Key questions about national identity and governance have not been fully resolved. Who is the country for? How should the country be run? Where are the external boundaries and internal jurisdictions? What powers should the central government have over the acceding units? When will powers be devolved so that the "concurrent list" (subjects on which both central and provincial governments legislate) expire and be abolished?

Regarding the "who" question, the original argument was that a homeland for the Indian subcontinent's Muslims was needed. But Muslims, although concentrated in the west and east of British India, were also spread throughout the region and beyond. Language was not an easily unifying factor. Urdu, a courtly language developed under Mughal dynastic rule in India, was spoken by many Muslims. But there were many other languages too: Punjabi, Bengali, Balochi, Pashto, Sindhi, Seraiki, Hindko—to name some prominent ones. Language became a critical issue driving nationalist sentiment in Bengali-speaking East Pakistan, and language has also been the basis for ethnic violence between Sindhi's and Urdu-speaking Muhajirs in Sindh. There are inequalities in the weight given to different groups. Punjab is commonly believed to play a hegemonic role, due partly to its large population and representation in the armed forces. There are socioeconomic inequalities, with enormous weight for some privileged groups as detailed below; the landed aristocracy has high influence. The weight given to the federating units in Pakistan, and their rights and autonomy with respect to the center, remain an ongoing negotiation, as discussed below.

Pakistan was born amid severe communal violence, and religious minorities remain contested terrain. A fear among Muslims in Uttar Pradesh province had been that under a Hindu-majority government, Muslims would lose their rights and privileges. Some thought that Hindus in Pakistan could be potential hostages to prevent mistreatment of Muslims in post-Partition India (Interview, 2009). Jinnah's famous speech outlining secular principles declared that religious practice was private and had nothing to do with the business of state. A senior Hindu figure who was once an Indian National Congress activist and chose to remain in Pakistan complained that the constitutional setup had prevented minorities from even dreaming that they could achieve higher office, by restricting it to non-Muslims (Interview with Hindu former activist, 2009). The Hindu minister J.N. Mandal left Pakistan altogether after the Objectives Resolution was passed, although his reasons may have been more complex and tied to other rivalries (Interview with senior Hindu community member, 2009).

Sectarian agitations have long included violence. The Ahrars' activism in the 1950s against the Ahmadi community is an early example. The Ahmadis are a

Weak state, strong society, negotiable polity 37

religious sect that claim to be Islamic, but have run into opposition due to the prophetic status ascribed to the sect's founder. Mumtaz Daultana, Chief Minister in Punjab province, had little personal passion on the issue, but did not suppress the 1953 anti-Ahmadi agitation, which led to a central government crackdown, Daultana's dismissal, and eventually martial law (Ziring, 2005: 175). A political survival interpretation may be that he sought to coopt potential challengers and also shore up his political influence by allowing the Ahrars, an extreme anti-Ahmadi group, to escalate violent acts against the Ahmadi community. Some support for this suggestion can be found in the fact that the Ahrars, originally founded in 1931 by Punjabi Muslims opposed to the Muslim League, ended up supporting the provincial Muslim League (Daultana's party) in the 1951 elections.

The Ahmaddis, who were previously considered "Muslim" by law, eventually found themselves declared non-Muslims. This may have been due to political pressure, a cynical play to a particular religious lobby by Zulfikar Bhutto as he sought to shore up support, or a genuine religious argument (Interview with Asad Ali Thanvi, 2009). Formerly full members in a polity were stripped of their status— so much so that Pakistani passport forms require a "declaration in the case of Muslims" affirming that the signatory does not belong to the Ahmaddi community. Sectarian tensions have contributed to some groups declaring their rivals non-Muslims, as some Sunni militants have done to Shias.

In sectarian interactions in Pakistan, *manazra* refers to disputational debate or confrontational dialogue between scholars from different fiqh orientations (Haydar, 2001: 29). Maulana Haq Nawaz Jhangvi (b. 1952) had a *madrasa* training and also learned this polemic art. Maulana Jhangvi focused on the respect due to the Prophetic companions, a central and contentious issue between Sunnis and Shias. Jhangvi's biographer, Maulana Farooqi, suggests that Maulana Jhangvi was motivated by the fact that powerful Shia landlords permitted open *tabarrabazi* (slander) against the Prophetic companions (Haydar, 2001: 270). There was an international context: in Jhangvi's view, post-revolutionary Iranian Shia literature allegedly impugning the companions was flooding Pakistan (Haydar, 2001: 271). (Another way to understand this is that the sociopolitical conditions were such that a uniting common grievance would quickly provide needed legitimacy to mobilize people against the landlords; class divides had lined up with religious divides.)

Jhangvi founded the Sipah-e-Sahaba Pakistan SSP on September 6, 1985, in his mosque. The SSP program, as stated in a published brochure, included restoring the Caliphate, to have Pakistan declared a Sunni state, with public laws conforming to Sunni fiqh, severe punishments for those slandering the companions, and to get legislation declaring Shias to be *kafirs* (Haydar, 2001: 273–279). At one SSP rally, a reported slogan was *shia kafir, Shia kafir, jo naheen maana wo bhi kafir*: "Shias are Kafirs, Shias are Kafirs, anyone who disagrees is also Kafir".

Most landlords in Jhang District are Shia (and also claim to be Syed, meaning belonging to the Prophet's family). Jhang's rural and urban population, however is mainly non-Syed and Sunni (Haydar, 2001: 267–268). There is thus a revolutionary challenge element with a material political economic basis. Sectarian solidarity may enable collective action despite repression or retaliation by powerful landlords.

38 *Political survival in Pakistan*

Religious or sectarian affinity groups may be mobilized for material and economic benefit.

The blasphemy laws introduced under Zia ul-Haq prescribe life imprisonment or death to those who desecrate the Quran or insult the Prophet. Although no one has been actually put to death or imprisoned for life based on this law, it nevertheless remains a stick that can be used against minorities. Alleged desecration has fueled mob violence targeting minorities, such as the seven Christians killed and many homes gutted in Gojra in August, 2009; the allegations may be cover for other enmities, but are immensely destructive nevertheless.

As for how the new country was to be governed, Pakistan's founder, Mohammed Ali Jinnah, was a non-practising Muslim with a secular outlook on Pakistan's polity. However, he was ill and died shortly after Pakistan was created. His lieutenant, Liaquat Ali Khan, who followed as a national leader, was assassinated in 1951. Depending on how they are counted, Pakistan has had up to six constitutions. On attaining office, incumbent leaders repeatedly tried to deploy, suspend, or modify basic rules in ways that allowed them to consolidate their authority.

Constitutional instability

Pakistan's founding vision was to be a parliamentary democracy, but military takeovers and the often-deployed power to dissolve legislatures have led to political and economic instability (Bashir, 2008: 6). The president's discretionary authority to dissolve the Parliament emerged from the Government of India Act 1935 (which allowed for a continuing powerful governor-general) and the Independence Act 1947 (which created a constituent assembly to both legislate laws and frame the constitution). From 1786, the East India Company's governor was empowered to act unilaterally when he judged that Company interests or British possessions were at risk. Jinnah introduced Section 92A into the Independence Act, which empowered him to declare governor's rule in the provinces; the Chief Ministers of Sind and NWFP were ousted when they clashed with Jinnah (Almeida, 2008).

The constituent assembly clashed with the governor-general. As constitution-making under a "transparent, popularly accepted process" was in process, the Assembly was dissolved, and the highest court upheld the dissolution on a "purely technical and unpersuasive interpretation of the law" (Bashir, 2008: 6). This was a blow to democratic institutions. Subsequent attempts to frame and sustain a constitution (in 1956, 1962, and 1973) were ended by martial laws in 1958, 1969, and 1977, respectively.

Pakistan's first constitution established a parliamentary system and was passed nine years after foundation. Pakistan was modeled as a federal republic with a National Assembly (elected directly by the people), senate (with representation for each federating unit), prime minister, and governor-general (later president), and an independent judiciary. Provincial assemblies would legislate on provincial subjects. This did not last and was quickly supplanted by martial law under Ayub Khan in 1958.

The 1962 Constitution promulgated under Ayub Khan gave the president extensive legislative and executive powers and influence over the National Assembly.

Although the system was federal, the provincial governor and government were basically the president's agents (Rizvi, 2001: 121–122). Ayub Khan's 1962 constitution, although "president-centric" with a presidential form of government, nevertheless had restraints on the president's power to dissolve the assembly, including Article 23 (3) which "precluded the possibility of the president dissolving the assembly as a pre-emptive strike" and Article 24, which would require the president to also leave office if he dissolved the Assembly (Bashir, 2008: 7). According to Ayub's constitution, after his resignation the legislature's speaker should have assumed the Presidency. Instead, Chief of Army Staff Yahya Khan took over, and in 1969, he abrogated the 1962 Constitution.

Zulfiqar Ali Bhutto's 1973 constitution produced a decisively parliamentary system with a very weak president, empowering the prime minister. It also had "safeguards against the PM's abuse of dissolution as a pre-emptive tactic against a vote of no-confidence or a revenge measure if the PM had already been unseated by such a successful vote" (Bashir, 2008: 7). Z.A. Bhutto swiftly issued emergency declarations that effectively removed these protections. The 1973 Constitution also promised that the "Concurrent List," subjects, on which both the federal and provincial governments legislated, would be abolished in 1983, enhancing provincial autonomy and authority. This has not taken place.

Constitutional rule was suspended under Zia ul-Haq's martial law regime, which began in 1977. In 1985, Zia ul-Haq restored the 1973 Constitution with controversial alterations, the most notorious being the 8th Amendment. Article 58 Clause 2 (b) allowed the president discretion to dissolve the National Assembly (and dismiss the prime minister and cabinet) "where, in his opinion, 'a situation has arisen in which the Government or the Federation cannot be carried on in accordance with the provision of the Constitution and an appeal to the electorate is necessary'" (Akhtar, 1992: 258). Between 1985 and 1997, there were five elections, but no Assembly finished its term, and each was dissolved by the president using Article 58 Clause 2 (b) (Zafar, 2000: 3). The Supreme Court tended to argue that Article 58 2 (b) provided checks and balances that could reduce the likelihood that martial law would be imposed, but parliamentarians disagreed (Zafar, 2000: 5). In 1993, President Ghulam Ishaq Khan moved to dismiss Nawaz Sharif's government. In an unprecedented action, the Pakistan Supreme Court accepted Nawaz Sharif's appeal, and ordered his government reinstated. Revelations about political influence-peddling in the Supreme Court played a role. Former Chief of Army Staff General Aslam Baig had disclosed that he had secretly pressured the Supreme Court to not reinstate the Junejo government, which had been dismissed in 1988. This compelled the Supreme Court to take a different course and respond to Nawaz Sharif's appeal (Ziring, 1997: 542–543).

A functional, respected judiciary is vital for the rule of law. As appointees without a constituency, judges with insecure tenure are "more vulnerable to coercive pressure than the larger body politic" (Bashir, 2008). Collusion between judicial figures and powerful social actors and intimidation are persistently suspected and reported; bribery of judges is increasing (Interviews, 2009). In 1997, Prime Minister Nawaz Sharif's supporters disrupted a courtroom proceeding and sought

40 *Political survival in Pakistan*

to intimidate Chief Justice Sajjad Ali Shah, as a court case against the prime minister was underway.

In 1997, Prime Minister Nawaz Sharif's government amended the constitution to remove the president's ability to dismiss a prime minister (Zafar, 2000: 4). In 1999, General Musharraf put the constitution into abeyance. In 2002, General Musharraf issued the Legal Framework Order establishing a military-dominated National Security Council, and also restored the Article 58 2 (b) power to dismiss the prime minister (Talbot, 2005: 401). In 2007, when the judiciary was about to consider his eligibility to contest an election for President, Musharraf put the constitution into abeyance, and required the judiciary to take a new oath, making "as many as sixty one (61) Judges of superior judiciary including Chief Justice of Pakistan and Chief Justices of three Provinces dysfunctional for many of them either did not agree to take or were not given the oath" (Chief Justice Iftikhar Chaudhry, Supreme Court Judgment, July 31, 2009). Musharraf suspended the constitution, in other words, to ensure his political survival and remove a potential judicial veto to his candidacy. Ironically, the judiciary had originally provided cover for his actions after 1999. Chaudhury's resistance, and the eventually successful lawyers' movement to restore him to office, may have been a turning point in enforcing constraints on executive power, but it is too early to make that claim, particularly given the controversial positions taken by some movement members.

Pakistan and Islam

"Islam" or Muslim identity was the "raison d'être" that justified Pakistan's very existence; in seeking to mobilize public support for the soon-to-be-born state, the Muslim League used the slogan "Islam in danger." "Islamic" consciousness was palpable and a motivating symbol. Incumbents and challengers have in diverse ways sought to deploy Islamic symbols and frames in mobilizing support and rationalizing choices. Pakistan is host to numerous Sufi saints (*pirs*) and their followers (*mureeds*). These can be politically consequential, and *pirs* have played important roles in guerrilla resistance movements (Pir Pagaro in Sind being a prominent example; his Hur militia confronted British rule, and his descendants remain politically powerful). *Sajjada nasheens* (who have authority in religious shrines) were significant in mobilizing support for the Muslim League victory in the important pre-Partition elections in Punjab in 1946 over the more secular Unionist party.

Islam is unlike Roman Catholicism in that there is not a clear "church" (Mottahedeh, 2007). There is not a single hierarchy that defines who speaks authoritatively for the religion. Instead there are sources, starting with the Quran, Islam's scripture, which Muslims hold to be God's word. Next is the Sunna, referring to the wisdom and teaching of the Prophet Muhammad. Finally, there are *ulama*, religious scholars seeking to act as custodians of the tradition (Zaman, 2002). Diverse views within an interpretative tradition that is over 1000 years old have lent stature to specialists. With lithograph, print, and other transmission

Weak state, strong society, negotiable polity   41

technologies, traditional authority has in places been supplanted by an interpretative anarchy (Bulliet, 2004). New communications technologies have further augmented this process—Pakistan's television program "Aalim Online" provides one example amid a myriad.

Just as there is not a single Islamic "church," so there is not a single Muslim "pope" to explain how to make Pakistan's constitution authoritatively "Islamic." It is not that there were no answers to questions in Pakistan about what "Islam" says; rather, there were too many answers, sometimes vague and themselves open to contested interpretations, as well as zealots and believers who were convinced that their interpretation was superior. Various interested groups and parties have come up with different answers while generally agreeing that an "Islamic" government was sought. The Jamiat Ulema-e-Islam (a Deobandi pro-Pakistan *ulama* group led by Maulana Shabbir Usmani, whose son Taqi Usmani became Chief Justice and a well-known Islamic scholar) was prominent (Interview with Maulana Asad Thanvi, July 2009). The Jamiat Ulema-e-Pakistan was a Barelvi group (there has been an acrimonious history between the Deobandi and Barelvi sects in South Asia). The well-disciplined Jamaat-e-Islami distributed literature describing its vision for the Islamic state. In 1948, a Shariat group was set up in the Pakistan Muslim League to work toward an "Islamic order" in Pakistan (Afzal, 2001: 65). Jinnah reportedly declared that the future constitution would be based on Shariat (Afzal, 2001: 65–66).

Shortly after Pakistan's founding, the "Objectives Resolution" specified an Islamic orientation for the country, as well as a democratic polity: the polity would be one "Wherein the principles of democracy, freedom, equality, tolerance and social justice as enunciated by Islam shall be fully observed" and "Wherein the Muslims shall be enabled to order their lives in the individual and collective spheres in accordance with the teachings and requirements of Islam as set out in the Holy Quran and the Sunnah." At least two interviewees declared their strong belief that the Objectives Resolution was Liaquat Ali Khan's compromise with religious leaders and was responsible for Pakistan's later problems with religious agitation and sectarian conflict (Interviews, July 2009). An interviewee who participated in the Nizam-e-Mustafa popular agitation against the Z. A. Bhutto regime asserted that the Objectives Resolution only captured in words what the Muslim League pre-Partition appeals had stated in numerous speeches (Interview with Dost Muhammad Faizi, July 2009).

Translating the religious lobbies into a workable prescription for an Islamic government appeared to many to be an intractable problem. The *Munir Report*, a 1954 Commission of Enquiry publication, noted that:

> "no two learned divines [...] agreed" on the definition of a Muslim: "If we attempt our own definition as each learned divine has done and that definition differs from that given by all others, we unanimously go out of the fold of Islam. And if we adopt the definition given by any one of the *ulama*, we remain Muslims according to the view of that *alim* but *kafirs* according to the definition of every one else".

(cited in Jalal, 2008: 270–271)

42 *Political survival in Pakistan*

The inability to define who counted as a Muslim made it correspondingly difficult to define an "Islamic state," as Jalal (2008) observed. Despite these challenges, Pakistan was identified with Islam and Muslims in official narratives. This was a "loaded and untenable equation," difficult to reconcile with the fact that most Muslims in post-Partition India stayed on in India rather than migrate to the homeland for Indian Muslims (Jalal, 1995: 87). The Sind Provincial League and others saw the defense of Pakistan as the defense of Islam; Pakistan's subjection to India would have implications for other Islamic countries (*Dawn*, September 24, 1953, cited in Rizvi, 2001: 59). Liaquat Ali Khan stated that "the Muslims of the sub-continent wanted to build up their lives in accordance with the teachings and traditions of Islam, because they wanted to demonstrate to the world that Islam provides a panacea to the many diseases that have crept into the life of humanity today" (Rizvi, 2001: 62). The Pakistan Muslim League's early leader Khaliquzzaman was interested in "Islamistan," a vague plan for unity among Muslim states in the world, while Liaquat Ali Khan actively discussed economic and military cooperation (Afzal, 2001: 53, 83–84).

Virtually all rulers in Pakistan have sought to use Islam to enhance their legitimacy, undermine opposition, and increase their authority. Military ruler Ayub Khan, not usually considered an Islamist, sought to enhance his legitimacy by mobilizing support from Sufi *pirs* when confronting his Jamaat-e-Islami supported rival, Fatima Jinnah, in the 1962 election. His successor, the hard-drinking Yahya Khan, invoked God in the 1971 war. Zulfikar Ali Bhutto referred rhetorically to "Islamic" socialism and the quest for an Islamic bomb; he also outlawed gambling and drinking, and declared Ahmaddis non-Muslims, in an effort to obtain religious support and divide a challenger coalition.

Zia ul-Haq, described variously as a "thoroughgoing" Islamizer (Nasr, 2001a), and a "revolutionary Islamist" (Husain, 2002), established the Federal Shariat Court in 1980. The well-known Hudood Ordinances of February 10, 1979 proclaimed that Islamic law would be applied to the four offences subject to Hudood (literally, boundaries): intoxication, theft, *zina* (adultery/fornication), and *qazf* (slander or false accusation). The Offence of Zina [fornication and adultery] Ordinance provoked special controversy due to its negative consequences for women's ability to prosecute rape crimes without themselves being charged with adultery. Zia ul-Haq also added two sections to the penal code, prescribing life imprisonment or death for blasphemy against the Quran or the Prophet.

Successors to Zia ul-Haq included Benazir Bhutto, who visited a Sufi shrine in Lahore immediately upon her arrival, and under whose tenure the Pakistani-supported Taliban made major territorial gains in Afghanistan; Nawaz Sharif, who headed the Islami Jamhoori Ittehad (the Islamic Democratic Alliance) and was Zia ul-Haq's protégé from the 1980s, sought Shariat rule to enhance his control; and Musharraf, who compromised with the Muttahida Majlis-e-Amal, a religious coalition in NWFP, in their wish to effective religious law (the *Nizam-e-Adl*).

Wickham (2002) argues that authoritarian regimes seek to remove sites, agents, and targets of mobilization. State Islamization in effect tries to remove targets by making the state legitimate "Islamically" and by coopting some agents—in effect, giving them a seat in the winning coalition. Official Islamization can also remove sites for mobilization, by bringing locations and resources challengers might use under the regime's surveillance and purview. Incumbent leaders in Pakistan, whether military or civilian in origin, have adopted "Islamic" postures for these and other reasons. Nasr (2001a) argues that Islamic postures were used to try to expand the state's reach into society, made difficult by the landed "oligarchy" that constrained state action:

> the alliance between the state and the oligarchy impeded the state's efforts to either effectively pursue development or satisfactorily contend with inequities in distribution of resources through state institutions, forcing the state to instead look for alternate channels for alleviating poverty and to even contemplate a different structure of authority through which to expand its capacity to rule. The result has been that the state turned to Islam and its social institutions to achieve both ends. The turn to Islam in Pakistan is therefore a product of the attempts by a state that is held captive by the oligarchy to augment its power and autonomy of action.
>
> (Nasr, 2001a: 58)

Specific extraction initiatives under Islamization, however, did not profoundly alter the low tax revenue or land inequality problem that Pakistan has faced, as described in the next chapter. The Council on Islamic Ideology argued against land reform, posing one obstacle to legislation, although there is not unanimity on this question. Maulana Asad Thanvi of the Jamiat Ulema-e-Islam expressed a dissenting view, arguing that the original land distribution under British rule was illegitimate, and therefore land redistribution was justified, and furthermore that Islamic inheritance laws would over generations naturally divide up large holdings (Interview with Asad Thanvi, 2009).

Political parties

According to the "responsible party government" ideal commonly suggested in politics textbooks (e.g. Sodaro, 2004), a party declares a particular political platform, is elected amid competitors, tries faithfully to implement its proclaimed governance preferences, and then is held accountable as the public evaluates the party's performance and votes in the next election. This ideal-type is far from the ground realities in Pakistan, where elected governments have not usually fulfilled their full term in office, and where horse-trading and floor-crossing have made official platforms appear florid and hollow. Political parties in Pakistan are typically weak entities suffering from factionalism, low party discipline, and frequent defections and "floor-crossing." Individual party members often seek to ally with the victor to receive some spoils. Factions are brought together for opportunistic reasons, and rivalries lead to party splits. Struggles for patronage are routine, and defections plentiful, in what may be a South Asian pattern (Sobhan, 2002: 153). Personalities rather than platforms appear to dominate parties.

44 *Political survival in Pakistan*

The Muslim League, whose demand had originally supported Pakistan's creation, did not provide a unified and lasting force for national coherence and mobilization. Founded in 1906, the Muslim League only became a mass party in 1939; India's Congress, in contrast, started in 1885 and was transformed into a mass party in 1920 by Gandhi. The Muslim League was dominated by Jinnah and did not have effective procedures for resolving internal conflicts and aggregating diverse interests (Rizvi, 2001: 61–62). The Muslim League has had various groups, such as a Pir Pagaro group, referring to the powerful Sindhi Leader Pir Pagaro. The Qaiyum Muslim League was a split-off creation from the Muslim League, and resulted from Abdul Qaiyum Khan's rivalry with Mumtaz Daultana (Talbot, 2005: 434).

Across the five general elections to the National Assembly from 1988 to 2002, the Pakistan Muslim League won 43 percent of the seats. But this is deceptive, as it arguably functioned as a unified party only in 1993 and 1997. More often, competing factions claimed the party mantle, making the PML label closer to an "ad hoc election-driven gathering of independents," taking various factional guises (known by the factional leader's initial, such as C, J, N, and Q) (Gazdar, 2008: 1). The 2008 elections in Pakistan saw the Musharraf-associated PML-Q lose significant numbers to their opposition, the PML-N (referring to Nawaz Sharif's faction). One opportunistic faction was sardonically described by detractors as the "Al-Faida Group" (the benefits group)—a play on "Al-Qaeda"; that label captures the belief that special privileges and private benefits (rather than ideology or principled stances) drive party loyalties.

The Pakistan People's Party was the most successful at getting votes in West Pakistan in the 1970 election. It demonstrated an ability to generate votes in different provinces. Despite its name and its populist rhetoric under founder Zulfiqar Ali Bhutto, the Pakistan People's Party is more a dynastic family enterprise than an organization based on transparent rules beyond any personality or clique. Party funds are not distributed transparently and upward mobility within the party ranks is based predominantly on the party chief's direction (Interview with Ghazi Salahuddin, March 2009). The Pakistan People's Party, although dominated by the Benazir Bhutto/Asif Zardari group has a faction associated with Murtaza Bhutto, known as the *Shaheed* (martyr) group after he was killed.

Religious parties have not been immune; for example, the Jamiat Ulema-e-Islam's powerful faction, JUI-F, is associated with Maulana Fazlur Rehman. The Jamiat Ulema-e-Pakistan, Jamiat Ulema-e-Islam, and the Jamaat-e-Islami are established names among religious political parties. The religious groups had generally opposed the Muslim League's demand for a separate state and therefore "needed to reestablish their credentials as loyal citizens of the state, not to mention build political bases of support among the more religious segments of the urban lower middle-classes—the commercial and trading groups in particular" (Jalal, 1990: 282). The Shariat lobby in the Muslim League, as well as the Deoband *ulama*, quickly called for an Islamic constitution. Qasim Zaman argues that the *ulama* have been "custodians of change"; rather than fixed, atavistic throwbacks rigidly adhering to medieval ideas, the *ulama* have sought to retain authority, influence, and power by posing as gatekeepers and sole authoritative interpreters in the

Islamic tradition (Zaman, 2002). Moreover, in an Islamic system, the *ulama* would have significant veto power, as they would presumably judge whether public laws were in keeping with Islam.

The Jamaat-e-Islami may be a relatively "modern" party in its institutionalized internal rules, disciplined cadres, and resilience to personalized factions. Although their proclaimed agenda is "revolutionary," in practice they tend to be orderly participants in the polity, and generally fairly rule-bound. Syed (2001) has a dissenting view, describing coercive tendencies in the organization.[3] The JI has shown tactical flexibility, such as when it supported Fatima Jinnah, a female presidential candidate, against the military ruler Ayub Khan in the 1965 elections. It is a vanguardist political party with longer-term ambitions, and a disciplined corps, as well as a middle class support base. The Jamaat-e-Islami has had three leaders: Maulana Maududi from 1941 to 1972; Mian Tufail until 1987, and Qazi Hussain Ahmed from 1987. Furthermore, the JI's "reputation for being corruption-free, its internal democracy, and the discipline and dedication of its workers set the JI apart from other parties" (Cohen, 2004: 176).

From an early stage, the JI's leaders were involved in polity design, and had aspirations for using a selection institution—elections—to gain office or join a winning coalition. Maulana Maududi distanced himself from the *ulama*, although he had undertaken some study in the traditional *nizami* curriculum that is taught in *madrasas*. Maududi also referred to his aristocratic Sufi lineage and his relationship to the vast Chishti order—a reference that may have bolstered his leadership (aside from his formidable, precocious intelligence and rhetorical mastery of Urdu). The JI has a reputation for superior internal discipline, compared to other groups. Despite this reputation and the relative ideological unity in its cadre ranks, the JI's success in elections has been limited at a national level. It achieved some recent success in the local and provincial elections in NWFP as a coalition partner to the religious group called the Muttahida Majlis-e-Amal (MMA, the Allied Action Congregation). Yet even the JI's reputation was somewhat tainted with the appearance of nepotism when its head appointed a relative to a "reserve" seat in the legislature (Interview with former MMA member, 2009).

Disputed borders

The most prominent border dispute in Pakistan's history has been over Kashmir. Kashmir is typically described as being strategically important for Pakistan. The Pakistani defense analyst Hasan Askari Rizvi writes that the Indian military occupation in Kashmir raised serious geostrategic concerns:

> Kashmir is so strategically located that it can be used to cripple Pakistan economically and militarily. Two of the important rivers flow from Kashmir. The Mangla Headworks on the river Jhelum is only a few miles inside the Azad [Pakistani-held] Kashmir border. The presence of Indian troops could constitute a direct threat from the rear to the North West Frontier Province and parts of the Punjab including Rawalpindi-Islamabad. Kashmir can therefore be used

46   *Political survival in Pakistan*

for an offensive strategy against Pakistan, whereas the possibility of a Pakistani attack on India via Kashmir is very remote.

(Rizvi, 2001: 53)

A pattern of confrontation over Kashmir has emerged. Local insurgents and the Indian and Pakistani militaries have repeatedly clashed, escalating several times into all-out war. For Pakistan, about 15 percent of the size of India, and with fewer inherited resources from the British, this meant a proportionately greater defense burden on its national budget. That extraordinary concern for national security has had profound consequences for Pakistan's development, particularly the oversized role the Pakistani military plays in national political and economic decision-making.

In 1893, a treaty between British India and Afghanistan had included a border drawn by British representative Sir Mortimer Durand. Known as the Durand Line, it separated the Pushtun tribes in Afghanistan from the Pushtuns in British India (Rizvi, 2001: 28–30). This became West Pakistan's western border and was rejected by Afghanistan's government, leading to the Afghani refusal to support Pakistan's membership in the United Nations, and to several clashes. This border is frequently in the news today as a porous region where the Pakistani military is heavily engaged. In 1993, the British treaty expired. This may provide legal cover to irredentists.

Internal jurisdictions

Calling Pakistan's central government "federal" as is sometimes done in official documents is misleading. The country has more frequently acted as a unitary state, or as a highly centralized federal one. The center has retained the power to dissolve all legislative assemblies. Provincial autonomy remains a bone of contention. The provincial autonomist perspective has historical roots. According to Sindhi nationalist Mumtaz Ali Bhutto, Muslim-majority areas considering accession to Pakistan believed they would be joining a confederation. Unlike the Indian plan for a federal state under which a Muslim minority might be made subservient to a Hindu majority, the provinces would retain their autonomy and self-governance, excepting those powers that they chose to give to the center. This promise was not kept. The consequence has been that the country has not worked, has broken, and more than half the country's history has been played out under martial law or military rule. Democracy has not taken root because in a multinational state like Pakistan, a "highly centralized federal system" cannot work. When free elections are held, as in 1970, then the provincial divide asserts itself (Interview with Mumtaz Ali Bhutto, February 2009). (As comparable cases which could not hold together, M. A. Bhutto mentioned the USSR, Czechoslovakia, and Yugoslavia.)

Center-unit tensions are often stoked by demands by provincials and subgroups for greater financial resources. The National Finance Council, which distributes development funds to the provinces, has a population-based formula for award sizes. An ongoing grievance from sparsely populated Balochistan is that allocated

Weak state, strong society, negotiable polity 47

funds do not match that province's contributions from natural gas production. This is complicated by budgetary strains from defense and debt-servicing burdens.

Ayesha Jalal (1990) argues that defense spending needs have contributed to state centralization. In this process, non-elected institutions (the military and civil service) became dominant over elected institutions. Since the colonial era, however, those unelected institutions had not recruited evenly from the population. This has exacerbated Pakistan's integration problem. For example, military personnel in British India were recruited largely from the Punjab and NWFP, ostensibly because they were "sons of soil" and "martial races" (a British colonial-era notion describing an ethnic grouping primordially inclined to soldiery). Sindhis and Balochis are underrepresented in the army, particularly at the officer level, and this has become a major grievance (Rizvi, 2001: 270–271). This disproportionate ethnic representation undermines the military's image as a national force. Military operations against Balochi insurgents may be tainted as attempts at ethnic domination rather than an exercise in maintaining law and order.

Author interviews with polity members from varied backgrounds revealed a widespread belief that "agencies"– referring typically to Inter-Services Intelligence (ISI, military) and Intelligence Bureau (IB, civilian)—were actively involved in manipulating ethnic, sectarian, and other leaders and organizations. According to a former provincial assembly member, these agencies are driven by "hyper-patriotism." They believe they are best able to judge the national interest, and their mission justifies law-breaking, conspiracy, and violence. Their activities have repeatedly created "monsters," outcomes that backfired or created unintended consequences, in what might elsewhere be called "blowback" (Interview, 2009). In Ayesha Jalal's terms, this exemplifies the way unelected institutions consolidate their supremacy over elected ones (Jalal, 1995).

Although India was seen as the major threat to Pakistani territorial claims, there was also significant friction with their western neighbor. Afghanistan supported an independent Pakhtunistan (a homeland for the Pathan ethnic group that populates the NWFP and parts of Balochistan). Afghani Prime Minister Hashim Khan suggested in 1947 that the NWFP could join Afghanistan. There were Afghani raids and military clashes with Pakistani troops. A diplomatic break occurred in 1955 when Pakistan moved to incorporate NWFP into the "One Unit Scheme of West Pakistan," rejecting Afghani objections as meddling in internal Pakistani affairs. Relations with Afghanistan were resumed in 1957 only to break again in 1961 before resuming in 1963 (Rizvi, 2001: 54–55).

Pukhtun nationalist Wali Khan famously stated that he had been a Pukhtun for 4000 years, a Muslim for 1400 years, and a Pakistani for 40 years. This neatly summarized the identities layered in the Pukhtun regions, and suggested an order of precedence. Pukhtunwali, the unwritten code that underlies Pukhtun tribal society, emphasizes protection and hospitality toward guests and revenge for all insults, embedded within self-pride and honor (Jalal, 2000: 26). Pukhtunwali has been compared to medieval chivalry (Foust and Koogler, 2008). Pukhtuns have "defied external pressures more effectively than their own internal fissures"; they are reputed to have a competitive spirit, and emphasis on individual identity that

48   *Political survival in Pakistan*

nevertheless "coexists with a binding communitarian code, which, when it conflicts with Islamic strictures, invariably prevails" (Jalal, 2000: 26).

Wali Khan's National Awami Party was inherited from his father Ghaffar Khan's famous Red Shirt organization, a nonviolent movement which had supported the Indian National Congress and opposed British rule. The NAP was strong in four out of six settled districts in NWFP, and had little presence in the Fata areas or elsewhere. The Pakhtoonistan demand had little attraction for Pukhtun who were well-integrated into the military and who were integrated economically with Punjab and Karachi (Cohen, 2004: 217–218). A Muhajir observer from an elite civil service background traced the large Pukhtun influx into Karachi to the time when Gohar Ayub, son of national leader Ayub Khan (a Pakhtun), held power there. Pukhtuns have subsequently come to dominate the trucking and transport sector (Interview, 2009). Their "docile" labor undermined unionizing activity among shipyard workers (Khan and Jacobsen, August 11, 2009). The implication was that the national leadership facilitated their ethnic group's success over others. Such perceptions point to the sense that the affinity groups who are politically favored are those with whom the leader shares ethnicity.

The "tribal" Pukhtuns have posed another challenge for Pakistan's consolidation as a state. Concerned about Russian influence in Afghanistan, the British had worked to retain a modus vivendi with the various tribes in what were then the "unsettled areas" in the north-west. Nevertheless, there were tribal agitations which had dealt serious defeats to the British (under the Faqir of Ipi in 1936). These issues did not disappear with Pakistan's creation; several tribal leaders have sought secession. Some agitating tribes from the British era such as the Wazirs and the Mahsuds remain familiar to those analyzing the recent "Taliban" insurgency. Prominent among these was the Faqir of Ipi, Haji Mira Ali Khan, from the Tirah border between Pakistan and Afghanistan (Ziring, 1997: 87). Afghanistan had friendly relations with tribal Pukhtuns, and this brought some support to local secessionists. Gandhi and the Congress had promised Afghanistan a route to the sea in return for opposing Pakistan. In early 1948, an emissary from the Afghan king tried unsuccessfully to convince Jinnah to grant sovereignty to the tribal belt. However, Afghanistan did not intercede when Pakistani forces defeated the Faqir of Ipi.

In independent Pakistan, there are seven tribal agencies, "frontier regions" with "administrative enclaves in six settled districts and provincial tribal areas abutting on nine settled districts" (Riaz, 2008). Fata (Federally Administered Tribal Areas), and FRs (Frontier Regions), which are directly under presidential authority. The president also has final authority in Pata (Provincially Administered Tribal Areas), which are under the provincial governor. Governance in the tribal areas has usually been by customary law applied by chiefs, elders, and councils called *jirga*. One difficult political issue is whether Fata can be merged with NWFP. "The Fata has proved to be a kind of black hole for successive civilian governments which have tried to introduce reforms or integrate it with the province" (Riaz, 2008). The Durand Line, a disputed boundary between Pakistan and Afghanistan, complicates the effort to place Fata clearly under Islamabad's control.

Weak state, strong society, negotiable polity 49

Frontier Crimes Regulations, a colonial-era creation, provide the governance interface between the government (represented by a political agent) and the tribes. The central government's authority was restricted to communications, foreign affairs, and defense. When the princely state of Swat acceded to Pakistan, there was effectively no change in legal status. British involvement in administrative decision-making was often greater than the formal legal limits would suggest, as the local ruler consulted with the British administrative appointments, and the system worked "fairly smoothly" as both "knew their limits"; the nearby princely state of Chitral saw the Frontier Crimes Regulations invoked only once during a particular political agent's tenure (Interview, 2009).

East Pakistan and some other units appeared more eager to push for a confederation than a genuine federation. There were numerous grievances, including resistance to Urdu as the national language, disputes over customs revenue collections and disbursements, and a widespread belief that policies were economically unjust to East Pakistan. In 1955, the "One Unit Scheme" was introduced, creating an integrated "West Pakistan Province" incorporating states and provinces. There was political resistance to the scheme.

In March 1957 the East Pakistan Assembly voted for a more radical autonomy in the federation; this was resisted by Iskandar Mirza and Ayub Khan, who believed that only mild autonomy could safeguard national integrity and security (Afzal, 2001: 216). In July 1957, the West Pakistan Assembly demanded that the One Unit Scheme be dissolved. Resistance to the One Unit Scheme grew during the 1960s' anti-Ayub movement.

Under Ayub Khan's successor, Yahya Khan, West Pakistan was reconstituted into Punjab, Sind, NWFP, and Balochistan provinces on July 1, 1970 (Rizvi, 2001: 187). This difference, fed by perceptions that West Pakistan was treating East Pakistan unfairly, escalated to a severe national crisis.

East Pakistan's regional elections had brought the East Pakistan-based Awami League to power. In the 1970 elections to the National Assembly, the Awami League won 160 seats from the 162 allocated to East Pakistan. The Pakistan People's Party had contested the same election, found support in West Pakistan, and was the second major winner, receiving about half as many votes as the Awami League (Rizvi, 2001: 190–91). Rather than a compromise or coalition government, these regionally polarized results led to the federation's dismemberment. West Pakistan did not allow the Awami League to assume the power it had won at the polls. The PPP's support was based in West Pakistan, and it was able to cultivate support with the Pakistani military and elite. A brutal military crackdown in East Pakistan took place, and a full-fledged rebellion arose, which included Indian military engagement. The result was a humiliating defeat for the Pakistan army, and the creation of Bangladesh.

Policy-makers in Pakistan's early decades feared a national breakup (Brines, 1968: 234). This fear was realized in the 1971 war, which culminated in the secession of East Pakistan and the creation of Bangladesh. For Pakistan, this was actually two wars, a civil war in the face of East Pakistani dissent and a war with India (Sisson and Rose, 1990: 1). A central government bias against East Pakistan

50 *Political survival in Pakistan*

was discernible in the relatively little attention that region received. December 1970 elections had produced two regionally dominant political parties: the Awami League, led by Sheikh Mujibur Rahman in East Pakistan, and the Pakistan People's Party, led by Zulfiqar Ali Bhutto in West Pakistan. Each sought to wield power at the national level. Mutual suspicions about trustworthiness and West Pakistani concerns about the fidelity of the Awami League led to the civil war and brutal military crackdown in East Pakistan, which commenced in late March, 1971. A total of 7 million refugees fled to India (Talbot, 1998: 208), including most Awami League leaders who set up a "Government of Bangladesh" in Calcutta (Sisson and Rose, 1990: 2–4).

Bangladeshi nationalist guerrillas continued raids into East Pakistan, and increasing direct Indian interventions took place (Talbot, 1998: 210). On December 3, 1971, a Pakistani air raid on Indian military bases took place. An Indian counter-attack that included naval bombardment of the Karachi port followed. Pakistan also attacked into Kashmir and the Indian Punjab. The Indians counter-attacked into multiple places and several major tank battles resulted. The war was not as intense on the eastern front, as marshes provided East Pakistan (what became Bangladesh) with natural defenses. India launched an air and ground attack into East Pakistan and imposed a naval blockade, and the Indian forces reached the outskirts of Dacca (which became the Bangladeshi capital) on December 16, 1971.

On December 17, the Indian Prime Minister Indira Gandhi and the Pakistani President General Yahya Khan made reciprocal ceasefire announcements. Losses included up to 9000 Pakistani men, 200 tanks, and 75 aircraft, and 2500 Indian men, 80 tanks, and 45 aircraft (not including Bangladeshi fighters). A Pakistani submarine and an Indian ship were also sunk (Ganguly, 1994: 81–84). Pakistan Television's Hamid Rajput described the secession as a psychological blow. The world's largest Islamic state had broken up, and its aftermath was a grave, depressed period for many Pakistani nationalists (Interview with Hamid Rajput, July 2009). Zia-ul-Islam Zuberi, who became a Sindh Province Assembly member in the 1970 election on a Jamiat Ulema-e-Pakistan ticket, described the fall of Dhaka as a terrible moment, sparking disappointment and anger. From that point on, people started to wonder if Pakistan itself would survive (Interview with Zia-ul-Islam Zuberi, 2009).

As the numerically dominant province in West Pakistan and the main recruiting center for the army, Punjab enjoyed special strength. Clive Dewey (1991) has argued that military dominance in Pakistan is derived from a special relationship between the peasantry and the army in Punjab (Talbot, 2005: 64). This is not spread evenly throughout the province, but rather found most emphatically in some districts, such as Attock, Rawalpindi, and Jhelum. One lesson from the Army Staff College is that all countries have a "heart" or "core." In Pakistan, this is Punjab; the other three provinces are all potential invasion routes (Cohen, 2004). Perceived Punjabi hegemony and efforts to constrain it remain a repeated theme in Pakistani politics.

There was also the security claim that "the security of East Pakistan lies in West Pakistan." This was used to justify to East Pakistanis why resources were being

Weak state, strong society, negotiable polity 51

appropriated for use by a military that largely recruited from West Pakistan. The claim was perceived to have been proved false in the 1965 war, because India was deterred from attacking East Pakistan only due to fear that the Chinese would intervene (Interview with senior retired military officer, 2009). This was one factor precipitating the massive support that Mujib ur-Rehman enjoyed, because it made resource appropriation from East Pakistan look more like predatory exploitation than action for East Pakistan's security. A key rationale for Pakistan—that it could provide security—was undermined and, with it, the argument for taking resources from East Pakistan and placing them into West Pakistan.

Tensions in Sind have been fed by income inequality, resentment against Punjab's dominance, and strained relations with Mohajirs settled in urban centers. Land ownership was most concentrated in Sind, where "8 per cent had holdings over 100 acres which accounted for 55 per cent of the total area, while those in possession of 500 acres or more constituted less than 1 per cent of all the owners and controlled 29 per cent of the land" (Jalal, 1990: 87). *Haris* were sharecroppers without occupancy rights, and may have constituted as much as two-thirds of the peasantry (Jalal, 1990: 87). The leaving Hindu landlords had made as much as 1,345,000 acres available, and up to 800,000 acres were taken by Sindhi landlords (Jalal, 1990: 87).

Shah (2008) suggests that socioeconomic changes played a role in Sindhi ethnonationalism:

> In 1970s, Prime Minister Bhutto started to transform Sindh society by developing its middle class. The emerging middle class began becoming foundation stone of the nationalist movement in Sindh. Almost all major nationalist parties were founded in this era. After Bhutto was executed, Sindh took to resistance against the military. Hundreds of civilians as well as armed personnel were killed.
>
> (Shah, 2008)

A related development that may have spurred on Sindhi and other nationalist parties is likely to have been Bangladesh's secession after the Awami League's massive electoral victory in 1970. That may have spurred on ethnic activists elsewhere. Shah suggests that such boosts from the successes of nationalist movements elsewhere can be seen in the encouragement Sindhi activists receive from Balochistan: "If there is a resistance in Balochistan, the morale of the nationalist movement in Sindh becomes high" (Shah, 2008). Furthermore, "Musharraf government's policies have escalated the sense of deprivation in Sindh. Besides, the murder of Benazir has aired the flame of separatism in Sindh, which is spreading day by day" (Shah, 2008).

Regionalist and ethnic tensions are partly disclosed by the National Assembly seat tallies from 1988 to 2002. It appears that only the PPP has an ethnically and regionally diverse base. In contrast, the PML is based strongly in Punjab; the various Balochi and Pushtu nationalist parties are located in their regions. The religious parties are concentrated in NWFP, and have some spread elsewhere, but

52 *Political survival in Pakistan*

are comparatively small. MQM appears to be tiny, but derives its power from its relative dominance over Karachi, with its sizeable population, port, and commercial centrality.

Regional and ethnic tensions can be discerned from election results. Haris Gazdar used election results to try to identify patterns in support of various political parties (*Dawn*, February 13, 2008: 1, 4); however, the patterns are difficult to describe as alignment or realignment because there are few data points. The 1970 elections showed what observers and citizens suspected: that East Pakistan and West Pakistan had markedly different political loyalties, and that no parties won significant representation across the provinces.

Provinces can contain different ethnic "segments" or concentrations; a province like Balochistan contains different ethnic segments (Balochi, Pashto, and heterogeneous) and other ethnic groups, such as Seraiki, are located in both Punjab province and NWFP. Gazdar finds that the largest ethnic segments in Pakistan (Punjabi, Sindhi, Seraiki, and Pushto) are "healthy" in that there are parties straddling ethnic boundaries and that parochial electoral outcomes within particular segments do not persist (Gazdar, 2008: 4). The PPP and the Muslim League retain a presence in these areas.

Yet there is evidence from the electoral data that Pakistan remains regionally and ethnically fragmented, as seen in electoral "waves." The Muslim League appears dominant through its position in the Punjab, reducing the party's incentives to engage in "inter-provincial accommodation"; in contrast, the PPP relies more on both Punjab and Sindh and therefore is likely to "toe a more federalist line" (Gazdar, 2008: 4). PPP wins have generally drawn on a more diversified ethnic base. Muslim League victory electoral waves (1990, 1997, 2002) appear to reduce the PPP to a Sindhi party, and PPP victory waves (1988, 1993) appear to reduce the Muslim League to a Punjabi party. There is a difference, though. Gazdar notes that "a restricted PPP still retains a presence in Punjabi and Seraiki segments, whereas a restricted Muslim League virtually disappears from Sindhi-speaking segments" (Gazdar, 2008: 4). Gazdar argues that victories achieved by reliance on one ethnic group and by restricting others to narrow ethnic segments risks the federation's health (Gazdar, 2008: 4).

In the official party platforms for the 2008 National Assembly elections, various different approaches were taken to the provincial autonomy question. The parties devoted significant attention to this. The PPP, for example, promised to abolish the "Concurrent List" (policy areas in which both provincial and federal governments have a say) and to have economic justice for the provinces when natural resources were extracted or taxes collected. The MQM sought a national dialogue leading to consensus on the issue, and suggested that defense, foreign affairs, and currency be left to the federation. The Awami National Party (based primarily among the Pukhtun ethnic group) sought maximum provincial autonomy as well as holding federal forces (military and bureaucratic) responsible for past and future actions in the provinces (Rahman, 2008).

This uneasiness about national integrity and the federation's strength may partly explain PPP leader Asif Zardari's strong assertion after Benazir Bhutto's

Weak state, strong society, negotiable polity   53

assassination that the party was loyal to the federation: there was a reasonable prospect that his party could win national elections. Appealing to Sindhis alone was not a wise strategy because it would alienate other potential supporters, and because secession was not a reasonable prospect. In contrast, the Punjab governor offered safe refuge to Sind-based Punjabis at the Punjab governor's house, and thereby stoked fears of anti-Punjabi backlash after the assassination. To some observers, this seemed a thinly veiled effort to play on ethnic animosities and tensions.

Selection institutions and winning coalitions in Pakistan

"Selection institutions," or the actual means by which state leaders are chosen, have changed from time to time in Pakistan. They have included dismissal by the president, military coup, rigged election, free election, and attempts to embed a decisive constitutional role for the military in the leadership and winning coalition. Unstable, unreliable, and difficult to access selection institutions (combined with narrow winning coalitions) have encouraged revolutionary and secessionist challenges. The lack of repeat or regular elections, and the dismissals by presidents and coup-makers, can be understood as efforts to undermine parliamentary elections as a selection institution. The army has made it clear that it will belong to every winning coalition or take over leadership directly.

State institutions vs. government institutions

Historians Jalal (1995) and Ziring (1997) see not a simple battle between democracy and autocracy, but rather a competition between elected and unelected institutions. A related distinction is the contest between institutions of state and institutions of government; in theory the institutions of government (such as legislatures) are supposed to formulate and legislate policy while the institutions of state (such as military and civil bureaucracies) are supposed to provide professional implementation.[4] There are principal agent problems: as the principal, the legislature's authority is eroded if the bureaucratic agents shirk their duty or defect from their expected roles. Moreover, bureaucratic institutions can engage in the ultimate subversion by capturing government institutions, dismissing them, or replacing them.

In practice, state institutions and government institutions clash over who rules. A legislature must offer sufficient benefits or impose sufficient costs to state institutions to prevent them from the temptation to undertake a coup or otherwise subvert the legislature. Consequently, when there is an operating legislature, the institutions of state will normally be highly placed in the winning coalition, as well as be subject to attempts by elected leaders to manipulate bureaucratic structures and thereby prevent challenges. When the institutions of state are directly ruling the country (as happens with military coups, for example) they will usually undertake some electoral measures and innovations (such as Ayub Khan's presidential election based on the Basic Democrats, and Zia ul-Haq's referendum). Such moves can enhance the legitimacy that has

54 *Political survival in Pakistan*

been lost by subverting the institutions of government that are supposed to rule. Incumbents emerging from both the institution of state and institutions of government have used corruption charges against specific elected and bureaucratic figures to disqualify or dismiss them from office. The clash between institutions of state and institutions of government extends to rule manipulation, reflected in repeated wrangling over Article 58 2 (b) (which gives the president the power to dismiss the government and legislature).

It may be argued that leaders who emerge from legislatures would rely on a larger winning coalition than leaders who emerge from a bureaucratic background. The legislature-based leader must satisfy legislators and underlying constituents as well as thwart challenges from the institutions of state (by including some in the winning coalition and manipulating or repressing others). The *Logic of Political Survival* asserts that larger winning coalitions translate to more public goods provision but shorter-lived leaders. This is because in large winning coalitions, members divide up a larger pie between them so have less to lose by defecting against the incumbent. In comparison, in a small winning coalition, each individual member has more to potentially lose if the incumbent loses office. The elected governments in Pakistan (Z.A. Bhutto's government; the two iterations that Nawaz Sharif and Benazir Bhutto each enjoyed in the 1990s) were indeed short-lived, compared to the military regimes under Ayub Khan, Zia ul-Haq, and Pervez Musharraf. But the *LOPS* logic does not fully explain this, because each government did not simply reduce private goods provision, but expanded it. At the same time, elected leaders tended to take initiatives to centralize control and narrow their winning coalition. Z.A. Bhutto's tenure, particular as martial law was imposed and the Balochistan provincial government was dismissed, fits this description.

A common argument is that five "vested groups" have stalled genuine democracy in Pakistan: the military, feudals, big business, religious leaders, and bureaucracy (Iqbal, 2008). Some observers believe that private media organizations are an emerging force; Pakistan Television (PTV) monopolized television news from its creation in 1964 under Ayub until Musharraf's liberalization almost four decades later (Interview with former Pakistan Television administrator Hamid Rajput, July 2009). A prominent business executive argued that the media, students, and lawyers were also powerful groups (Interview, 2009). The "Establishment" refers to the long-lived winning coalition in Pakistan that has persisted in its key players.

Military and civil bureaucracy

To be successful and survive, any political leader's supporting coalition must draw some military support, or at least avoid military challenge. Unless the military is included, a political contender's supporters cannot form a winning coalition. Legislative institutions such as the Constituent, National, and Provincial Assemblies have been repeatedly constrained or dismissed by military and bureaucratic figures. In Hamza Alavi's view, "overdeveloped" military and administrative strength originated as colonialists emphasized law and order over popular representation (Talbot, 2005: 54). In the colonial period, the military kept order, quelled rebellions, and deterred invaders. The civil service bureaucracy administered laws and regulations, licensing activities and collecting revenues. Termed "vice-regalism," this pattern continues, characterized by paternalism, wide discretionary powers, and the centralization of authority (Talbot, 2005: 64). Post-colonial state managers explicitly maintained continuity with the colonial period. The unelected leaders from the bureaucracy and the military consciously followed a colonial pattern, seeing themselves as guardians of stability and national integrity. This was apparent in actions taken by Governor-General Ghulam Muhammad.

On Liaquat Ali Khan's assassination, Khwaja Nazimuddin agreed to step down as governor-general to become prime minister, an office that had appeared strong in Liaquat's time. Ziring notes that "Nazimuddin was an acknowledged lightweight, but Liaquat had strengthened the office of the Prime Minister, and if Nazimuddin received the approval of the army high command and gained the loyalty of the senior members of the bureaucracy, he could be the best choice" (Ziring, 1997: 121). In other words, Nazimuddin's strength and efficacy in office would depend on military and bureaucratic support, vital for implementing policies, and critical forces in his winning coalition. Civil servant Ghulam Mohammad, an important figure in creating financial institutions for Pakistan, was made governor-general (Ziring, 1997: 126).

Ghulam Mohammad invoked the 1935 Government of India Act to dismiss Nazimuddin, the sitting prime minister, without the advice or consent of the Council of Ministers; Nazimuddin appealed to the Commonwealth Relations Office but the queen offered no response (Ziring, 1997: 161). True to the vice-regal pattern with its dominant military and bureaucracy, Ghulam Mohammad's most important supporters were General Ayub Khan, commander–in–chief of the Pakistan Army, the defense secretary, Iskandar Mirza, and Chaudhri Mohammad Ali, secretary-general of the administrative services (Ziring, 1997: 149). Constituent Assembly members considered their body sovereign; this was threatened if they could be superseded by Ghulam Mohammad as governor-general. Under their speaker, Maulvi Tamizuddin Khan, the Constituent Assembly passed laws to curtail the governor-general's powers. In 1954, Ghulam Muhammad responded by dissolving the Assembly.

Governor-General Ghulam Mohammad's dismissal of the Constituent Assembly in 1954 represents a decisive juncture at which the military-administrative influence over the legislative body was established. The Muslim League disputed the governor-general's action, taking the issue to the Chief Court of Sindh, where speaker Maulvi Tamizuddin Khan argued that the dismissal was "unconstitutional, illegal, *ultra vires*, without jurisdiction, inoperative, and void" (Choudhury, 1959: 148, cited in Ziring, 1997: 171). (Police forces arrayed outside the Sindh High Court attempted to bar Maulvi Tamizuddin's entry; he apparently disguised himself in a woman's burqa and managed to enter the facility (Interview with Sind High Court Senior Advocate Rochi Ram, July 2009).) The Sindh High Court agreed with Tamizuddin's argument, describing the Constituent Assembly as dissoluble only by a two-thirds majority from the Assembly itself; "Furthermore, the Crown was no longer empowered to terminate the Constituent Assembly, and the Governor-General,

56   *Political survival in Pakistan*

whose power stemmed from the Crown, could not be deemed to possess power not granted to the monarch" (Ziring, 1997: 172).

Ghulam Mohammad's government appealed the ruling to the Federal Court (later the Supreme Court of Pakistan), which reversed it. A constitutional struggle was sparked because the reversal's legal basis also called into question the Constituent Assembly's other legislative actions, 46 acts which had become law. The Federal Court also made it clear that an Assembly must exist; a second Constituent Assembly was created using the Provincial Assemblies as an electoral college (Interview with Rochi Ram, July 2009). This Assembly generated the 1956 Constitution. It was shortly before the originally scheduled 1958 elections that Ayub Khan's military coup took place.

According to *The Logic of Political Survival*, "military skill has often been a critical qualification for membership in the selectorate" (Bueno de Mesquita et al., 2003: 369). The Pakistani military is sometimes described as an "army with a country" and remains key to any winning coalition: Moonis Ahmar, a Pakistani political scientist and longtime commentator, notes that "The only institution in Pakistan that retains its organizational coherence, power, and influence is the military, and some suggest that a short-cut to get the government to act on some domestic issues is to influence the military" (Ahmar, 1996: 1046). Specific policies are more likely to be adopted if they have military support. Civilian prime ministers incorporate the military into the winning coalition for the prime minister's survival. Eventually, however, prioritizing the military's interests means less to go around to other groups clamoring for government largesse, and the prime minister eventually loses. A civilian-led government typically has a somewhat larger winning coalition, and with that, greater prospects for defection from that coalition.

In the pre-Partition forerunner to the Pakistan Civil Service, the British selected middle and upper management based on merit. After Pakistan was created, pressures to recruit more evenly from different places in the country have contributed to an entrenched quota system. This grew from early concern that Bengalis were underrepresented, and by 1980, only 10 percent of positions were offered on merit alone, while others were designated based on population-weighted criteria to provinces and other areas (Jones, 1997).[5] This quota system was meant to help prevent alienation by increasing representation from excluded groups. But a different governance problem has resulted—incompetence, or less than the most competent people for jobs.

Senior civil servants from the 1950s in particular tend to retain an elitist self-image; they typically regard the military as less intellectually developed and even boorish. High placement in the competitive civil service examinations was an immediate merit-based leap into the power elite. High officials in the civil service typically have great discretion, and enormous patronage power and graft opportunities. This has social status consequences; to one successful candidate in the civil service examination, this meant that his mother started receiving marriage proposals. Each batch's common training period produced camaraderie that often lasted their whole lives, and a self-assured culture that valued professionalism, particularly in the early years after independence (Interviews, 2002, 2008, 2009).

Bureaucrats have historically enjoyed significant insulation from public prosecution. The Government of India Act 1935 and later Constitution framers retained provisions that prevented prosecution of government officials for offenses committed "while acting or purporting to act in the discharge of his official duty"; prior sanction by the government is required before that public servant can be prosecuted (Noorani, July 25, 2009). The consequence is great power for the bureaucracy, as a significant hurdle has to be overcome before holding them to account for their actions. Ghulam Mohammad was a bureaucrat who obtained the governor-general's office, and proceeded to dismiss the Constituent Assembly, an anti-legislative move that laid the basis for several future dismissals by the political executive.

A great complication arose when the military, a junior partner for the civil bureaucracy and national government, took formal power in a military coup in 1958. This significantly expanded the military's role in political affairs. Since the 1950s, the Pakistani military has played a dominant role, whether it is directly in charge or whether civilians are in charge. Defense analyst and former Director of Naval Research Ayesha Siddiqua argues that the military has become predatory, and no civilian politician can survive for long in national office if the military's political and economic interests are threatened (Siddiqua, 2007).

Under Iskander Mirza, the military was initially a junior partner. Ayub Khan eventually displaced Mirza and asserted military supremacy. Yahya Khan's take-over was only a top-level administrative change and maintained continuity with the Ayub period except that the One Unit province for West Pakistan was abolished; Yahya Khan held Pakistan's first universal franchise national legislature elections because he received the flawed intelligence prediction that no clear winner would emerge and he would stay a dominant powerbroker. With the Awami League's dramatic win in East Pakistan, civil war, and Pakistan's humiliating surrender to India, Yahya Khan was forced out and military rule was curtailed. Zulfikar Bhutto has been described as someone who was hostage to his class interests, setting aside his initially left-leaning populist promises and instead promoting landholding rural interests (these apparent contradictions are explored in more detail in Chapter 3). He had a "classical realist" outlook and promoted military power. A few years into his regime, the military asserted itself and displaced him, pressured the Supreme Court into convicting him, and executed him.

The military under Zia ul-Haq was able to institutionalize its role in the policy process through a constitutional provision for the National Security Council, seen as an advisory body for emergency and security issues. All civilian members are appointed at presidential discretion, excepting the senate chair; the military's domination in the NSC would provide a veto to any civilian effort, or make the military itself the chief decision-maker during a proclaimed emergency (Rizvi, 2001: 257). (The NSC was abolished, and later reintroduced under General Musharraf.)

The military is dominated by the army. Although the army is technologically "modern," it still reflects traditional values in two key areas. First, there is traditional religious practice. Second, there is a tendency to see landholding as the desired goal. According to Ayesha Siddiqua (February 2, 2008), this is due to a quasi-mystical

58   *Political survival in Pakistan*

symbolic value that is associated with land ownership. This may be because the rural landholding class, seeking to protect its privileges, provided essential support for creating Pakistan (a reason not cited by Siddiqua). Whatever the explanation, Siddiqua's basic point is valid: in contrast to the "modern" image projected by the military, it has become a new landed gentry class. Rural elite culture is apparently also aped in lavish social gatherings.

Thus, a vital player in the winning coalition at the national level is the military. At the subnational level, the military is an important patron or a threat. The military is a key veto-holder. Crony capitalism is rife, leading columnist Shakir Hussain to write: "The cardinal rule for business everywhere is 'survival of the fittest' while in Pakistan, it is survival of the fittest, and most connected" (cited in Siddiqua, 2007: 105). Generous loans are given to landlords and big entrepreneurs, and loan defaulters are typically not held accountable and punished. This is facilitated by the state's regulatory role over the banking sector (Siddiqua, 2007: 105). Civilian leaders have been as culpable as military leaders; both Benazir Bhutto and Nawaz Sharif gave land worth nearly 167 million US dollars to cronies (Siddiqua, 2007: 105). These are "private goods" and special privileges doled out to favored supporters.

The Fauji Foundation did not pay taxes until the 1970s. It is now a major taxpayer, but still pays less (at 20 percent) than the Shaheen Foundation and Bahria Foundation, associated with the air force and navy respectively, which pay at a 30 percent rate. Siddiqua's research attributes this to the army's greater size and influence (Siddiqua, 2007: 119–123). These Foundations enjoy deep connections with the armed forces, and those connections pay off in profit-maximization, through favorable lending and licensing practices, as well as unwillingness by authorities to enforce environmental and other regulations against military-origin business entities.

The military has tried to demonstrate its authority to the rural landlords, expropriating territory as favors to military personnel—particularly from Cholistan in South Punjab, which is not the military's recruiting ground. This may partly explain the support for PPP and opposition or nonestablishment politicians in that region. The dominant landlords in South Punjab have not put up significant resistance to the military's land acquisition because it serves their economic interests:

> Khursheed Zaman Qureshi, a prominent landowner from 2000–02 in Musharraf's military government, did not object to the armed forces acquiring land in Southern Punjab. Although the common people are anxious about the military getting preferential treatment over the indigenous poor population in the ongoing land distribution in the three districts of South Punjab, Qureshi did not feel obliged to challenge the military's interests. In fact, the former minister appreciated the association between the landowners of Southern Punjab and the military, sharing the view that military agriculturists brought development to the region, which the local landowners could not negotiate with their counterparts from the politically significant Central Punjab.
>
> (Siddiqua, 2007: 203)

In water distribution, there is pervasive suspicion that water is diverted to favored military personnel and supporters and away from other needs, particularly those in Sindh, where there are acute water shortages (Siddiqua, 2007: 203). The added water from the Thal Canal going to South Punjab will not benefit the indigenous Cholistani people as much as irrigate senior military officers lands (Siddiqua, 2007: 203, citing water distribution analyst Mushtaq Gaddi).

Rather than crush the civilian landholding elite, the military has worked to join that elite class. The military elite have:

> systematically used traditions or created norms to occupy state land for the benefit of the military fraternity. There is a constant threat of alteration in the use of millions of acres of state land that is under the organization's direct control, and for land which is not controlled by it. The military uses its political power to acquire land and to alter the use of state land from operations purposes to private ownership. The change in the use of land from public good to private benefit serves the interests of senior generals and the officer cadre at large, and in this they behave no differently from the big landowners and the landed-feudal class, especially in the treatment meted out to ordinary soldiers and poor indigenous people the military's authority and linkage with the political and institutional power base is instrumental in turning it into one of the prominent land barons in the country. The exploitation of land makes the generals no different from the top civilian landowners in the country.
>
> (Siddiqua, 2007: 205)

Land is taken in both urban and rural areas. Profit-making schemes are less transparent to public accountability procedures and are favored.

The army, a coherent, disciplined bureaucratic organization which safeguards its interests, is defined partly by its public image, as captured by the following description:

> The Pakistan Army's history also shows how it protects its corporate image and structure even against its own leadership when the leadership appears to be threatening the respect and operation of the army as an autonomous entity. It up-ended the Ayub Khan and Yahya Khan dictatorships, when public discontent arose against the army. It also failed to follow up on the investigation of the death of General Ziaul Haq and was reluctant to investigate the suspicious death of General Asif Nawaz. Interestingly, when a civilian prime minister removed General Jehangir Karamat, the army took the change in its stride and rallied behind its new leader.
>
> (Nawaz, 2008: xlii)

This impression is born out in the adamant statement that Musharraf had disgraced the military by indulging in politics and violating his military oath (instituted with the 1973 Constitution, which requires military personnel to swear to not indulge in politics), and by relentlessly pursuing his political survival while breaking his own

60 *Political survival in Pakistan*

promises (Interview with senior retired military official, 2009). The interviewee went on to blame the army's failures on deviance from its core mission, which is to protect the country. This bears out the argument made by Nawaz (2008): that the army members' self-image as professional soldiers working toward a patriotic mission is their highest value, to the point that they will speak against their own former leaders when those leaders have blatantly contravened these values.

Efforts by civilian leaders to control and influence the military have a lineage. Z.A. Bhutto tried to shake up the military command structure and build a parallel security force, the Federal Security Force, to balance the military and reduce his reliance on the military for his rule. Shuja Nawaz, whose brother Asif Nawaz was chief of army staff, recounts that Nawaz Sharif's family offered free BMW vehicles to senior army officials; Shuja Nawaz also points to documents purporting to show that Asif Nawaz was assassinated by arsenic poisoning, and suggests that someone in Prime Minister Nawaz Sharif's house may have been the perpetrator (Nawaz, 2008). The Chief of Army Staff is the dominant figure in the army; the longer the Chief stays in power, "the more likely he is to promote compliant clones. This deprives the senior military leadership of the useful capacity of argument and debate in making decisions" (Nawaz, 2008: xlii–xliii).

In an executive order creating a National Security Council headed by the president, Musharraf declared that "If you want to keep the army out, you bring them in" (*Dawn*, August 22, 2002; cited in Talbot, 2005: 401). Musharraf's statement spells out in practical form an assertion made in *The Logic of Political Survival*: "If the military was disenfranchised, they would overthrow the system" (Bueno de Mesquita et al., 2003: 369). If the military is permanently in the winning coalition and has decisive policy influence, then it has little incentive to foment coups and intervene. The military can dominate and overwhelm other institutions as it has increasingly secured its role through "legal" financial and economic "independence"—through preferential treatment for its business offshoots.

Recruitment into the bureaucracy continues and has been used for political patronage as well as to politicize administration (Sobhan, 2002: 162). Political scientist Aqil Shah argues that to understand the civil-military relationship in Pakistan, one must considered the heavy militarization of the bureaucracy, particularly since Zia ul-Haq's regime, when the military "created for itself a statutory quota both at the entry and upper levels" (Shah, 2008). Under Musharraf, "military penetration of civil departments and agencies has only deepened," as seen in the following evidence:

> the chairman and three members of the Federal Public Service Commission (FPSC) are former military officers. The Civil Services Academy (CSA), the National Institutes of Public Administration (NIPAs), and the Pakistan Administrative Staff College (PASC) are all militarized at the top. [...] Ex-military men have also been appointed as "master trainers" in the NIPAs and PAS. Even the Central Selection Board (CSB) and the Civil Service Reforms Unit are headed by retired military officials.
>
> (Shah, 2008)

Weak state, strong society, negotiable polity 61

Military leaders use civilian posts to reward military officers. A prominent business leader joked that the Pakistan Military Academy at Kakul should be given a higher ranking than any other learning institution, because unlike a Harvard Ph.D., a Kakul graduate is qualified to lead an electric company, a public administration academy, a fertilizer business, and numerous other occupations (Interview with business leader, 2009).

Shah opines that such appointments take away from merit and seniority-based hires and promotions, distorting performance incentives for career bureaucrats, undermining organizational morale by "subjecting civil servants to the ridiculously irrelevant military notions of order and discipline," and placing those trained for military purposes into civilian contexts for which they do not have appropriate skills (Shah, 2008). Military officers are trained in using coercive force, making them professional "managers of violence" in Harold Lasswell's terminology (Shah, 2008). They are unsuited to civilian posts because they are "by training and disposition, unsuited to performing civilian jobs which require voluntary subordination to civilian authority" (Shah, 2008). While this may be overgeneralized, Siddiqua (2007) has noted the contempt that military personnel, retired or not, appear to have for civilian authorities. There remains little civilian authority in the Ministry of Defence.

Thus, the military's intervention in the country has routinely subverted processes leading to a durable basic constitutional order; it is only when the military's rule is incorporated institutionally into the process (as happened with Article 58 2 (b)) that overt military coups are reduced. What this means is that rules at the national level are unclear but nevertheless have a central player, a veto-holder that cannot be ignored in any effort to construct a winning coalition. A challenger for national office must consider this carefully. Quasi-states are useful to the military in that they maintain some degree of public order and sometimes advance military interests.

The military has successfully demonstrated its supremacy to the civil service, by dismissing officers without regard for tenure traditions, and holding civil servants to account for alleged corruption. According to Mazhar Aziz, the military does not generally believe that civilians can offer "good governance"; the military believes that it has the "capacity, indeed duty, to contribute and engage in all the spheres of civilian life" (Aziz, 2008: 100). The military can undo the democratic process in mere hours with "two trucks and a jeep," as a politician noted recently (*Dawn*, August 4, 2009). Brigade 111 is positioned to take over key civilian offices and locations and has been deployed repeatedly in coups (Interview with senior journalist, 2009).

There is further evidence that the military has remained central to any winning coalition: at critical clashes for political influence, the side supported by the army chief has typically won (Rehman, 2008a). The support of the Chief of Army Staff is often a decisive factor, and he is widely believed to wield the greatest influence. At its outermost layer, the selectorate in Pakistan includes the national voting public. The selectorate range was controversial due not only to who should be franchised, but also whether joint or separate electorates were appropriate given the concerns of national minorities. The winning coalition in Pakistan

62   *Political survival in Pakistan*

may include rural landholders, the civil bureaucracy, some business interests, and most crucially, the military. Without these, it is difficult to sustain office. Iskander Mirza, Zulfikar Ali Bhutto, Benazir Bhutto, and Nawaz Sharif all found this out. In three cases, it was close friends or protégés that turned against their erstwhile patrons: Mirza, Z.A. Bhutto, and Sharif.

Economist Ishrat Husain has argued that ideological proclivity and governmental form has not mattered in Pakistan's growth policy choices, because the main beneficiaries (what the political survival framework would term the winning coalition) has remained narrow and relatively consistent:

> the same constellation of landlords, industrialists, traders, politicians, military and civil bureaucrats, and some co-opted members of the religious oligarchy and professional and intellectual groups dominated the scene under every single government [...] the stranglehold of this elite group, accounting for less than 1 per cent of the population, on the affairs of the state has remained unscathed. The capture of the institutions of the state and the market by the elite is complete.
>
> (Husain, 2000: xiii)

A political survival interpretation is that leaders have been held hostage to a winning coalition, and have been unable to escape the winning coalition sufficiently to construct a different coalition based on broader public interests.

Elections in Pakistan were not held until almost 25 years into the polity's founding (aside from a rigged referendum for Ayub; that election may be interpreted as the classic autocratic strategy of holding a referendum to show how vast the selectorate is, thereby increasing the loyalty norm in the winning coalition). "Universal suffrage is a way of signaling that almost anyone could, with a very low probability, make it into a winning coalition" (Bueno de Mesquita et al., 2003: 336–337). The universal franchise elections of 1970 resulted in a massive security crackdown and the polity's dismemberment. The winning coalition remained; large numbers of the disenfranchised simply broke away. Prominent Bengalis, former leaders of united Bengal province, were originally included in leadership positions in Pakistan's early days. This had a strategic consequence, suggesting to the East Pakistanis that they were in the selectorate. Also, slow changes in civil service quotas offered some pathways into the winning coalition's lower rungs and outer layers. But the creation of Bangladesh showed that pursuit of autonomy and secession was a way that a challenger who was denied office in the polity could nevertheless obtain an alternative role. That this took place successfully continues to shape Pakistan's challengers.

Landlords

Landlord power in Pakistan is derived from the extreme inequality in land ownership in the country. According to historian Imran Anwar Ali (2001), such rigidity and inequality has roots in British policy, which found it politically convenient to support landed groups. The 1901 Punjab Alienation of Lands Act disallowed land transfers from agricultural castes to non-agriculturists. This in effect meant that land could not be lost due to mortgage defaults, and it prevented the steady gains of the moneylenders. Ali argues:

> Rather than business development, at least of the indigenous variety, the British built up, through land distribution in the canal colonies, the social and economic power of the incumbent landholding groups. Canal land was predominantly allotted to landholding peasant lineages, and to medium and large *zamindars*. Commercial groups could only acquire land at auctions and at market rates, in contrast to the highly subsidized purchase prices extended to land grantees from the agricultural "castes".
>
> (Ali, 2001: 102)

This may have impeded capitalist development, because it was precisely such commercial trading that moved the British economy into the mercantile era:

> By constraining the social market for agricultural land, the colonial authority in the Pakistan area succeeded in retarding the very process that had expedited the transition to agricultural capitalism in Britain itself. Thus, in rolling back the emergence of a new class of more vigorous, commercially oriented owners, and in retaining an already entrenched, caste-based agrarian hierarchy, the British clearly preferred to trade off economic development for political expediency.
>
> (Ali, 2001: 103)

The true roots of landlord power lie not simply in dominance, but in support for landlord nominees from upper peasantry (Ali, 2001: 103). The landlord is viewed as a benevolent paternal figure. A *Mai Bap* (literally, "mother-father") culture lends a parental aura to landowners. According to this perspective, those low in social and economic status treat the powerful as both mother and father: providers who know better and are deferred to, at least on the surface. This was one reason why the British were accepted and even loved (Interview with former civil official, 2009). During a visit to a Sindhi landholder, old and young *haris* alike approached the author in a self-effacing manner and addressed their guest with the title "*Saieen*," connoting respect. This was interpretable as the warm and well-mannered hospitality so widely noted by visitors to rural areas in Pakistan, but it also reflected on the profound social and economic inequality that prevails in rural Sind.

The "hydraulic" political economy in the Punjab region contributed to close links between bureaucracy and landholders. Rainfed lands were only tangentially related to the state. In contrast, the massive linked canal network could be used for control purposes. This enhanced bureaucratic and military power. The bureaucracy had control over both the land settlement process and the canal irrigation network. Canal officials and influential landlords colluded for unequal water access and for coercion. Scholars such as Hamza Alavi and Mustafa Kemal Pasha see landlordism

64 *Political survival in Pakistan*

as a British colonial legacy, embedded in a political economy in which northwestern India (later West Pakistan) was the agricultural hinterland to the region.

The British had been unwilling to eradicate corruption and rent-seeking in their bureaucracy because it was politically inconvenient. The military benefited from land grants to veterans, and to land allotted for breeding military animals. After 1947, both the magnitude of bureaucratic corruption and of military control increased. According to Human Rights Commission member Rochi Ram, landlord power also increased, because landed gentry were well placed to capture legislative assemblies (Interview with Rochi Ram, July 2009). According to this view, landlord power increased further with the British withdrawal, as there had been some constraint by the external British government in the pre-Partition period.

Indicators for land ownership concentration in Pakistan have not changed much since Partition (Husain, 2000, Table 2.9). In the early 1970s, 5 percent of landowners controlled over 70 percent of the land (Siddiqua, 2007: 200, citing Alavi, 1976: 337). Sindh and southern Punjab are the areas best known for large landholdings. Landless peasants—known as *haris*—sharecrop the land, giving about half their produce to the absentee landlords, and paying some additional charges in a system called *batai*. Mechanisms for resolving disputes were biased toward the landlords, giving *haris* little legal recourse and permitting the "feudal" exploitation that is widely entrenched (Husain, 2000: 60).

Landlords in Pakistan, with private police and jails, already represent quasi-state entities. In rural areas, landlord writ has historically reigned in landed estates. They are reputed to live like medieval kings, and the newly rich class in Pakistan—particularly military higher-ups, but also newer professionals, such as prominent journalists—seek to emulate the landlord lifestyle for its symbolic power (Interview with former Provincial Assembly member, 2009).

One book source originally listed 81 families as the "political landlords"; an updated edition mentions 102 families, including 15 from NWFP, 36 from Punjab, 33 from Sindh, and 18 from Balochistan (Iqbal, 2008). Such landlord families are commonly believed to have produced most of the Pakistani leadership, on varying platforms including "republicanism," "Convention Muslim League," "Islamic socialism," and membership in Zia ul-Haq's "Majlis-i-Shoora." Landlord dominance is clearest in the provincial assemblies. They also have a disproportionate share in national politics: in 1962, landlords held 58 out of 96 National Assembly seats, and in 1965, 34 out of 82 (Talbot, 2005: 31). Increasing marriages between feudals and military, bureaucratic, and industrial/financial families have blurred their distinctions and further solidified their coalition, tying the "Establishment" to the landed classes (Interview with Hamid Rajput, July 2009). This means that the elites have increasingly merged, so that previous distinctions are blurry. The same family might be related to powerful landlords, bureaucrats, and military figures (Interview with former provincial legislator, 2009). Many if not most political opposition figures also come from the feudal group (Iqbal, 2008). These "feudal families" could be described as a major selectorate component, generating challengers in normal politics.

The "feudalism" debate

Whether Pakistan is or remains "feudal" has been a debate played out over columns and letters in *Dawn* in 2008. Economist S. Akbar Zaidi asserts that "feudalism" is no longer an applicable category in twenty-first century Pakistan (Zaidi, 2008). In a strict economic sense, feudalism is about a particular, narrow means of production that does not fit Pakistan today. A significant proportion of impoverished rural households are not involved in farming. Furthermore, the Pakistani middle class has been growing. Another column contributer, Haider Nizamani, also rejects the notion that there is feudalism in Pakistan because in 1999, 88 percent of cultivable farms were in farm sizes below 12.5 acres, and over half the total farms were less than five acres. Land ownership does not itself produce political power. However, the "rural gentry" is a "junior partner" to the state. Nizamani believes "feudalism" to be a politically expedient obfuscating term used by critics; using the term reduces the critical scrutiny that ought to be paid to production processes, labor organization, and non-economic coercion (Nizamani, 2008).

In contrast, columnist and former Defence Secretary Ayesha Siddiqua's strong view is that Pakistan remains "feudal" because high symbolic value is ascribed to land and the military and upper classes remain eager to acquire land holdings as well as to adopt feudal attitudes (Siddiqua, February 2, 2008). Landlords as a distributional coalition remain a significant bottleneck to Pakistani growth and development. Compared to peasants with insecure land tenure, landlords are few and wealthy. As a smaller group with more resources, landlords are more likely than peasants to overcome barriers to collective action. Moreover, a look at provincial and national assemblies shows that they remain populated and heavily influenced by large landholders. Another perspective describes Pakistan as "feudal" not in the European historical sense, but in the sense that powerful persons appear to dominate and overwhelm institutions and this happens time and again in both urban and rural settings (Conversation with journalist, July 2009). In Ishrat Husain's view, feudal-origin norms have spilled over to bureaucratic and industrial sectors, reinforcing an "elitist growth model" in which most benefits from "development" accrue to a narrow group (Husain, 2000: 62).

Business

Departing Hindu businesspeople created a vacuum in Pakistan. Prominent business families like the Habibs and the Ispahanis were invited by founding statesman Jinnah to bring industry to Pakistan (Husain, 2000: 84), and the Habibs were among the first to offer salaried positions in Pakistan (Interview, 2008). The business community in Pakistan was famously dominated by 22 families, as described by Chairman of the Planning Commission, Mahbub ul Haque. Under Zulfiqar Ali Bhutto's nationalizations, the dominance these families enjoyed receded, and they removed some business interests from the winning coalition. Nawaz Sharif's family was among those whose business interests were threatened by Z.A. Bhutto; unsurprisingly, Sharif became Zia ul-Haq's protégé in the

66 *Political survival in Pakistan*

1980s, and has been a rival to Benazir Bhutto and the Pakistan People's Party ever since.

Big business in Pakistan still tends to be dominated by families—as one senior business executive put it, boardroom pictures usually resemble a family album (Interview, 2009). Landlords have an advantage in businesses that process agricultural products, such as sugar mills. Because "agricultural income" is not taxed, schemes have been developed to avoid taxes through loan arrangements with landlords (Interview with Central Board of Revenue official, 2009). Some rivalry between business and rural landlords exists because there is resentment over the imbalance in tax policies.

In brief, the Pakistani winning coalition has drawn on the military, bureaucracy, landlords, businesspeople, and some religious figures. The military regimes have tried to enhance their legitimacy through referendums involving the polity at large—Zia ul-Haq and Pervez Musharraf both did this, and Ayub Khan in effect did so too by trying to mobilize support from *pirs* for his presidential election. But these were viewed with cynicism as rigged figleaves for dictatorship. Moreover, these offered little prospect for an increase in the winning coalition or change in distributive policies.

Although the judiciary has generally justified military coups by the "doctrine of necessity," there is a possible new assertiveness. In 2007, amid growing public clamor against the military-backed regime, a showdown took place as Chief Justice Iftikhar Chaudhry inquired into Musharraf's eligibility for election to the presidency. Musharraf responded by imposing emergency rule, suspending the constitution, requiring judiciary to take a loyalty oath, and dismissing those who refused. A lawyers' protest movement was sparked, and Musharraf eventually resigned in 2008. This was a high-stakes battle, because it suggested that the judiciary holds a functioning veto over candidates for high office. Moreover, those who are unhappy with the current status quo and prefer a larger winning coalition generally support such judicial actions, because they represent efforts to change selection institutions. It remains unclear how durable the judiciary's apparent assertiveness will be. One lawyer expressed skepticism because the conflict was driven by self-seeking personal interests; Chaudhry had validated Musharraf's original coup along with other judges, and given that he had been dismissed under the 2007 Provincial Constitutional Order, Chaudhry's 2009 judgment against the PCO as Supreme Court chief justice was tainted by his own involvement as a party to the conflict (Conversation with lawyer, 2009).

A key question is the degree to which outside powers (particularly Britain and the United States) remain powerful selectors in Pakistan. With independence, the viceroy's official influence ended, but that did not mean an end to outsideinfluence. When Governor-General Ghulam Muhammad dismissed the Constituent Assembly in 1954, Speaker Maulvi Tamizuddin tried to appeal to the Queen, showing the belief that outside power still mattered (she did not respond). It is commonly believed that American-friendly Ayub Khan's rising prominence and national leadership was enabled by the United States (Interviews, 2009). Despite formal independence, it is arguable that national leaders and

Weak state, strong society, negotiable polity   67

challengers saw a great power role in their national selection processes. Numerous examples show that this remains the case, particularly for smaller-coalition military-led governments. Opponents who saw Musharraf as US President Bush's lackey berated him with the derogatory label "Busharraf." A popular novel includes a darkly comic scene in which an ambitious military general misreads the US ambassador's comments over a football game as encouragement for a coup (Hanif, 2008).

As seen in the next chapter, international financing plays a key role in Pakistani state resources. Outside forces remain powerful in Pakistani leaders' and challengers' strategic calculus. A memorable line summarizing the "political survival" versus "ideology" dilemma came from General Pervez Musharraf to explain his policy U-turn on Afghanistan and the Taliban after the American "global war on terror" was declared. He asserted that "national interest" (a key symbol in political philosophy, used to appeal to and motivate people) had not changed and does not change. However, "the environment" had changed. He did not mention what most observers understood—that his political survival was under serious threat unless he complied with US wishes.

The current context

Some believe that the feudal system has kept the agricultural population depoliticized (Talbot, 2005: 31). Uncertainty, instability, rigged elections, political horse-trading, and military-bureaucratic dominance have meant that a significant component in the population feel disenfranchised. Low voter turnout in Pakistan suggests that people do not have much faith in elections as an authentic selection institution for meaningful governance change in their lives. Perceived disenfranchisement was expressed repeatedly in interviews with low-skilled workers. Noncompliance with taxes, and a general disregard for public policy pronouncements, also support the notion that a high proportion in Pakistan feel disenfranchised. Pakistan's selectorate is unequal; some have far more weight than others. The outer edges in the selectorate are difficult to distinguish from those who are entirely disenfranchised.

Consider an incumbent leader reviewing leadership in Pakistan's history. Numerous leaders have faced significant personal costs associated with leaving office: Liaquat Ali Khan was assassinated. Ayub Khan abdicated when ill and pressured to do so by Yahya Khan. Zulfikar Ali Bhutto was detained and then executed. Many have expressed the belief that Zia ul-Haq was assassinated. Nawaz Sharif and Benazir Bhutto were both charged with crimes, and faced detention or exile; Benazir Bhutto was assassinated. Pervez Musharraf faced assassination attempts. Aside from wanting to retain office for its benefits, removal from office is associated with high costs. A prominent business executive joked that Pakistan routine "exports" its leaders, either to Allah or to outside countries (Interview, 2009). Accountability is low: Liaquat Ali Khan's assassination remains mysterious, as does Zia ul-Haq's plane crash; the Hamoodur Rehman Commission's investigation into the events leading up to Bangladesh's secession were not made public for

68   *Political survival in Pakistan*

decades, and responsible figures were not held to account; Benazir Bhutto's assassins have not been brought to account through a transparent process.

Constitutional instability has reigned in Pakistan for years, and in that context, the military has been a powerful, organized, consistent force, emerging swiftly from secondary status to the civil administration (under the early civilian governments, and the government of civil servant Ghulam Mohammad). Article 58 2 (b) represents one step in a difficult political evolution which seeks to both constrain the military's involvement in domestic politics while also recognizing that completely sidelining the military will produce another military coup when its interests are threatened. The military has dealt with this by starting to dominate civil society through its foundations, businesses, and strategically-posted retired personnel.

In Pakistan, the rules of the game are unclear. Moreover, virtually all political actors try to rewrite the rules in their favor. The feuding over Article 58 2 (b) captures this rather well. In practice, the military coup is clearly one selection mechanism for leadership, having launched three military rulers who have governed directly for much of Pakistan's history. Military backdoor influence is another. Judicial judgment seems to be a method also—as when both Ghulam Ishaq Khan and PM Nawaz Sharif were forced to resign, in a deal that was facilitated by the Chief of Army Staff. There are rigged referendums to add legitimacy to an authoritarian ruler. There are some elections that have had a significant impact. In 1971, the country broke apart in the post-election upheaval, because an unexpected party from previously disenfranchised East Pakistan won a clear majority. The 1988, 1993, and 1997 elections all had significant consequences for turnover in national office.

The 2002 elections took place without the two main parties, in effect, and so did not have quite the same impact; moreover, the country was dominated by coup-leader Musharraf. The 2008 elections saw a resounding defeat for the PML-Q, a Musharraf-friendly creation termed the "king's party" by opponents. With enough repetitions, elections could become the chief selection mechanism in Pakistan. An accompanying challenge would be to reduce the power unelected institutions retain as compared to elected ones. But the lawyers' movement reduced their potential to a narrower, personality-based agenda: deposed Chief Justice Iftikhar Chaudhry's reinstatement, and Musharraf's impeachment (Khan and Jacobsen, September 17, 2008).

The PPP's power base is in the Sind. The military recruits mainly from the Punjabis and Pathans. Balochistan and NWFP have seen armed battles with the central government of Pakistan. Balochistan is the poorest province and there is a common belief that natural resources there have been exploited by the Pakistani government without adequate investment in Balochistan. In 2006, a major Balochi leader, Akbar Bugti, was killed in a military operation, further inflaming Balochi sentiment. In the NWFP, there are periods with near-daily violent interactions between different factions and the Pakistani government. At the same time, there is continuing pressure from the US on Pakistan to crackdown on militants. Popular feelings are strong against current US policies in the region; when the Pakistani government is perceived as carrying out US wishes, there is a popular backlash. Whether the military will successfully repress separatists is an open question.

Weak state, strong society, negotiable polity 69

In this context, one possibility raised by analysts and observers is that Pakistan might break up into several smaller countries, such as Balochistan, Pashtunistan, Sind, and Punjab. This remains unlikely because the military is still the dominant force-holder, and is strongly committed to a united Pakistan. Nevertheless, it is telling that Benazir Bhutto's coffin was draped not in a Pakistani flag but in a flag from her party, even though she had been PM twice. Also, the new PPP leadership affirmed its commitment to the Pakistani federation; this would have been unnecessary if there was no question about Pakistan's unity.

In civil-military relations, power continues to be skewed heavily in the military's favor. Pakistani judiciary and lawyers mobilized recently in protest against heavy-handed military interventions and the military's refusal to abide by Supreme Court decisions. This showed a broad wish among Pakistan's professional classes for curtailing the military's role in national politics and for the rule of law. However, these movements have so far been frustrated by the military's dominant hand, as well as international (mainly US) support for the military during the "war on terror." Civil society in Pakistan is weak and fragmented; rural landowners continue to be powerful members of the elite, there is a small industrialist class that has some weight, while religious forces are diverse and internally divided into factions. These factors indicate that the military will continue to be the key player in the future, and that small opposition groups are likely to continue to resort to political violence.

This chapter has provided a brief introduction to the context for leaders and challengers in Pakistan). The next chapter looks at leaders more closely, particularly with regard to extraction. As defined in the first chapter, extraction is a key state activity, and a leader may extract in ways that produce more public goods or more private goods. The political survival perspective predicts that small winning coalition leaders will generally provide more private goods and fewer public goods than large coalition leaders. The investigation in the next chapter examines ideologically diverse leaders in Pakistan who made strategic decisions driven by political survival constraints. Pakistan's social fractures have shaped the political survival strategies adopted by challengers; these are explored in Chapter 4.

3 Leadership and extraction

How rulers obtain resources affects national political well-being. Not all routes are equal. Transparent, uniformly applied taxation policies are associated with efficient property rights and public goods. A weakly enforced tax structure, or alternative financing located through non-tax revenues, is often more susceptible to reallocation into "private goods" and special privileges for small distributional coalitions. Moreover, direct taxation from a broader base in the polity will have a different fiscal sociological and state-building consequence than indirect taxation and a narrow tax base. This chapter focuses on extraction choices by examining specific leaders' records in Pakistan, particularly those of Ayub Khan, Zulfiqar Ali Bhutto, and Zia ul-Haq.

Among Pakistani national leaders, Ayub Khan has been called a "developmentalist"; Zulfiqar Bhutto, a socialist; Zia ul-Haq, an Islamist. These characterizations are commonly asserted. Each used the Islamic symbol to some degree. Critical decisions related to extraction, a key state activity with consequences for public goods and private goods, however, were not driven by ideological motives as much as by pragmatic considerations related to political survival. The paramount consideration and consistent consideration in each case has been maintaining a winning coalition and warding off challenges to rule.

Pakistani leaders have generally failed to tax agriculture substantially, which, given the agricultural sector's size, is a major reason that domestic extraction in Pakistan remains low. While agricultural taxation remains a "provincial subject" (meaning that the central government is not constitutionally permitted to tax agricultural incomes), constitutional instability, major changes through amendments, and martial law regimes mean that the constitutional bounds alone are usually soft compared to other polities. The provincial governments have not collected significant agricultural taxes beyond fees related to water (*aabiyana* canal tax) and land (land revenue). Introducing agricultural income tax assessed on up-to-date produce indices would be a major shift.

Agriculture has been a key sector from which extraction by the central government has historically been difficult or impossible. Combined with Pakistan's failure to develop agricultural taxation, rural ownership structures continue to present a significant hurdle blocking development-oriented policy changes. Meaningful land reform has the potential to radically restructure state-society relations, as land

Leadership and extraction 71

ownership confers status, wealth, and power. It may increase efficiency, and to the extent that it weakens the powerful landlord lobby, land reform better positions the state to increase agricultural taxation. With successful redistribution, state capacity grows, and the country's fiscal skeleton is strengthened.

According to Pakistani economist and former government official Shahid Javed Burki, reducing unequal land distribution can also increase efficiency. In Pakistan, agricultural productivity was estimated by one study to be 2.75 times higher in small as compared to large farms (Burki, 2008c: 242–243). The Green Revolution in the 1960s meant more productivity on larger mechanized farms. However, rural economic development was needed to provide a domestic market with which to sustain industrialization; this was a reason that Ayub Khan introduced his Land Reform Act in 1959 (Nasr, 1996: 257–258).

High military spending and debt servicing burdens have squeezed Pakistani public finance. It is widely argued that perceived security concerns have dominated and distorted Pakistani strategic planning and budgeting. Thornton (1999) describes Pakistan's mixture of ambitions and threat assessments as being "out of balance" and resulting in wasted budget resources (Thornton, 1999: 184). In *The State of Martial Rule*, Jalal (1990) describes Pakistan's political economy as being fundamentally directed by high perceived defense needs. Siddiqua (2007) has found that the military has progressively built itself into a dominant social class with vast business interests, landholdings, and a firmly ensconced political role, even when not in direct control.

This chapter makes several assumptions: that taxation, particularly direct taxation, is politically risky, that international financing is less politically risky, and that money creation policies bear the least political risk, to the extent that they remain undiscovered and do not create excessive inflation. However, in fiscal sociology terms, direct taxation is the best policy, international financing is worse, and money creation is the worst policy. Indirect taxation is easier to implement but is usually regressive and does not have the same fiscal sociological consequences as direct taxation. This chapter examines extraction choices in Pakistan. Sub-sections on international financing and taxation policies under each regime are included. Money creation or covert strategies are not subdivided into the time periods but treated separately. The purpose here is not to provide a comprehensive representation of all taxation, international financing, and money creation efforts in the Pakistan's history. Rather, some prominent initiatives are examined for their value in elaborating hypotheses on the relationship between political survival and strategic choice in public finance. A brief description follows.

In the international financing sections, the focus is on whether aid or non-aid international resources in any form are made available or not. The idea is that even aid tied to specific projects can form part of an indirect "international solution" to a government's policy problems in at least two ways. First, tied aid can potentially free up resources elsewhere for the government, if the externally funded project would otherwise have required domestic funding. Second, a foreign-funded project may produce acquiescence to the status quo among social beneficiaries of the project (such as employees). Morrison (2009) finds that non-tax revenues generally increase regime stability. Tied aid may serve a similar function by reducing the burden of welfare provision on the state and thus freeing up resources elsewhere. Material aid, such as shipments of machinery or arms, also have a relieving influence on the fiscal burdens by freeing up resources that might otherwise have to be spent on arms purchases.

The taxation sections include historically prominent actions that directed or affected the administrative capacity of the state or suggested that an effort to adjust state-society relations with regard to resource distributions was taking place. These include such efforts as increases in tax rates, changes in tax structure, and nationalizations, which may represent a 100 percent tax (Barnett, 1992). Other elite-driven efforts to change formal political institutions of governance, such as constitutional changes, have been ignored here unless they have a direct impact on the capacity of the state to tax the national income.

Deficit spending generally is a burden on future tax revenues. From a development perspective, policy-makers have preferred to use foreign savings for needed investment, because drawing on domestic savings only reallocates funds from the private to the public sector (Interview with Ishrat Husain, February 2009). The narrow tax base also has a fiscal sociological consequence; a large population segment (the non-payers) stay removed from the implicit social contract of accountability that comes with providing resources for rule. This in turn prevents a larger tax-paying coalition from becoming politically activated. Thus, the political leadership continues to rely on a narrow winning coalition, and remains oriented to providing private goods rather than public goods.

Money creation efforts (especially when they are exercises in seignorage) are frequently covert. As a result, while there is strong evidence to suggest that these have been repeatedly and consistently pursued, the actual coverage of such strategies here is disproportionately small. Often there is not clear information about money creation activity in the time period under consideration. Secondary accounts contain some general assertions and claims without specific reference to any but the most prominent policies. Consequently, observations about money creation have been gathered separately before introducing the other strategies in depth.

The choice of public finance strategy affects state power. Money creation and international strategies tend to reinforce the current condition of state power

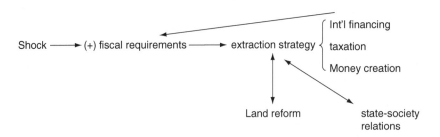

Diagram 3.1 Summary diagram of suggested extraction relationships

Leadership and extraction 73

(Barnett, 1992: 211). Restructural strategies, however, have the potential to alter state power. The linkages between public finance policy and state power are multiple and influence flows in both directions.[1] This is rather abstract and can potentially take different and unexpected forms in actual cases, as shown by the Egyptian and Israeli experiences.

Robert Bates has argued that international strategies are a chronic condition in developing countries (Levi, 2006). The Pakistan leaders' experiences reviewed below adds an additional aspect—the constraints faced by regime leaders as they sought political survival by retaining a winning coalition.

Pakistan is not usually considered a "strong" state comparable to Israel. Even Egypt would be considered a stronger state, especially when compared with Pakistan's early years, but also in comparison to India. Barnett's finding was that a strong state like Israel was able to engage in some domestic extraction increases in wartime and for war preparation (Barnett, 1992). Nevertheless, there were important limits to what could be achieved. Similar and greater limits have existed in the Pakistani cases. Taxation is generally politically risky because it may allow challengers to mobilize (Interview with S.M. Fazal, July 2009). One interpretation is that the political survival perspective predicts that all states, irrespective of state strength or political capacity, will avoid seeking increased domestic extraction whenever possible. If the attempts to increase domestic extraction have been severely constrained in all states, then the political survival perspective receives support.

One factor to consider in public finance is that subnational state governments also collect taxes. In Pakistan, the central government's revenue collection far exceeds the provinces.[2] Interprovincial tension often accompanies the awards given by Pakistan's National Finance Commission, which distributes the federal revenue's "divisible pool" among provinces. Former State Bank Governor Ishrat Husain refers to this as the "vertical imbalance" issue in Pakistan's taxation: the provincial governments spend largely from resources that are obtained through taxation at the federal level (Interview with Ishrat Husain, February 2009). In expenditures, defense spending is wholly central and borrowing is mainly central. Therefore, the central government bears the resource burden for war preparation. It is also the central government that has the option of an international or seignorage strategy open to it. Fiscal decentralization remains an ideal to many, but has not been implemented (Interviews, 2009). Hence, the focus here is on the central government in Pakistan.

Anecdotal and scholarly accounts report corruption, inefficiency, and ineffectiveness in Pakistani tax collection. For example, Nawaz Sharif, the former prime minister of Pakistan, belongs to a well-known, wealthy, industrialist family. That family reputedly paid a minute total tax bill, and was lambasted in the press. There is a general sense from the man on the street that major reform in tax policy and collection is required. It is widely acknowledged that Pakistan continues to have problems in getting the well-off to pay their "fair share" of taxes (Almeida, July 3, 2009; Weinbaum, 1999: 89). Horizontal inequities are rife: citizens in different sectors who make comparable incomes but pay different amounts in taxes create resentments (particularly among salaried corporate workers in public

74 *Political survival in Pakistan*

and larger private enterprises who find their incomes taxed) (Interviews, 2001, 2009).

According to Martinez-Vazquez's international comparison based on regression analysis of developing countries (controlling for GDP composition and per capita income), Pakistan's tax/GDP ratio should be four percentage points higher than it is (Martinez-Vazquez, 2006: ii). Others point to the lack of a "tax culture," low education, and mistrust of tax collectors, as well as a cumbersome filing process, as culprits (Interviewee B, 2000). A prominent business executive ranked himself among the top individual taxpayers in Pakistan, but emphasized that this was not because he was among the richest people in Pakistan—others evaded taxes while he simply chose to pay for personal reasons that did not have anything to do with enforcement or policing (Interview, 2009). While there have been some efforts at tax reform, they have been short-lived, and this, according to a former finance official, is responsible for the ongoing fiscal crises that Pakistan found itself in during the 1990s and beyond (Interview with former finance official, 2001).

Extraction in Pakistan: the early years

Raising needed revenues for government expenditures in a war context is a problem that can be dated to Pakistan's formation. Pakistan sought a share of the cash balance of the former government of undivided India; the cash balances of undivided India had been left in the hands of the successor Indian state (Brown, 1963: 166). Although an agreement was reached in December 1947 to transfer a cash sum to Pakistan, the Indian deputy prime minister used the pressure of the Kashmir conflict as a justification for not releasing the funds to Pakistan in January 1948 (Chaudhry, 1968: 63). Initial Pakistani customs taxes placed on jute and cotton were justified by the need to generate revenue, but viewed by the Indians as hostile economic acts (Brown, 1963: 169).

Pakistan's early years were preoccupied with bolstering the defense establishment, and this pushed the state to consolidate its authority (Jalal, 1990: 49). In the first three years of independence, up to 70 percent of the national budget was allocated for defense (Talbot, 1998: 118). The conflict with India shortly after independence meant pressing demands on meager central government funds. A sense of insecurity about the survival of their state plagued Pakistani policymakers. This was not the result of fears of military defeat alone. India's strategic location at the head of the Indus River meant that it could potentially "shock" and disrupt the Pakistani economy by interfering with the flow of irrigation waters (Choudhury, 1968: 155–159). (The World Bank was intimately involved in attempted negotiated settlements to this issue in the 1950s, and eventually an agreement was reached.)

Other major spending needs faced the Pakistani government, including the resettlement of millions of refugees and the installation of basic industries, as well as building the central government apparatus generally (Jalal, 1990: 54). It is estimated that 7 million refugees entered West Pakistan and 1.25 million entered East Pakistan (Ahmed and Amjad, 1984: 71). In general, Karachi was

Leadership and extraction 75

"quite unprepared to accommodate the administrative machinery of a nation then numbering somewhere around 70 million persons" (Brown, 1963: 205).

Substantial and creative efforts were required to build the state apparatus.[3] Domestic political dissent made this difficult. High defense-spending demands meant that the central government sought to control the provinces' finances as a way to appropriate needed resources (Talbot, 1998: 119). Within a year of independence, societal dissatisfaction manifested itself in labor and agrarian unrest, and the provinces resisted central government directives as encroachments on their authority (Jalal, 1990). Further incidents of agrarian unrest occurred in the early summer of 1950 in the Punjab, and severe communal disturbances took place in Bengal in February and March of the same year. In both cases, disillusionment with the Muslim League (the political party supporting the creation of Pakistan) and the financial policies of the central government were partially responsible (Jalal, 1990: 104–105).

In the aftermath of Partition, India appeared to enjoy "marked superiority in military resources, both in being capable of mobilization over an extended period, and in having greater material resources" (Kavic, 1967: 37). In comparison, "Pakistan had no domestic source of modern arms and military stores and her ability to wage war could be severely restricted by an Indian blockade of Karachi" (Kavic, 1967: 37). Thus, international strategies for obtaining resources for war-making were an imperative for Pakistani policy-makers. Furthermore, India was aware of this and could act to restrict the possibilities that Pakistan had of obtaining such international resources. Therefore, strategic anticipation and action could affect the extent to which an international solution was obtained.

Pakistan initially sought to buy military supplies using hard currency. Finance and commerce officials sought strategies to increase the dollars at their disposal and in the process began to "learn the ropes" of the international financial system (Jalal, 1990: 96). Thus, there was an early understanding that international sources of revenue needed to be tapped. Pakistan experienced what may be described as a minor international economic shock in the 1950–51 fiscal year. Import prices had risen sharply and export prices had dropped. The worsened terms of the trade situation were combined with depleted foreign exchange reserves (Jalal, 1990: 141). The low foreign exchange reserves situation was exacerbated by a liberal import policy, and it was hoped that foreign grants and loans would help make up the gap (Jalal, 1990: 141–142).

The governor of the state bank, Zahid Husain, was alarmed by Pakistan's revenue and spending situation featuring sharp budget deficits,[4] indebtedness, and unsatisfactory tax collection (Jalal, 1990: 100). A controversial decision not to devalue the Pakistani rupee left consumers facing higher prices and was potentially bad for the economy. However, the outbreak of the Korean War and the rise in raw cotton prices opened new markets for Pakistan's jute and cotton exporters, and the Pakistani government could increase revenue by imposing export taxes (Jalal, 1990: 100, 104). Such indirect taxation is typical of a weak state because customs duties on import and export take place at ports and are relatively easy to collect.

76 *Political survival in Pakistan*

Jalal (1990) suggests that the central government's efforts to procure and allocate financial resources affected relations between the center and the provinces. Economic grievances and social dissatisfaction produced great uncertainty in central and provincial politics partly because there was no well-organized political party to channel diverse interests (Jalal, 1990: 100–101). The central government's expenditure was focused on building industry and defense capabilities against the Indian threat. These priorities and the related efforts to expand the newborn central government's resource base and administrative capabilities had an impact on the socioeconomic conditions of the provinces. Very early on in its national history, however, the Pakistani central government had encountered significant political instability and dissent and found itself blamed.

International financing

The effort to obtain international resources for funding government activities began immediately with independence and continued thereafter (Sisson and Rose, 1991). Initially Pakistan sought this from the Islamic nations of south-west Asia, but was stymied by differences within that bloc. There were unsuccessful efforts to borrow from Commonwealth countries also. A significant loan (200 million rupees) from Hyderabad in October 1947 helped, as the treasury was nearly empty (Afzal, 2001: 17). In late 1947, a $2 billion loan request was made to the US but was turned down (Talbot, 1998: 119). Although the US imposed an arms embargo on both India and Pakistan after the Kashmir clashes of March 1948, Pakistan was able to obtain credit of $10 million from the United States (the US also sold chemical plants, jute presses, and textile machinery to Pakistan) (Afzal, 2001: 44–45). This was ostensibly for refugee rehabilitation, but was in fact used to obtain military supplies (Jalal, 1990: 76–77). The USSR was seen as a threat and China appeared uninterested, so by the early 1950s Pakistan settled on the US as the only viable choice for reliable outside support (Sisson and Rose, 1991: 47). By the middle of 1952 Pakistan was seeking both wheat grants and long-term military credit from the United States (Jalal, 1990: 171). Ten million dollars of economic aid was received from the US in 1952, and a $15 million loan was also received in the same year (Brown, 1963: 381). Such economic assistance came on generous terms, allowing for 80 percent of the payments' expenditures to be controlled by the central government of the recipient country (Brown, 1963: 382).

In addition to its revenue budget, the Pakistani central government had a "capital" budget which relied on borrowing through such means as treasury bills and other floating loans (Brown, 1963: 294). The "war footing" at the time of Partition continued and military expenditures contributed to rising Pakistani indebtedness (Brown, 1963: 294). Pakistan was facing a cash shortage, but the country appeared a poor bet for international creditors and had a difficult time obtaining international financing (Jalal, 1990: 45). India had initially inherited the entire public debt and this meant that Pakistan had no basis for a credit history (Jalal, 1990: 35–36). Even lending agreements would be under unusual constraints. For example, international creditors "would sometimes demand advance deposits in foreign banks to guarantee

Leadership and extraction 77

payment when due" (Brown, 1963: 294). Nevertheless, the Pakistani government did engage in some international private borrowing by issuing securities.

In 1953, Pakistan decided to enter into an alliance with the United States (Sattar, 1997: 66). Initially, US assistance to Pakistan was "half-hearted" in relation to Pakistani expectations (Sattar, 1997: 73). Military assistance during this period and earlier from the US was received but the amounts are not public (Brown, 1963: 382). In 1954, Pakistan and the US signed the Mutual Defense Assistance Agreement. Providing military assistance to Pakistan was part of the US anti-Soviet strategy, but it raised concerns among Indians that the arms would be used against them (Brown, 1963: 371).

Pakistan joined the South East Asia Treaty Organization (SEATO) in 1954. Although there was no immediate increase in military aid, economic aid was increased from $15 million in 1954 to $114 million (Sattar, 1997: 74). Pakistan also joined the Baghdad Pact, a security alliance, which was established by Turkey and Iraq in 1955. This was renamed the Central Treaty Organization in 1959 (Iraq engineered a coup against the royal regime in 1958 and subsequently pulled out).

Taxation

When British direct rule started in 1858, an effort was made to introduce an agricultural income tax. The 1886 Income Tax Act ended this, and restricted the payments from the agricultural sector to the land revenue system. The 1922 Income Tax Act exempted agricultural incomes. A national taxation committee in 1926 argued for taxing all income and the 1935 India Act gave the provinces power to tax agricultural land and income. However, opposition to agricultural taxes has a long history. Landholders were key political support for British administration (Mahmood Hasan Khan, 1999: 136). Consequently, efforts to extract more from the agricultural sector were circumscribed.

Pakistan's independence was followed in 1948–9 with taxation measures attempting to cover rising budget deficits. These produced political dissent in the form of civil unrest. The potentially explosive consequences of attempting tax increases therefore became apparent at an early juncture in Pakistani history. For example, substantial rifts arose between the central and provincial governments over their respective shares of the export duties levied on jute (Jalal, 1990: 107). These fed what would become increasingly strident demands for provincial autonomy in East Pakistan.

Revenue-raising through taxation in the 1950s was difficult, and Jalal's summary below also points to the intersubstitutability with other revenue-raising strategies.

> With defence and civil administration swallowing most of the foreign aid as well as nearly 80 per cent of its annual revenue, and increased debt servicing liabilities, the central government had to seriously consider reforming the tax structure. Yet the dramatic fall in world prices of its two main export crops, jute and cotton, foreclosed the possibility of raising indirect taxes which already provided approximately 73 per cent of its ordinary revenues as well as those of

78 *Political survival in Pakistan*

the provincial governments. Increasingly the role of direct taxes in public finance was out of the question; it would almost certainly erode the government's support among the propertied classes. [...] So the only real alternative to easing financial hardship was to rely on a mixture of deficit financing and ever larger inflows of foreign aid.

(Jalal, 1990: 242–243)

This excerpt underlines the weakness of the Pakistani state. Taxation as an extraction strategy was difficult to pursue. Even indirect taxation, normally relied upon by weaker states, could not be increased. Borrowing and foreign aid were the preferred (and, realistically, the only available) strategies for obtaining needed funds.

There was an outside push to get the Pakistani state to increase its extractive capacity. American Secretary of State Dulles noted in 1954 that Pakistan had to expand its economic base and increase its ability to raise domestic resources for military spending (Jalal, 1990: 241). An expert panel, known as the Harvard Advisory Group, helped Pakistan in developing its five-year development plan.

A Planning Board was instituted in July 1953 to oversee the government role in economic development in Pakistan. The Planning Board made recommendations about scale and priorities in allocating financial resources for development. The Board operated through a series of five-year plans that set objectives and targets for economic growth in specific sectors. There were also goals for managing the fiscal deficit (Khan, Aftab Ahmad, 1997: 183–221). Focusing on the plans in order to assess actual government policy can be somewhat deceptive. For example, the first Five-Year Plan (1955–60) was not backed by the government until 1958 (Brown, 1963: 322).

The weakness of Pakistani extractive capacity is reflected in the fact that Pakistan's first Five-Year Plan left 36 percent of the development expenditure to be financed by foreign capital (Jalal, 1990: 245). The difficulties of domestic extraction are notable in the following description of events surrounding the budget proposal in 1958:

In an unusual move during an election year, the finance minister proposed a whole series of taxes [...] [the] taxes were not expected to raise more than Rs. 4.5 million in central revenues. But they were greeted by an almost universal outcry. [...] Business interests for their part saw it as a wanton attempt to strangulate industry. A number of trade associations observed token strikes. The unkindest cut for the government was the decision by the board of directors of the Karachi stock exchange to close down business for three days. Interestingly enough, increased allocations for both defence and civil administration—and the main reason for the centre's taxation proposals-were only mildly criticized; an indication of the extent to which the so-called representatives of the people had resigned themselves to letting these two main institutions of the state get the better part of the national revenue.

(Jalal, 1990: 270–271)

Leadership and extraction 79

The proposed taxation structure increased the income of public companies that was taxed (Jalal, 1990: 270, n. 203), and business interests were therefore strongly opposed to it. Thus, both agrarian and urban business opposition stymied taxation proposals and efforts. There were efforts to cut down on smuggling, such as the East Pakistan Smuggling of Food Grains Act (1950).

Land reform

Land ownership reform has commonly been seen as essential to counter the social and economic ills that accompany inequality, such as "feudalism," poverty, and uncertainty for landless agricultural workers. The need for land reform was clearly recognized throughout South Asia's development plans. One risk with expropriating capital is capital flight. Expropriating land is different, because land cannot flee. Landlords might be regime clients or, alternatively, they might mount challenges against incumbent leaders. Land reform under Pakistan's early civilian regime failed to be implemented. The political leadership depended on a winning coalition that included the powerful landlords, as seen in the Pakistan Muslim League positions held by landlords in Punjab, and the political resistance successfully mounted in Sind by landlords.

The Pakistan Muslim League (the dominant political party) attempted an ambitious reform program, based on a working committee's deliberations, but political opposition from the landlords scuttled this in West Pakistan.

> In August 1949, on the report of a PML Agrarian Reforms Committee, its working committee decided to abolish, with immediate effect, all hereditary *jagirs* (land granted in lieu of meritorious services, the land revenue being assigned to the grantee) without compensation; to grant proprietary rights to occupancy tenants; to abolish feudal and customary cesses and dues; to provide security of tenants for tenants-at-will; to replace *batai* (landlord's share) with cash rental. The committee also resolved to abolish the *zamindari* system and fix land ceiling at 150 acres for irrigated and 450 acres for non-irrigated land. It directed its governments in the provinces to implement these recommendations but, except for East Pakistan where the Hindu landlords owned 75 per cent land, the PML failed to introduce any meaningful reforms primarily because the landlords dominated its ranks and the ceiling fixed was too unrealistic. This failure tarnished the party image.
>
> (Afzal, 2001: 53)

The *jagirs* and *inams* (awards) "conferred by the British Government in return for services rendered to the cause of imperialism were to be expropriated, and occupancy tenants were to be owners on the payment of a nominal price" (Rizvi, 2000: 111, citing Ahmad, 1970: 201). Although the PML Agrarian Reform Committee's recommendations were accepted by the PML Council, their report was filed without action. Nevertheless, the report became an important reference point for future land reform documents and may have influenced tenancy reform

80 *Political survival in Pakistan*

acts in Punjab, Sindh, and NWFP in the early 1950s (Mahmood Hasan Khan, 1999: 126).

Many landlords in Bengal were Hindu, and a good number had moved to India in Partition (Rizvi, 2000: 112). Relatively successful land reform took place in East Pakistan, where the East Bengal Estate Acquisition and Land Tenancy Act of February 16, 1950 was to "abolish the *zamindari* [landholding] system within ten years, to give security to tenure to the tenants, to eliminate intermediary rent collectors, and to fix the land ceiling at 33 acres per head"; by 1956, 421 landlords had petitioned against the expropriation, but the Dhaka Court and the Supreme Court upheld rulings against them, and the government took over the lands by 1957 (Afzal, 2001: 54–55).

The Punjab Muslim League won the 1951 Provincial Assembly elections, in an election where only landlord candidates were expected to win. Mumtaz Daultana, the biggest landlord in Punjab, was the party leader, and he was made chief minister. Later in 1951, the draft Land Reform bills were discussed, seeking

> to give security of tenancy to occupancy tenants; to exempt from tax all owners of under five acres of land; to limit the size of landholding to not more than fifty acres; and to change the traditional division of crops between the landlord and the tenant from 50 per cent each to 75 per cent for the tenant and 25 per cent for the landlord. Mumtaz Daultana, supported by [Governor-General] Liaquat Ali, remained firm for a while against opposition to the Bills from a section of the landlords, threatening to go back to the electorate for a fresh mandate. However, his attitude softened after Liaquat's assassination. The Bills that were finally passed failed to cut down big landholdings, although all *jagirs* [fiefs and land grants] were abolished except those conferred in lieu of military service or endowed to religious shrines. The share of the tenant was fixed at 60 per cent and that of the landlord at 40 per cent. These reforms satisfied none; one faction condemned these as "half-hearted", and the other regarded these as "un-Islamic".
>
> (Afzal, 2001: 58)

The Land Reform Bills originally sought dramatic change, but were heavily diluted due to landlord resistance, and eventually scrapped in Punjab. Sind Province also resisted land reform, with landlords (*zamindars*) and land grant-holders (*jagirs*) rallying around Ayub Khuhro, who simply asked to shelve the PML Report calling for the landlord system to be abolished (Afzal, 2001: 59). The failure can be summarized in the assertion that a few thousand landlords possessed over 50 percent of the Punjab, a little less than 50 percent of land in NWFP, and over 80 percent of land in Sind (Rizvi, 2000: 112).

The Ayub Khan regime (1958–1969)

A military official observed (in a more evocative Urdu phrase) that "America sits in our roots," and pointed to Pakistan's security alliances and Ayub Khan's close

Leadership and extraction 81

relationship with the US prior to his coup and during his regime (Interview, 2009). Moreover, sizeable foreign aid reduced the need for Ayub to push for greater domestic extraction. Ayub drew on the Harvard Advisory Group for national planning advice. Ayub's ideology might be called "secularist developmentalist"; his decade in power was officially celebrated as the "Decade of Development." Subsidies and incentives helped private enterprise and thereby fed national economic growth, but with increasing income inequality. Unemployment and inflation added to the majority's woes. Drinking water shortages in Karachi and a sugar shortage in the country belied the "development" gains that Ayub's regime had claimed. In 1968, Mahbub-ul-Haq, the Planning Commission's Chief Economist, made his memorable declaration that "twenty families controlled 66 per cent of the entire industrial capital, 80 per cent of the banking and 97 per cent of insurance capital" (Rizvi, 2000: 163). A Pakistani corporate executive suggested that this was similar to Japan's support for 14 trading houses, except that in Pakistan these families lost clout in the 1970s nationalizations (Interview, 2009).

Ayub Khan's 1958 coup was followed by crackdowns on smuggling and corruption. These included 1662 civil servants who were charged with misconduct, corruption, and inefficiency, and were demoted, forcibly retired, or removed (Rizvi, 2000: 100). Out of 823 who were dismissed outright, 84 were top grade civil service officers (Rizvi, 2000: 100, Table IX).

Numerous politicians and public officials (such as ministers, deputy ministers, and parliamentary secretaries) were also charged with misconduct and corruption. The military government used disqualification orders (known as PODO (Public Offices (Disqualification) Order)) and EBDO (Elective Bodies (Disqualification) Order) to bar specific politicians from public offices for periods ranging for about six years. Unofficial sources claimed up to 6000 people were disqualified, however, this was a clear exaggeration because the total membership in the two Constituent Assemblies and all Provincial Assemblies from 1947 to 1958 was not over 1600 (Rizvi, 2000: 101–102).

Ayub's allies and supporters did not face an equivalent crackdown. Open corruption appeared as Ayub's own family members benefited from their relative's powerful position:

> Two of his sons secured their release from the army and decided to enter civil life. One of them, Gohar Ayub, and his father-in-law, General Habibullah entered business and industry. Gohar emerged as a powerful business magnet in a relatively short span of time. [...] What added fuel to the fire were the efforts of Gohar Ayub to become the political over-lord of Karachi.
>
> (Rizvi, 2000: 164)

Thus private goods were clearly gained despite the rhetoric against corruption. This was particularly the case in the business licenses granted to Ayub's relatives; it was also apparent in the lands acquired at Haripur (Interview with retired civil servant, July 2009). Ayub's image was tarnished (Interview with retired military official, 2009).

82 *Political survival in Pakistan*

The winning coalition did not need the politicians, as the Ayub regime's actions show. They also firmly demonstrated that the military could hold the civil service accountable. The military was not itself accountable to the civil service or civilians (Siddiqua, 2007). Ayub Khan's decision to move the capital to the Potwar plateau "was motivated by his desire to keep a close contact with the G.H.Q., which was in Rawalpindi" (Rizvi, 2000: 107).

Ayub made an effort to "civilianize" his regime by introducing the "Basic Democracies" system, in theory to empower local level officials and councils. The reality was that these minor positions were heavily circumscribed by the civil bureaucracy and national government. Justifying these small steps, Ayub Khan declared:

> There were certain basic requirements of the western democratic structures which did not exist in our country. Western democracy presupposes a high degree of social and political awareness and mass literacy, so that the people know the value of their vote in terms of broad national policies and an advanced system of mass communication for speedy and accurate dissemination of information [...].
>
> (Rizvi, 2000: 115)

Ayub made similar remarks at other times. The 1959 Basic Democracies Order gave the bureaucracy enough power to control the local self-governance institutions, and ensure they were subservient to the Ayub regime. Under the order, "the controlling officer had the power to quash the proceedings, suspend the execution of any resolution passed or an order made by the local council, prohibit the doing of anything proposed to be done and require the local council to take such action as may be specified by him" (Rizvi, 2000: 119, n. 72). "The CSP [Civil Service of Pakistan] became an increasingly important partner in Ayub's ruling coalition as a result of the central role accorded Commissioners and Deputy Commissioners in the Basic Democracies scheme and the control over development funds which they acquired under the Rural Works Programme" (Talbot, 2005: 161). Not surprisingly, "due to fear of victimization and the desire to win favour, the [local council] members did not take steps to displease the bureaucrats associated with these institutions" (Rizvi, 2000: 119). Rizvi speculates that the Basic Democracies system had been designed to provide Ayub with a political base independent of the military and the bureaucracy. If that analysis is accurate, the effort was unsuccessful.

That Ayub's winning coalition was centered on the military is evidenced by the fact that his eventual resignation resulted from declining support among his commanders. The anti-Ayub sentiments had begun with the Tashkent Declaration, and grew.

> When the regime faced the serious political crisis of 1968–69, the military dissociated itself from Ayub Khan. The main indicator of the military's unhappiness with Ayub Khan was the emergence of Air Marshal Asghar

Khan and a few other retired Generals as active and vocal opponents of the Ayub Regime. Air Marshal Asghar Khan, being the first Pakistani C-in-C of the Pakistan Air Force was still respected in the military circles. [...] The military was also not happy with him due to his decision to withdraw the Agartala Conspiracy Case. The accused were in the custody of the military and most of the evidence of the case was collected by the military intelligence. Its withdrawal put the military in embarrassing position.

(Rizvi, 2000: 179)

The military found it difficult to tolerate damage to its public image, a key interest. This suggests that there were ample reasons for Ayub to seek his political survival through an effort to construct a new winning coalition, a tricky task for any political leader. It is improbable that his regime would have survived even with solid support from the Basic Democracies.

If a broad winning coalition mattered, then Ayub's decision to not seek re-election would have ended his official position. However, it was not this decision alone, but the fact that it further detracted from his support in the military and the bureaucracy. This is summarized in the following quote from Rizvi:

The civil administration was already ineffective and after Ayub Khan's decision not to seek re-election, it also did not render as much support to him as was done in the past. Ayub Khan had not ruled out the possibility of such a situation when he could not depend upon the military and the bureaucracy. He established the system of Basic Democracies to provide him a political base independent of the military and the bureaucracy. But his efforts did not yield satisfactory results. The erosion of these sources of power was the major cause of his decision to step down from Presidency.

(Rizvi, 2000: 179)

Eventually, Ayub resigned under pressure from his close collaborator General Yahya Khan, having lost the army's support. Yahya himself left office two years later after the military's humiliation over the East Pakistan crisis and war with India. One reason he was not followed by another military leader is that there was not an obvious candidate up to the task. Yahya Khan's leadership did not result in substantive policy changes from Ayub Khan's path, except in two areas. The One Unit Scheme was dissolved and West Pakistan was reconstituted as the Punjab, Sindh, Balochistan, and NWFP. Ayub's constitutional initiatives were abrogated. Nevertheless, Yahya Khan's takeover was typically viewed as a top-level replacement within the military structure that Ayub Khan used as his primary resource of rule. "The Ayub Khan and Yahya Khan governments were not two different regimes but one continuous military rule in which the only change was in the topmost leadership" (Siddiqua, 2007: 72). As a result, Yahya Khan's brief tenure can be described as a change in administration, but one that continued the regime that Ayub Khan had started.

84 *Political survival in Pakistan*

International financing

Pakistan's dependence on American military and economic aid increased from 1954. One analyst describes the 1954–65 period as being especially significant in terms of receipts of economic and military aid to Pakistan (Cohen, 1999: 191). In this period, Pakistan received $4 billion in economic aid and $1.372 billion in military aid (Sattar, 1997: 77). Other estimates of military aid to Pakistan in this period have included figures of $1.5 billion and $750 million (Brines, 1968: 127). This aid included American aircraft and heavy armor, such as 200 Patton tanks and a squadron of supersonic F-104 fighters (Brines, 1968: 127). Despite this alliance, the Americans did not provide clear support for the Pakistani side on the Kashmir issue. Nor were the Americans unequivocal in their support for Pakistan over India.

Under Ayub Khan, US economic aid to Pakistan tripled from its 1958–59 level, going from $61 million to $184 million (Siddiqui, 1972: 99). The decade of the 1960s, particularly its first half, was a "heyday" of foreign assistance to Pakistan (Zaidi, 1999: 113). However, the Sino-Indian border war of 1962 impacted Pakistan's foreign relations. American military assistance to India from 1962 onwards produced a "deterioration" in the US-Pakistan relationship, although the material cost is not clear (Chaudhri, 1970: 26).

Pakistan's relationship with China has been friendly since 1959 (Sattar, 1997: 72), but it is not clear what direct aid, if any, Pakistan received from China prior to 1965. The Sino-Indian border conflict was associated with a warming in Sino-Pakistani relations, following the dictum "my enemy's enemy is my friend," or "my enemy's neighbor is my friend" (as once described by Kautilya).[5]

Corruption in Pakistan meant that international financing or resource and commodity transfers were often siphoned off by black marketeers and smugglers (Jalal, 1990: 250). A consortium of Western countries (the US, UK, Canada, France, West Germany, and Japan) pledged a $945 million credit to Pakistan for the first two years of its development plan; of this amount $320 million was actually allocated in 1961 and was mostly provided by the US (Brown, 1963: 323).

The 1965 war with India and other circumstances raised the demands on central government revenues beyond expectations. The Third Five-Year Plan (1965–70) witnessed a squeeze on government funds that was associated with increased defense expenditures since the 1965 war with India: "drastic cuts" in foreign aid, more difficult loan terms and an increased repayment load, as well as ecological disasters of droughts and floods in 1965–66 and 1966–67 (Khan, 1997: 190). Two Pakistani economists have described the years 1965–67 as a period characterized by crises connected with poor harvests in 1966–67, large hikes in defense expenditures after the 1965 war, and reductions in foreign loans received (Ahmed and Amjad, 1984: 81).

In the 1965 war with India, Pakistan received support from Indonesia, Iran, Turkey, and Saudi Arabia in the form of six naval vessels, jet fuel, guns and ammunition, and financial support, respectively. A slew of smaller outside patrons were therefore useful in wartime (Sattar, 1997). Nevertheless, one observer notes that the Pakistani President Ayub was unable to create an Islamic bloc for ongoing

Leadership and extraction   85

assistance that would support continued fighting (Brines, 1968: 353).[6] During the course of the actual war, both the US and Britain embargoed military assistance to both sides (starting on September 7 for the US and September 8 for Britain) (Brines, 1968: 355). China also became a foreign patron for Pakistan. China gave Pakistan $60 million in development assistance in 1965, $40 million in 1969, and pledged an additional $200 million. In 1966, the Chinese also gave military aid, including MiG aircraft and army equipment (Sattar, 1997: 97).

Two Pakistani economists describe the war period as a time of overall cutbacks in foreign aid (Ahmed and Amjad, 1984: 81). The need for large food imports were paid for through a combination of Pakistani cash reserves and US and Canadian food assistance (Ahmed and Amjad, 1984: 81). The uncertain economic conditions associated with the war, in particular, resulted in a delay in the launching of the Third Five-Year Plan (Ahmed and Amjad, 1984: 87).

Late in 1965, Pakistan's President Ayub made a public statement to the Pakistani National Assembly reflecting the pitfalls of reliance on foreign military assistance. In the same statement, however, he affirmed Pakistan's internationalist strategy for locating resources. Asserting that he would search the world for weapons, Ayub stated that "[in] obtaining military assistance from foreign sources, we have to be on our guard against the danger of relying too heavily on any single source of supply. Already we have suffered on this account" (quoted in Brines, 1968: 395). His phrase "suffered on this account" referred to the effects of the embargo of American military assistance during the war. Pakistan's decision to support an end to the war was closely related to the US arms ban of September 7, 1965, in the context of destructive tank battles and the run-down of non-replenishable equipment (Talbot, 1998: 178). There was a belief that the US betrayed Pakistan in the 1965 war; damaged or destroyed tanks, for example, were not replaced to retain regiment strength, and ammunition stocks ran low, causing grave concern (Interview with retired military officer, 2009). In other words, there was a sense that the US had not behaved well as a foreign patron in wartime.

Such strategic difficulties did not produce a call for substituting the international strategy with a domestic strategy for locating war-making resources. Instead, Ayub called for a refinement and strategic sophistication of the international strategy under which locating diverse patrons would ensure Pakistani security. A military mission sent to Moscow in July 1966 reflected this spirit (Brines, 1968: 409). As if to symbolize the diverse sources of foreign support, Chinese aircraft and tanks were displayed alongside American-supplied arms in a Pakistani military parade in early 1966 (Brines, 1968: 413).

The Anglo-American embargo during the war led to an emphasis on China and the USSR as foreign patrons (Brines, 1968: 414). The USSR became more active in managing regional security affairs, and departed from its previous hostility to Pakistan by starting an arms supply relationship (Baldev, 2000: 17). A Soviet mediation effort between India and Pakistan took place late in 1965 in Tashkent (Brines, 1968: 396). This was preceded by Soviet efforts to move closer to Pakistan, through economic barter agreements with East Bloc countries as early as 1963, to hints of support for the Pakistani position on Kashmir (Brines, 1968: 261–262).

86   *Political survival in Pakistan*

Embodying this shift, a military officer who had previously traveled to the US for training was now sent for training to the Soviet Union (Interview with retired military official, 2009). The deal was to obtain about 250 tanks from the USSR, as well as helicopters, guns, and other items; however, Pakistan eventually received only 50 tanks, and some other items. A Soviet-Pakistani military aid agreement was made in July 1968 that provided Pakistan with $30 million of Soviet military equipment (Sisson and Rose, 1991: 238). Small Soviet military sales to Pakistan were discontinued, however, after Indian protests (Sattar, 1997: 98).

In both 1965 and 1968, Ayub's government made one year standby arrangements with the IMF, worth over SDR 125 million (Zaidi, 1999: 315).[7] Substantial borrowing from the IMF thus took place. In 1970, US support for aid to Pakistan increased, and some B-57 and F-104 aircraft were sold to Pakistan (Sattar, 1997: 99). Kissinger and Nixon both used Pakistan in initiating contacts with China, signaling the closeness of the US-Pakistani relationship. The Aid-to-Pakistan Consortium (a group of Western countries and institutions) continued to be an important source of foreign assistance to Pakistan (Khan, Aftab Ahmad, 1997: 189). The USSR also gave a steel plant as aid in 1968 and committed more than $1 billion in soft loans for development projects in Pakistan (Sattar, 1997: 98).

Taxation

Pakistan had started with a very low tax/GDP ratio (less than 4 percent). Ayub Khan's regime showed some gains in domestic extraction as tax dodgers were forced to declare income and smugglers faced a crackdown (Siddiqui, 1972: 100).[8] In the agricultural sector, the Taxation Enquiry Committee of 1959 endorsed a federal income tax, and the Taxation and Tariffs of 1964 recommended that provincial land revenue should be merged with federal income tax levies. Neither proposal was accepted by the federal government (M.H. Khan, 2002: 193–194). The 1959 Taxation Enquiry Committee had also recommended a wealth tax; this was introduced in 1963. Formerly, agricultural lands had been subject to the land revenue tax, collected by provinces. The wealth tax was to be collected by the central government. Due to exemptions and the fact that land value was set at ten rupees per Produce Index Unit (Mahmood Hasan Khan, 1999: 134), agricultural land generally escaped the wealth tax. By 1969/70, the tax/GDP ratio rose to 6 percent. The increase was mostly due to excise taxes resulting from industrial growth; "To encourage industrialization, many tax exemptions were granted and wealth taxes (direct taxes) were less than 1 per cent of GDP" (Shahrukh Khan, 1999: 16).

Despite the increased extraction, Pakistan had difficulty paying for the relatively short 1965 conflict. An austerity program had been set in place by late October 1965. This began with a $217 million cut in the government's development expenditures (Brines, 1968: 402). It was followed by a reduction in private investment opportunities (meaning the reduction of selected state loans to private ventures, for example). There was also a 25 percent increase in excise, customs, and sales taxes (Brines, 1968: 402). A combination of spending cuts and tax increases were therefore used to reallocate resources and increase the funds available to the national government for the heightened spending needs associated with the war and war threat.

The 1964 Taxation and Tariffs Commission strongly recommended merging provincial land revenue with the federal government's existing income taxes (Mahmood Hasan Khan, 1999: 137). If successful, the move would have raised the taxes collected by the federal government. The report was published in 1967; the recommendation was not accepted due to opposition from West Pakistan's provincial government (the provinces of West Pakistan had been conjoined under the One Unit Scheme).

Income and corporate taxes as a percentage of total tax receipts actually fell to less than 6 percent in 1970/71 (as compared to 15.7 percent in 1957/58). This happened in the context of some industrialization and widely acknowledged dynamism in the economy. The Pakistani economist Zaidi believes that this was due to tax fraud, and suggests that "it seems that the pattern of tax evasion and underreporting may have been established very early in Pakistan" (Zaidi, 1999: 203). The Pakistani state was not very successful in increasing direct taxation, which stagnated and may have seen an actual decrease.

Land reform

Ayub Khan originally sought significant land reforms, whose aim was to reduce the large landholdings. One hope was that rural economic empowerment would increase the market for industrial goods, helping to sustain national industrialization (Nasr, 1996: 257). The Land Reform Act of February 1959 abolished *jagirs* without compensation and imposed a limit on individual landholdings, but the ceiling remained high and evasion and intra-family transfers subverted the process (Mahmood Hasan Khan, 1999: 128). The implemented reforms were not as radical as they appeared, due to high land ceilings (Talbot, 1998: 165) and because actual retained holdings were in numerous cases larger than the prescribed limit (Rizvi, 2000: 112). More extensive land reform may have succeeded in creating a new class of capitalist farmers (and an expanded tax base and a bigger market for industrial goods). Scholars have found the results of these attempts to be "unimpressive" and argue that "landlordism remained virtually unchanged" (Talbot, 1998: 165). There were beneficiaries among small and medium-sized landowners, but Ayub's Land Reform Act did not change the existing tenancy laws of the province of West Pakistan (Mahmood Hasan Khan, 1999: 128).

According to economist Shahid Javed Burki, Ayub Khan's planned reforms were originally more extensive. However, he chose to appoint the aristocratic Nawab of Kalabagh to a key governance post. This ensured landed interests were firmly in charge, and meant that land reform efforts were stalled (Burki, 2008c: 246–247). This compromise with landed interests had a lineage: Ayub originally sought to bring landlords into his winning coalition and thus draw their support away from his former partner and later rival, Iskander Mirza. This view is supported by historian Lawrence Ziring's narrative summary:

88 *Political survival in Pakistan*

> In need of political leverage, Mirza fell back on the landed aristocracy who had flocked to the Republican Party. Ayub had appointed a Land Reform Commission, and the feudals at first feared the loss of their vast holdings and hence a diminution in their influence and power. Ayub laboured to offset that alliance and to overcome such fears. He appealed directly to the agrarian elite, and he assured them that his plans did not entail a reduction in their stature, or the loss of their property.
>
> (Ziring, 1997: 222–223)

Ayub thus thwarted a challenge from Mirza by convincing rural landlords that his Land Reform Commission would not reduce landholdings or landholder influence.

Why Ayub Khan, despite his "developmentalist" agenda, did not more aggressively pursue land reform fits neatly into the political survival approach. As the incumbent, there was simply not much benefit to be gained for his winning coalition from enacting significant land reform. There was little immediate political benefit in promoting an equitable income distribution too. On the contrary, there was some risk in both cases from the distributional coalitions that enjoyed privileges. At the same time, ample foreign aid reduced the need to penetrate society and extract more domestically. As a result, these "majority goods" or "public goods"—land reform and income redistribution—were not supplied. Ironically, unwillingness to restructure state-society relations with redistributive policies may have undermined his rule in the longer term. A large-scale agitation that reflected dissatisfaction with income inequality and the 1965 war, and pressure from Chief of Army Staff Yahya Khan, compelled an ill Ayub to resign in 1969. Yahya Khan's takeover produced little practical difference in land distribution or income inequality.

The Zulfikar Ali Bhutto regime (1971–1977)

This period is frequently identified as a substantial departure from the past for Pakistan. Elections brought a populist leader with a socialist philosophy, Zulfiqar Ali Bhutto, to power. The fact that elections on a universal franchise brought a challenger to national office suggested a different and larger winning coalition than the military coup-based regime. Yet this picture is complicated by the lack of repeated fair elections, and the failure to institutionalize such elections as a stable, recurrent mechanism for determining leadership contests and political survival outcomes. Furthermore, the electoral result saw a division and a disastrous civil war in which the country disintegrated; the perceived underlying machinations influenced future challenger behaviors (as described in Chapter 4). As regime leader, Z.A. Bhutto arguably tried to prune his winning coalition substantially in an effort to ensure his political survival. Z.A. Bhutto's rise had cobbled together disparate groups into a difficult to manage coalition fraught with internal contradictions. The PPP factionalized and there were defections, his popularity dwindled, an opposition alliance emerged, pleading for the *Nizam-e-Mustafa* (a religious political order), and his personally created security force was

Leadership and extraction 89

inadequate for the needed repression. Z.A. Bhutto's legitimacy declined and he had to rely more exclusively on the military. There were credible and widespread allegations that the 1977 elections were rigged by the Z.A. Bhutto regime. Several polity observers and participants expressed their belief that this was a tragic choice, because he would have returned to office under fair elections (Interviews, 2009).

Z.A. Bhutto had been foreign minister under Ayub, but became distanced and eventually left his post after the post-1965-war Tashkent Agreement. The 1971 war dismembered the country, and led to the loss of substantial revenues from the export produce of East Pakistan. Additionally, an assured market for 40 percent of West Pakistani manufactures was lost (Talbot, 1998: 217). However, the loss of East Pakistan (which became Bangladesh) was not necessarily a pure negative. It has been described as a plus in terms of relieving certain pressures on the Pakistani economy and budget (Interviewee A, 2000). Furthermore, a rupee devaluation shortly after the war meant that Pakistani exports were competitive, and therefore the blow to earned foreign exchange was cushioned (Zaidi, 1999). Maintaining East Pakistan was an administrative nightmare. A bias had existed in government spending, favoring West Pakistan over East Pakistan (Jalal, 1990: 244). However, it was difficult to govern territory located across 1000 miles of hostile territory.

The war itself, however, had been costly, as Pakistan lost "half its navy, a third of its army, and a quarter of its air force," and 93,000 troops had been surrounded and taken as Indian prisoners of war (Talbot, 1998: 212). It is difficult to overestimate the psychological costs. Some soldiers in the West Pakistan theater reportedly wept on hearing the news that the contingent in East Pakistan had lost (Interview with retired military officer, 2009). Some believed that a US fleet was on its way to aid Pakistan, but it never arrived. Others described a national depression with the realization that the world's largest Islamic state had been split (Interview with PTV correspondent Hamid Rajput, 2009). An Urdu-speaking Karachiite who would have been a teenager at the time described the fall of Dhaka as Pakistan's biggest historical catastrophe (Conversation with Karachi resident, 2008).

In the post-1971 period, the military was humiliated by its defeat and Pakistan's breakup. The military's image and legitimacy as the guardian of the state was damaged. There were calls for military leaders to be tried, and the Hamood ur-Rehman Commission (named after its chairperson, the chief justice of Pakistan) began inquiring into the failures that produced the debacle. The press had pub-licized lurid reports about Yahya Khan's drinking and womanizing. Bhutto made a clear and concerted effort to sideline the military and make it subservient to his authority. He spoke about a "People's Army" model similar to the North Vietnamese. Returning from a high-profile foreign trip, he was greeted by paramilitaries from his party organization, rather than the customary military guard (Rizvi, 2000: 208–220). In an address to the nation in March, 1972, Bhutto asserted his commitment to reducing the military's influence in political life:

> What has happened in Pakistan since 1954, and more openly since 1958 is that some professional Generals turned to politics not as a profession but as a plunder and as a result the influences that had crept into socio-political life

90 *Political survival in Pakistan*

> destroyed its fabric as the influence of bonapartism had affected Europe in the 18th and 19th century. But come what may, these bonapartic influences must be rooted out in the interest of the Armed Forces and the People of Pakistan.
>
> (quoted in Rizvi, 2000: 210–211)

Bhutto was a practiced populist, and his rhetoric was powerful in part because public opinion in parts had grown critical and hostile to the military. Perhaps ironically, he was also designated "Chief Civilian Martial Law Administrator."

Z. A. Bhutto took significant steps to reduce the military's political power and veto over his leadership. A political survival interpretation is that he was able to do this at first based on an ostensibly larger and different winning coalition from that of the previous regime. Rather than relying on support from corps commanders, Z. A. Bhutto's rise to power had drawn on his PPP organizational machine, and mass electoral support in West Pakistan. By April 1972, as his first four months in office came to a close, 43 senior military officers had been relieved of service. The chief of army staff and chief of air staff were removed for interfering with the Hamood ur-Rehman Commission, and for not making the army and air force available to the government during a police strike (Rizvi, 2000: 213). In October 1972, Bhutto's government also created the Federal Security Force, which was tasked with assisting the police and civil administration with law and order. Its strength rose from 13,875 personnel in 1974 to 18,563 by 1977. The force had semi-automatic weapons, mortars, grenades, and communication and transport equipment, and planned to acquire used tanks from the army. In February 1976, its assignments were expanded to include nation-building, development work such as housing construction, flood control, and adult education (Rizvi, 2000: 216). The FSF itself became politicized, becoming notorious as "a kind of private force at the disposal of the ruling party which was used against the political opponents and the dissidents within the ruling party" (Rizvi, 2000: 216).

The military's organization was changed: the three services' chiefs had their tenure reduced to three-year periods and were put under the Joint Chiefs of Staff Committee which was under the president, the commander-in-chief. The three forces had been based in Karachi, Rawalpindi, and Peshawar, and in 1974, the naval HQ had been shifted to Rawalpindi (in 1983, the air force HQ was also shifted to Rawalpindi). Moreover, Z. A. Bhutto's stated commitment to building a nuclear program may be understood as more than purely a response to the Indian nuclear test of 1974: a nuclear program in civilian hands would help sideline the military's political centrality by reducing its stature as the guardian of state security.

The 1973 Constitution (enforced on August 14, 1973) explicitly defined the military's role, and defined attempts to subvert or abrogate the constitution by force as high treason. Furthermore the constitution required all military personnel to take an oath to uphold the constitution and to not engage in political activities (Rizvi, 2000: 214–215). A 1973 parliamentary law made treason punishable by capital punishment or life imprisonment. The 1973 Constitution swung power toward the legislature, supporting a "parliamentary system with a very weak President, bicameral legislature with sufficient law making and financial powers, federalism with provincial autonomy, independent judiciary and a guarantee of fundamental rights" (Rizvi, 2000: 227).

These lofty ideals were not sustained in practice, as the federal government continued controversial interventions affecting the provinces, and as fundamental rights were suspended. When Bhutto dismissed Ataullah Mangel's government in Balochistan in 1973, the military was sent in to counter the insurgency in that province (Rizvi, 2000: 217). Another challenge came in when the NWFP government cabinet resigned in a protest action (Rizvi, 2000: 227). This indicated that the institutional arrangement over provincial and federal powers was failing, and was all the more troubling because the most populous province, East Pakistan, had so recently seceded and formed Bangladesh.

Protest actions and organized political dissent were repressed. The Awami National Party was banned and its leader and 43 other workers were detailed and put on trial for "anti-state activities" and alleged involvement in a PPP leader's assassination (Rizvi, 2000: 228). Bhutto's personal popular appeal had declined, particularly as he subverted institutions for patrimonial purposes. Nine opposition parties, including primarily religious parties and rightist parties, created a coalition called the Pakistan National Alliance in January, 1977 (Rizvi, 2000: 232). Elections were held in March that year, and the PPP won 155 out of 200 seats. The PNA won 36 seats and alleged massive rigging. It boycotted the provincial elections, launching a national strike on March 11, and a "mass protest movement" to demand that that Bhutto and the chief election commissioner resign and fresh polls be held; although the demand for Bhutto's resignation was later withdrawn (Rizvi, 2000: 234). Bhutto resorted to martial law in major urban centers. After expressing concern at the political situation, the military, led by Zia ul-Haq, executed a coup and detained Bhutto.

International financing

The aid consortium supporting Pakistan stopped discussions on new aid to Pakistan on June 21, 1971 (Siddiqui, 1972: 168). Siddiqui, writing at the beginning of the 1970s, saw this move as a major shift in Pakistan's relations with international sources of financing:

> The Consortium's changed attitude meant that the Pakistani bureaucrats had at long last lost the support of their international backers. The era of the "favorite child" treatment of Pakistan by the western aid-givers was at an end. To stop succour reaching Pakistan from the west had been a prime objective of Indian foreign policy for almost two decades. This had been achieved at a most propitious moment.
>
> (Siddiqui, 1972: 168)

However, Pakistan was to eventually receive massive foreign aid infusions in the 1980s (under Zia ul-Haq's regime). In the meantime, foreign resources continued to be vitally important. Despite a shift in American willingness to act as a patron for

92 *Political survival in Pakistan*

the Pakistani regime, the Zulfikar Bhutto era saw a continuing international strategy for obtaining needed resources, which unfortunately added to the debt burden.

In the 1971 war, the US State Department embargoed arms deliveries to Pakistan (Sattar, 1997: 105). As in the 1965 war, Pakistan actually lost foreign patronage. In July 1971, the US suspended $75 million of economic aid to Pakistan for that fiscal year. Except for food aid, practically all American military and economic aid to Pakistan was suspended by late summer 1971 (Sisson and Rose, 1991: 257–258). A small amount of prearranged US aid (worth about $5 million) was nevertheless provided (Sisson and Rose, 1991: 191–192). A major new American aid package to Pakistan was not forthcoming during Bhutto's tenure as national leader.

Although China honored previous aid commitments, it was generally unwilling to approve new arms aid through spring and summer 1971. Pakistan made a specific appeal for some equipment, in particular aircraft, but China did not agree to the request until several months later (Sisson and Rose, 1991: 251). Thus, Chinese aid was reduced at the time that Pakistan needed it urgently. China's belated military and economic aid and limited diplomatic support was a disappointment to the Pakistan government (Talbot, 1998: 212). In the 1965 war, by contrast, worry about Chinese intervention had prevented India from escalating the war to East Pakistan (Interview with senior journalist, 2009).

Based on a Soviet-Indian understanding, Soviet arms sales to Pakistan had been suspended in spring 1970, although actual shipments on existing contracts continued until 1971 (Sisson and Rose, 1991: 198). The USSR's position as a patron of Pakistan after the 1965 war thus waned. This reinforced the common perception that foreign patronage tended to desert Pakistan in high stress periods of wartime (as evidenced by the experience of the 1965 war). In 1975, the US began the process of resuming supply of arms to Pakistan by removing the embargo that had been placed during the Bangladesh crisis (Baldev, 2000: 30).

Foreign aid to Pakistan maintained a dominant, significant role in development expenditures by the central government. The level saw little change from 1968, the late Ayub period (Noman, 1990: 89). By mid-1971, high defense expenditures and collapsing foreign exchange earnings from jute placed stress on the resources of the central government. Pakistan had to negotiate short-term loans as the IMF and World Bank did not provide support for debt rescheduling (Talbot, 1998: 210). The oil shocks of 1973 and 1979 placed additional stress on state funds for Pakistan and heightened fiscal requirements. The worldwide recession associated with the first oil shock hurt Pakistan's exports, and as a result Pakistan's balance of payments deteriorated further (Zaidi, 1999: 6). From September 1973 to September 1974, oil prices rose from $2.70 per barrel to $11.20 per barrel. For oil-importing countries unable to quickly adjust to domestic demand for oil, this meant a sizeable increase in the import bill. See Diagram 3.2 below for a graph of the average price of crude oil. The jumps in 1973 and 1979 are notable.

At the same time, expanding social welfare provided by the state combined with high defense expenditures to squeeze the Pakistani budget. Cotton crop failures in 1974/75 and devastating flooding in 1976/77 had negative economic consequences for Pakistan in this period also (Zaidi, 1999: 101). Anecdotal evidence suggests

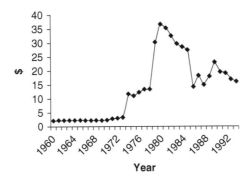

Diagram 3.2 Average price of crude oil
Source: *International Financial Statistics Yearbook* (IMF, 1999).

seignorage activity, but high inflation in the 1973–4 period was blamed by the government on the increase in oil prices (Ahmed and Amjad, 1984: 95).

Speaking for the government, Shahid Hussain asserted to the Pakistan Aid Consortium that worsened terms of trade over the 1972–76 period meant that the regime had to either retrench on domestic spending (on consumption or development), or to increase foreign inflows, and the country had chosen the latter option (cited in Noman, 1990: 93). What this left out was the money creation policies that were also rampant (as described below).

Foreign loans became more important, and an acrimonious relationship with the World Bank grew as Zulfikar Bhutto's regime resisted increases in domestic extraction. In consequence, the World Bank did not provide loans needed for social service (health, education, and welfare) spending by the Zulfikar Bhutto regime (Noman, 1990: 90). Additionally, Z.A. Bhutto's government concluded four standby loans with the IMF worth, in total, SDR 330 million (Zaidi, 1999: 315). In the 1970s, Pakistan also received some rebates on purchases of oil from the Middle East. These lightened the impact of the oil shocks to a minor degree (Interviewee A, 2000). It became easier for Pakistani workers to obtain passports and related documents. One interviewee suggested that this was a tactical policy decision to increase the number of overseas Pakistani workers (particularly in the Persian Gulf) and thereby obtain greater remittances (Interview, 2009). Annual disbursements from oil-rich Islamic countries helped also (by the late 1970s, Pakistan was receiving $50 million, $30 million, and $100 million from Kuwait, United Arab Emirates, and Saudi Arabia, respectively (Talbot, 1998: 33–34)).

Taxation

Zulfikar Bhutto's government espoused a populist and socialist philosophy and engaged in nationalizations and land reform legislation. This was in keeping with

94 *Political survival in Pakistan*

the spirit of the times (Interview, July 2009). However, this was selective: there is evidence that business groupings that supported the PPP enjoyed favorable outcomes, and many large business families were unaffected by the nationalizations in net asset terms (Noman, 1990). "Nationalizations" provide an indication that some specific business groups were not in Zulfikar Bhutto's winning coalition. The nationalizations began in 1972 and included major industries (ten categories of industries were nationalized). Ardeshir Cowasjee, a shipping business owner and well-known public figure, found the nationalizations illegitimate, and declared that his ships had been "stolen." Resistance or recalcitrance produced repression; Cowasjee was himself jailed after declining to put some people on his payrolls (Interview with Ardeshir Cowasjee, February 2009).

A group of "scheduled" banks were also nationalized in 1974 (Stewart and Sturgis, 1995: 17). While one way to think about nationalizations is that they are an extraordinary domestic extraction, the net effects in this case were different. The nationalizations often increased costs to the central government without adding equivalent revenue. Company heads were told that they were being taken over and they would be compensated. Compensation included payment for the machinery as well as a "nominal" rent payment for land and buildings. There were some legal challenges, but these generally failed. The new state-owned enterprises now operated with more overhead expenses and the profit motive did not force the administrators to watch costs carefully. Instead, administrators reputedly had lavish personal expenses, which they charged to company accounts; at the same time, their manipulated figures showed increased productivity, and made it appear that the company was profitable when in fact it was making a loss. Accounting practices were opaque, deceptive, and did not accurately represent real returns (Interviews, 2000, 2008, 2009).

Public sector growth was thus associated with rising inefficiencies. It is appropriate to write that the "main beneficiaries of [Z. A. Bhutto's] policies were his party leaders and their families, bureaucrats, and others employed by the industrial empire acquired by the state" (Kukreja, 2005: 152). The nationalization efforts also produced a prolonged "entrepreneurial strike" and some entrepreneurial emigration, undercutting the productive base of the economy from which revenue for state purposes could be extracted. Capital also fled the country along with the industrialists (Zaidi, 1999: 430). The nationalizations may have also helped enhance landlord power and wealth by vertically integrating it with such related industries as food processing and cotton milling industries (Kukreja, 2005: 150).

It is also not clear, however, that these ostensibly extractive actions were directly linked to the war or war threat as an effort to build state extractive capacity. The potential linkage is confounded by at least three factors. First, the socialist political philosophy espoused by Bhutto was one justification used for the nationalizations. Second, a wide perception exists that the rapid public-sector expansion was used for patronage purposes (Interviews, 2008, 2009). More jobs could now be handed to the winning coalition's members, especially Bhutto's party workers. Finally, the war was over, Bangladesh had become an independent state, and the unique administrative and strategic demands of defending territory 1000 miles away were gone. This meant that, in one way, the war had resulted in a lessened burden on the central government. This would imply that the nationalizations could not have been sought as a way to generate resources to control or administer distant East Pakistan.

Land reform

Z.A. Bhutto was from a prominent landholding family. Among his close supporters was Ghulam Mustafa Khar, a well-known landlord colorfully described in the book *My Feudal Lord* (Durrani, 1991). This suggested an affinity group that was interested in maintaining the highly unequal status quo in land ownership, and not in the radical redistribution that initially appeared to be high on Z.A. Bhutto's agenda. Within three years of Z.A. Bhutto's tenure, those party affiliates that advocated radical redistribution were expelled, and in some cases, sentenced to prison terms. The repressed included the Mukhtar Rana grouping with trade union support in Punjab, former Z.A. Bhutto cabinet member Mairaj M. Khan, who accused Bhutto of class betrayal, and Industrial Production Minister J.A. Rahim (Noman, 1990: 102–103). Urban worker threats of *gherao* and *jalao* (literally, "encircling" and "burning"; violent direct action against industrial entities) were met by police repression, and Z.A. Bhutto responded to such threats in 1972 by stating unless the workers desisted, "the might of the state would meet the might of the street" (Ali, 2005: 83). Thus, significant elements in his support coalition were denied their preferred goods, and arguably jettisoned from the winning coalition. Yet Bhutto's rhetoric was populist, and his appearance sometimes emulated Chairman Mao, who was viewed as a revolutionary in an agrarian setting. Under Z.A. Bhutto, there were two land reform acts, the first relatively minor and the second more extensive, but these did not have a radically redistributive effect, for reasons largely related to Bhutto's political survival goals.

The Land Reform Act of 1972 did favorably affect the legal position of sharecroppers, although its effect on land redistribution was "far more limited than the 1959 Act in terms of the area resumed by the state" (Mahmood Hasan Khan, 1999: 128). In theory some portion of large landholdings could have been appropriated by the state without compensation. In his rhetoric, Bhutto declared that land would be taken from the rich and given to the poor. However, the proposed land reforms were not fully implemented (Khan, 1998: 15). Among the problems faced by Bhutto's attempted land reforms were: "landholding ceiling fixed on individual basis, exemption for owning tractor and tubewell, etc, the loopholes in implementation, and the policy of landlords to surrender uncultivable land which could not be purposefully redistributed" (Rizvi, 2000: 225). The hope that land reform would mean greater tax revenue was counteracted in part because small farmers did not enjoy the economies of scale found on larger farm units (Interview with high-ranking former civil service official, 2000). Even such things as getting farmers to pay "Canal tax" or "Aabiyaana" water tax (specifically designated for agricultural services) were not pursued because of fear of political opposition.

96   *Political survival in Pakistan*

Ingenious evasion tactics allowed large land possessions to persist (Khan, 1998: 284). Landlords would bifurcate their holdings, and transfer them to their servants' names while retaining a *mukhtar nama* (power of attorney) because the servant is under the landlord's influence. Consequently, the land would stay effectively in the landlord's control (Interview with former civil official, 2009). Additionally, specific land expropriations were used to target political enemies among Balochi nationalist leaders (Noman, 1990: 94). Land redistribution was most effective (in terms of landless peasants receiving tenure) in NWFP, and this was arguably an effort to build PPP popular support against the provincially powerful National Awami Party (Noman, 1990: 94). In general, however, despite accompanying rhetoric against "feudal" landlords, the reforms "did not really break the hold of the large landowners and were more a showpiece political ploy" (Zaidi, 1999: 430). A pro-Bhutto student activist expressed his disillusionment, saying that the Mao cap Bhutto wore and populist slogans were a conspiracy by the feudal class to retain their privileges (Interview with former student activist, 2009).

On the surface, this view would be contradicted by the far-reaching 1977 land reform legislation. By putting forward the 1977 reforms, the Bhutto regime in effect admitted that the 1973 land reforms had been inadequate. The new land ownership ceiling was reduced to 100 acres for irrigated and 200 acres for unirrigated land. Moreover, the January 1977 Finance Act replaced land revenue (simple tax on land, a minor revenue earner) with a tax on agricultural incomes, to be determined by Produce Index Units (PIUs) per hectare (despite the fact that the 1973 Constitution retained the rule (from the 1935 Government of India Act) that agricultural taxation would remain a provincial matter). However, interview data suggests that the 1977 land reform and agricultural income tax legislation was a ploy that apparently married irreconcilable goals: to keep landlords within Z.A. Bhutto's winning coalition while retaining his appeal to the broader electorate, as seen below. Bhutto was contending with a growing opposition that became known as the Nizam-e-Mustafa movement (see Chapter 4 for details), and proposals for breaking rural elite power had populist value. But this was belied by the many PPP legislative seat tickets that were given to the landholding rural elite, leaving what appears to be a paradox: how Bhutto, renowned for his guile, hoped to obtain simultaneous support from diametrically opposed interest groups in a way that saw him through to victory in the election and retained powerful interests in his control after the election.

Interview data suggest that the apparent contradiction can be resolved through a strategic, political-survival based interpretation. A former Central Board of Revenue official suggested that the agricultural reforms were a sophisticated way to threaten landholders, because the agricultural tax legislation was to take effect in July 1977, after the election (Interview with former CBR official, March 2009). The suggestion was that Z.A. Bhutto would nullify this legislation if elected to office. Otherwise, the legislation may have proceeded and landowners brought more thoroughly into the tax base. As partial evidence for this theory, the official pointed to the timing of the agricultural tax legislation. Such legislation is normally expected to come out at the time the budget is being prepared, but the Finance

Act of 1977 did not. Thus, a strategic maneuver related to Z.A. Bhutto's peculiar political survival needs may explain the agricultural reform package and its curious timing.

Another civil administration official from that period, who as a student had been a dedicated Bhutto supporter, also viewed the 1977 land reform legislation as a stick to those feudal landlords who did not remain in Bhutto's coalition. The threat was that the legislation would be enforced selectively against those who opposed Bhutto. As support for his theory, the official pointed to the fact that many among those who held PPP tickets in the 1977 legislative elections had run on tickets opposing Bhutto in the 1970 elections (Interview with former civil administration official, 2009). Land reform legislation was not meant to be carried out, but was rather used as a strategic bargaining tool to ensure that landlords remained in Bhutto's support coalition.

The Zia ul-Haq regime (1977–1988)

Zia ul-Haq's 1977 coup brought him to office at a time when challengers to Bhutto's regime had been calling for the Nizam-e-Mustafa. Zia ul-Haq actively and repeatedly courted religious-rightist sentiments to enhance his legitimacy. The label "Islamizer" is most associated with Zia ul-Haq, despite religious references by virtually all previous office-holders, because he advocated specific policies labeled "Islamic." According to a senior military official who knew him, Zia ul-Haq was a humble, professional, hard-working, and religious person. He declared that elections would follow in 90 days after his coup. Zia ul-Haq had apparently come to believe that God would give him a chance to Islamize Pakistan, and religious cronies encouraged and nurtured this belief. There was also a fear from political advisers that holding elections would put Z.A. Bhutto in a position from which he could punish Zia ul-Haq, potentially for treason. Consequently, Zia ul-Haq clung to power and did not hold the promised elections on time (Interview with former military official, 2009). In 1979, Zia ul-Haq's government executed Zulfiqar Ali Bhutto on a murder conspiracy charge. This helped Zia ul-Haq's political survival by eliminating a challenger; the trial remains tainted, sometimes described as a "judicial assassination." There was an international outcry, but not a large-scale domestic mobilization to defend Bhutto at the time.

In the early 1980s, a multiparty alliance called the Movement for the Restoration of Democracy was set up, and demanded an end to martial law and free and fair elections. The MRD called for civil disobedience, and countrywide agitation was initiated. While there was not a strong response in Punjab, Balochistan, and NWFP, militancy arose among ethnic Sindhis in Sindh (Afzal, 2001: 254). A Pakistan International Airlines plane was hijacked by Al-Zulfikar, a group led by Z.A. Bhutto's eldest son, Murtaza. This tainted the MRD and PPP, although they condemned the hijacking.

In 1983, non-party polls were held for local bodies. In December 1984, Zia ul-Haq held a curiously worded referendum calling for Islamization to be approved rather than a straightforward yes or no to his continued tenure. The referendum was

98   *Political survival in Pakistan*

passed by 97.7 percent in favor with a 62.15 percent turnout. These figures were disputed. This was followed by general elections in 1985 on a non-party basis. The MRD, JUP, and some other political parties boycotted the election; some (e.g. PML Pagaro sent in candidates on a "like-minded persons" basis) (Rizvi, 2000: 261). Campaigning instruments such as public meetings and loudspeakers were disallowed. The feudal, tribal, and commercial elite performed well (Rizvi, 2000: 262–263).

Zia ul-Haq announced the Revival of the Constitutions Order (RCO) on March 2, 1985, shortly after the election. The president's discretionary powers made it impossible for autonomous prime ministerial power to emerge. The controversial Article 58 2 (b) gave the president the discretion to dismiss the federal government and dissolve the National Assembly (Rizvi, 2000: 263). The parliamentary joint session was held on March 23, 1985, and Zia ul-Haq took oath as the elected president for five years. He appointed Muhammad Khan Junejo, a feudal from Sind, as prime minister. This arrangement developed strains due to temperament and style, which worsened when the civilian government, led by the PM, demanded that martial law be withdrawn. Zia ul-Haq conceded, once an amended RCO was endorsed. The National Security Council was abolished and the PM was to be elected by parliament after 1990.

Zia ul-Haq executed another near-coup when the military's interests (and his own political survival) were threatened. Along with divergences on policy issues, Zia ul-Haq's protégé, Prime Minister Mohammad Khan Junejo also planned to decrease military spending. There was also potential damage to the military's prestige and legitimacy due to an ammunition dump explosion:

> The growing criticism of the military, especially the defense expenditure and the perks of the senior officers, inside and outside the parliament in 1986–87 perturbed the military circles who felt that the civilian government was deliberately encouraging anti-military sentiments. On top of all this was the blowing up of the Ojhri ammunition dump in Rawalpindi in April 1988 which caused much havoc in the area. Whereas Zia ul-Haq and the Army wanted to hush up the matter, the political circles demanded punitive action against those Army personnel whose negligence had caused the incident. Zia ul-Haq felt that if the civilian government took action against some officers his role as the guardian of the interests of the military would be compromised. Furthermore, after removing some senior officers, the government could feel confident to ask him to quit as the Army Chief.
>
> (Rizvi, 2000: 265–266)

In May 1988, Zia ul-Haq removed the civilian government, assumed executive authority, and began work to coopt more leaders; however, he was killed in an air crash in August 1988, ending his administration. There are many conspiracy theories regarding his assassination, satirized in a popular novel (Hanif, 2008). Among them is the view that American "agencies" were concerned about Zia ul- Haq's plan to extend the jihad to Kashmir as Afghanistan de-escalated (Interview with ex-military official, 2009).

The Soviet-Afghan conflict colored much of this period for Pakistan. Other factors, however, were also prominent in affecting the revenue-raising requirements of the central government. In discussing Pakistan's Sixth Five-Year Plan (1983–88), for example, Khan described Pakistan as being vulnerable to external shocks because of its narrow export base (Khan, Aftab Ahmad, 1997: 208). Fluctuations in international markets could, therefore, have severe consequences for the Pakistani economy, producing what Nouriel Roubini would term a "revenue shock" (meaning a decrease in the tax base).

SAARC (South Asian Association for Regional Cooperation) was announced at a summit in Dhaka in 1985. It included Bangladesh, Bhutan, Maldives, Nepal, Sri Lanka, India, and Pakistan. The major aim was regional economic welfare, but there was cynicism from the outset about the possible outcomes of such an arrangement (Sattar, 1997: 134). Substantive changes to such things as import-export duties, for example, are not clearly linked to the creation of SAARC.

Hussain (1989: 167) asserts that Pakistan's foreign exchange earnings in the 1980s have been based on agricultural exports and remittances of expatriate workers in the Middle East. Approximately 40 percent of Pakistan's foreign exchange earnings in the 1980s came from foreign workers' remittances (Talbot, 1998: 42). Hussain (1989: 167–168) describes some aspects of the economic burden of foreign loans. The total level of annual loans has increased from $.15 billion in the 1950s to $2.2 billion today, a 17-fold increase. The steady increase in external indebtedness comes with additional international pressures, particularly in the form of conditionality. Although not a specific exogenous "shock," the pressures of indebtedness have the potential to escalate to crisis proportions.

International financing

The Soviet occupation of Afghanistan starting in 1979 and the associated "second Cold War" between the US and USSR revived US-Pakistan military ties and substantially increased US aid. In 1980, US President Carter offered $400 million for an 18-month period in military and economic aid. Pakistani President Zia ul-Haq rejected this as "peanuts" (Sattar, 1997: 120). Reagan offered a significantly larger package amounting to $3 billion in loans and grants over five years (Sattar, 1997: 121). Pakistan became the base for American support for the Afghan resistance but still sought a closer security relationship with the US, particularly a guarantee of US aid in the event of a Soviet or Soviet-supported Indian attack on Pakistan; the hope was to elevate the 1959 executive Agreement on Defense Cooperation into a binding treaty (Sattar, 1997: 120–121). Overall, "Pakistan received over $7 billion in military and economic assistance before the George Bush administration concluded (in 1990) that Pakistan's covert nuclear weapons program violated U.S. law" (Cohen, 1999: 191).

According to a former highly placed civil servant and finance official, such international support was accompanied by a recognition that relatively small, weak Pakistan was being asked to confront the USSR, a superpower, and that this would dramatically increase military spending requirements. Moreover, many

100 *Political survival in Pakistan*

developing countries had "structural imbalances" after the 1979 oil shock, and after international financial institutions imposed increasing constraints. In comparison, prior borrowing from the International Monetary Fund had been primarily to provide short-term balance of payments support, while development project funding was obtained from the World Bank. This began to change with conditionality in lending. There were now political costs, such as eliminating subsidies and phasing out favored projects. Other economies in Latin America, for example, were more badly managed, but could get funding on more favorable terms than Pakistan. Domestic borrowing was an alternative way to obtain funds, but raised interest rates, reducing resources for spending in other areas (Interview with former finance official, 2001). An associated problem is that higher interest rates negatively affect the resources available for private sector investment, further dampening economic prospects. Zia ul-Haq's regime at first accepted a structural adjustment loan, and then backed away from later disbursements; increased international aid as the Afghan War proceeded may have reduced the urgency of obtaining conditional loans.

Expatriate labor remittances from the Middle East were an important source of increases in income in Pakistan (Khan, Aftab Ahmad, 1997: 208). However, these fell from the expectations of the Sixth Five-Year Plan, and thus constituted an external economic shock of the "shocks to revenue" category described by Roubini (1991). A boom period of such remittances in the early 1980s was then followed by a slow down (Stewart and Sturgis, 1995: 55). Through official channels, expatriate Pakistanis remitted over $20 billion to Pakistan; it has been estimated that unofficial channels might account for an equivalent additional amount of remittances (Zaidi, 1999: 431).

Taxation

According to a highly placed former government servant, Zia ul-Haq's regime saw notable efforts toward fiscal reform (under a broader economic reform plan). There were successes in organizing in indirect taxation, in such areas as sales taxes. Direct taxation, however, did not see much success. Documentation was strong primarily in large corporate organizations, but was weak in large sections of the economy, such as retail and transport. There was resistance to initiatives in self-assessed tax payments. Importantly, government resolve weakened as the Movement for the Restoration of Democracy gained strength and the "survival instinct" took over (Interview with retired senior civil servant, 2001). Another former civil servant noted that an "Iqra" (from the Arabic command "read," a Quranic reference) surcharge on imports was meant to fund literacy programs, but was diverted elsewhere (Interview with former civil service official, 2001).

The 1983–88 period saw increased pressures on government spending as a result of increased debt-servicing, defense spending, and poor revenue-raising efforts. This was accompanied by a sharp increase in domestic debt (Khan, Aftab Ahmad, 1997: 208). It appears that domestic spending was financed by domestic borrowing because political opposition prevented tax increases and international financing was not forthcoming.

Leadership and extraction   101

The tax ratio had stagnated after reaching 14 percent by the end of the 1980s. There was an increase in land revenue from 1985 as Punjab, Balochistan, and NWFP provincial governments increased their land revenue taxes on an ad hoc basis; however, land revenue is collected by provincial governments, unlike the wealth tax, which is collected by the federal government. That landholders were beneficiaries under Zia ul-Haq's rule can also be seen in that he appointed M.K. Junejo, a Sindhi landlord, to be prime minister, and in the development funds he distributed to National Assembly members from 1985 to 1988. Landlords dominated the assembly, and they had discretion in how development funds were spent.

A notable extraction shift under Zia ul-Haq was the 1980 "Zakat and Ushr" Ordinance, one component in an "Islamization" effort. *Zakat* refers to an obligatory annual contribution that financially able Muslims are required to make for particular social purposes, and *ushr* refers to a 10 percent contribution based on crop production. Under Zia ul-Haq, *zakat* collection was centralized under the Ministry of Finance. In 1983, it included 37,000 *Zakat* committees employing 260,000 people, and placing 126,000 preachers under government supervision (Nasr, 2001a: 145). Zia ul-Haq's winning coalition included some religious figures, but there was ambivalence and dissent. While *ulama* were eager for resources and state patronage, they also wanted to retain control over seminaries. There was concern that centralized *zakat* funding would give the government leverage over religious seminaries and other institutions. The JUI leader Mufti Mahmood instructed his seminaries to not accept *Zakat* funds; some *ulama* in Sindh criticized the funding as a political bribe, and there were complaints that state funding was reducing voluntary contributions (Nasr, 2001a: 143).

Importantly, given the failure to tax agricultural income in the past, the *Ushr* levy was to be taken from Sunni Muslim landowners in place of land revenue. One survey in 1984 showed that the *Ushr* agricultural tax was still in planning and had not been implemented (Clark, 2000: 203). Moreover, evasion of this tax was widespread (Interviewee B, 2000). Dost Muhammad Faizi, the former Sind provincial minister for Zakat and Auqaf, asserted that *Ushr* was not implemented in a significant way due to the lack of a bureaucratic apparatus for assessing agricultural income well (Interview with Dost Muhammad Faizi, July 2009). Zia ul-Haq's regime did not create such an apparatus, although collection and assessment rules were introduced in 1983. Together, *Zakat* and *Ushr* taxes provided only 2 percent of government revenue, and *ushr* collection was generally a quarter or less of *zakat* revenue (Nasr, 2001a: 145).

"Milbus" is a term former Naval Secretary and Defense Analyst Ayesha Siddiqua has developed to capture the military's increased involvement in commerce (Siddiqua, 2007). During Zia ul-Haq's regime, Milbus grew and became more entrenched. Such commercial involvement serves to develop and steer social resources to maintain the military's resource needs without depending on civilian sources. This can be interpreted as either an effort to preempt the relevance of other veto-holders or to keep the "winning coalition" narrow (depending on civilian revenue sources would mean that the military alone could not dictate policy, but

102 *Political survival in Pakistan*

would have to consider what is acceptable to those civilian revenue sources). The military worked to create "independent" revenue sources by cornering economic contracts and offering subsidies and loans to its own foundations (such as the Fauji and Shaheen Foundations). A political survival interpretation is that Zia ul-Haq protected his winning coalition in the name of "service solidarity" (service meaning military personnel).

Milbus methods employ subtle, near-covert ways to reallocate domestic resources toward the military without the direct aggravation and redistribution experienced by imposing higher income taxes. It reflects state weakness, and cannot count as true domestic extraction, but an activity that thrives in part because it is distant from public accountability and transparency. Three common mechanisms or methods are subsidies (including loan forgiveness, or soft loans), no-bid contracts, and allocating lands. These all result from the executive's discretionary power and represent ways to allocate social resources to the military without the political backlash that direct extraction might bring. Ayesha Siddiqua's highly publicized work also expresses the growing realization in Pakistani civil society that there are significant development and resource allocation costs to the military's role. Siddiqua's work has been partly challenged by the claim that the military has acted within the law, particularly in a prominent land allocation matter (Interview with Lt. Gen Moinuddin Haider, 2009). But the overall theme in Siddiqua's work remains unscathed, and the military's foundations and commercial projects are often rationalized as being appropriate compensation for patriotic personnel (Interviews, 2009).

Land reform

The Qazal Bash case had challenged land reform legislation from the Z. A. Bhutto period. The Federal Shariat Court ruled against the challenge on a technicality. The case was later appealed to the Supreme Court, a process that was not resolved until after Zia ul-Haq's demise (when the Supreme Court's Shariat Bench ruled in the case eventually, they upheld the challenge to land reform laws in the Qazal Bash case).[9] Zia ul-Haq himself did not pursue land reform initiatives. This may have been because he did not believe land reforms to be "Islamic". But it is also the case that Zia ul-Haq simply did not have an urgent reason to push for significant land reforms. Nawaz Sharif, nurtured under Zia ul-Haq and belonging to a wealthy Punjabi business family, was a potential candidate for leadership, and had rivalry with landed interests. Zia ul-Haq also sought support from landed groups, as noted above.

Overview of money creation

A history of currency manipulation existed in British India (Rothermund, 1988: 76). A precedent for seigniorage was established. In the initial period after independence, India retained control over the instruments of monetary policy. As a result, Pakistan did not have the money creation option for meeting the revenue needs of

Leadership and extraction 103

the central government (Jalal, 1990: 45). Initially, Pakistan did not even have the capacity to print and circulate its own currency. Instead, a common monetary system under the supervision of the reserve bank of India was used until at least the end of March 1948 (Jalal, 1990: 34). Indian banknotes and coins continued to be legal tender as late as March 1948 and September 1949, respectively (Talbot, 1998: 128). Currency notes issued under the British era was used, having been stamped "Pakistan" (Interview with retired civil service official, 2001). Thus, it was not possible to generate funds by tweaking monetary policy because the necessary monetary instruments were absent.

As the instruments of currency issue and central banking were developed, however, the possibilities for money creation policies grew accordingly. Money creation became a government strategy for providing needed funds in times of fiscal stress. The demand for food subsidies occasioned such policies:

> Crop failures in 1956–7 saw rice and wheat disappearing from the bazaars. [...] Anxious to stem the drift towards political unrest, the government not only bought food imports at much higher rupee costs but also introduced price subsidies, thus imposing an excruciating burden on an exchequer crippled by escalated rates of defence and administrative expenditure. The creation of paper money to meet the government's current account deficit, nearly 40 per cent of which was due to food subsidies alone, saw the inflationary spiral assuming monstrous proportions.
>
> (Jalal, 1990: 250)

Thus, money creation had clear inflationary effects (as suggested by Goode, 1984). Such activities were not without domestic critics. Jalal describes central bank warnings against increasing the money supply and the legislative approval required for further domestic borrowing during this period (Jalal, 1990: 251).

One former finance official noted that inflationary financing increased after the 1965 war, and over time became a source of support for inefficient public enterprises such as the Tarbela Dam, the steel mill, and cement works (Interview with finance official, 2001). Another observer noted that some corporate interests were eager to obtain credit on easy terms and so supported money creation policies. The propensity to create money as a solution for budgetary problems probably had its best-known manifestation in the 1974–77 period. When seeking to bankroll spending in the aftermath of the first oil shock, Prime Minister Z.A. Bhutto was informed that the desired funds were simply not available. Bhutto's reputed response was: "well, print more money." This was associated with a severe inflationary period in the Pakistani economy (Interview, 2000). Prior to this, in 1971, new currency notes were issued in Pakistan. These provided an additional seignorage opportunity for state managers (Interview, 2000). In addition, borrowing from state-run banks as a way to deal with inadequate revenues was a persistent feature of government behavior throughout the 1970s. Without underlying economic changes, additions to the money stock fueled inflation (Stewart and Sturgis, 1995: 56).

104 *Political survival in Pakistan*

Government borrowing from state-run banks as a way to deal with inadequate revenues continued from the 1970s to the 1980s. Higher rates of inflation resulted from this credit expansion (Stewart and Sturgis, 1995: 56). This was especially true from 1990/91 onward, when bank borrowing contributed a "very large share" of the financing of the budget deficit (Zaidi, 1999: 242). In the 1980s, foreign funds meant that money creation was not resorted to as often to finance the deficit, and inflation remained low as a consequence (Zaidi, 1999: 242). A State Bank official described the process of money stock addition. A nominal overdraft limit for government spending exists. When spending exceeds that limit, new ad hoc treasury bills are printed on demand. Although the process is not hidden, the "common man" does not make the linkage between such activity and inflation (Interview with State Bank official, 2001).

Some "strong" central bank governors had the reputation of resisting government spending beyond the approved limit and not honoring checks. However, a strongly independent central bank (one that could constrain such money creation activity) had yet to come into existence in Pakistan by the early 1990s; Pakistan's State Bank (central bank) remained a tool of the Ministry of Finance and was not an independent policy-maker (Stewart and Sturgis, 1995: 91). Former State Bank Governor Ishrat Husain agrees that the central bank in Pakistan was an extension of the Pakistan government through the 1980s and into the early 1990s, but asserts that things have changed. The State Bank was given autonomy in 1993/94, and in "evolutionary process" received increased autonomy in 1997 and 2002, so that at present its leadership is autonomous, cannot be removed by the political executive, draws on a group of economists for advice, and is no longer subservient to the Ministry of Finance (Interview with Ishrat Husain, February 2009).

The Pakistani state was born with few resources at the disposal of the central government, and only an embryonic apparatus for governance. Very early on, efforts to increase revenues through agricultural taxation were blocked. Indirect taxation was also difficult in the context of low prices for basic Pakistani commodity exports. In this context, international financing and indebtedness became the favored means of procuring government resources. Inflationary financing through short-term borrowings from the central bank and printing money have also been persistent features of government financing in Pakistan. Pakistan's experience, however, remains more contained than the disastrous inflationary periods in some other developing countries, and this indicates better monetary management (Interview with former finance official, 2001). Measures to increase central bank autonomy have been taken, and provide a promising basis for insulation from political pressures, but it is too early to determine whether seignorage actions have ended.

Conclusion

In 1956, a young military officer was about to leave for a training course in the US. A senior lawyer told him that military aid was Pakistan's second curse, the first being evacuee property. When Pakistan came into being, 70 percent of urban and rural property was owned by non-Muslims in West Pakistan, who emigrated. These two factors produced a quick-grab mentality, where individuals and groups vied to capture resources (Interview with retired military officer, 2006). This was a far-sighted observation, because both international aid and windfall property bonanzas allow governments to circumvent the key proposition underlying fiscal sociology: that citizens pay for public goods that they receive, and in return hold authorities to account for service and provision quality.

Increasing domestic taxation and engaging in land reform are policies in the public interest because they lay the foundation for solvency and a fiscal sociology that would favor further political development. Pakistan's history has seen modest efforts in these areas, and some stagnation. Ideological variation among leaders—secular developmentalism, Islamic socialism, or Islamic fundamentalism—did not shift the country's fiscal sociological path, nor produce a decisive change in public goods provision. Instead, using public office to obtain private goods only seems to have become more entrenched.

Arguably the broadest support coalition bringing a contender to power has been in the 1970 election. The elected PPP government under Z. A. Bhutto sought significant redistribution at first, and committed itself rhetorically to providing majority goods. But political survival goals overtook this as Z. A. Bhutto tried to narrow his winning coalition, remove contradictions, and ensure his political survival. Repeated, regular elections before the full electorate might have altered his political survival strategy, by requiring a clear majority at the polls in order for the incumbent to retain office. The possibility of rigging elections, overriding or manipulating constitutional provisions, and generally adjusting selection institutions for personal political survival meant that a smaller winning coalition could be pursued. A smaller winning coalition generally means that individual members are more loyal to the incumbent, because they stand to lose more private goods, and because they are less likely to obtain similar favor under an alternate regime. Consequently, an incumbent would prefer a smaller winning coalition to a larger one. Rather than political settlements with troublesome political forces in Balochistan (and allied ones in NWFP), it was easier to deploy the military for heavy-handed repression. In Z. A. Bhutto's case, polarized and incompatible policy preferences among his supporters meant that a smaller winning coalition was even more necessary. These factors meant that the public or majority goods that might otherwise have been expected were underprovided.

War threats and concern about state survival can produce heightened extraction, and stronger states with respect to society. In Pakistan, amid war threats and heightened fiscal requirements, money creation and international financing have been favored over increased domestic extraction as revenue-raising strategies in Pakistan. The wars themselves have been short, with international assistance in such situations becoming "almost extinct," so immediate relief must be found from within the system, usually by reappropriating resources and by soliciting voluntary contributions (Interview with former finance official, 2001).

After the 1965 war, there was a national sense that reliance on international resources had endangered Pakistan's national security by constraining the materials

106   *Political survival in Pakistan*

needed to wage war. While minor initiatives in improving domestic extraction were pursued, the international strategy retained its dominance with adjustments to diversify international patronage. Similarly in the aid freezes of the post-1971 period, international borrowing and other resources were located as ways to obtain essential funds for central government expenditure. Experience with constraints on its international strategy produced a more sophisticated international strategy, rather than a decisive shift to greater domestic taxation.

The one notable effort to impose agricultural taxation, and to unveil corrupt, nonperforming loans to well-placed elites, was led by Moeen Qureshi, a caretaker prime minister who did not have the same political survival pressures as incumbents because his tenure was limited by design. This is explored further in Chapter 5.

Despite official recognition by state leaders (Ayub and Z.A. Bhutto) that land reform was necessary, there was not a sufficient leadership push to make these goals a reality. Over the 1959, 1972, and 1977 Land Reform Acts, about 8 percent of cultivable land was resumed from large landowners, mostly based on the 1959 Act. The distributed land was mostly low quality, and many recipients were already landowners rather than sharecroppers (Mahmood Hasan Khan, 1999: 129). Incumbents did not act to seal loopholes or prevent backtracking, and non-implementation prevented needed structural changes. Vigorous, consistent efforts to provide these public goods, however, risked mobilizing challengers, and also threatened to remove the private goods enjoyed by the winning coalition's members. Incumbent political leaders maintained their position by continuing to deliver private goods to a small winning coalition. Among the three leaders examined in this chapter, all winning coalitions have included the military and the bureaucracy, although specific figures in each have been removed by incumbents seeking political survival, and bureaucracy in particular has become more subservient and politicized. Landlords, business groupings, and some religious figures (and some ethno-nationalists) played roles in all winning coalitions, and as potential challengers whose nuisance value could be reduced and whose allegiance could be gained by delivering private goods. Some rivalries between these groups are notable, such as business resentment over agricultural non-taxation; on balance, however, inter-marriage and other ties and mutual influence have grayed the boundaries between these groups.

The land ceiling, appropriation, and redistribution approach to making land distribution more equitable was tried under Ayub Khan (in 1959) and Zulfikar Ali Bhutto (in 1974 and 1977). In Pakistan, this approach did not work because government institutions were influenced by landed aristocrats, both at the planning and implementation levels. Built-in loopholes allowed large landholdings to persist, and landlords could use influence over bureaucracy and policing to subvert implementation (Burki, 2008c: 247). Moreover, because land redistribution was not accompanied by a functioning institutional context, new farm owner-operators were often unproductive. According to prominent landlord and politician Sardar Mumtaz Ali Bhutto, Sind chief minister under his relative Zulfiqar Ali Bhutto's national government, the Bhutto family surrendered 40,000 acres of land in Sind under the land reforms, but increased productivity did not result. The land used to

Leadership and extraction 107

be 90 percent fertile, but more than half the land is now barren; small cultivators did not have the tools and skills needed to cope with great corruption in the bureaucracy, the revenue system, the irrigation system, and law and order problems. Where there used to be a railway depot to take away produce, the railway tracks are now covered from disuse; the same land now produces one fourth of what it used to (Interview with Sardar Mumtaz Ali Bhutto, 2009). One lesson is that profound social change sought by policy-makers requires follow-through support and care in governance.

In the preface to *Pakistan in the Twentieth Century: A Political History* Lawrence Ziring states that his work is "a critique of the country's leaders, of men and women who were not only burdened with awesome responsibilities, but who were called to realize a noble, but nevertheless illusive, objective. Unfortunately, these same men and women too readily succumbed to the scramble for power and privilege, and in so doing, they did great damage to the nation" (Ziring, 1997). A former finance official similarly declared his conviction that the challenge with fiscal reform for the public good was due to "a lack of courage, not a lack of foresight" (Interview, 2001). These assertions reflect a common belief: that insincerity and compromise by national leaders is responsible for the failure to pursue the public good. However, this only describes an outcome without explaining why Pakistani leaders were particularly insincere in comparison to rulers elsewhere. The political survival logic offers an explanation: Pakistani leaders have usually depended upon a small winning coalition, and retaining office has depended on amply rewarding that small coalition. This has been detrimental to the public. Not until the polity allows for different political survival pressures—such as those produced by a sufficiently large winning coalition—is this likely to change. Even "insincere" leaders or those seeking power will be more likely to provide public goods when the winning coalition is large.

The political survival depiction has an important other side: challengers who pose threats to incumbent leaders. The theoretical assumptions relating to challengers in the political survival model as suggested by Bueno de Mesquita et al. (2003) apply primarily to well-established polities where boundaries and expectations are relatively clear. In weak states with fluid institutions, there are additional considerations and possibilities. Furthermore, the roles played by ethnic splits and political Islam in shaping challenges must be incorporated. The next chapter examines how the political survival logic has shaped challengers in Pakistan.

4   Challengers in a weak polity

In a weak polity "normal" and "revolutionary" challenges are difficult to distinguish from each other. There have not been enough patterned, routinized leadership contests to establish what constitutes "normal." The polity's weakness means that there are alternative nascent or active or parallel polities at work. In a fluid polity, attempting to rewrite the rules in one's favor is common. Where there are multiple, overlapping authorities, a "challenger" (better described as a political entrepreneur, since the goal may not be to unseat the incumbent state leader) will seek to maximize autonomy in the domain with maximal political survival prospects. Where the ground rules are not well-established or enforced, one way for challengers to unseat incumbents and obtain office is to change the rules, thereby appropriating powers for themselves and restricting the political authority enjoyed by the incumbent leader.

In this chapter, statements by leaders, affinity group members, and polity observers shed light on strategic paths to de jure and de facto quasi-states in a weak state context. While the examples given here are embedded in a historical context, the purpose is not to offer exhaustive historical narratives, nor is it to survey all contenders for political ascendancy. Rather, it is to demonstrate that across challengers from different backgrounds, a common political opportunity—the chance to pursue de facto and de jure quasi-states—has frequently been exploited. The broadly shared strategic expectation is that building a quasi-state may further political survival goals. If these efforts are accommodated within the polity's institutional framework, then the state will likely survive and even thrive in the long term. Incumbents' inability or unwillingness to either fully repress or institutionally accommodate quasi-states risks state failure, as has been demonstrated through Bangladesh's secession.

Post-colonial South Asia has seen numerous secessionist and "autonomist" movements. In India, the Naga, Mizo, the Bodo, Assamese, Meitei, Sikh "Khalistan," and Kashmir movements; in Sri Lanka, the Tamil Eelam movement; in Bhutan, the Lothshampa autonomist movement; and in Bangladesh, the Chittagong Hill Tracts autonomist conflicts. There have been four international wars and 18 armed "internal conflicts" in the first 50 years since independence, as well as numerous violent unrest incidents, resulting in 4.3 million deaths according to one measure. "Civil" society is often militarized, with death squads, private

Challengers in a weak polity 109

armies, militias, and armed organized crime operating in sizeable areas. At least six national leaders have been assassinated (Stewart and Hyat, 2002: 108–112). Agitational politics are a persistent phenomenon. Contentious tactics such as public demonstrations, strikes, and organized violence all show that a leader or group has the ability to mobilize and deploy force.

Religious and sectarian rivalries, termed "communal" tensions, have been expressed in violent forms between Muslims, Hindus, and Sikhs, as well as intra-Muslim sectarian tensions. Population displacements are sizeable. Conflict groups inside Pakistan often draw on external support and become domestic conduits for international rivalries. While there are autonomist or secessionist groups elsewhere, the perceived threat is severe in Pakistan. In interviews, several Pakistanis asserted that some substate groups actively seek to destroy the Pakistani federation (Interview with former Sindh province official Ghazi Salahuddin, March 2009; with *Daily News* editor S.M. Fazal, 2009; and others). Crucially, Pakistan has experienced disintegration. The process leading to East Pakistan's secession in 1971 both exemplifies and amplifies quasi-state political opportunities for challengers.

According to *LOPS*, revolutionary challengers aim to bring the disenfranchised into the selectorate. Challengers in Pakistan have often mobilized the disenfranchised by offering political inclusion in a new polity, in which they are better off than they were under the prior arrangement. Challengers who do not attain leadership office in a weak polity may nevertheless obtain or retain office in a quasi-state. A challenger's political survival may be obtained or even furthered by failure to obtain national office. A maximal assumption is that challengers prefer their own leadership on the largest, most secure scale they can possibly attain. Whatever ideology a challenger espouses, it is assumed that greatest jurisdiction is preferred. Quasi-states allow such jurisdiction. Authority in a quasi-state gives one the ability to be a "general in one's own army," rather than merely a lieutenant in another's army.

This Venn diagram shows aspirants to "Quasi-state," and "national office," and additional possibilities. Set A represents those aspiring for national office; set B represents those aspiring to quasi-state leadership. Someone can pursue leadership that is simultaneously quasi-state and national office (intersection of sets A and B;

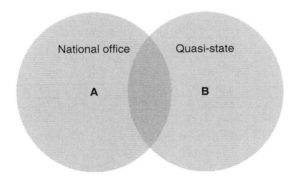

Diagram 4.1 Office-holding possibilities

110 *Political survival in Pakistan*

this means leading a quasi-state that captures the state, or obtaining state leadership and then creating a quasi-state or both together) or both (union of sets A and B (this would be a feudal lord who obtains high office and has separate authority in both domains)). Or aspirants could be A and not B, or B and not A.

In a weak state, there are three challenger types: those who seek formal office defined by the state, those who seek to rule in quasi-states, and those who seek both and will settle for one, and advocate for the maximum authority possible for whichever they acquire. Creating a quasi-state or threatening a secessionist challenge could be a route to office, a way to bargain for membership in the national rulership structure, or a way to pursue special privileges and benefits.

Not all quasi-states are overtly secessionist. Not all secessionists have a quasi-state. But quasi-states tend to be autonomist and/or secessionist, and secessionist threats are made more credible by quasi-states. A quasi-state performs certain state functions, but does not have recognition as a sovereign entity, and may not have sought such recognition.

Powerful landlords represent small-scale quasi-states. They have coercive instruments, such as private jails and armed supporters, to help control tenant farmers and others within their fiefs. State agents such as police and bureaucracy are typically under landlord influence (Interviews, 2009). Frequently, landlords are associated with a local religious leadership, such as a *pir* or *sajjada nasheen*, or the landlord family itself may lay claim to religious leadership status. Landlords also have participant power in the electoral political process, being able to mobilize people for the polls. One Sindhi migrant to Karachi described carrying out this behavior pattern in her new home—she simply voted for whomever her landlord told her to (Interview, 2008). It is not unusual to have several political parties represented in one landlord family, so that whoever dominates the legislature or other formal office, the family remains a favored constituent.

Most challengers who successfully obtained office were closely linked to a previous ruling coalition, and then embarked on their own and broke away. Ayub Khan was in Ghulam Mohammad's ruling cabinet, as was Iskander Mirza. Ayub Khan's presence placed a sitting commander-in-chief in a civilian cabinet for the first time. Yahya Khan and Z.A. Bhutto were both close collaborators with Ayub Khan. Zia ul-Haq was picked by Bhutto to be chief of army staff. Nawaz was supported by Zia ul-Haq and the ISI, which helped cobble together the IJI coalition. Musharraf was elevated by Nawaz over other choices for the role of chief of army staff. Being in the leadership circle enables one figure to make a power grab and consolidate personal authority over others. This pattern seems to have been the prevalent one—even in the 1970 election Bhutto, although a civilian, had allies from previous military connections as well as wide support. Mujib ur-Rehman had no such allies.

As identity markers that demarcate difference, define groupness, and bind political communities, "Islam" and "ethnicity" are comparable. Ethnicity carries less formalized debates about "law," and may not have the same coherent yet contested normative prescriptive element. But ethno-nationalism does bring with it a political program that is tied to "ethnicity." Similarly, Islamism brings with it a

Challengers in a weak polity 111

political program tied to "Islam." Each mobilizes symbol, and attempts to convert social capital into political mobilization. Just as ethnic associations can be considered "civil society," so can religious associations (Varshney, 2002).

Sharply demarcated affinity groups and clear outgroups (particularly scapegoats) provide conducive contexts to challengers seeking quasi-states. Religio-nationalism and ethno-nationalism provide such social divisions. Religion and ethnicity are not necessarily mutually exclusive. In an extreme analogy, "Islam" and "ethnic identity" are cards in a deck that a challenger has. The particular deck and the strength of "Islam" or "ethnicity" or other mobilizing symbols and instruments varies challenger by challenger. Playing the ethnicity card threatens agitation, conflict, and trouble for a national leader. Hence, it makes sense for the leader to coopt or repress this. Replying with the Islam card is one way to retain political legitimacy. Appeals to religious affinity are ways to weaken ethnic affinity group ties. But the Islam card helps other challengers that can seek to outbid the state competitively on its Islamic-ness or choose a sectarian challenge. In some cases, an ethnic affinity and a religious affinity may overlap, providing an affinity alliance on which quasi-state authority can rest.

Challengers have a political survival option not available in the same form elsewhere. In Pakistan, a failed candidate for national leadership can nevertheless carve out space in which to exercise authority, in some cases. The endgame is never entirely clear, except by death. Even exile can be reversed. Entire polities can be reorganized and boundaries redrawn. Existing rules can and will be reworked, often to favor the incumbent; the challenger will try to do the same thing by redrawing boundaries and emphasizing different jurisdictions. This "revolutionary" option is close to normal political behavior in Pakistan. What might be considered normal in a stable democracy, such as free and fair elections on a universal adult franchise, constitutes a revolutionary change in Pakistan and may produce a revolutionary outcome. The new selection mechanism may enhance the selectorate and bring new groups into the winning coalition and outsiders to national office. That happened with Mujib ur-Rehman's election in 1970. Then, the electoral result was disregarded, and civil war followed.

The common thread here is challenger paths under particular incumbents. The two major themes that arise are: challengers from within one's winning coalition and leadership circle (appointees themselves try to consolidate authority at their patrons' expense, often rewriting rules in the process), and challengers who can when it suits them pursue autonomism, redrawing polity boundaries in de facto and de jure ways that maximize their authority. Challenge is a process reflecting strategic interdependence, a complex decision-making condition under which anticipated choices by other actors affect one's present choice. This chapter has not attempted to provide a comprehensive account of the socioeconomic circumstances leading to unrest. Those belong to the macro forces that impact group consciousness and affinity ties, and provide fuel for mobilization.

Challengers seek plum assignments to enrich themselves and their supporters. In other words, they may simply join the winning coalition if the price is right. This may alienate some in their affinity group. Another facet in challenger

112   *Political survival in Pakistan*

behavior is that the challengers' parties can themselves split as internal challengers pursue a secessionist logic, sacrificing party unit to obtain office in a splinter group.

Like states, quasi-states need resources to survive and engage in war-making, state-making, and protection. In a more primitive fashion, quasi-states replicate state extraction strategies, emphasizing a taxation strategy or an external financing strategy. They can rely on member donations, coercive extraction, and financing by external or distant agents with other agendas. These are difficult to map out for specific groups because they are largely clandestine activities. Nevertheless, interview data yield some near-unanimous perceptions. The two most common forms are *bhatta*, which taxes individuals and business, and financing from "agencies."

The term "*bhatta*" which can be translated as "bonus" can be found as far back as at least the eighteenth century, when Lord Clive found the civil servants, military officers, and soldiers of the East India Company all taking *bhatta*. Clive took steps to cut down on such bribery and corruption (Mahmud, 1988: 191). In addition to side-payments given to predatory state agents, *bhatta* has increasingly come to mean protection money and involuntary donations to non-state actors. In my own fieldwork, numerous shopkeepers described *tanzeems*—social organizations, usually politically affiliated militias or thugs, who come to collect *bhatta*—in practice an extorted "donation," or protection money. Non-contribution invites assault or worse. The merchants interviewed in fieldwork were understandably reluctant to share details, but most acknowledged making routine *bhatta* contributions to *tanzeems*. This shows "extraction" behavior, one state characteristic.

It is widely believed that "agencies" finance and manipulate religious and ethnic groups. Interviewees from many backgrounds expressed their conviction that "agencies" were involved. Usually this term refers to the Inter-Services Intelligence and the Intelligence Bureau, the military and civilian intelligence agencies in Pakistan that have provided covert aid to specific groups. One interviewee described these agencies as driven by "hyperpatriotism" that gave them license to manipulate domestic political processes with aggressive action without regard to law or conventional morality (Interview, 2009). Their actions might be designed to splinter a troublesome organization or to prop up one against another.

In some cases, "agencies" refer to wealthy patrons inside "The Establishment," or foreign backers seeking to extend their influence, undermine rivals, and carry out proxy wars on Pakistani soil. A group's leadership might have businesses such as restaurants, but the income generated is significantly greater than that which restaurants ordinarily make. In general, service industries like restaurants can be used as fronts for money-laundering because their products, customers, and receipts are difficult to monitor. Profitable criminal activities such as smuggling are also widely suspected (Interviews, 2008, 2009).

Politically relevant group identity and religious affiliation are intricately intertwined in the Pakistani case. This may be because the state was founded on "Muslim" or "Islamic" nationalism, as seen in the Muslim League's pre-Partition slogan "Islam in danger." "Muslims" were declared a nationality based on a

Challengers in a weak polity 113

coherent, distinctive common culture and language. Jinnah proclaimed in his 1944 letter to Gandhi:

> We are a nation. We maintain and hold that Muslims and Hindus are two major nations by any definition or test of a nation. We are a nation of a hundred million, and what is more we are a nation with our own distinctive culture and civilization, language and literature, art and architecture, names and nomenclature, sense of value and proportion, legal laws and moral codes, customs and calendar, history and traditions, aptitude and ambitions; in short, we have our own distinctive outlook on life and of life. By all canons of international law, we are a Nation.
>
> (quoted in Stepaniants, 2001)[1]

Yet these well-known words contain seeds that have been reaped by quasi-state founders. Jinnah defined "nation" according to components that are largely met by ethno-nationalist narratives in Pakistan, and they have the potential to subdivide the "Muslim" or "Pakistan" collective entity.

Secessionism in Pakistan may be particularly likely because it replicates the impulse behind the country's formation. Jinnah represents a powerful archetype, a successful case which can be emulated in form. As a minority and a distinct nation worried that the majority would oppress them, Indian Muslims had justified separatism. Groups inside Pakistan who identify themselves as minority groups and distinct nations could similarly justify separatisms. Adopting Islam and making it the dominant identity fits the Pakistani state's foundation. Separatist ethnic minority groups who are religious Muslims must find a way to decouple loyalty to the Pakistani state from loyalty to the Islamic faith. This can be accomplished by challenging the official Islam supported by the state leader on a sectarian basis, through religious "outbidding," painting the regime leader as not genuinely or sufficiently Islamic.

A political survival interpretation would see secessionism as something that has worked for challengers in the past. At the local or provincial level, secessionism has often been the alternative for challengers when a satisfactory political office is not found. A weaker political platform that risks less repression calls for provincial or regional autonomy, which give more power to provincial leaders.

Provincial and local leaders have often resisted the central state's efforts to consolidate power and authority. Ethno-nationalists found further legitimacy for their claims to greater autonomy from the Lahore Resolution, which asserted that the new state would have "autonomous and sovereign" constituent units. An autonomist call or a secessionist claim may be posturing to both retain more radical affinity group members and to bargain for a better deal from the state leader. There is strategic interdependence between challengers and leaders; they sometimes make choices that are conditioned by behavior they anticipate from each other. Leaders are usually former challengers.

Given these circumstances, the strategic problem for Pakistani national leaders was to try to "stamp out the fires of provincialism with solemn messages of religious

114 *Political survival in Pakistan*

unity without sparking off an Islamic conflagration" (Jalal, 1990: 280). Leaders at the "center"—the government that is less than genuinely federal, given its unitary tendencies—displayed extreme insecurity, describing any criticisms of the center as "Indian-inspired," and "refusing to tolerate even the mildest expression of provincial loyalties" (Jalal, 1990: 280). Incumbent leaders were fixated on internal and external rivals for their authority, and repeatedly suggested that India, the principal external rival, was supporting the internal rivals. This belief was widely shared (as demonstrated by the assertions of the Hamoodur Rehman Commission Report). Whether or not the leaders themselves genuinely believed this, the allegation was strategically beneficial as it delegitimated provincial and other internal rivals.

Jinnah behaved in a somewhat authoritarian fashion during his brief tenure as governor-general. As Pakistan's founder, however, he was a towering figure, and carried a legitimacy and force to his decisions that did not require reliance on purely coercive means. He had obtained support from the Pir of Manki Sharif in the Frontier region by promising an Islamic political order. His views remained ambiguous. Jalal (1990) contrasts his declaration urging attendees at a Sind bar association meeting to "sacrifice and die in order to make Pakistan [a] truly great Islamic state" with his statement at Pakistan's first Constituent Assembly meeting:

> You are free to go to your temples, you are free to go to your mosques or to any other place of worship in this State of Pakistan [...]. You may belong to any religion or caste or creed—that has nothing to do with the business of the State [...]. We are starting with this fundamental principle that we are all citizens and equal citizens of one State.

Jalal's concludes that although a secularist, Jinnah "was above all a hardened politician, ready to take refuge in Islam to survive the cross-fire of provincialism and religious extremism" (Jalal, 1990: 279–280).

Thus, "Islam" provided an identity to balance provincial forces, but it needed to be deployed carefully so as to avoid alienating the less religiously inclined, and also to avoid stoking religious extremism. Leaders had

> no real alternative except to continue making increasingly more cynical uses of Islam. This entailed issuing seasonal statements urging the people to order their lives according to the high ideals of Islam, condemning the spread of corruption with catchy quotes from the Quran and making a big play for religious piety during ramazan. The rhetoric was couched in an idiom designed to reinforce Islamic sentiments, but one which was sufficiently ambiguous as to allow the "liberal" citizens to get on with their lives unaffected by the counter-propaganda of the religious parties.
>
> (Jalal, 1990: 292)

In other words, the task was not to create an opposition, but to deploy religious symbol for legitimacy and retain religious groups in the winning coalition.

Challengers in a weak polity 115

Disparate groups tapped "Islam" for moral claims. Given that support for private property as well as a broad orientation to social justice can be found within well-established Islamic traditions, "Islam" provided a way to forestall communist agitation, prevent agrarian reforms and thereby support landlords, give business the ability to profit, give the urban propertied property security, and ensure state interest in capital development:

> For the landlords of west Pakistan, anxious to cut short all moves towards agrarian reforms, for the trading and commercial groups, determined to make a killing without let or hindrance, for the urban propertied classes, looking to secure and augment their wealth, and for a state needing to consolidate and expedite the processes of capital accumulation, Islam offered a moral escape from one too many awkward realities. As Liaquat Ali Khan pontificated, the people of Pakistan should "follow the teachings of the [P]rophet and not those of Marx, Stalin or Churchill [sic]."
>
> (Jalal, 1990: 280–281)

For leaders and their winning coalition and clients, appeals to Islam made sense strategically. If Muslim solidarity could overwhelm ethnic affinities, then ethnically based autonomist or secessionist challengers would be defanged.

Appeals to national unity based on religious affiliation stirred anxiety among religious minorities. The Objectives Resolution was passed with a preface that referred to Allah's sovereignty. Former Jinnah associate J.N. Mandal, a Hindu leader of scheduled castes and the central Labour minister, resigned in protest and then left for India (Ziring, 1997: 107). Mandal not only gave up on continuing political challenge but also exited the polity altogether; this was interpretable as a forceful statement rejecting the preface to the Objectives Resolution. Others ascribed Mandal's action to a more personal grievance that Mandal had with Liaquat Ali Khan, and also to Mandal's belief that he had been snubbed and bypassed in committee decision-making (Interview with Rochi Ram, July 2009).

Early quasi-state challenges to Pakistan came from those that had pre-existing organizations and affinities, and ambiguous or hostile feelings about joining the new state. Among these, two notable examples are Abdul Ghaffar Khan and the Khan of Kalat. Both were repressed. Coercion worked in Pakistan's early history in maintaining the state's coherence and integrity. When coercion failed in 1971, and Bangladesh was created, challengers had a new model to emulate, and the Pakistani state looked more vulnerable. This vulnerability seemed to increase as the country's fiscal sociology remained dysfunctional and winning coalitions stayed narrow.

Different "Islamic" groups may have differed in how they defined an "Islamic state," but they united in "condemning the un-Islamic lifestyles of Pakistan's most influential managers—the politicians quite as much as the civil and military officials" (Jalal, 1990: 282). Such allegations undermined leaders' legitimacy. Khaliquzzaman, the Muslim League president, was an "aspiring pan-Islamicist," who

116 *Political survival in Pakistan*

dubbed the advocates of "Shariat government" "hypocrites" who had no purpose other than to exploit the catch-phrase for personal ends. True Islamic democracy, according to him, could only be established by the constituent assembly and the Muslim League when the people had been properly educated.

(Jalal, 1990: 282)

In other words, incumbent leaders could counter-attack by presenting an alternative "progressive" Islamic interpretation as more legitimate, and accuse the religious challengers of being obscurantists. This competitive bidding for an Islamic credentials dynamic thus has an early manifestation in Pakistan. Official Islamism can be a way to undermine challenger credibility and to coopt Islamists. In *Islamic Leviathan*, S.V.R. Nasr explains the "turn to Islam" not as an ideologically driven phenomenon, but as resulting from complex bargaining over resources, power, and legitimacy between the state and social forces. In the interplay between incumbents' efforts to acquire legitimacy and weaken challenger affinity groups, Islam has played a recurring role.

Religious political parties were either susceptible to the tendency among other groups to organize around personality-driven factions. Maulana Maududi's Jamaat-e-Islami was relatively disciplined, but has not become an effective dampener against local quasi-state tendencies. This is traceable to its often oppositional stance to the national government, among other factors. In 1948, the government declared that the fight in Kashmir (during a ceasefire with India) was a jihad. Maulana Maududi rejected this, because a jihad could only be proclaimed by a government, while the Kashmir fight, according to Pakistan, had been declared a jihad by local religious leaders and fought by volunteers (Nasr, 1996: 74). In other words, Maududi demonstrated that he could constrain and shape an important warmaking symbol (jihad) by argument and through his public standing and following.[2]

Ayub Khan had removed the electoral process to which the JI was committed, and repressed the organization (Nasr, 1996: 73). When the JI supported Fatima Jinnah as an opposition candidate to Ayub, he rallied support from *pirs* with whom he had close ties (Siddiqui, 2001: 4). The *pirs* "provided religious fire-breaks from the incandescent attacks of Islamist groups and parties such as the JI" (Talbot, 2005: 30). Confronted with the challenge from the Jamaat-e-Islami, Ayub found support not among secularists but by allying with a different Islam.

When open elections on a universal franchise were held in 1970, the Jamaat-e-Islami was soundly defeated, winning only 6 percent of the vote, while the Awami League swept to victory. JI supporters explained this by saying that the "Islamic spirit" had not taken hold, and that others had misled the people. The JI is reputed to have collaborated with the Pakistan army in trying to suppress the insurgency in East Pakistan. Maududi believed that Bengalis were under Hindu and Communist influence (Bahadur, 1975). The Islami Jamiat Talaba (a student organization associated with the Jamaat-e-Islami and formed in 1947) agitated against the Awami League and the PPP and undertook paramilitary operations in East Pakistan under military direction (Cohen, 2004: 178). Yet the failure to maintain Pakistan's integrity demonstrates that these efforts did not achieve their objective.

Challengers in a weak polity 117

Z.A. Bhutto's PPP government repressed the JI in 1972. A JI Member of the National Assembly was assassinated, and Mian Tufail Muhammad (the JI amir) and some other leaders and activists were jailed and mistreated. Over this PPP period, Mawdudi urged the JI to retain its commitment to the constitutional process. However, a cycle of violence did emerge, and it "damaged the party's moral standing" (Nasr, 1996: 73). Mawdudi saw this as a response to government brutality, and continued to insist on peaceful methods even as the JI and especially the IJT (its student wing) became more involved in violence (Nasr, 1996: 74). The JI was close to Zia ul-Haq's regime, particularly in its early phase. But violent sectarian conflict between Sunni and Shia groups also grew during this period.

Jinnah as challenger/leader

A prototypical challenger, one that set a historical example for other political aspirants, is Mohammad Ali Jinnah. Before Jinnah was acclaimed as "Quaid-e-Azam," he belonged to Congress, the Indian independence-seeking party. He was arguably a bridge-building politician who stressed the common cause found among the entire subcontinent's native residents, rather than Muslim separatism. After it became apparent that Jinnah would be excluded from political leadership in the Congress, he took a polarizing route, and joined the All-India Muslim League in pursuing Muslim autonomy and political rights; he wanted to found a sovereign Muslim state. Jinnah became aware at a point in his advocacy that he had lung cancer and not long to live; this may firmed his resolve to pursue maximum autonomy or sovereignty. Others assert their belief that Jinnah was using a secessionist posture to bargain for Muslim rights within an Indian polity. Sayeed Hasan Khan, for example, states:

> I myself believe that Jinnah did not really want Pakistan as such; rather he was fighting for the rights of Muslims in an Indian federation. He used the slogan as a bargaining counter but mishaps of history forced him to accept the Pakistan in a severely truncated, split-apart shape.
>
> (Sayeed Hasan Khan, 2005)

Whether secessionism was truly the motive, or simply the strategic means to pursue Muslim rights within a united India, remains debatable. Whatever the motivation, Jinnah's stance was justified by the two-nation theory, one that Gandhi deeply opposed. In early September 1944, Jinnah and Gandhi met in a last-ditch summit, seeking a plan for peace in South Asia after World War II. They failed to reach agreement.

> "[Can] you not appreciate our point of view," Jinnah wrote to Gandhi, "that we claim the right of self-determination as a nation and not as a territorial unit, and that we are entitled to exercise our inherent right as a Muslim nation, which is our birth-right?" Yet Gandhi was "unable to accept the proposition that the Muslims of India are a nation, distinct from the rest of the inhabitants of

118 *Political survival in Pakistan*

India [...]. The consequences of accepting such a proposition are dangerous in the extreme. Once the principle is admitted there would be no limit to claims for cutting up India [...] which would spell India's ruin".

(Wolpert, 2006: 74)

Gandhi's fear was that one secessionist call would encourage others—such as Sikhs seeking Khalistan. Francis F. Turnbull, a private secretary to the secretary of state, recorded and communicated a similar fear over (Viceroy Wavell's) British deliberations about supporting "Pakistan," suggesting that it may lead to balkanization (Wolpert, 2006: 97). The fear was that fragmentation would accelerate as leaders, driven by parochial interests and local loyalties, sensed a political opportunity to push for autonomy and secession.

This was apparent as leaders gathered at the Simla summit seeking a workable formula for an Indian constitution. A British cabinet mission had traveled to India for this purpose, meeting with various leaders during early 1946. The two schemes discussed were a three-group loose federation, comprising Muslim-majority provinces NWFP, Punjab, Sind, and Balochistan in the first group, the Hindu-majority provinces in the second group, and Bengal and Assam in the third. The second scheme was a divided India, with Pakistan "consisting only of the majority Muslim Districts that is roughly Baluchistan, Sind, North-West Frontier Province and Western Punjab [...] and Eastern Bengal without Calcutta but with the Sylhet District of Assam" (Communication from the cabinet delegation and Viceroy Wavell to Attlee, April 11, 1946; cited in Wolpert, 2006: 103). Agreement between the Muslim League and Congress was vital to either plan's success. Jinnah appeared inclined to agree to the second scheme if Calcutta, a Muslim minority city, was included in Pakistan.

The federation plan, called Scheme A, was refined into:

a three-tier all-India federation, with a powerful middle tier of three "Groups of Provinces": Group A: the Muslim-majority Provinces of Sind, Punjab, Baluchistan, and the North-West Frontier; Group B, all the Hindu-majority provinces of most of the rest of India; and Group C, Bengal and Assam. The upper central government tier would be much less important that the groups, responsible basically only for defense, foreign affairs, and communications. Each group would have its own bicameral legislature to raise taxes and maintain order among its predominantly Muslim or Hindu populace, enjoying the virtual autonomy of a sovereign state. Provinces would enjoy traditional local powers over education and law and order but remained dependent on their own group legislature for most of their funding. After ten or fifteen years, moreover, any group or any one of its provinces could opt out, to reconsider its constitutional position.

(Wolpert, 2006: 104)

The hope was that the great autonomy given to the group level (taxation and internal security) as well as the option to secede after a decade or more would appeal to Jinnah, while maintaining a coherent all-India national government, even a weak one, would generate support from Congress.

The "groups" were thus near-states—significantly autonomous, with an option to assess and revise their participation in the loose federation. In effect, they were to be de jure quasi-states, brought about by formal design through a legal process.

The key task from a political survival perspective was to satisfy the need for secure office for leaders. If Jinnah could not have leadership office within Congress—as he had apparently decided—he could obtain this in Pakistan, ideally the biggest, strongest Pakistan possible. Congress leaders aspired to rule an undivided India. All wanted independence from Britain. This does not imply insincerity—rather, it reflected Jinnah's expressed belief in Muslim nationhood, and the widespread fear that Muslim rights were at risk in a Hindu-dominated India. Intricate disagreements and tensions prevailed in the 1946 Simla conference. The British sought a withdrawal, and Indian nationalists sought independence. However, disagreement prevailed on what independence should look like. The disagreements were based on fears that one community would dominate another. In terms of political survival "grouping" would better protect Jinnah's influence, both by presenting a large domain over which his authority would likely extend, as well as a bargaining chip for future negotiations with Congress and the Indian federation. Pursuing a de jure quasi-state was a vehicle that served political survival.

East Pakistan and Mujib ur-Rehman

The East Pakistan clash with the central government and its later secession encapsulates an important lesson for Pakistani challengers: strong affinity distinctions combined with external support can provide the basis for significant autonomy or successful secession. It also threw the appeal to Muslim solidarity as well as the selection process into a legitimacy crisis. As a Sindhi nationalist put it, the Bengali secession resulted from a broken covenant. The elections were held on the presumption that the victor would form a government, but there was a failure to respect the *aksariat* (the majority) and its wishes (Interview, 2009). To the Sindhi nationalist, this demonstrated the end of Pakistan's promise and a signal that only secession or autonomy could provide acceptable resolutions for disenfranchised communities. Others voiced the shock and great dismay that came from Pakistan's dismemberment as an "Islamic state" and the painful lesson that Muslim solidarity was not sufficient to hold the state together (Interviews with Hamid Rajput, PTV correspondent, and others, 2009).

Elections in East Pakistan were delayed until March 1954, making it the last province to have elections. The Muslim League greatly feared losing to local parties that were opposed to Urdu as a national language and had other grievances. The Bengal legislature, elected in 1947, was to expire in 1951, but the chief minister resisted calling elections and the legislature extended its term until a public outcry and brewing rebellion forced elections to be held. A "United Front", which represented various groups, was organized (it included the Awami League, the Krishak Sramik Party, the Gantantri Dal, the Nizam-i-Islam, and the Youth League). The

120 *Political survival in Pakistan*

United Front won overwhelmingly, and the Muslim League obtained only ten of the 309 contested seats (Ziring, 1997: 153–155).

East Pakistan was Pakistan's chief foreign exchange earner (Ziring, 1997: 156). This was based largely on exported jute. Yet Bengalis were generally underrepresented compared to their demographic majority, especially in the army officer corps (5 percent in 1963) but also in the CSP (139 out of 467 officers in 1967) (Talbot, 2005: 161). The CSP recruitment system was changed in 1968 to redress this imbalance (Talbot, 2005: 161, cites Burki, "Twenty Years of the Civil Service of Pakistan"). Bengalis were also underrepresented in the numerous commissions of inquiry that were instituted in such varied fields as "land reform, franchise and constitutional recommendations, and the press" (Talbot, 2005: 161).

The 1965 war had caused "significant psychological as well as physical damage" to a young officer corps (Ziring, 1997: 323). One prominent civil servant found it "tragic that at a later stage Field Marshall Ayub Khan himself called it a 'futile' war" (Siddiqui, 2001: 71). There was dissent and conflict over the Tashkent agreement that followed. Z. A. Bhutto used this issue and the Kashmiri cause as a way to build political support and break from Ayub.

There was further fallout from the 1965 war: it had galvanized Bengali nationalism. One reason was that the security mantra from the time was that the security of East Pakistan lies in West Pakistan. But when it actually came to the war, the Bengali perception was that only the threat of Chinese intervention had prevented India from attacking East Pakistan. The common perception was that Pakistan's security efforts (and the revenues collected from both East and West Pakistan) were devoted primarily to West Pakistan (Interview with retired military officer, July 2009). A key state function, protection from external threats, seemed to be lacking, and this further undermined the legitimacy of the central government.

Mujib ur-Rehman, the Awami League leader, was an activist and a challenger for office. He had been accused of participating in the Agartala conspiracy in 1968 against the Ayub regime. The Pakistani junta viewed Mujib as being complicit in a secessionist plot. This was despite the fact that raising the Bangladeshi flag at Paltan Maidan—a secessionist, anarchic display in a prominent location—was done by Shadin Bangla Kendriya Chattra Parishad (Independent Bangladesh Central Student's Union), and that the Awami League sought to try to control such actions (Ziring, 1997: 356).

Ayub Khan had suppressed wages, fueling resentment, urban agitation, and eventually a protest movement that helped to dislodge him. The anti-Ayub movement was semi-organized or not centrally organized by a principal challenger (Jalal, 1990: 301). An observer described enormous marches and processions in Karachi, with protestors climbing electric poles to mount banners and flags; he also noted apparently anarchic behavior as people carried sticks, threw stones, and sometimes rampaged (Interview with PTV correspondent Hamid Rajput, July 2009). Ayub had fallen ill, and was pressured to resign. His close colleague and Chief of Army Staff Yahya Khan stepped in to replace him (rather than allowing the speaker of the National Assembly to acquire national leadership, as was legally required).

Challengers in a weak polity   121

The anti-Ayub agitation can be described as an effort by the disenfranchised to influence political outcomes and obtain a voice. When Yahya stepped in and promised elections on a universal adult franchise, a broader selectorate was, in effect, promised. The Awami Party based in East Pakistan won a majority but was not permitted to form a national government. When their preferences were rejected, the result was the biggest crisis in Pakistan's history—extreme repression and armed resistance, and then dismemberment and state failure. Intervention by India played a critical role, as well as the decision by Pakistan's erstwhile allies to not intervene to prevent its defeat and the country's breakup.

The Awami League's demands, known as the Six-Point Program, sought to make Pakistan a confederation, calling for separate currencies, with the power to tax vested in the provincial governments, a separate provincial militia and internal security apparatus, and the provincial right to negotiate trade relations with other countries; the central government's responsibilities would be limited to defense and foreign policy (Ziring, 1997: 329). The December 1970 national elections gave the Awami League 167 seats out of the 169 allotted East Pakistan. This clear victory—in elections widely perceived as fair—gave Mujib enough seats to establish a majority-party government in the parliamentary system, without the need for a coalition. (Ziring, 1997: 333). Yahya Khan and his regime held these elections, described as the freest in Pakistan's history, based on an incorrect intelligence assessment that no clear winner would emerge, and that the regime could retain its dominant position by playing one side against another (Interview with informed observer, 2009).

After the election outcome, Yahya at first announced that Mujib ur-Rehman would become prime minister; after a meeting with Z.A. Bhutto, however, Yahya Khan withdrew that pledge (Interview with PTV journalist Hamid Rajput, July 2009). Denied the political office that his majority showing in the National Assembly elections should have produced, Mujib began to make independence or autonomy-leaning gestures. Yahya Khan traveled to East Pakistan on March 15, as a supposed final effort at preserving the Pakistani federation:

> Mujib was already addressing East Pakistan as Bangladesh when Yahya arrived. Indeed he referred to the President of Pakistan as the "guest of Bangladesh" ... Mujib had literally taken control of East Pakistan. All government offices answered to his directives, and those officials still loyal to the government in Islamabad found themselves under extreme pressure, or forced to seek refuge for themselves and their families. Observing the situation from West Pakistan, Bhutto publicly declared Mujib's action a violation of all understanding, and said that in the circumstances, the rule of the majority no longer obtained. Bhutto seemed to be leaning toward the recognition of two governments, but his public posturing insisted on the maintenance of Pakistan's territorial integrity.
>
> (Ziring, 1997: 349)

Mujib had warned Bengalis that "an artificial crisis is being fabricated to sabotage the making of the constitution" (Ziring, 1997: 355). The Mukti Bahini in East

122 *Political survival in Pakistan*

Pakistan was supported by the Indian army and the 1970–71 internal war cost between 300,000 and 3,000,000 lives (Stewart and Hyat, 2002: 111). Pakistan had excluded the majority of the population, East Pakistanis, from membership in the winning coalition and the effective selectorate, producing a secessionist challenge. Mujib had "near-sovereign control," a solid quasi-state overlaid with the province that positioned East Pakistan well for a bid for full independence, which it achieved. His quasi-state came partly from obtaining control over government offices.

Yahya Khan used heavy Islamic symbolism in his address to the nation as the 1971 war with India unfolded: "The Indian aggressors should know that they have to face twelve crore [120 million] Mujahids of Pakistan, imbued with the love of God and the Holy Prophet. The Indians know that in 1965, our brave forces had smashed them into pieces. But this time, God willing, we shall hit the enemy even harder than before" (quoted in Nawaz, 2008: 298). Others picked up on this theme. An editorial in *The Pakistan Times* stated that "He [Yahya] spoke in the name of Islam [...]. Overnight the ethos is deeply Islamic [...]. If crisis truly mirrors the condition and nature of a nation, today our character is transparently clear and no dust of controversy can blur its shining image" (quoted in Nawaz, 2008: 298). Yahya Khan sought legitimacy and unity by invoking religious symbolism. He used the evocative term "Mujahid," mentioned what is sacred and venerated, God and his Holy Prophet, and used a common term emphasizing one's faith when he said "God willing" to condition his assertion that the enemy would be hit harder than before. Thus he clearly sought to give the war an "Islamic" frame. Yet the same frame would be severely strained by Bangladesh's successful secession. The country's largest province had broken away despite claims that Pakistan was fighting an Islamically legitimate war. This showed that Muslim solidarity was not sufficient to prevent secession, and had an emboldening effect on others— particularly in the conscious choices by Sindhi political leader G.M. Syed, as well as the terms in which unrest in Balochistan was understood by observers, described below.

Zulfikar Ali Bhutto as challenger/leader

As a challenger, Z.A. Bhutto's career describes an intricate process by which the path to national office is paved with border adjustments. Z.A. Bhutto was Ayub's foreign minister and had played a major decision-making role in the 1965 war. Significant miscalculations caused Pakistani losses. After the war, Bhutto gave the impression that Ayub had caved in to Indian pressure at the Tashkent summit and not supported Kashmiri interests despite Pakistan's self-proclaimed success in the war. Bhutto received a visit by Chinese leaders in March 1966. The Chinese affirmed support for Pakistan and Bhutto rode with them as throngs greeted them with a "tumultuous welcome" (Ziring, 1997: 309). These factors boosted Bhutto's national stature and Bhutto announced the Pakistan People's Party in October 1967.

After the elections in which the Awami League won a majority, Bhutto "began hinting at there being two majority parties in the nation, and that the country needed two Prime Ministers. Yet, intensifying his intimacy with Generals Peerzada, Gul

Hassan, and Omar, who he knew would never sanction two separate and distinct governments, Bhutto shifted his themes to Islam and democracy, stating that the elections should not be a prelude to the disintegration of the Muslim state" (Ziring, 1997: 344).

In other words, his desire for office superseded his wish for national integrity; yet when needed, he adjusted his stated preferences to fit what he perceived would be the winning coalition's preferences: the generals' wish for "Islam" and integrity.

Ziring (1997: 352) suggests that Yahya had gambled on possible success by Bhutto and Mujib in last minute talks, but the junta had already decided to intervene militarily even if Mujib yielded on the Six Points.

Ziring's political history suggests that a conspiracy was at work:

> The last minute Mujib-Bhutto-Yahya talks were programmed to fail. Before leaving Dhaka, Yahya knew that the army was about to strike. Bhutto, also, was fully apprised of the situation, but remained in Dhaka so as not to give the appearance of colluding with the junta.
>
> (Ziring, 1997: 352)

Bhutto's famous words after returning to Pakistan on March 26, 1971, were "By the grace of God Pakistan has at last been saved." Did "saved" mean saved under his leadership but without East Pakistan, or did it mean that the federation was to remain intact? According to historian Lawrence Ziring, "the record reveals that the PPP leader was apprised of the more intimate details of Operation Searchlight and, indeed, was himself a party to the action" (Ziring, 1997: 353). Ziring asserts that Bhutto rejected efforts that would have allowed a caretaker civilian government to oversee a political transition that ended military rule while retaining the federation.[3]

Without proving that there was political collusion between Bhutto and the junta, it nevertheless appears that Bhutto's veto meant that any accommodation with Mujib in a Pakistani federation was impossible. Interpreting this from the standpoint of seeking political office, it could be described as an effort to launch a repression and thereby eliminate a challenger. A related interpretation is that a redistricted state was one way to further Bhutto's political survival ambitions, even if that redistricting included a severe truncation. This is lent some credence by Bhutto's alleged statement "*udher tum, idher hum*" (you over there, and us over here) to Mujib ur-Rehman. The implication was willingness to accept two near-sovereign units within Pakistan, as long as one was Z.A. Bhutto's domain.

The rallying point in the movement against Bhutto was a call for Nizam-e-Mustafa (the Order of the Prophet). In the 1970s, there was an oppositional Islamist agitation that took various forms—eventually the Nizam-e-Mustafa mobilization. Deobandi and Ahl-e-Hadith *madrasas* played a documented role in the 1974 anti-Ahmadiya movement and in the Pakistan National Alliance agitation for the Nizam-e-Musatafa in 1977 (Ahmad, 2000: 190). Bhutto was seen as secularist, despite his efforts to deploy Islamic symbols. In 1975 opposition leaders formed the United Democratic Front (a multiparty, anti-PPP group); the group chose Mufti

124 *Political survival in Pakistan*

Mahmud, an *alim* and JUI leader, as its head (Nasr, 2001: 98–99). When the 1977 elections were announced, the group changed its name to the PNA, and espoused a platform called the Nizam-e-Mustafa. The JI was the most prominent and significant member (Nasr, 2001: 99).

The IJT had been active against the PPP by challenging its post-civil-war stance. "Bhutto had not only failed to create a strong state, but presided over further erosion of state power as politics became mired in agitational politics in a climate of growing Islamic consciousness" (Nasr, 2001: 98). The IJT developed a "psychology of dissent" in which it supported such anti-PPP agitational campaigns as the "Non-Recognition of Bangladesh movement of 1972–74, the anti-Ahmediya controversy of 1974, and the Nizam-I Mustafa (Order of the Prophet) of 1977" (Nasr, 2001: 96). "While the Jama'at advocated Islamic constitutionalism, IJT had been harping on the demand for Islamic revolution" (Nasr, 2001: 96).

Z. A. Bhutto "played the Islamic card":

> he tried to present himself as a born-again Islamic reformer. Bhutto approached the Islamic world for aid, offering nuclear technology in exchange. This conversion was so transparently insincere that it fooled few people. His portrayal of his policies as Islamic as well as socialist made no impression Pakistan's Islamist parties, further alienated his leftist supporters, and only set a precedent for successors: when in trouble turn to Islam.
>
> (Cohen, 2004: 144)

Z. A. Bhutto's personal reputation and admitted drinking made his claims appear opportunistic.

G. M. Syed and Jeay Sindh

Cohen believes Sindh to have been in one period the "most likely case of separatism after East Bengal" (Cohen, 2004: 214). This is due to the fact that Sind has a sea border and a well-developed, distinct culture and language. Yet a separate Sindh would block Pakistan's access to the sea. A critical problem for Sindhi independence is Punjabi consent, because Sind is a lower riparian to Punjab. Some Sindhi ethnic activists frame their ethnic identity and history with reference to numerous "great figures," heroes in Sindhi cultural history, which can be taken as role models or exemplars. These are celebrated with a cultural vision in which rural Sindhis cherish Shah Latif's poetry, Sufi sayings, and wisdom spouted by intellectuals and fakir singers alike. Sometimes, folk heroes are described in stark opposition or defiant confrontation with others.

Sindhi nationalism gained appeal and traction as Mohajir self-awareness grew, and as the Mohajirs became better placed in national leadership. Sindi nationalism grew partly in response to heightened interaction and competition with Mohajirs. Mohajirs had an advantage in national civil service examinations because Urdu, their native language, was one of the two official languages of Pakistan. Sindhi ethno-nationalism grew partly in response.

In 1972, a movement began among the Sindhis that would make Sindhi the medium of instruction in schools; compel government employees to learn Sindhi; raise a Sindhi-speaking paramilitary force; return land taken from Sindhis in the resettlement program; regain provincial control over railways, the postal service, and electronic media; increase Sindh's share of the Indus waters; and declare Pakistan to be "four nations living in a confederation".

(Cohen, 2004: 213)

Pakistan has been closer to a unitary state than a federal one in practice, and there has been resentment among those who believed that the Lahore Resolution suggested confederalism. During the 1970s, Sindhi was made an official provincial language, and university and provincial civil service positions for Sindhis were increased.

G.M. Syed was a Sindhi political leader who came from a *pir* (Sufi saint) background and founded Bazm-e-Soofia-e Sindh, an organization that held events at religious shrines (Talbot, 2005: 37). He was a Muslim League leader before partition. But when Pakistan was made, policy differences arose, and G.M. Syed did not receive a significant political office under the civilian order. He broke away from the Muslim League as a result. The fact that Zulfikar Ali Bhutto, the incumbent, was Sindhi was not sufficient to defuse the sense that Sindhis were underrepresented in powerful positions. The PPP was a national party although it was based in Sindh. This meant that Sindh separatists or autonomists operated through separate organizations. Some Sindhi nationalists even questioned Z.A. Bhutto's Sindhi-ness, suggesting that he was a migrant from India, or a Punjabi agent (Interview, 2008). Such statements bolster a narrative that describes Sindhis as being locked out from influence and resources by powerful and antagonistic Punjabi and Muhajir forces.

Based on these differences, G.M. Syed founded a party called "Jiyai Sindh" (Long Live Sind). The party's goal was to ensure the provinces had "khud-mukhtari"—choice, and independence, although the degree to which Westphalian sovereignty is emphasized has varied. At one point, G.M. Syed asserted that "Sindhu Desh" meant a sovereign United Nations member state (Talbot, 2005: 302). G.M. Syed eventually questioned "Pakistan" altogether when he opined that with "minor adjustments in the British Cabinet Mission Plan of 1946, the confederacy of the Indian subcontinent be established" (*Dawn*, January 18, 1991; cited in Talbot, 2005: 5, n. 11).

Unsurprisingly, there were polemic and propagandic efforts to both elevate and denigrate G.M. Syed. Even after his death, narrating his personal and political biography remains a contentious affair. One interviewee who did not sympathize with the Sindhi nationalist narrative claimed that Syed's mother tongue was actually Saraiki and that he was descended from Fatimid Arabs settled in India; a Jeay Sindh interviewee disputed this and said G.M. Syed's mother tongue was Sindhi (Interviews, 2008). A former Jeay Sind Qaumi Mahaz (Jeay Sind National Movement) activist expressed deep respect for G.M. Syed's thought and sacrifices,

126   *Political survival in Pakistan*

and regretted that despite Syed's three decades in jail, his two sons have repudiated Jeay Sindh's original agenda, and the people have not provided enough support (Conversation with former Jeay Sindh activist, March 2008).

The Muslim League in the 1945 federal elections and 1946 provincial elections had a one-point manifesto: if you want Pakistan, vote for Muslim League. This was precisely what G.M. Syed tried to do with Jeay Sindh. Detractors have criticized Jeay Sindh for its "one point agenda," and argued that this did not have much to offer the electorate (Interview, July 2009). Apparently "Islamic socialism" beat "Sindhu desh" at the polls (an ideological spin on this electoral outcome). The Bengali language movement provided an example for G.M. Syed. He described Sindh as a primordial nation, and Pakistan, in contrast, as an "unnatural accident" ("Sindhu Desh was born with the birth of Mother Earth. Our attachment with it, too, is as old and ancient as that" (Syed, 1974, Ch. 1)). According to G.M. Syed, "For the period of full 25 years, Pakistan could not give itself a constitution for the simple reasons that the People of East Bengal stood firm against any Constitution that could legalize and perpetuate the Muhajir-Punjabi imperialist hold on them" (Syed, 1974, Ch. 2). He viewed the attempt to constrain provincial units as "imperialism" by outside forces.

G.M. Syed stated that according to the Lahore Resolution of 1940, Pakistan's constituent units were to enjoy autonomy and sovereignty, but this promise was betrayed:

> In 1946 at Delhi, a convention of Muslim League parliamentarians, without any mandate of the mother organization and in total disregard of its basic constitution, subverted this solemn declaration of intent behind the political demand of Pakistan and adopted a resolution aimed at the establishment of unitary state for Pakistan.
>
> (Syed, 1974, Ch. 2)

G.M. Syed blamed Pakistan's failure to develop a working constitution on the fact that East Pakistanis would not accept anything less that autonomy. Once East Pakistan separated, an exemplar was provided for other communities with similar claims and grievances. Thus G.M. Syed sought a break based largely on Bengali success, and based on a similar reasoning.

G.M. Syed explicitly quoted Jinnah and asserted that Jinnah's argument for a separate Muslim nation applied exactly to Sindhi nationhood:

> The same Mr. Jinnah, on the 23rd of March 1940, at the Lahore session of All India Muslim League, said the following:
>
> "There is no doubt that Musalmans are to elect their representatives on the constituent Assembly through separate electorate. That is a good thing but decisions on Constitution are nevertheless to be taken by majority. Should there be difference on any issue between the minority and the majority, who will decide the point?"

Challengers in a weak polity 127

"All the talk today takes place on the assumption that Musalmans are a minority. We have got so used to this that we are not able to think any other way. We have totally forgotten the fact that Musalmans are not a minority but, in every sense and from all view points they are a separate nation."

The political argument developed, by Mr. Jinnah in his speech quoted in these extracts can exactly apply mutandis to the claim of Sindhi people to be treated as a notion and not as a minority in Pakistan.

(Syed, 1974)

Jinnah's quote can be used time and again in Pakistan, to devastating effect: "The problem then in India is not of an inter communal character but manifestly of international character and it must be treated as such" (quote from Jinnah's speech of March 23, 1940, at the Lahore Session of the All India Muslim League, quoted in Syed, 1974, Ch. 1). This provides the root justification for de jure quasi-states to flourish.

G.M. Syed justified his activism in favor of the Pakistan movement by arguing that it was tactically and pragmatically necessary to break the power of "British Stooge" (personal rival Hidayatullah) and Hindu vested interests, among others. It was a strategic necessity:

We found ourselves thus compelled to organize and rouse the Muslim masses on the basis of the communal platform of the Muslim league to confront the Hindu vested interests. Immature and in-experienced in politics and social works as we were, we prepared a religious-political program based more on self-complacency and wishful thinking than on anything else, to popularize among the masses, through the Muslim League Organization.

(Syed, 1974)

Thus, religious identity politics and affinity boundaries were selected for tactical reasons, because communal ties would mobilize people in ways that served G.M. Syed's agenda and leadership.

Moreover, G.M. Syed pointed to the role played by learning that is grounded in a historical trajectory:

It did not occur to us then that by organizing Musalmans on communal basis, we were not at all serving the interest of the Muslim masses, but on the contrary putting the same under grave jeopardy, since among their exploiters, along with the Hindu vested interests there were equally, if not more ravenous Muslim vested interests as well, conversely among the exploited and oppressed millions, too, there were the Hindus as well as the Muslims.

(Syed, 1974)

Here, G.M. Syed has claimed that his goal was the province's development and progress, but he needed an appropriate political vehicle. Religious and ethnic

128 *Political survival in Pakistan*

appeals have provided such vehicles at different times, facilitated by both his personal background and due to his organizational activities. A political survival interpretation could be that G.M. Syed's exclusion from a national position based on his contributions to the Muslim League shaped his later emphasis on a de jure quasi-state in Sind, as his provincial influence would likely secure him leadership. Moreover, the Sindhi role in national leadership had been thoroughly occupied by Z.A. Bhutto. According to this interpretation, something more than mild advocacy for Sindhi rights was needed in order to further Syed's prospects for obtaining political office.

A different emphasis would be that G.M. Syed's stated goal—provincial development—remained consistent, but the means to pursue it varied according to the political opportunities that presented themselves, through a historical learning process. Muslim League-oriented communal agitation was pursued when it seemed to promise freedom from exploitation by Hindu vested interests. The emphasis on a Sindhi quasi-state came about because the central government in Pakistan and "Muslim vested interests" proved to be exploitative and predatory. This learning process produced a more rigid Sindhi nationalism.

Both emphases are possible interpretations, and it is difficult to decisively reject one over the other. The first is skeptical about the role ideology plays in driving challenger choices. The second accepts the arguments made by G.M. Syed on their own terms. Whatever motives one ascribes to G.M. Syed's position, however, the core political survival mechanism that is exhibited by challengers in Pakistan remains intact: quasi-state pursuits provide a means for aspiring to political office.

G.M. Syed was held in detention more than once. Since his death in 1995, he remains a revered figure among Jeay Sindh activists. A nationalist narrative drawn largely from G.M. Syed's writings and experiences, and extended to better relate to present circumstances, can be found among his affinity group. Violent interactions with the national regime and other groups have spurred de facto quasi-state elements in Jeay Sindh. An armed uprising in Sind in 1983 posed a major threat to Zia ul-Haq's regime's survival. According to a Sindhi nationalist, the uprising was partly fomented by Jeay Sindh. Rasul Bux Palejo, who provided leadership in the rebellion, was formerly from Jeay Sindh, and created the Sindh Awami Tahrik after breaking away (Interview, 2008). The agitation was distinguished by participation from rural as well as urban groups, and was eventually suppressed by three army divisions and helicopter gunships (Talbot, 2005: 253–254).

In May 1989, Benazir Bhutto described the Sindh situation as a "mini-insurgency"; Ziring's account offers details:

> Instability in Sind also prompted the Jiye Sindh leader, G.M. Syed, to renew his call for an independent or autonomous Sindhu Desh. His followers turned out in significant numbers to demonstrate their resolve, and in the ensuing riots, they temporarily seized Sukkur airport. The anger of the protestors was dramatized by the burning of the Pakistan flag, and only the army was able to

Challengers in a weak polity 129

restore law and order, but not before 3,000 followers or the Jiye Sindh movement had been arrested.

(Ziring, 1997: 515–516)

Flag-burning is a symbolically charged act, and in this case demonstrated that the activists were rejecting the Pakistani central government's authority.

Jeay Sind activists narrate a history in which some ancestors came from Iraq to settle in Sind, and prospered, until they were permanently displaced, subjugated, and impoverished by Muhammad bin Qasim's invasion (Conversation with former Jeay Sind activist, 2008). The invasion is portrayed as a usurpation rather than a liberation of oppressed non-Muslims. In contrast, the Pakistan national narrative describes the history as a near-blank until Mohammad bin Qasim's glorious arrival, and refers only obliquely to the social structure and culture among the indigenous peoples. The Pakistani nationalist narrative describes Hindus as British allies, a "fundamentally insecure people" who "hated Muslims and would have oppressed them in a one-man, one-vote democratic India" (Cohen, 2004: 205). One political smear against the East Pakistani Bengalis had been that they were too influenced by Hindus.

Because Sindh remains deeply Islamic in its cultural affiliation, Jeay Sind activists run into a potential problem if the central government appeals to Muslim solidarity. One way Jeay Sind activists get away from this problem is to pursue a sectarian approach that challenges the Tablighi Jamaat and Deobandi schools, associated with Punjab and Muhajirs, and to emphasize a distinct Sindhi Islamic culture based on famous Sufi poets and festivals. A related development is the growing alliance or identification Jeay Sindh activists have with Sunni Tahrik, a Barelvi-affiliated militant religious organization. Deobandi approaches (and others that denigrate popular religious shrines) have a built-in animosity toward the Barelvi sect.[4] One Jeay Sindh activist declared that he felt hatred for the Tablighi Jamaat (a popular evangelizing grassroots movement that is loosely affiliated with Deobandi Islam). He accused the Tablighi Jamaat of smuggling narcotics into Sind, among other despicable acts (Interview, 2008). Barelvis can be found among non-Sindhis too, but Deobandis are fewer in number among Sindhis. A religio-ethnic nationalism may provide a sharper affinity boundary around which activists can organize. If religious sectarian affinity can overlap with ethnic affinity, then the risk increases that intergroup conflict will escalate to a broader conflagration. The security dilemmas that this generates may be the spur for further quasi-state building.

The Sindhi independence movement continues to have its martyrs, which reinforce ingroup solidarity and enhance perceived differences with outgroups. Interviewees from various backgrounds did not generally view Sindhi secessionism as a serious threat to Pakistani integrity (Interviews, 2008, 2009). One interpretation is that the 1971 war that led to Bangladesh in effect represented a choice by the Pakistan military to express their preference for securing a workable arrangement with Sind (Nasr, 2001). The national independence narrative associated with founder G.M. Syed nevertheless persists among Jeay Sind activists, even though

130 *Political survival in Pakistan*

they remain a minority with scant success at the polls (Conversation with a former Jeay Sind activist, 2008).

Violence targeting the Jeay Sind Qaumi Mahaz persists. For example, in March 2008, a Jeay Sind Qaumi Mahaz activist was kidnapped and murdered in Karachi; JSQM chairman Basheer Qureshi announced a three-day mourning period in Sindh and described the event as a conspiracy against the Sindhi people. A rally was held and a complete strike was observed in Larkana (Soomro, 2008). More recently, *Dawn* (July 25, 2009) reports that the car of the JSQM chairman, Bashir Khan Qureshi, was attacked, and a district chief for Thatta was killed as the JSQM leadership and party members traveled for a public protest against the lack of investigation into the killing of another JSQM worker. Bodyguards killed one attacker and captured another; apparently the attackers were identified as Pakistani intelligence agents. There were violent protests by Sindhi nationalists afterwards throughout the province. While the attackers' identity is not definitive, the consequences are significant. Decapitating an organization is one way to decrease its prospects for successful collective action and mobilization. At the same time, the violent attack and brewing conflict spiral may radicalize or polarize the population and generate additional recruits.

Mumtaz Ali Bhutto

Sardar Mumtaz Ali Bhutto, who was educated in law at Oxford, has a political lineage: his family was politically involved ever since the British allowed a political process in India. In the 1926 election, his uncle contested from Sindh and obtained the highest votes (Interview with Mumtaz Ali Bhutto, 2009). A landlord with influence in Larkana and elsewhere in Sind, M.A. Bhutto was Sindh's chief minister during his cousin Zulfikar Ali Bhutto's tenure in national office. During this period, the Sindh Assembly undertook to make Sindhi an official language in the province. This played to those with Sindhi nationalist affinities; it made educational advancement and government job prospects harder for Urdu-speaking Muhajirs, while improving the chances of native Sindhi speakers (Interview with Muhajir observer, 2009). Ethnic divisions between Sindhis and Muhajirs were exacerbated.

M.A. Bhutto's ability to pursue national political office was severely curtailed during the Zia ul-Haq years. With Zia ul-Haq's death and the opened political process, Benazir Bhutto made a successful bid for national office. M.A. Bhutto broke with the PPP and established the Sindh National Front. He proposed a formula that devolved significant autonomy and near-sovereignty to Pakistan's constituent nations. Army cantonments would be eliminated, and each unit would have the right to make foreign agreements (Ziring, 1997: 516). M.A. Bhutto also led the Sindh-Balochistan-Pushtun Front that advocated a confederation and favored curtailing the central government's power on defense, foreign affairs, currency, communications, and interstate transportation (Talbot, 2005: 245). He explained that while he identifies with Sindh, his position was not as radical as some "nationalists" because he chose to ally with others seeking a confederation (Interview with M.A. Bhutto, 2009).

At present, M. A. Bhutto argues for "total decentralization of power," stating that

> the center is just government and bureaucracy. There are no people in the center, no land in the center, and no income in the center. Everything comes from the provinces. The center is unnecessarily meddling; it takes income away from provinces, redistributes it to provinces, and takes the lion's share. We feel that is not fair.
>
> (Interview with Mumtaz Ali Bhutto, 2009)

M. A. Bhutto further asserts that Pakistan, as a multinational state, could not sustain a highly centralized system, much as Yugoslavia or the USSR could not. The basic flaw was that the original confederalist bargain, which attracted accession to Pakistan, was not implemented:

> The strongest argument for creating Pakistan was that if you stay in India, you will be yoked to federal system, where majority rule will prevail, [and] where you will be under a Hindu majority, [with] Muslims subservient; but if you come to Pakistan, we offer you a confederal system, you are master of your own land and province; and you do what you like, and center is there only to exercise the powers the provinces confer on it. So it is fundamental to Pakistan's creation and existence that there should be a confederal system. Unfortunately, this promise was never kept, [and] was violated from the day that Pakistan was created, with the consequence that the country has not worked, has already broken once, [and the] greater part is gone. [The] rest has been under military rule, more than half its age under military rule and martial law. Democracy has not taken root, [and] does not last more than a year or two.
>
> (Interview with M. A. Bhutto, 2009)

Taken together, these statements represent strong claims that the central government has transgressed its promised limits. Moreover, M. A. Bhutto blamed the East Pakistani secession on an overbearing central government.

As a solution, M. A. Bhutto prescribes a maximally strong de jure quasi-state. His vision for autonomy goes beyond Mujib ur-Rehman's "Six Points" because it advocates for a provincial right to undertake a unilateral declaration of independence in the event that the constitution is violated. M. A. Bhutto argues that the judiciary has shown itself to be unreliable in upholding key constitutional requirements. In particular, the judiciary have compromised and legitimated military rule repeatedly, whereas Article 6 in the constitution describes such military intervention as treason. M. A. Bhutto's position is that if the military takes over the central government, then the provinces should retain the right to secede; only this, he believes, will check military intervention (Interview with Sardar Mumtaz Ali Bhutto, 2009).

A political survival interpretation would be that Mumtaz Ali Bhutto saw provincial autonomy as a means to securing political ascendancy, given that he was not

132 *Political survival in Pakistan*

pursuing national office or that he had low prospects for attaining national office. M.A. Bhutto's sophisticated reasoning demonstrates the difficulty in separating methods from motives in unpacking the political survival mechanism in Pakistani politics. He formerly served under Z.A. Bhutto's PPP umbrella. After Zia ul-Haq's coup, Z.A. Bhutto's mantle was taken up by his daughter Benazir. For M.A. Bhutto to pursue a de jure quasi-state makes strategic sense because it would enhance his jurisdiction in the area in which he has influence and ascendancy. It is where he has strong prospects for further political office. At the same time, his confederalist ideology is a coherent argument for implementing Pakistan's original promise in a just fashion. His ideological position and his political survival interests are thus compatible.

Challengers in Balochistan

In Balochistan, Baluchi speakers made up only one third of the population; the other linguistic communities were Brahuis and Pathans (Jalal, 1990: 93). Ahmed Rashid (2008: 283) describes the Baloch as being "secular" because "mullahs have no standing in Baloch society, which has remained untouched by the waves of Islamization that have swept the region" as compared to the Pushtuns. In response to a question about his primary affiliation and loyalty, a Balochi journalist emphasized that his first identity was Muslim, before "Baloch" or "Pakistani" (Interview, March 2008). This statement may have been a diplomatic effort to not appear overtly disloyal to Pakistan because religious identity's primacy is widely respected. There are distant irredentist possibilities for Balochis, who can be found across the border in Iran also; a united cross-border Balochi movement (difficult as it may be to imagine under current circumstances) might provide a serious challenge to both Pakistan and Iran. Another complication is the Balochi clans that are divided between Pakistan and Afghanistan, such as the Zehris (Interview with Balochi journalist, 2008).[5]

Prior to the current borders identified as "Balochistan" there were other subunits, such as princely states, among which Kalat was the largest. The Khan of Kalat (Ahmad Yar Khan) acceded to Pakistan in 1948, although there are claims that the terms of accession permitted revocation or that accession happened under duress. In 1951 his state had become part of the Balochistan States Union. On October 6, 1958, the Khan of Kalat reacted to the military bases placed in Balochistan by seceding from Pakistan. The Khan of Kalat lowered the Pakistan flag from a fort and raised his ancestral flag. There was brief "armed defiance" (Talbot, 2005: 152). This gesture provided the pretext for martial law to be imposed, based on the threat to national integrity and security that this allegedly secessionist activity posed. Early on October 8, 1958, Ayub Khan's coup took place (Jalal, 1990: 274). The army's deployment to coerce Kalat and three other princely states "simply lent weight to the view, common among some Baluch sardars, that independence rather than subjugation to the Pakistani state was the only logical option" (Jalal, 1990: 93). Ahmed Yar Khan, who led the Kalat revolt, was arrested for conspiracy against Pakistan. He was released in 1962 and "all his privileges were restored" (Baloch, 2008).

The Kalat case describes a former state that has de jure claims and that sought, briefly, to obtain full independence. In some form, its legacy has continued, although something approximating a more modern secessionist nationalism has emerged.

Two armed conflicts between Balochi forces and the Pakistani military took place between 1948 and 1958. Another armed engagement began in 1962 and ended in 1968. These were precursors to further violent interactions in the region under later regimes. A third military engagement between Balochis and the Pakistan military took place between 1962 and 1968, and a fourth between 1974 and 1978.

The 1970 elections, with the success enjoyed by the Bengalis, the National Awami Party, and the JUI raised provincial expectations (Ziring, 1997: 333). The fourth military engagement took place between 1973 and 1975 after Bhutto dismissed provincial governor Ghaus Buksh Bizenjo and the government, led by Chief Minister Sardar Ataullah Mengal, resigned in protest. Bizenjo had become known as Baba-e-Balochistan (father of Balochistan) due to his early and forceful advocacy of Balochi nationalism (Axmann, 2009: 230). The Pakistan army launched a major operation, and the Baluchis suffered 3300 casualties, with 7000 families fleeing to Afghanistan for refuge (Cohen, 2004: 220). Mengal left for England, where he convened the "Pakistan Oppressed Nations Movement." Bizenjo, who led the Pakistan National Party (PNP), argued for a "loose" federation reflecting the Pakistan's four nationalities (Talbot, 2005: 245).

In February 1973, Z.A. Bhutto dismissed the NAP and JUI government in Baluchistan; the NWFP's JUI government resigned in protest. The armed revolt by Baluchi tribesmen embroiled the military once again in "a full-scale civil war to protect the integrity of the state," with differences:

> Instead of chasing Bengali guerrillas in the swamps of the Sunderbans it had to contend with the no less determined Marri, Mengla and Bizenjo tribesmen in the mountainous terrain of Baluchistan. And, most important of all, instead of acting on behalf of a military regime it had to take orders from a civilian government whose leaders ought to have known that the martial spirit once given its head stops at nothing short of total solutions, positive or negative.
>
> (Jalal, 1990: 317)

Pakistan's internal war with the Baloch in 1974–8 may have cost 8000 lives (Stewart and Hyat, 2002: 111). Bhutto's winning coalition did not include those in Balochistan, and he had coercive instruments at his disposal. It was relatively easy to repress the challengers. This had a delegitimating consequence for Bhutto's image, but it was likely that Bhutto's support was by this point already concentrated in the more narrow "Establishment." The question is whether this process can be identified before the fact. There is uncertainty and incomplete, imperfect information, even for heavily involved actors intimately familiar with situational intricacies.

In 1996, Sardar Attaullah Khan Mengal (formerly the first elected chief minister of Balochistan) formed the Balochistan National Party. His party's perspective is that the "army establishment" makes decisions regarding Balochistan, and that low trust makes it difficult to start meaningful negotiations. Mengal has recently

134   *Political survival in Pakistan*

asserted that the federal government was dominated by Punjabi interests, and that the conflict revolved around exploitation of Balochistan's resources; he called for military to withdraw and for maximal provincial autonomy, with only foreign affairs, defense, and finance in the federal government's control (*Dawn*, April 3, 2008: 18).

Akbar Bugti, a leader in the Bugti tribe and a former federal cabinet minister, headed the Jamhoori Watan Party (Talbot, 2005: 448–449). A former military officer who knew Bugti several decades earlier described him as a fun-loving, wealthy young man (Interview with retired military officer, 2009). Several incidents, including an alleged rape by an army officer, and the killings of Chinese engineers who were to work on the Gwadar port, fed tensions between the Musharraf government and Balochis. Gas reserves in Balochistan, an important natural resource that supplies other areas in the country, are concentrated in Dera Bugti (the Bugti tribe's land). Nawab Akbar Bugti, who led a force numbering up to 10,000, was killed in a missile strike after a dispute with the Musharraf's government over gas royalties. His killing has become a symbol for protest and public resentment against central government policies.

Prince Mohyuddin Baloch, a former federal communications minister, now heads the Baloch Rabita Ittefaq Tehrik. His father was Ahmed Yar Khan, who led the Kalat revolt in 1958. Prince Mohyuddin Baloch asserted that growing alienation in Balochistan had become an international issue, and that as armed conflict continued, outside powers such as a neighboring country would intervene. He termed this a "Great Game," referring to the imperial machinations and rivalries that drove territorial disputes and acquisitions in nineteenth-century Asia. According to Prince Mohyuddin Baloch, previous to the agreement with Pakistan, Balochistan enjoyed an independent status akin to Nepal or Afghanistan. The prince demanded a UN investigation into the killings of Akbar Bugti and nationalist Balaach Marri (Baloch, 2008).

A political survival interpretation may be that this "official transcript" offered by an acknowledged influential figure, combined with the irredentist threat, may lead an incumbent national leader to offer patronage and private benefits in return for political quiescence. Secessionism and de jure quasi-state pursuits may be a bargaining posture, a strategic self-representation designed to obtain private goods. This interpretation may be supported by the fact that various Balochi nationalist leaders have previously held government posts. Cabinet positions are sometimes seen as patronage from the incumbent leader to provide private rewards to the appointee and prevent nuisances. Moreover, the request for a UN investigation also follows a pattern—an appeal to an authority outside the federal government for a more credible investigation, both to bring an international audience to the conflict, and also to give voice to the belief among the disenfranchised that the federal government is a partisan rather than a neutral law-providing actor. (After Benazir Bhutto was assassinated, her husband Asif Zardari similarly called for a UN investigation.)

A Pakistani economist believed that Balochistan's situation replicated the East Pakistan province: a poor area where people felt that their cultural and economic rights were not being given to them (Conversation with an economist, 2002). Balochistan has natural resources such as gas. The Gwadar port development is also inequitable, positioning non-Balochis for large gains if the port becomes a major hub. According to a government agricultural census officer, road infrastructure in Balochistan under Musharraf's rule improved significantly (Interview, March 2008). The trip from Turbat to Gwadar—which took him 18 hours in 2000—was made in two hours in 2007. There was public benefit, and people appreciated it, whatever Musharraf's motives may have been. One obvious gain for the polity is that better infrastructure provides public goods to Balochis, and this reduces the incentive for revolutionary or secessionist challenge. Additionally, sociological changes may follow improved access and further economic integration, tying Balochis to the other Pakistanis through trade and increased interaction. But rising expectations and invidious comparisons can lead an ethnic group's members to feel relatively deprived, and relative deprivation can stoke political violence (Gurr, 1970).

A retired high military officer expressed deep worry over sentiments expressed by students in Balochistan: they openly stated on live television that what happens in Islamabad or elsewhere in Pakistan does not concern them, because Balochistan is entirely separate. The Pakistani flag has been replaced in places with nationalist banners (Interview with retired military officer, 2009). Thus, an affinity group oriented toward Balochi independence exists and appears to have grown in size and boldness. Moreover, as the Gwadar port project has reached completion, Balochi nationalists have argued that an independent Balochistan would bring great wealth. With a small native population, access to the sea, and projected revenues from natural resources, Balochistan could be the "richest country in the world" in per capita terms (Interview with corporate executive, 2009). While there are some secessionist appeals that appear to be primarily bloggers, it appears that the affinity group for a strong de jure quasi-state or full secession has spread and become more deeply entrenched. Some observers dismiss this phenomenon as being restricted to a narrow strip inside Balochistan (Interviews, 2009). However, the frequent violent interactions with the Pakistan military and open declarations against the state suggest a less confined activism.

Altaf Hussain and the MQM

Altaf Hussain's advocacy has seen both de facto and de jure quasi-state elements, and has simultaneously produced a political party that has representation in the provincial and national legislatures, as well as Karachi district control under the devolved powers system. This makes the MQM a particularly rich case for describing political opportunities for challenge in a weak state.

In pre-Partition India, the demand for a separate Muslim state originally came from the Muslim minority provinces, Bihar, UP, New Delhi, Bombay, and Gujarat. Muslims in Punjab, NWFP, and less so in Sindh were "comfortable with their situation under the British," and "not particularly enthusiastic about the idea of Pakistan" (Burki, 2008a). Eight million Muslims came to Pakistan. Six million

136 *Political survival in Pakistan*

Hindus and Sikhs moved to India. The Muhajirs (migrants) had a disproportionate share in political leadership in Punjab, Sind, and NWFP; their power depended on a powerful central government as well as on Karachi as the country's capital. The 1951 population census showed that refugees were one tenth of the population, approximately 7 million people. They formed a sizeable minority. Seventy percent of the refugees into West Pakistan were Punjabis, but they assimilated and did not adopt the "Muhajir" label. In contrast, Urdu-speakers and others did retain the label:

> the Urdu-speaking refugees from the United Provinces, Delhi, Central Provinces, Bihar, and Hyderabad Deccan, who settled mostly in Sindh, have continued to maintain the Mohajir label for their group identification. Recently, as a result of political mobilization on the basis of Mohajir identity in the urban areas of Sindh, many Kutchi Memons and other individuals who migrated from Bombay, Gujrat, and other parts of India, and their descendants have also come to identify themselves as Mohajirs.
>
> (Ahmed, 2002: 27)

According to historian Ayesha Jalal, Islam assisted cultural fragmentation rather than national integration: "Urdu and the aristocratic culture of Mughal India were presented as the indubitable link between the people of Pakistan and their Islamic heritage" (Jalal, 1990: 289). This elicited a sharp reaction in East Pakistan, and had effects in West Pakistan, particularly in Sind where Urdu-speaking Muhajirs were gathered (Jalal, 1990: 289). Islamism's early appeal was to the Muhajirs, who felt that they had sacrificed the most for Pakistan, and who were major early recruiting grounds for the JUP and the JI (Jalal, 1990: 289–290). Ayub Khan's decision to relocate the capital to Rawalpindi in northern Punjab, as well as his accommodation with landlords in politics, weakened the political position Muhajirs enjoyed (Burki, 2008a). As migrants became more marginal, they no longer had the same incentive to support a strong central government. Agitation for autonomy increased.

Bangladesh's creation created an additional grievance for the Muhajir community: the "stranded Pakistanis," mostly Urdu speakers, were not repatriated to Pakistan. Mohajir observers note the non-Bengalis (called "Biharis") in East Pakistan were not allowed to move to West Pakistan, and over 250,000 still live in camps around Dhaka (Cohen, 2004: 215). One suggestion was to create "Muhajiristan," a Muhajir region cut from Sindh, with a population boosted by Biharis stranded in Bangladesh (Haq, 1995: 993). This suggestion came following the language controversy in 1972, when the Sindh Assembly passed a bill requiring all students to take Sindhi language instruction, and for provincial officials to learn the language. This disadvantaged Muhajir students and jobseekers, and provoked an autonomist, quasi-state-oriented reaction.

The Muhajir Qaumi Mahaz's emergence is commonly regarded by analysts as an "ethnic mobilization" case (e.g. Ahmar, 1996; Haq, 1995). The MQM grew from the All Pakistan Muhajir Student Organization (APMSO), founded by Altaf Hussain in 1978 in Karachi University. Karachi University had a Punjabi Student Organization and a Baloch Student Organization. Major student parties at the time included the

NSF (National Student Federation, a leftist organization) and the IJT (Islami Jamiat-e-Talaba, a rightist group partly affiliated with the Jamaat-e-Islami). The Muslim Student Federation represented the Muslim League. Unlike most student political organizations, which emerged as "student wings" of established political parties, the MQM is a political party that grew from a student movement (Interviews, 2008, 2009). The APMSO founders left student life, and in 1986 created the Muhajir Qaumi Mahaz.

The year 1986 saw spiraling ethnic tensions between Muhajirs and Pushtuns in Karachi. In a famous incident at the bus transport juncture called Sohrab Goth, a Mohajir girl named Bushra Zaidi was run over by a bus driven by a Pushtun. Mohajirs rioted, and attacks on Pushtuns quickly spread elsewhere in Karachi. In another incident, mosque loudspeakers contributed to collective action: on December 14, 1986, a Pirabad mosque issued a signal, and several hundred Pushtuns launched attacks on Biharis and Mohajirs (Jones, 2002: 123). Revenge attacks began and arson quickly spread. These incidents and others have remained in collective memory as important points for Muhajir mobilization.

The key decision-maker in the MQM remains the leader and founder Altaf Hussain, described as Quaid-e-Tehrik ("Leader of the Movement") by his supporters. His portrait is displayed in many Karachi MQM-dominated neighborhoods, along with MQM flags. He resides in the UK, and a coordination committee works between there and Pakistan on issues regarding MQM-related policy and appointments. According to MQM member Hamid Abidi, adviser to the Sindh chief minister, Altaf Hussain solicits input from various expert sources as well as the general public before making decisions which are generally consensus-based (Interview with Hamid Abidi, July 2009).

Zia ul-Haq's regime would have been well served by a party in Sind that would compete with Sindhis and reduce their political influence. Several writers have claimed that "the ISI [Inter-Services Intelligence] sponsored the MQM to weaken the PPP and the MRD in Sindh"; Altaf Hussain has denied these allegations (Talbot, 2005: 264–265, n. 83). An interviewee suggested that Zia ul-Haq sponsored the MQM to try to deflate the "independent Sindh" slogan (Interview, 2009). Sindhi nationalists would realize that unfettered appeals for independence based on Sindhi ethnicity might provoke a reactive Muhajir mobilization, and divide Sindh further. One observer noted that the MQM never actually pursued independence or emigration explicitly, but the threat was there by implication (Interview with former civil servant, 2008). Hamid Abidi, editor of the pro-MQM daily *Amn* and adviser to the Sindh chief minister, also asserts that the MQM did not seek independence (Interview with Hamid Abidi, July 2009).

The MQM initially received plaudits as a positive force, giving direction to Mohajir youth; it transformed a centrist community to an opponent of the state (Haq, 1995: 1004). The MQM filled a leadership vacuum; "it was Altaf Hussain who came to embody the ordinary *mohajir's* concern for the protection of life and physical property," drawing primarily on "lower-middle-class descendants of the Pakistan Movement" (Ziring, 1997: 495). Hamid Abidi, then employed by the Intelligence Bureau and monitoring an MQM rally in 1986, reports that Altaf Hussain was speaking effectively to a constituency that had previously not had

138 *Political survival in Pakistan*

its interests represented. He spoke at length about perceived disrespect to Muhajirs, as seen in labels like *"muttarwala"* (meaning those who are all talk), and also pointed to quotas that worked against Muhajir opportunities in education and government employment. Moreover, Altaf Hussain demonstrated an ability to mobilize people successfully into large gatherings (Interview with Hamid Abidi, July 2009).

As the MQM's power grew, particularly in Karachi, it came to have a reputation as heavy-handed *bhatta* collector. The MQM spearheaded the anti-Benazir Bhutto opposition, holding a political gathering at Jinnah's Mausoleum in Karachi in January 26, 1990, that "was undoubtedly the largest political gathering in Pakistan's history" (Talbot, 2005: 306–307). An MQM-organized strike in February 1990 produced disorder, violence, arson, and looting, and the army was eventually called in. A *Dawn* editorial describes the 1992 military action as a crackdown on MQM "strongholds," during which the military "bulldozed the security walls that had turned large parts of Karachi into ghettoes and opened up 'no-go' areas" (*Dawn* July 16, 2009: 7).[6] According to Hamid Abidi, editor of the pro-MQM *Amn* newspaper, this description was propaganda for consumption by the rest of the country, while Karachiites knew the reality. He asserted that the military operation cost 15,000 lives, and the MQM still collects funds to pay to the *shuhada* (martyrs') families (Interview with Hamid Abidi, July 2009).[7]

The very fact that the MQM survived a major military crackdown in the early 1990s and has retained its power as the dominant political force in Karachi says something about its ability to deliver security (or, in terms consonant with Charles Tilly's framework, war-making and protection). Welfare services are also provided by the MQM. One observer, not an MQM member, expressed awe at its organizational resilience and strength (Interview, 2009). The MQM has sought to demonstrate grassroots orientation and sharpen its populist credentials by providing social services, such as neighborhood cleanups in places under their control, and health care. Prominent social service Khidmat-e-Khalq (service to Creation) works include ambulance and medical services, as well as support for families of MQM *shaheeds* (martyrs) and other needy persons. The Khidmat-e-Khalq division launched a fund-raising drive for persons displaced by the insurgency in Swat in 2009, after the MQM joined Jeay Sindh in a city-wide strike to protest the influx of Swat refugees.

In a rally in February 1987 in Hyderabad, Altaf Hussain asked whether those attending would rise to defend Pakistan if an attack by India took place, and they responded negatively, sending a message that Muhajir loyalty could not be taken for granted and Pakistan should do more for Muhajirs (Jones, 2002: 124). In other words, an alternative allegiance, or a compound allegiance, was implied. Altaf Hussain distributed a questionnaire in 1994, and claimed responses numbered in the hundreds of thousands, with the overwhelming majority favoring a fifth Muhajir province (Jones, 2002: 128). That autonomist message has waned recently. Hamid Abidi, editor of the pro-MQM *Amn* newspaper, asserts that the MQM has moved beyond Muhajirs into the educated urban populations in Sind generally, and a separate Muhajir province was not the MQM's goal. MQM leader Altaf Husain now describes the Muhajir community as "Urdu-speaking Sindhis" (Interview with Hamid Abidi, July 2009). A former Jeay Sind activist reacted negatively to this characterization of the Muhajir community (Interview with former Jeay Sind activist, July 2009).

Large segments in Karachi report making donations to the MQM. Within this base, allegiance to the MQM appears to be high. There have been visible changes in Karachi's traffic infrastructure since Musharraf's devolution plan produced an MQM-affiliated city nazim (mayor). While some Jamaat-e-Islami supporters ascribe Karachi's development projects to a previous city nazim associated with the JI, Nematullah Khan, most interviewees believed the city's development was due to efforts by MQM-affiliated Nazim Syed Mustafa Kamal. There were various reasons ascribed to this: among them, technical competence, personal dedication, and the fact that MQM constituency was mainly educated middle and lower-middle class urbanites (Interviews, 2008, 2009).

Unlike most political parties, the MQM's constituent base and primary affinity group is urban middle class, although it is largely Urdu-speaking and geographically restricted to urban centers in Sindh. Observers from different backgrounds have noted that MQM appointments to legislative and ministerial positions tended to be drawn from the middle class (rather than the elite business or landlord families which are overrepresented in other political party officers) (Interviews, 2009). The MQM has ambitions to be a broad-based party representing an educated, middle class constituency, among others (Interview with Hamid Abidi, July 2009). But its background as a Mohajir Qaumi Mahaz (Mohajir National Movement) rather than its newer name, Muttahida Qaumi Movement (Allied National Movement), means that it remains widely perceived as the party of Urdu-speaking migrants from India.

One MQM supporter suggested that Karachi is relatively stable because it has one "bhai" (big brother; he was referring to Altaf Hussain, the MQM leader, who is referred to as Altaf Bhai, or Brother Altaf, by his supporters); Karachi, claimed the MQM supporter, was more stable than strife-torn places elsewhere that have many "bhais" (Interview with MQM supporter, 2008). This summarized the "stationary bandit" problem. According to one observer, Altaf Hussain by the late 1990s; "looked far less like an energetic campaigner for Mohajir rights and far more like a would-be mafia boss determined to hang on to control of Karachi" (Jones, 2002: 131). Under Musharraf's devolution plan and the Local Government Ordinance, the separate administrative structures for Karachi have enabled a Mohajir-dominated jurisdiction, given the MQM's strength in the city. With Musharraf's exit, there are increasing tensions between the MQM and the Sindhi-dominated provincial government, who both seek jurisdiction over Karachi.

Pushtun ethnonationalism

Pushtuns have had autonomist impulses demarcated by both ethnic and religious affinity markers. Abdul Ghaffar Khan, the "Frontier Gandhi" with his Khudai Khidmatgar organization (its members known as the Red Shirts) had established his influence through a struggle against British rule and influence in the North-West

140 *Political survival in Pakistan*

Frontier. His personal ties to Gandhi and nonviolent philosophy placed him closer to Congress than the Muslim League. He was opposed to "Pakistan" and saw it as a divide-and-rule stratagem for continuing European influence, enabled by the Anglophile Jinnah (Ziring, 1997: 85). British Viceroy Lord Mountbatten refused Ghaffar Khan's wish to include an "independence" option into the referendum, leading Ghaffar Khan to boycott the vote (Cohen, 2004: 217).

The Khudai Khidmatgar (servants of God) movement can be understood as "an attempt by the smaller landlords to mobilize support among the peasants to challenge the authority of the big Khans" (Jalal, 1990: 91). In NWFP, the big landlords (called Khans) who had been British collaborators had supported the Muslim League's demand for Pakistan. Jinnah's statement supporting Shariat rule, made to the Pir of Manki Sharif, helped mobilize support for accession to Pakistan. The NWFP plebiscite expressed a preference for the Muslim League; Jinnah removed Dr Khan Sahib, Abdul Ghaffar Khan's brother, from his post as chief minister of the NWFP after the plebiscite.

Abdul Ghaffar Khan and his brother Dr Khan Sahib met with Jinnah after Gandhi's assassination. Jinnah invited them to join the Muslim League, but they remained intransigent. It is likely that they recognized Jinnah's weak health and believed Pakistan would not outlast Jinnah. "Khan Sahib reminded the Quaid-i-Azam that he had refused to swear loyalty to Pakistan, and that the Red Shirts would not be disbanded. Ghaffar Khan noted that his party would continue its programme to provide the Pathans with a higher profile than that envisaged by the Muslim League" (Ziring, 1997: 85).

Jinnah was convinced that the brothers sought to secede and create "Pakhtunistan," land of the Pakhtun. The Pukhtun politician Khan Abdul Qaiyum Khan was skilled at political survival; he had initially denounced the Muslim League and then joined it when it became clear that Pakistani sovereignty would be achieved. The provincial Muslim League came under his control. As chief minister, he imprisoned Ghaffar Khan in May 1948, invoking the Frontier Crimes Regulations (Ziring, 1997: 86).

Religio-autonomism

The Muttahida Majlis-e-Amal, an alliance of religious parties, enjoyed a victory in the 2002 elections in NWFP and also obtained a role as a coalition government partner in Balochistan. Musharraf's strong support for US policy after September 11, 2001, produced a backlash. His policies added fuel to rising anti-American feeling in NWFP and Balochistan, the provinces contiguous with Afghanistan. This raised "the possibility of a very different kind of separatist-nationalist movement in the NWFP, one based on religious symbols and alliances" (Cohen, 2004: 219). *Madrasas* in the area have also provided a basis for mobilization: the Jamiat Ulema-e-Islam's electoral success in some constituencies was likely due to the many Deobandi *madrasas* in the area (Ahmad, 2000: 191). Among the MMA's most prominent actions was to pursue Sharia law in the province under their Nizam-e-Adl (System of Justice) program. General Musharraf accepted their efforts in an

Challengers in a weak polity 141

unspecified political compromise under which the MMA reduced opposition to Musharraf's constitutional changes (Taylor, 2005: 225). In effect, the MMA traded autonomy inside NWFP in return for withdrawing their challenge to the national incumbent. This fits the de jure quasi-state thesis in that the MMA used the polity's existing processes to pursue an autonomist agenda. The MMA sacrificed principle (opposition to Musharraf's policies) for political survival and ascendancy (political survival in their province, and acknowledgement that the military is a vital winning coalition member). In office, the MMA's image was tarnished due to alleged nepotism, when reserve women's seats in the legislative assembly were given to relatives of MMA leaders (Interview with former MMA member Maulana Asad Thanvi, July 2009).

The JI may have found itself outside the winning coalition often enough to seek complete overthrow and revolutionary change. But this has not happened. Instead, the JI, along with JUP and JUI, other MMA members have found opportunities for office and private benefits, such as support for favored causes in Afghanistan and Kashmir, and local authority. In this way they have been associated with the winning coalition and have not been wholly disenfranchised.

The MMA was not as successful in the 2008 elections, however. One reason may have been the nepotism displayed by its leaders, who appointed family members to reserve seats and thereby reduced their legitimacy as public goods providers (Interview with Maulana Asad Thanvi, 2009). Over the February 2008 election period, the Awami National Party (led by Asfandyar Wali Khan, Abdul Ghaffar Khan's grandson) described itself as "secular" in counterpose to the MMA bloc in the NWFP and Balochistan. This may have been a strategy to appeal to international audiences rather than domestic ones. Its agenda is more ethnic than Islamist. One ANP goal was to have the province's name changed to "Pakhtoonkhwa," meaning the "Pakhtun Brotherhood."

The name Pukhtoonkhwa was originally suggested by Ghaffar Khan as an alternative to the more secessionist-sounding "Pukhtunistan." The politics of naming include a "cultural nationalism" that might embolden secessionism, as well as provoking other ethnic groups without their own territories to seek such recognized homelands.

The Federally Administered Tribal Areas region is probably the clearest "anarchic" example in Pakistan, although it is partly anarchy by design, as the area has been designated for self-rule (excepting the areas covered by the Frontier Crimes Regulations, as described in Chapter 2). FATA covers 27,000 kilometers and is populated by 7 million Pushtuns; it lacks socioeconomic development, with three fifths of the population in poverty and 17 percent literacy (Ahmar, 2008). The region provided a haven for jihad groups fighting Soviet forces in Afghanistan, due partly to the porous border. An insurgency broke out against American-Pakistani attempts to root out the Taliban fighters that took refuge in FATA after US invaded Afghanistan.

A "war economy" has persisted in the border areas, sustaining training camps and fighters. Militants have established parallel governments in North and South Waziristan (Khan, M. Ilyas, 2008). Some leaders in FATA hold authority over

142 *Political survival in Pakistan*

"fiefs"; an example is the jihadist Maulvi Haqqani, whose roots go back to the war against the Soviet occupation of Afghanistan (Gall, 2008). A de facto quasi-state phenomenon is amply visible among Taliban leaders such as Baitullah Mehsud, whose boasts about his war-making capabilities included threats against American territory. Militias thrive on insecurity and anarchy because they are able and willing to deploy coercive force. It makes sense for militia leaders to intimidate or eliminate existing, traditional authority figures (such as tribal elders) to increase local anarchy, as this removes rivals while enhancing their own long-term prospects (Conversation with NWFP migrant, 2008).

Taliban leaders (and allied groups) typically issue declarations about what is "Islamic," and use these to legitimatize their attacks on internal and external claimants to authority. These acts help to consolidate their control within specific territory and to ward off outsiders who try to intervene. Defeats suffered by the Pakistani military in its attempts to control the area add to the Taliban's prestige as a successful war-maker. Fata has become "the most armed and militant region where the writ of the Pakistani state appeared almost nonexistent"; narcotics and weapons smuggling (and official "connivance") have "rendered the tribal areas ungovernable and controlled by the 'mafias' " (Ahmar, 2008). Consequently, people are often in overlapping polities. It is unclear which polity will survive; in the meantime, all inhabitants have to weigh the risks and opportunities the complicated situation offers.

Baitullah Mehsud (reportedly killed in August 2009) led the Tehrik-e-Taliban Pakistan, which is an umbrella organization including 40 militant groups (Walsh, 2008). The Tehrik-e-Taliban Pakistan, Sufi Mohammad's Tahrik-e-Nifaz-e-Shariat-e-Mohammadi and the Pir of Manki Sharif represent attempts to use Islamic legitimacy to justify creating a quasi-state. It may be helpful to distinguish whether these are simply Pushtun-led religiously conservative movements or whether they represent an active revolutionary Islam-based agenda that is more religiously inclined than ethnic. There have been efforts to displace traditional tribal leadership, often with assassination. Some analysts, such as Olivier Roy, believe the Taliban to be Pushtun nationalism in a different garb (Grare, 2006). Other observers draw a sharp distinction between the nonviolent Pushtun nationalism espoused by Khan Abdul Ghaffar Khan and the current aspirants to leadership who claim religious legitimacy, as seen in designations and titles such as "*Mufti*," "*Qari*" and "*Mullah*" (Yousaf, 2009).

Insurgency in the tribal areas

According to an editorial in *The Times*, London:

> Pakistan is already an anomaly. Without being labeled a failed state, it comprises large swaths of territory where its central government's writ does not run and its forces dare not deploy [...] in Swat, where troops have been withdrawn and Sharia has largely replaced Pakistani law; and in South Waziristan where the power vacuum has been filled by Baitullah Mehsud, leader of the Taliban faction that is not encircling Peshawar.

Challengers in a weak polity 143

Officially, Islamabad has not ceded control of Peshawar to anyone. Yet the Taliban are already closing down music shops and internet cafes. Those business owners who can are leaving [...].

(quoted in Irfan Husain, 2008)

The insurgency might spread into a broader internal war because Islamist sympathizers and allies elsewhere could react to the heavy-handed government crackdown in Waziristan and Fata. This possibility is somewhat alarmist but not entirely—as *The Times* accurately notes, the central government have tried to make deals with "separatist militants" to appease them, rather than risk an "unwinnable civil war that could engulf the whole country." Others skeptically note reports that Baitullah Mehsud commanded fewer than 1000 fighters (Foust and Koogler, 2008).

Irfan Husain (2008) describes wide areas in Pakistan as undergoing a "creeping insurgency" in which violent, emboldened law-breakers have "used classic salami tactics, slicing off bits of land and sovereignty," and using negotiation respites to consolidate their position. This notion—chopping away the Pakistani polity and establishing quasi-states—suggests that the quasi-state strategy is becoming more prevalent and relying more on de facto power (through war-making and state-making, rather than juridical appeals). In the shorter term, these will surely make the writ of state more difficult to enforce.

Moreover, as Irfan Husain (2008) notes, there is a morale problem—the army does not want to fight locals, partly because the army is drawn from Punjab and NWFP. Ideologically, the army believes that the insurgents are fighting for Islam. This may be a way to see how the largely Pushtun "Islamic" challenger problem is worse than the Bengali "ethnonationalist" challenger. In the 1971 war, the Bengalis were seen as aliens, so Pakistani soldiers had less compunction about killing them. Islamists have ideological allies in the military; moreover, there are more ethnic ties with Pushtuns in the tribal areas and Pushtuns in the military.

"Taliban" means "religious students," usually referring to those studying in *madrasas*. The Dar-ul-Uloom Haqqania, a *madrasa* in Baluchistan, has 2500 students, and taught the Taliban leadership (Cohen, 2004: 182). In a society where religious learning is valued and gives the scholar social position, the label "Taliban" had the possible strategic benefit that it gave the movement legitimacy. Moreover, traditional egalitarianism in Pushtun tribal society has meant that religious legitimacy often provides the basis for leadership. According to Maulana Asad Thanvi of the Jamiat Ulema-e-Islam, the appellation "Taliban" should only apply to a small minority within the movement. Only a few were actually religious students, and this mainly in the early 1990s. The current forces called Taliban are not generally religious students (Interview with Asad Thanvi, July 2009).

The Taliban were originally seen by Pakistani security strategists as a way to extend Pakistani influence into Afghanistan and perhaps further into central Asia; now, their presence continues to justify appeals for US aid. For both reasons, there is significant ambiguity in how the Taliban have been treated (Remarks by a retired diplomatic official, 2009). If controlling the internal war in the tribal areas becomes

144 *Political survival in Pakistan*

the military's new rationale, then one would expect the conflict to continue for the foreseeable future—otherwise, the rationale will disappear. This disturbing reasoning matches the "war-making and state-making as organized crime" argument by Charles Tilly, where states are compared to protection rackets. Without a credible threat, the racket cannot last.

It is a tricky proposition to withdraw the military from the tribal belt and still retain the state's authority. In a peace deal, the military agreed to withdraw from South Waziristan. The Taliban then demanded that the military also leave Darra Adamkhel in Frontier Region Kohat, district Swat, and all of Waziristan. An editorial in *Dawn* April 30, 2008 notes that local administration is not strong enough to establish the writ of state and rule of law; instead, militants "dictate terms in their strongholds and from those bases export their ideology to the rest of Pakistan" ("Mehsud's walkout": 7).

The search for new provinces: de jure quasi-states?

The logic behind appeals for de jure quasi-states is well articulated by the recent effort to carve a new Pukhtun province beyond the NWFP, where Pukhtuns are in a majority. Rafiq Pashtoon, leader of Pashtoon Qaumi Tehrik, has called for a new "southern Pashtoonkhwa" province comprising areas from Sibi to Zhob in Balochistan. Rafiq Pashtoon argued that existing governance posts in Balochistan should include more Pashtoon representation, saying "it was unjustified to give top posts of chief minister and governor of Balochistan to Balochs and demanded that till the creation of the new province one of the posts should be given to a Pashtoon" (Kasi, July 1, 2009). He blamed Yahya Khan for merging the area of Sibi to Zhob into Balochistan and "turning a majority into a minority," creating problems for local people. Moreover, he noted that "there were political movements in Punjab, NWFP, and Sindh for Saraiki, Pothwar,and Mohajir provincies and there was no harm if the PQT demanded that Balochistan be divided for the creation of a Pashtoon province" (Kasi, 2009). This last statement spells out the de jure quasi-state logic: a minority could be turned into a majority by redrawing jurisdictions, and examples set by other de jure quasi-state actors made this a reasonable move.

As one who claims the leadership mantle in the effort to obtain the new province, Rafiq Pashtoon is well-positioned to gain high office if the province is in fact created. In an effort by Balochistan's provincial leaders to defuse this secessionist posture, they may try to coopt key figures by offering them governance posts. Rafiq Pashtoon's quote hints at this possibility, when he pointed out that key government posts are too concentrated in Balochi hands. From a political survival perspective, such a posture promises the challenger two possible political offices: leadership in a new jurisdiction, or a compromise-based high office in the existing jurisdiction. The danger to challengers is repression, but the proliferating appeals for new jurisdictions suggest that existing repression (or threatened future repression) is not a sufficient deterrent. Further examples can be found in appeals from Saraiki-speaking areas as well the Northern Areas.

Challengers in a weak polity 145

Saraiki ethno-nationalism

Saraiki speakers (a language related to Sindhi) reside primarily in the Punjab. In the 1981 Census, Saraiki was listed as a separate language (rather than a dialect of Sindhi) for the first time.

> As a result of this, Punjabis, for the first time, were shown to be less than the majority of the present Pakistan's population (48.2 per cent). Seraiki was reported to be the language of 9.8 per cent of Pakistan's and 14.9 per cent of Punjab's households. Seraiki self-identification has grown amongst the intelligentsia, and political mobilization on the basis of ethnic identification is attempted during the elections and at other times, although without much popular response at this stage. Although the census numbers are quite disappointing for the advocates of a Seraiki province who claim themselves to be the largest—even the majority—linguistic group in Pakistan, they are large enough to be considered the fourth largest community after Punjabis, Pushtoons, and Sindhis.
>
> (Ahmed, 2002: 26)

The Saraiki Qaumi Movement (Saraiki National Movement) was formed in October, 1989, and called for a new Saraiki province drawn from the Bahawalpur, Multan, Dera Ghazi Khan, Dera Ismail Khan, and Jhang (Talbot, 2005: 302). The Saraiki Qaumi Movement undermined Nawaz Sharif's Punjabi stance, by demonstrating that Punjab was not single-voiced (Talbot, 2005: 302). By the mid-1990s, the Saraiki Suba Mahaz (Movement for a Saraiki Province) was calling for a Saraika Suba, a Saraiki-speakers' province (Talbot, 2005: 16).

A Saraiki speaking semi-literate rural villager who had migrated to Karachi provided some insight into the push for a Saraiki province (Conversation with Saraiki speaker, July 2009). He believed that Saraiki speakers deserved their own province, just as there was a Sindhi or Balochi province. The Punjab government had done relatively little for the Saraiki people; it had taken them 60 years to build a road to his village. Perhaps a separate Saraiki province would mean more development funds for infrastructure and textile manufacturing. Around his village, there were some large landholdings and some smaller ones. There was a family of "makhdooms" (landlords) who were extremely powerful. They had several brothers, each one representing a different party or faction. If one did not have assembly seats, the other would; they alternated in power within the same family. No one, he said, can say a word against them because they are powerful. The situation under the *chaudhries* in Punjab, or at least the ones he was familiar with in southern Punjab, was better than life under the *waderas* of Sind, where the landlords could kidnap someone's daughter and assault her without repercussion.

The Saraiki speaker described a *tanzeem* in the 1990s that was active in agitating for a Saraiki province. There was a woman organizer and leader named Shahida who used to take people in buses for gatherings, sometimes picking up Saraiki speakers from as far away as Karachi. She would pay for the transport and related

146 *Political survival in Pakistan*

costs, as well as payments to individual participants, totaling up to *lakhs* (several hundred thousand) rupees. The argument made to the Saraiki-speaking ethnic affinity group members was that the central government paid attention and distributed funds to Punjab and to Karachi, but overlooked the people in between. Obtaining a Saraiki province would be beneficial to Saraiki speakers because it would bring development funds to their region. The Saraiki speaker believed that it was in Shahida's interest to see a new province formed because she would be well-placed to become its chief minister or hold some other high post, and reap *crores* (tens of millions) of rupees (Conversation with Saraiki speaker, July 2009).

This conversation captured a savvy strategic assessment by an individual with a Saraiki ethnic affinity. He recognized that if a Saraiki province was created, the political organizer who had funded the drive would earn windfall wealth (presumably from corrupt kickbacks and perks) but nevertheless believed that a Saraiki province would mean more development funds for his region. Moreover, activism was enabled because someone was willing to pay him and other individuals to congregate and publicly agitate for a political goal. A political survival perspective might see this autonomist drive as a bargaining chip or a posture by a challenger; in return for defusing the agitation, the politician might accept a lucrative ministership with the Punjab provincial government. If excluded from such a post, then obtaining a separate province would position her for provincial leadership, and with it, more wealth and power.

Following back-and-forth opinion-editorial columns on creating new provinces, Maria Malik from Ahmedpur East presented a narrative supporting autonomy for Bahawalpur (in a letter to the editor, *Dawn*, June 20, 2009: 6). Bahawalpur was one of the largest states in British India, and was ruled by Sir Sadiq Mohammad Khan Abbassi V, who acceded to Pakistan in 1947 on the condition that there would be no internal interference in Bahawalpur's affairs. On October 14, 1955, Bahawalpur was merged into the new province of "West Pakistan" under the One Unit Scheme. Pakistan "stipulated that the princely state would revert to its original status if the One Unit was dissolved" (Malik, 2009). But this promise was not kept. Shehzada Manoor-ur-Rashid Abbassi, Makhdoom Noor Mohammad Hashmi, and Chaudhry Farzand Ali led a movement for Bahawalpur's independence, but their efforts were suppressed. Maria Malik claims that the amir of Bahawalpur remains authoritative in people's hearts; his supported candidate in the 2008 election beat the candidates supported by Tariq Bashir Cheema, a powerful nazim.

Riaz Hussain Pirzada, a legislator from Bahawalpur, described the basis for an autonomy claim as follows:

> Bahawalpur existed as a province before the Partition. It enjoyed the status of a state after Pakistan came into being, but it was made part of the Punjab rather than giving it the status of a province. This was sheer injustice with the people of Bahawalpur. It still retains its constitutional status, and to make it a province will require a simple notification supported by a two-thirds majority in the national Assembly.
>
> (Tariq, 2009)

Challengers in a weak polity 147

This view may be overly optimistic about Bahawalpur's chances to become the fifth province, not least because a two-thirds majority in the National Assembly is required. Any move to create another province will surely be accompanied by intense agitation from other aspirants to provincial status. Pirzada went on to argue that creating other provinces (such as a Saraiki province next door) was an enemy plot against Pakistan.

A political survival speculative interpretation would argue that the strategic possibility that another unit might be created opens political opportunities. Well-placed individuals may wish to leverage their existing positions into a bid for leadership of the new entity—particularly if that leadership brings more resources and more decision-making autonomy. At the same time, it makes sense to reject similar calls by rivals: each additional autonomous unit will reduce the space one's own unit enjoys, particularly if there is an overlapping jurisdiction in question.

Northern areas

Pakistan includes "micro-nations" (Cohen, 2004: 222). The Northern Areas Thinkers' Forum "advocates the formation of two independent states in the northwest region of the subcontinent" (Cohen, 2004: 222). Once belonging to the Jammu Kashmir princely state, Gilgit-Baltistan now has 2 million people (Ahmed, 2009). A secessionist or autonomist narrative may be found in the perspective articulated by Abbas Ali (*Dawn*, July 26, 2009). According to Ali, on July 31, 1947, the British left Gilgit Agency; on October 27, 1947, "the people of Gilgit Baltistan defeated the forces of Gansara Singh (Dogra Raj) and achieved independence to celebrate their own 'Yaum-e-Azadi' [Day of Independence] on November 1 and founded a new country 'Islamic Republic of Gilgit'."; "the people of Gilgit-Baltistan" wanted to join Pakistan, and on November 16, 1947, "Pakistan established its administration in the area" (Ali, 2009).

In a familiar pattern, local strongmen were used to ensure stability. "The Pakistani administration first ruled through the local Mirs and Rajas but when people turned against them the process of reforms began under Zulfikar Ali Bhutto regime, which did away with oppressive systems of Begar, Hukumi Kharid, Rajigi, ending Miri systems and restoring people's human rights" (Ali, 2009). These powerful intermediaries were swept aside. According to Abbas Ali, these 1974 reforms left Gilgit Baltistan on "the verge of becoming a fifth province," but the process was stopped by General Zia ul-Haq's coup. Since martial law ended, a movement for its recognition as a province has begun again. An elected "Northern Areas Legislative Assembly" advises the federal government but has "no authority to change laws or raise and spend revenue" (Ali, 2009). Thus, the Gilgit-Baltistan autonomists aspire to gain the power to extract and distribute resources, a key state-like function according to Charles Tilly and other theorists described in Chapter 1.

In Abbas Ali's narrative, people sought independence from Dogra Raj because they desired "self-governance," and this same goal is now alienating them from Pakistan. A specific grievance is the belief that local recruits into the Pakistani armed forces have sacrificed their lives, and the region in return received "nothing

148 *Political survival in Pakistan*

other than repression and deprivation of fundamental human rights." With the post-Musharraf civilian government, there is further talk about a constitutional package; there are high expectations. Ali expresses the view that "true political, legislative and administrative power should be transferred to the people of Gilgit-Baltistan [...] It is in the interest of both Pakistan and the people of Gilgit-Baltistan to immediately give the rights of self-rule to the people of this area, establish an assembly, reform the administration and justice departments where the elected Assembly of the Gilgit-Baltistan should be the supreme authority. This assembly should be responsible for all legislative and executive matters of the area, except currency, foreign affairs and defence" (Ali, July 26, 2009). Thus, Ali's narrative concludes with a plea for autonomy, while suggesting that if Pakistan is unwilling to devolve powers, there might be a push for all-out secession. Ali's narrative is based on claims about "the people of Gilgit-Baltistan." The Balawaristan National Party's Nawaz Khan Naji warned that a "Balochistan-like" situation would arise if Islamabad followed old colonial policies (Ahmed, 2009).

Sectarian conflict has been rising and nationalism is getting stronger in Gilgit Baltistan; "[t]he rhetoric of Muslim unity is no longer in vogue" (Ali, July 26, 2009). In the 1970s, there were Hanafi *madrasas* built there to counter Aga Khani influence (The Aga Khan heads the Ismailis, an Islamic sect) (Interview with former civil servant, 2003). There are Aga Khanis in Hunza; some have migrated to Karachi and work at the Aga Khan University Hospital. Some observers suspect that the press for autonomy will receive support from the Aga Khan; one allegation is that Z.A. Bhutto negotiated a possible land sale in the region to the Aga Khan (Interviews, 2008). A common conspiracy theory is that the Aga Khanis will try to establish a state in this area. Suspicions about an Ismaili state in the northern areas are high because people recognize that an ethnically distinct, disenfranchised area that has a clear different sectarian identity is a natural candidate for splitting away. In particular, when this coincides with a well-funded political dynasty with future ambitions, it seems a likely candidate. Whether accurate or not, the fact that informed Pakistanis perceive this to be the case shows a recognition that there are political opportunities for autonomy or secession to be pursued.

Conclusion

The Pakistani state project has been eroded and directly attacked by challengers using both de jure and de facto quasi-state strategies. This has been driven by political survival pursuits combined with the political opportunities presented by a weak state. Challengers who are unable to obtain national office, or choose not to seek national office, can seek to gerrymander the polity in a way that provides them with an autonomous jurisdiction. A purely de jure strategy seeks to reshape the polity and change the rules of the game, but does not in itself undermine the state's efforts to monopolize the means of violence. The de facto quasi-state strategy, however, threatens further breakdown in the rule of law and civil war in some cases. The Taliban represent an enormously destabilizing de facto and de jure challenge; their war-making capacity includes fearsome, destructive tactics such as suicide

Challengers in a weak polity   149

bombings, and they have shown an ability to resist and humiliate the Pakistan army in its attempts to wrest control.

There are complex and sometimes contradictory ways in which quasi-state leaders relate to the central state apparatus. Successful quasi-state leaders need tacit or explicit military support, military indifference, or enough war-making capacity to resist the military. The Taliban were at various times sponsored, accepted, or tolerated possibly by those with ideological affinities in central state organizations, and likely also because they were originally seen as a means to extend influence into Afghanistan and further into Central Asia (Remarks by former diplomatic official and conversations, 2009). Later, they became a bargaining chip in Pakistan's appeal for resources as a frontline state in the "global war on terror," and continue to offer a justification for the continuing priority the military receives in national government spending.

A key question is whether pursuing de jure quasi-states may in the long-term provide for a healthy and resilient polity, if incorporated through authentic devolution. Some note that resistance to Pakistan was embedded since the referendums that led to the country's creation; any political opening would provide secessionist groups to vie for their original goals and with it to undermine the central state (Interview with S.M. Fazal, 2009). But repression risks more de facto quasi-states: it risks a dysfunctional polity where the writ of state and rule of law is further eroded amid, violent confrontations, and potential civil wars.

A common thread among state leaders has been the effort was to equate "Islam" with the central government leadership in a quest for unity, or to borrow legitimacy by religious appeals through symbolic gestures. Ayub's reversion to an "Islamic Republic"; Z.A. Bhutto's move against the Ahmedi sect and support for key elements in the Nizam-e-Mustafa platform, Zia ul-Haq's Hudood Ordinances (and later, in Nawaz Sharif's championing of the Shariat bill, Benazir Bhutto's support for the Taliban, as well as Pervez Musharraf's "Enlightened Moderation") may broadly fit this mold. Each sought to retain legitimacy, to coopt or discredit Islamist challengers, and to promote Islamic unity against autonomists or secessionists, and thereby pursue political survival.

Yet the Pakistani experience suggests that appeals to religion are not limited to state leaders, nor are they sufficient to deter quasi-state efforts. In particular forms they may even fuel quasi-state strategies. An early exemplar was Jinnah as a challenger in British India; the Muslim League used the slogan was "Islam in danger," suggesting that a Hindu-dominated united India was a threat to Muslims' well-being. Quasi-state actors have managed to use Islam or appeals to Islam as ways to signal to affinity group members; some examples are described in the next chapter. More broadly, the next chapter considers the continuing role that quasi-states play in Pakistan as a mutually reinforcing process with ongoing governance failures and persistently poor fiscal sociology. This three-way relationship is not inescapable. Tax reform, land reform, and devolution may happen, but are unlikely to do so without significant shifts in political survival opportunities and constraints.

5 Quasi-states, extraction, and governance

The period after Zia ul-Haq's death in 1988 saw formal civilian rule for a decade, but no government completed its elected term. Benazir Bhutto and Nawaz Sharif both held office as prime minister twice; each government was dismissed, and caretaker governments were in charge in the interim until General Pervez Musharraf's coup against Nawaz Sharif in late 2000. The efforts undertaken by caretaker governments bolster the thesis that political survival pressures have perpetuated the above cycle. Caretaker governments have a brief time in office only, without prospects for retaining a seat in the long term. Consequently, caretaker prime ministers do not have the same strategic need to preserve a winning coalition. Major income tax changes, particularly in the agricultural income tax area, have been attempted by a caretaker PM rather than a "regular" officeholder. This provides some evidence supporting the thesis that political survival conditions have conditioned extraction choices by incumbents. Yet caretaker governments, by their limited powers and short-term expiry, are unable to fully enforce and sustain their decisions. As the debt-servicing burden has grown and high military expenditures have continued, dysfunction in the polity has grown.

A complex three-sided relationship, propelled by political survival needs, has crystallized. Poor extraction keeps the state weak, and governance poor. Quasi-states persist because the state is weak and governance is bad. Quasi-states continue to keep large segments of the political economy removed from the formal legal apparatus; they contribute to keeping extraction poor and this keeps governance poor. The relationships are interdependent and simultaneous: because governance is poor, extraction is poor. Because extraction is poor, quasi-states become de facto extractors. Landlords are often quasi-states; mafias are quasi-states; quasi-states form "no-go areas" for the formal government; quasi-states resist the writ of state; quasi-states mean an informal economy. This cycle is perpetuated by mechanisms traceable to political survival pressures.

The diagram below summarizes these relationships:

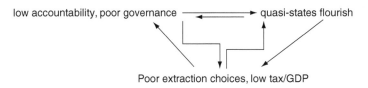

Diagram 5.1 A three-sided relationship

The arrows should be understood as pointing to reciprocal, reinforcing processes rather than a monotonic cause-and-effect sequence. As the political survival mechanism operates in one period, structural conditions and patterns for later periods are put into place.

State weakness is perpetuated through this cycle, which involves a non-developmental fiscal path due to political survival-driven extraction choices. Another challenge to effective state policy-making and policy implementation comes from quasi-states, which are alternative implicit or explicit ways to adjudicate conflicts and to determine who gets what, when, and how. Importantly, quasi-states need not directly politically challenge a given government. Instead, they can be junior partners to a particular government. In the longer term, however, such partnering, when it is not explicitly formalized into polity rules, can undermine the writ of state, particularly when a conflict arises between an incumbent's policy goals and the quasi-state leadership.

In order to function, quasi-state organizations and their leaders require resources, and this requires strategic choices about extraction. The available choices resemble the choices available to incumbent leaders at the state level. They can seek to appropriate resources from their constituents. They can seek to obtain resources externally. Money creation or seigneurage options are generally not available to quasi-state leaders because they do not issue their own currencies. It is notable, however, that some autonomist demands have sought the right to issue currency (e.g. Sheikh Mujib ur-Rehman in Bangladesh).

For external actors, financing a quasi-state actor is a path to extending influence, countering political enemies, and shaping outcomes. External financing can become the basis for patron-client relations, a phenomenon replicating at the quasi-state level what Pakistan does at the state level in seeking and accepting foreign aid. Distant patrons for quasi-state actors are not necessarily foreign actors; there is evidence that funding has in some cases come from domestic intelligence agencies. Interviews with various politically engaged Karachi residents reveal numerous conspiracy theories regarding the "agency-wallay" (covert operatives from unnamed intelligence agencies). Where quasi-states rely primarily on an external financing source, they continue to also be narrowly based, and consequently not as oriented to providing public goods within their perceived constituency, territory, or polity. Rather, the quasi-state incumbent leader's political survival is predicated on retaining the patron. The extent to which quasi-state

152 *Political survival in Pakistan*

leadership rests on a narrow coalition may well determine how much quasi-state behavior is "predatory" rather than "developmental." The incumbent leader in a quasi-state that draws its resources from a broad cross-section of its base is likely to be more oriented to providing broadly dispersed goods. In those quasi-states where most extraction comes from resource capture or from external assistance, the leader is more likely to provide private goods to a narrower winning coalition.

Incumbents generally seek to reduce provincial autonomy while challengers seek to increase provincial autonomy. This is unsurprising from a political survival perspective because an incumbent will generally try to reduce political space and opportunity or prevent challengers from consolidating their own support coalitions, and maximize their own control over resources and influence. Challengers will try to circumscribe the authority enjoyed by the incumbent at the political center as a way to undermine the incumbent's winning coalition, and as a way to nurture leadership within their provincial zone, both as a possible quasi-state and as a springboard from which to pursue higher national office. This may be seen in the behavior political parties display when in office compared to when they are in the opposition; in opposition, political parties generally seek more provincial autonomy.

"Governance" is used in diverse ways and by distinct literatures. This study has proceeded from the fiscal sociology literature, which argues that broad, direct tax-based extraction approaches are associated with more effective and accountable governance processes.

National leadership after Zia ul-Haq

In assessing national governance after Zia ul-Haq, the president, PM, and army chief are often depicted as important actors whose political machinations drove major national developments and changes in high office. Since 1988, there have been short-lived civilian governments, twice in Benazir Bhutto's PPP and twice with Nawaz Sharif's PML. These "failed to sustain themselves in power, not least because of the unresolved tensions between the army leadership, the president, and the party leaders" (Taylor, 2005: 225). Political instability has reduced the impact that development programs might have had. Broadly based supporting coalitions might have been a countervailing force to powerful individuals such as the president or the chief of army staff. A political survival-based interpretation would be that the prime ministers' tenures were short partly because they could not develop and sustain such broad-based support.

The post-Zia ul-Haq period saw Benazir Bhutto and Nawaz Sharif each hold the elected prime minister office twice, with caretaker prime ministers interspersed for brief periods. Ayub Khan, Z.A. Bhutto, and Zia ul-Haq, the leaders examined in Chapter 3, had significant ideological differences on questions regarding economic policy. Since 1988, there has been a "fundamental consensus on basic economic polices, but a lack of continuity of programmes and policies" (Husain, 2000: 35). Fiscal reform remains a high stated priority for all regimes that followed Zia ul-Haq, and they inherited a difficult macroeconomic situation. Significant spending cut-backs were needed, according to a structural adjustment program developed in

Quasi-states, extraction, and governance 153

collaboration with international financing institutions. Zia ul-Haq's regime had relied on domestic debt to cover large budget deficits. This had delayed the need to raise taxes, but squeezed out investment. Inflationary monetary strategies became one recourse, and average annual inflation in the first half of the 1990s rose to 12 percent, compared to the 1980s average rate of 7 percent (Noman, 1997: 197). Foreign and domestic debt levels rose, particularly as more commercial loans were tapped. Commercial loans are shorter in duration and more expensive, and bring a potential future cost in affecting the country's credit rating. International borrowing, seen as a "boon" in Pakistan's earlier period, has encountered some vocal criticism.

Despite broad ideological agreement on economic issues among competing leaders after Zia ul-Haq, policy continuity has not been achieved. A highly placed former finance official asserted that continuing with reforms for more than two years would have brought economic benefits with them that would have been difficult for any president to dismiss. However, a myopic "survival instinct" has "superseded the fiscal instinct" and scuttled the needed fiscal reforms (Interview with former finance official, 2001). One factor has been eagerness by new leaders to employ or reinstate favored supporters in state administrative positions. That turn-over, combined with the belief that the leader will not last long in office, encourage rent-seeking and predatory behavior for personal enrichment. According to one revealing report, an incumbent prime minister's appointees sought exorbitant bribes under their explicitly acknowledged belief that they had several months to take whatever they could appropriate before the incumbent was forced out (Conversation with security officer, 2009).

Brief tenure, however, cannot be the full explanation for governance failures. Ayub Khan and Zia ul-Haq each held power for over a decade, and Z. A. Bhutto saw what amounted to a full term in office. Musharraf's regime enjoyed nearly eight years in power. He started his tenure by asserting that domestic extraction had to be increased. As the following quote from *Dawn*, a national circulation Pakistani newspaper, suggests there also remains an official perception that Pakistani performance in domestic extraction is poor and must be improved:

> Pakistan's military ruler General Pervez Musharraf today said the country's survival lies in everyone paying tax. "For the country to be sovereign, everyone has to pay the tax due from him," he said, announcing that a survey would be launched on Saturday in 13 big cities of the country to nab tax evaders and to document the economy. "I will not allow any hurdle in our way," he warned the traders' community which is resisting the survey. Musharraf said 3,000 corrupt and inefficient tax collectors are being dismissed. The figure represents 10 per cent of the total strength of the tax department. "It is shameful that only 1.2 million people in our population of 140 million people pay taxes," the general said.
>
> (*Dawn*, May 25, 2000)

General Musharraf sought "nation building" through "national reconstruction." In practice, this meant plans to broaden the tax base and increase tax revenue, in addition to cutting expenditures by reducing civil service jobs. These plans were

154 *Political survival in Pakistan*

weakened and diluted, and eventually did not dramatically change the tax revenue situation; the tax/GDP ratio in Pakistan has actually declined. The simplest explanation for this is that the large aid infusions received for cooperation with the "War on Terror" made aggressive domestic taxation measures less urgent. Musharraf had the revenues needed for political survival without a radical shift in domestic tax extraction.

American aid to Pakistan reduced after the Soviet Union withdrew from Afghanistan in the late 1980s. Worker remittances to Pakistan also reduced due to instability occasioned by Saddam Hussein's invasion of Kuwait. Khan (1997: 212) describes the 1991 Gulf War as one of a set of international conditions that contributed to slowing growth in Pakistan. Persistent high budget deficits have meant that both domestic and external debt have increased substantially in the 1990s (Khan, 1997: 229). Today, most Pakistani national spending goes to debt servicing and military expenditures. This picture does not substantially differ from Pakistan's early days except that then the debt burden was less. Outstanding foreign debt has increased dramatically so that by 1993 it was two and half times its 1977 level (Stewart and Sturgis, 1995: 55). Cutting spending is one way to reduce the fiscal deficit. But security commitments make cutting military spending difficult. Moreover, development spending is desperately needed. Ishrat Husain argues that cutting development expenditures is the wrong way to reduce fiscal deficits (Husain, 2003: 207). Consequently, the need to raise adequate domestic resources is felt even more strongly. The national savings rate remains low, adding to the difficulty in locating resources.

Conditionality in lending has brought new constraints to Pakistani political leaders. Observers have noted (sometimes indignantly) the expanded influence of the IMF and World Bank on domestic economic policies in this period. One Pakistani economist describes the period from 1988 onwards as the "era of structural adjustment" and writes that "an examination of World Bank and IMF documents since 1988 reveals that almost every decision of any consequence taken by the various governments that have been in power has been predetermined by the two Washington agencies, and that Pakistan has merely followed diktat" (Zaidi, 1999: 7). Structural adjustment programs in Pakistan have generally set targets for a lower fiscal deficit (Zaidi, 1999: 7). A former civil servant in finance asserted that lending from international financial institutions became more dictation than negotiation, with decreasing decision space left to domestic leaders; the lender justification for stringent conditions was that the country's past record had eroded the government's credibility (Interview, 2001).

Privatization, a common approach associated with structural adjustment, offers one solution to fiscal deficits, but there is a strong perception that the process has delivered more private than public goods. Privatizations and nationalizations, variant attempts to restructure state-society relations, have both provided rich opportunities for side payments, rent-seeking, and patronage, undermining their public purpose. Nationalizations cannot be called a tax or extraction increase for the government, although they were clearly attempts to control social resources. As seen in Chapter 3, nationalizations undermined efficiency and became private goods for the favored and well connected. Privatizations also are not necessarily "withdrawals of the state" or deficit-reducing reforms, as much as patronage favors

Quasi-states, extraction, and governance 155

to preferred clients and opportunities for rent-seeking. Rather than encouraging competition and market efficiencies, they further complicate the shadowy private goods that thrive under opaque and unaccountable conditions.

Observers noted that privatization sales often had "open tenders" inviting public bids, but the reality is that political considerations played a role in determining who actually won the bidding process. For example, under Benazir Bhutto privatization, electricity generation agreements were made at a higher rate than international market production, for "Mr. 10 per cent"'s commission (Mr 10 Percent was a popular nickname given to Benazir Bhutto's husband, Asif Zardari, for his alleged kickbacks from government contracts). As a result, electricity became more expensive, and this multiplied through the economy with increased inflation. Electricity distribution remains a major source for public discontent. The unannounced "load-shedding" episodes (partial blackouts) that take place on a near-daily basis in Karachi are disruptive to businesses, schools, and residents, and have sparked riots. To many, dissatisfactory electric distribution is due to rent-seeking behavior by deal-makers at high levels; some observers accuse leaders of betraying the public good and preferring suboptimal options in electricity generation because there are greater opportunities for kickbacks (Various interviews, 2009).

A notable example from the early 1990s is the sale of Zeelpak Cement Factory, one of the few profitable state-owned enterprises. The tender advertisements did not note the minimum required bid nor the present value of the Zeelpak factory. One retired civil servant observed that the winning bid was successful because the bidder exerted political pressure on the prime minister through connections (Conversation with retired civil servant, 2008). A more recent example is the attempted steel mill privatization by PM Shaukat Aziz. Through a proxy company, he made a low offer for the steel mill. Public protest followed. Eventually Chief Justice Iftikhar Chaudhry and the High Court disallowed the sale. Also under Shaukat Aziz and the Musharraf regime, bank privatizations followed a similar path. The higher bidders were not awarded the company; rather, the preferred buyers were selected based on informal, personal ties.

Alternating Prime Ministers: Benazir Bhutto, Nawaz Sharif

The general tendency in South Asia is for a powerful prime minister to consolidate executive authority and use ministerships as patronage (Sobhan, 2002). To many observers, the alternating civilian governments after Zia ul-Haq were ineffective and corrupt, and punctured democratic idealism. A business professional asserted that state-owned enterprises like Pakistan State Oil and Sui Gas become patronage bonanzas for new elected governments. Benazir apparently packed Sui Gas (a major government corporation) and other state-owned enterprises with thousands of her favored hires, irrespective of merit—and Nawaz Sharif's government, when it came in, dismissed them all. When Benazir was restored, she rehired all the dismissed workers, and also arranged for them to receive arrears—compensating back pay stretching back for two years. One leader was rumored to receive 100,000

156 *Political survival in Pakistan*

rupees delivered in cash daily with no record, suggesting bribery and side payments (Conversation with business professional, April 2008).

Rochi Ram, a longtime observer of Pakistani politics, Sind High Court advocate, and Pakistan Human Rights Commission member, asserted that both Nawaz Sharif and Benazir Bhutto failed as leaders because they aimed low, seeking private goods and enrichment. They were more interested in business licenses and small handouts rather than the big vision for the country (a version of private goods versus public interest). He expressed disappointment that a grand opportunity for developing the country and working for the public good had been sold out for a petty price. The civilian leaders did not recognize the pragmatic need to cooperate and compromise with other powers such as the president as a way to invest in institutional durability (Interview with Rochi Ram, July 2009).

Civilian prime ministers, in office after more than a decade of military rule, and having the military-supported "judicial assassination" of previous Prime Minister Z.A. Bhutto fresh in memory, were well aware that they needed to retain military support. It is commonly perceived that key military backing helped Benazir. "Benazir enjoyed the support of the new army high command, and it was General Aslam Baig who sheltered her from the opposition and neutralized the impact of their attacks on her government" (Ziring, 1997: 515). Moreover, there was additional pressure on civilian political leaders: they were obliged to reward supporters who had struggled to end military rule. Sharing the common perception that corruption has been higher in civilian regimes, Kunwar Idris lists examples from his time as Sindh chief secretary under Benazir Bhutto's government: party functionaries demanded expensive land in a posh Karachi area as a handout, and junior engineers and finance professionals sought to leapfrog their careers to top-tier leadership positions. It was not easy to resist such pressures, and Benazir Bhutto "could not bring herself round to tell a youth who had set himself on fire for her sake that she couldn't give him the job he wanted" (Idris, July 26, 2009).

Political organization leaders at different levels also had an acute awareness about a covert military role. Perhaps the most frequently mentioned military agency involved in local political machinations is Inter-Services Intelligence. Hamid Gul, appointed ISI chief by Zia ul-Haq in 1987, "had developed the ISI into a formidable institution that was relatively free of [Chief of Army Staff] Baig's authority" (Ziring, 1997: 517). According to Ifitkhar Malik's *State and Civil Society in Pakistan*, "the ISI has destabilized Pakistan's fragile democracy through its unchecked interventions, unaccounted for funds and uncompromising rivalry with other intelligence-gathering agencies" (cited by Talbot, 2005: 269). The "agency" hands are seen everywhere as manipulative actors intervening in or undermining movement, community, and party unity, and often encouraging factionalism. This belief was expressed by interviewees from varied backgrounds (Various interviews, 2008, 2009).[1]

Rumors connected Hamid Gul, the ISI head, with Nawaz Sharif; they "intimated that both had consorted with the President in a maneuver aimed at undermining the Benazir-Baig relationship" (Ziring, 1997: 517). A political survival interpretation would be that if this was true, it demonstrated again how central the military was to

Quasi-states, extraction, and governance   157

any winning coalition or successful challenge for national office. Like Prime Minister Muhammad Khan Junejo before her, Prime Minister Benazir Bhutto sought support from the Civil Intelligence Bureau to counterbalance the ISI. Benazir Bhutto replaced Hamid Abidi as head of the Intelligence Bureau; apparently, his Muhajir background led to suspicion that he had pro-MQM leanings. When Benazir Bhutto was removed from office, Hamid Abidi was restored to his position at the Intelligence Bureau (Interview with Hamid Abidi, July 2009).

The MQM and ANP broke from the PPP after an army crackdown in Karachi. The opposition to the PPP filed a no-confidence motion calling for a vote on November 1, 1989. It appeared to observers that President Ghulam Ishaq Khan was supporting the motion. Ghulam Ishaq Khan, president after Zia ul-Haq and a powerful figure, was a career civil servant who had played numerous roles throughout Pakistan's history (Ziring, 1997: 505–510). Under Zulfikar Ali Bhutto, the Holders of Representative Offices (Prevention of Misconduct) Act was enacted (Ziring, 1997: 525). Ghulam Ishaq Khan used this through a caretaker government to pursue charges against Benazir. "Benazir was charged with having allotted hundreds of costly residential plots in Islamabad to PPP stalwarts at 'throwaway prices'. She also was accused of using gifts and bribes to win the support of members of the provincial assemblies" (Ziring, 1997: 525). Her husband, Asif Ali Zardari, was arrested for kidnapping and extortion and targeted by several investigations, alleging that he used his connections and office to enhance his personal wealth. (Benazir had appointed her mother minister (without portfolio) and father-in-law to a government office.)

A key fracture took place when a split emerged between Benazir and Mirza Aslam Baig, the army commander and her key supporter, after Karachi's riots in February 1990 had weakened Benazir's administration:

> Hundreds of demonstrators were arrested, but the movements that they represented continued to press their demands, while terrorist bombings and the deaths of innocent bus travelers in Karachi caused Benazir to cancel a trip to the Middle East. Holding fast to her diminishing authority, differences over tactics as well as strategy emerged between the Prime Minister and her Army Commander. Baig wanted a free hand in Sindh. He also wanted the opportunity to strike at PPP militants who, along with their counterparts in the MQM, prevented the restoration of law and order. Benazir refused to grant Baig his request, however, and their once solid relationship began to fall apart when the General was forced to acknowledge the uneasiness among his senior officers.
>
> (Ziring, 1997: 523)

Shortly thereafter, Ghulam Ishaq Khan invoked the Eight Amendment (Article 58 2(b)) to dismiss Benazir's government and dissolve the National and Provincial Assemblies.

Benazir Bhutto was vulnerable to challengers from Islamists because her gender was a liability; many Islamists believed that national leadership should be restricted to men. (The Jamaat-e-Islami supported Fatima Jinnah's campaign in the 1960s,

158   *Political survival in Pakistan*

however.) Cohen expresses a common view about Benazir Bhutto and her father: "Both Bhuttos, personally very secular, cynically used Islamic causes for short-term political gain" (Cohen, 2004: 174).

Nawaz Sharif's family fortune was based on the Ittefaq Foundry. Zulfiqar Ali Bhutto had nationalized the Ittefaq Foundry, the "heart of the Sharif family's industrial empire" (Cohen, 2004: 146). This was one root from which Nawaz Sharif's political stance against the PPP emerged. Nawaz was seen as Zia ul-Haq's protégé. He was finance minister in Punjab during the Zia ul-Haq era and later became chief minister of Punjab. As someone from a business rather than a "feudal" background, Nawaz Sharif was somewhat unusual.

One interpretation is that Nawaz Sharif belonged to Zia ul-Haq's winning coalition. Alternatively (and not necessarily excluding membership in the winning coalition), Nawaz Sharif could be seen as a challenger supported by Zia ul-Haq to offset the PPP threat. In either case, he affiliated with the "Establishment." It is widely asserted that the Islami Jamhuri Ittedad (the Islamic Democratic Alliance, which included Nawaz Sharif and the Jamaat-e-Islami) was sponsored by the ISI to keep the PPP in check (e.g. Cohen, 2004: 178). This relationship has grown significantly more complex and contradictory since that time, more so with the recent showdown between Nawaz Sharif and Musharraf.

Benazir Bhutto had come into office in 1988 (her first term). As Punjab chief minister, Nawaz Sharif was in the opposition against the central government, and a challenger seeking national office. He played up Punjabi national symbols: the logo used for the Bank of Punjab that he inaugurated on November 15, 1989, was taken from Maharaja Ranjit Singh, the last ruler of independent Punjab (and a Sikh). At the end of that November, the Punjab revenue minister announced a planned Punjab television station because "Pakistan Television, under instruction from the Federal Government, was not projecting Punjab's point of view on various issues" (Talbot, 2005: 301–302).

Talbot describes Nawaz Sharif's stance as "wearing the turban of Punjab" (Talbot, 2005: 302). This is an apt phrase, because it touches on the identity politics that Nawaz sought to mobilize. It also shows that the secessionist or quasi-state aspect to provincial politics is not restricted to the small provinces alone. Even if "secessionism" is too strong a claim, it is appropriate to describe an identity-based political confrontation in Punjab that pursued greater autonomy. Nawaz's Islami Jamhoori Ittehad included anti-Sindhi and anti-Indian sentiments (Talbot, 2005: 300).

In her first formal press conference as prime minister, Benazir Bhutto accused Nawaz Sharif and the Islami Jamhoori Ittehad of stealing the Punjab provincial election, and she condemned Nawaz as a separatist, "branding him 'the G.M. Syed of the Punjab' " (Ziring, 1997: 511–512). Benazir had been able to head a coalition government through an alliance with the MQM and the ANP. Of 215 contested seats in the November 1988 election, the PPP had won 92 while the IJI had won 54. Neither had enough votes to form a majority alone.

The leadership in Pakistan's dominant province frustrated Benazir Bhutto. On one level, this resembled the confrontation between Prime Minister Liaquat Ali Khan and Punjab's Mian Mumtaz Daultana, which "had terrible consequences"

Quasi-states, extraction, and governance 159

(Ziring, 1997: 513) for both. Benazir, however, was heir to a political party with a significant mobilization record, and had personal connections with landed gentry; Liaquat Ali Khan did not have a strong personal constituent base, beyond his original close tie to Jinnah.

The October 24, 1990 elections led to a PPP defeat in all the provinces and 105 seats for the IJI in the National Assembly. IJI allies won 50 additional seats in the National Assembly, while the PPP People's Democratic Alliance only received 45. Nawaz Sharif went from his position in Punjab to becoming the prime minister. In his first tenure as prime minister, starting in 1990, Nawaz Sharif declared that his government would be for national reconciliation, inviting other parties to collaborate on common issues (Ziring, 1997: 530). Defections from Nawaz' party alliance opened a point for PPP attacks. The defectors included Jatoi's National People's Party, the MQM, and the Jamaat-e-Islami (Ziring, 1997: 537). The corruption and abuse allegations against the Bank of Credit and Commerce International, as well as the failed Co-operative Societies in the Punjab (where two million people lost their savings) reduced Nawaz Sharif's credibility further (Ziring, 1997: 537–538).

Benazir Bhutto's second tenure as prime minister featured a significant effort at economic reforms, including fiscal reforms. These, however, were not sustained. A former finance official asserted that failure to stabilize gains from earlier reforms was partly responsible for the loss of public support. There was agitation raised by the small traders that responded to sales tax initiatives and joined Nawaz Sharif in opposition. This formed an acute threat to Benazir Bhutto's rule. In his second tenure as prime minister, Nawaz Sharif did start "so-called homegrown fiscal reforms," among which a universally applied General Sales Tax was at the top of the agenda. However, this only repeated a declaration without "serious implementation because of fear [of a political backlash]." A gap emerged between discussions with the IMF on the one hand and with supporters on the other, with the actual actions chosen somewhere in between (Interview with former finance official, 2001).

Nawaz Sharif supported a bill to enshrine Sharia in the Pakistani constitution. Cohen (2004) suggests that this was probably an effort to "outflank" parties on the religious right. "Playing the Islamic card would have enabled him to determine what was 'Islamic,' thus complementing his already formidable executive powers with the sanction of religion" (Cohen, 2004: 173). Prior to the 1999 coup, Nawaz Sharif "appropriated almost absolute powers in the office of the prime minister and, under the guise of a *Sharia* bill, was aspiring to make his powers virtually unassailable" (Sobhan, 2002: 151). This exemplifies the incumbent pursuing political survival by consolidating authority around his person.

In his second tenure as prime minister, Nawaz Sharif also introduced a controversial bill to prevent "floor-crossing" (moves by individual party members to switch sides). Floor-crossing indicates that party organization is weak, and that whoever becomes the leader may suddenly receive band-wagoned support as many National Assembly members try to join the winning coalition. Nawaz Sharif's bill was an attempt to enhance party discipline and his own control over the legislature by legal means. The Fourteenth Amendment, passed on July 1, 1997, amended the constitution by adding Article 63A which

160 *Political survival in Pakistan*

> provided for disqualification of elected members on the grounds of defection and also provided a comprehensive clause to include within the definition of defection: (a) a breach of party discipline; (b) voting contrary to any direction issued by the parliamentary party to which he belongs; and (c) abstention from voting in the House against party policy.
>
> (Zafar, 2000: 6–7)

Disciplinary powers and final authority for procedures against offenders was given to the party head. This anti-defection clause was swiftly appealed amid concerns that it would curb party members' freedom of conscience, was first suspended, and later upheld by the Supreme Court. The leading opinion by Justice Ajmal Mian found that the clause did not clash with basic constitutional features, and stated that the new Article

> will bring stability in the polity of the country and will be instrumental in eradicating cancerous vice of the floor crossing. It is also in consonance with the tenets of Islam and Sunnah as the same enjoined its believers to honor their commitments
>
> (quoted in Zafar, 2000: 8)

S. M. Zafar, a senior advocate of the Supreme Court of Pakistan and former minister of law and parliamentary affairs predicted that the article, if implemented with transparency and sincerity, would promote party stability and "reduce the tendency of changing of changing horses midstream for personal gain rather than a genuine concern on any issue" (Zafar, 2000: 9). The above quote from Justice Ajmal Mian also includes an Islamic rationale for the amendment, suggesting the perceived need to preempt possible "Islamic" dissent. A critical challenge would be to prevent the Article 63A from become a dictatorial instrument used by party heads to silence criticism.

There were other efforts to consolidate executive authority by Prime Minister Nawaz Sharif. He ended the president's Article 58 2 (b) power to dismiss the PM and the Assembly. But Nawaz Sharif's government was removed by a military coup after a dramatic showdown during which Chief of Army Staff General Musharraf's plane was not given permission to land in Karachi. Brigade 111 is notorious because it is well-positioned to detain civilian leaders and take over the federal government's administrative centers as a coup unfolds. The showdown between Musharraf and Nawaz Sharif ended with a familiar move by Brigade 111: displacing Nawaz and permitting Musharraf to launch what he termed his "counter-coup."

Musharraf's rulership strategies

In 2001, Pakistan's Supreme Court ruled that the military could retain power for three years provided that its term in power contributed positively to democratization and development (Sobhan, 2002: 159). In other words, the Supreme Court's

Quasi-states, extraction, and governance   161

action acknowledged the coup's reality and gave it a legal veneer—mildly akin to Justice Muneer's opinion describing Ayub Khan's coup-based military rule as a legitimate condition. Musharraf's first two years saw efforts at significant economic reforms, including fiscal reforms. There was an acknowledgement that agricultural taxation was needed, among other initiatives. These were promising and received support from international financial institutions (Interview with former finance official, 2001). International support may have been more forthcoming once the "War on Terror" created a strategic interest in larger aid packages for Pakistan, and this likely reduced the urgency for politically difficult fiscal reforms.

Musharraf's Referendum, on April 30, 2002, was designed to secure another five years in office before the October 2002 election (as required by the Supreme Court ruling in May 2000, general elections were required within three years of the October 12, 1999 coup) (Talbot, 2005: 398). The referendum was challenged by constitutional petitions, and was seen skeptically by some as "little more than an attempt to cover authoritarianism with the fig-leaf of a popular mandate," and probably an effort to undermine the regime's major opponents (Talbot, 2005: 398). Musharraf's devolution plan is discussed below.

The Council of Defense and National Security institutionalized a formal role for the military in decision-making alongside the elected representatives (Talbot, 2005: 351). This was similar to what Zia ul-Haq had proposed after the martial law regime (Talbot, 2005: 351). "Seen in a longer historical perspective, the CDNS appears to be a continuation of the viceregal tradition which has disastrously emphasized governance over participation; no provincial politicians were included in its membership" (Talbot, 2005: 351–352). Another way to put this is that a state bureaucratic institution—the military—was given a permanent and dominant seat in the government's policy-setting process.

Musharraf issued the Legal Framework Ordinance on August 21, 2002, prior to the parliamentary elections that were scheduled for that year. The executive order set up a National Security Council headed by the president rather than the prime minister, and restored the Article 58 2 (b) presidential power to dismiss the prime minister. Once again, the executive was favored in the tug and pull with legislative powers traceable to Constituent Assembly leader Maulvi Tamizuddin's clash with Governor-General Ghulam Mohammad and previously in Jinnah's actions as Governor General (see Chapter 2 for details). Article 58 2 (b) "negates the very essence of a parliamentary form of government" and "threatens to subvert the democratic process and the broad-based consensus it implies, especially as a besieged president refuses to accede to popular demand for his resignation" (Bashir, 2008: 6). Article 58 2 (b) remains a key point of contention, and presidents are loathe to give up extraordinary influence that comes with the power to dismiss a prime minister and entire Assembly.

After Chief Justice Iftikhar Chaudhry was removed from office by Musharraf, a lawyers' movement in Pakistan agitated for the judiciary to be restored. The movement, portrayed by supporters as a move to bolster the rule of law against unchecked executive power, threatened and undertook a "long march" (in vehicles, mostly). Eventually Musharraf, who had left his army post and become formally a

162 *Political survival in Pakistan*

civilian president, accepted a compromise. To the extent that a decision on the judiciary was made in response to the lawyers' agitation, this civil organization demonstrably increased its weight within the selectorate. Such actions may carry demonstrative value, helping to show that an alternative winning coalition can be created. This raises a question of whether the army (and to a lesser extent, the civil bureaucracy) could one day leave the selectorate, or have their dominant role in winning coalitions eliminated. Conversely, one may ask whether a challenger or incumbent not supported by the army and bureaucracy can obtain or retain power.

Maintaining the military's patriotic image remains a key goal among the senior leadership (Interview with retired military officer, 2009). Moreover, the military oath requires noninterference in politics. Consequently, shaming may be a viable pressure tactic to reduce the army's direct influence in national politics. This might backfire if it is seen as threatening to the army's morale, budget share, or to military businesses; if so, an attempt to shame might only trigger a more heavy-handed military action. In Musharraf's case, one interpretation is that he left office in effect because the new Chief of Army Staff, Pervez Kayani, had signaled a desire to keep the army out of politics. According to this view, the anti-Musharraf agitation alone was not sufficient to elicit these compromises, and the chief of army staff's role was necessary.

Caretaker governments

Caretaker governments have a limited time horizon. Caretaker leaders worry relatively little about their political survival because there is a clear, near-term time limit to their tenure. As a result they have had latitude not enjoyed by other politicians. Caretaker leaders are not constrained by the need to retain a winning coalition, as they cannot retain office. Their transitional, bounded role is difficult to convert into a lasting national leadership role. As a result, caretakers are less concerned with challengers, and also about rewarding a winning coalition. Freed from such constraints, they can undertake politically painful measures that incumbent leaders are reluctant to pursue.

Thus, caretaker leaders represent a partial test for the political survival thesis: they show cases where the usual logic about rewarding a winning coalition is absent. Some seek excessive personal gains, such as a recent caretaker who requested an extravagant, lavish compensation package, including lifetime benefits for himself and his family. Others are accused of implementing foreign donor and International Monetary Fund agendas. Yet others have crossed these red lines in Pakistani politics—most dramatic among these was probably Moeen Qureshi. As is repeatedly asserted, no Pakistani government has ever imposed an agricultural tax (e.g. Cohen, 2004: 143). The exception was Moeen Qureshi's caretaker government, which did impose a temporary agricultural levy.[2]

Arguably, other political actors who recognize that unpopular steps are needed may tacitly support "caretaker" prime ministers. Talbot argues that Moeen Qureshi was accepted by Benazir Bhutto and Nawaz Sharif because there were important economic reforms that had to be made:

Quasi-states, extraction, and governance 163

Qureshi had been accepted as a compromise caretaker leader by both Nawaz Sharif and Benazir Bhutto. However, it was clear from the outset that his major role was not to oversee fresh elections, but rather to introduce major economic reforms under cover of army support. The professional politicians were prepared to accept this turn of events as it absolved them from the responsibility for unpopular measures.

(Talbot, 2005: 330)

Moeen Qureshi's caretaker government released a list of 5000 bank loan defaulters—a "who's who" of powerful and influential figures whose total bad debt was 62 billion rupees. This shed some light on government-supported bank activity, revealing corruption and special privileges for a well-connected favored set. This move toward transparency unveiled what looked like government largesse to political supporters.

Ministries and embassies are often used as patronage opportunities, and are expensive to maintain. Moeen Qureshi's caretaker government closed 15 ministries and ten embassies. His government pursued a structural adjustment program that reflected the "Washington Consensus" policies implemented by the IMF and World Bank. As a "caretaker" prime minister, he was able to undertake such efforts without the backlash fears elected politicians such as Benazir Bhutto and Nawaz Sharif may have had. Qureshi devalued the rupee. Essential commodities rose in price, rousing criticism. Perhaps most strikingly, his government extracted a temporary agricultural levy:

As Pakistan's fiscal system came under growing pressure, the interim government of Moeen Qureshi, for the first time in the nation's history, instituted an agricultural income tax, which was vehemently opposed by the large feudal and land-owning interests. Based on a system that would assess income according to the productive capability of land (PUY), this new tax could bring in some semblance of inter-sectoral equity in tax burden.

(Husain, 2000: 41)

Caretaker Prime Minister Meraj Khalid's economic advisor was Shahid Javed Burki, who tried to raise taxes on agricultural income (Talbot, 2005: 349). Thus, there have been efforts under caretaker governments that are not found in other governments. As political survival constraints are lessened, these caretaker governments, despite their limited mandates and short durations, have room to maneuver and freedom of action not found in other governments.

Administrative capacity and political will

A crucial area in public goods provision is an apparatus for efficient and effective policy implementation. According to the *Logic of Political Survival*, what might be considered technical issues with efficiency are largely treated as deliberate choices by an incumbent seeking to retain a winning coalition:

164 *Political survival in Pakistan*

The leader collects taxes, allocates resources, and produces public and private goods without concern for inefficiencies in provision. If such inefficiencies exist, it is because they are in the leader's interest as a way to reward followers. Special exemptions from taxes and corruption are examples of these inefficiencies. Questions then of how to organize bureaucracy to provide government services most efficiently lie outside our theory, except to the extent that one thinks of efficient organization as itself being a public good.

(Bueno de Mesquita et al., 2003: 74)

Thus, *LOPS* presumes that inefficiencies and exemptions are often intentional rewards for followers. Reorganizing bureaucracy for increased efficiency can be considered a public good. But bringing in transparency, accountability, and feedback mechanisms to improve governance threatens the private benefits that accrue to bureaucrats with discretionary powers. Consequently, these are resisted. The incumbent tendency to use bureaucracy for political favors contributes to ineffectiveness:

By appointing favourites to key positions, ignoring seniority and merit-based promotions, inducting outsiders with little or no expertise or competence, purging civil servants without due legal process, allowing corruption and sycophancy to flourish, discouraging dissenting views, debates and thorough professional analysis of issues and failing to enforce standards of accountability, the political rulers from successive regimes have created a culture of fear, apathy, indifference, inertia and lack of initiative among the bureaucracy.

(Husain, 2003: 154)

In other words, leaders have in practice given out key positions as patronage to winning coalition members. This contributes to a poor bureaucratic apparatus in the long run. Bureaucrats have seen arbitrary retribution after regime changes, and therefore avoid taking initiative.

One retired civil servant believed that when bureaucrats "give options" and "describe consequences" when they make a recommendation, "political" leaders (elected civilians) are more likely to override them. The military, in contrast, is not likely to make "risky moves" and will accept bureaucratic advice (Interview with retired civil servant, 2001). This is an arguable point, as both military and civilian leaders have to some degree intervened in ways that reduce bureaucratic autonomy. The willingness displayed by civilian leaders to override bureaucratic recommendations may also be due to their somewhat broader winning coalition, which gives them a preference for policies that provide goods to their supporters.

In the Pakistani experience, highly placed civil servants have been sometimes minor and at other times major players in the winning coalition. Poor advice can undermine leaders' political survival, and it is arguable that poor and perhaps deliberate counsel led several leaders to make disastrous appointments to high office (for example, Z.A. Bhutto and Nawaz Sharif with Zia ul-Haq and Pervez

Musharraf, respectively). Compared to survey data from five South Asian countries, Pakistanis reported the most corruption in tax and land revenue bureaucracies (Transparency International, 2002).

A key problem for taxation is "scientific" assessment—how to ascertain exactly where taxable income can be found. A second problem is enforcing the law so those who are liable pay the appropriate amount. The apparatus for monitoring and sanctioning is weak.

Pakistan has seen efforts to survey the economy and expand sales and income taxes (Interview, 2000). The effort to broaden the tax base has received a push from various factors, including a rising debt burden and conditional loans, as well as requirements by the World Trade Organization that Pakistan reduce tariffs. These efforts have become notable in the late 1980s and through the 1990s (Interview, 2000). Tariff reduction increased fiscal requirements elsewhere (Interview with former finance official, 2001).

Specific efforts include an attempt to increase transparency and public accountability in the taxation process by standardizing tax rates and creating an office to deal with citizens' complaints (Interview, 2000). Yet the covert financing problem, with its inflationary effects, remains acute:

> The State Bank of Pakistan has advised the government to exercise fiscal responsibility, restrain and restrict direct borrowing from the central bank to finance its expenditures. This is necessary to arrest the spiraling price trend as the deficit financing has a strong direct relationship with inflation.
>
> (Subohi, 2008)

This quote, taken from a 2008 news article, expressed concern about widening fiscal deficits and the central government's continuing reliance on short-term borrowing from its central bank. This is despite the fact that central bank independence has been growing. Ishrat Husain, former State Bank governor, suggests that 1993–94 was the beginning of an evolutionary process whereby the central banking function received increasing autonomy (Interview with Ishrat Husain, 2009). This process was strengthened in 1997 and then 2002. Decisions regarding exchange rates and other key aspects of monetary policy are made by a group of economists. The central bank has autonomy in governance and is institutionally separated from the Ministry of Finance, compared to its historical position directly under the political executive.

"Pakistan's narrow tax base" has meant that "development activities have had to be funded through foreign capital flows rather than internal resource mobilization" (Talbot, 2005: 38). But foreign capital typically adds to the debt-servicing burden, and is often unreliable. Domestic debt has negative consequences. Deficit-financing through bank borrowing squeezes investment capital, creating problems for private business:

> the financial repression which resulted from the government's deficit financing strategy has diverted valuable capital from the private sector and created a

166 *Political survival in Pakistan*

credit crunch, thus making it financially impossible for private firms to buy manufacturing units

(Husain, 2000: 40)

The "deficit financing strategy" referred to above is non-bank borrowing by the government at higher-than-market rates, which drives up interest rates.

There is room for debate over whether administrative capacity or political will is the key ingredient in determining whether the tax-GDP ratio can be increased. The argument that capacity is chiefly responsible focuses on limited assessment capabilities as well as corruption. The tax net for direct tax collection (including income, corporate, and wealth taxes) has remained low, although tax rates have been lowered to encourage compliance. Economists S.M. Ali and Faisal Bari explain this by referring to capacity:

> The government has not been able to document the economy so that large segments do not fall in the net, and the government has no way of catching them. This includes agriculturalists, traders, small and medium sector business owners, and the working population of the informal sector. [...] Apart from the information asymmetry issues, reported corruption levels in the tax department have also been quite high. So even for people who are in the tax net it is relatively easy and "profitable" to pay employees of the tax department a percentage of the tax and underreport their income officially. Tax evasion through underreporting is a large problem in Pakistan.

(Ali and Bari, 2000: 55–56)

One problem is ineffective record keeping. Ayub (2008) reports that a fire destroyed the Sindh Board of Revenue's office in March, burning land records worth billions of rupees. A police investigation concluded that arson was the cause. How can property rights be monitored and enforced through impersonal law, and how can agricultural taxes be levied, when the records themselves can be so easily wiped out? The equivalent might be a debtors' mob that raids a bank and burns its loan records. The records can be difficult to reconstruct, particularly given that they are usually not held in multiple storehouses in electronic form, and property rights are notoriously difficult to identify and ascertain with ease and clarity.

The problem remains severe, as noted by former State Bank governor Ishrat Husain:

> After fifty-six years of independence we still do not have a computerized, transparent, well-maintained set of land records for agriculture or urban lands. The land revenue hierarchy and the urban development authority functionaries have deliberately kept the system opaque so that they can manipulate the records for maximizing their personal benefits. The enormous cost to the economy in terms of foregone capital formation through active land markets or expensive litigation involving disputes in claims to titles has put the country behind in achieving its growth potential. Crude estimates suggest that

Quasi-states, extraction, and governance   167

Pakistan's GDP would grow at least by two percentage points faster if the land titles were clear, actively traded, mortgaged and exchanged without much hassle. Similarly, if tax assessment, tax code and tax collection methods were simplified, made less arbitrary and free from discretion of tax officials, the tax base would be much wider and Tax-GDP ratio much higher.

(Husain, 2003: 217–218)

Institutional strengthening is a complex process that is difficult to generate with a single executive order. In other words, to some degree this is political capacity, which is difficult to enhance quickly. Nevertheless, leadership decision-making, and sustained commitment, does matter. Engaging in "efficient institutional supply" is a public good, and small winning coalition governments are focused on private goods and insufficiently energetic about public goods.

The focus on capacity does not negate the role played by political will. Rather, it compounds the difficulties faced by a leader who seeks to increase domestic taxation, and raises a second order challenge. If administrative capacity is the problem, then political leaders must invest more in administrative capacity. One problem is that administrative posts at all levels are seen as opportunities for personal enrichment, and a share in every side payment is reputed to go to higher-ups through to the very top. Needed administrative reforms are not carried out because they would undermine the opportunities for private goods that the incumbent and winning coalition members enjoy.

Tasneem Siddiqui, a civil servant who received Pakistan's highest civilian medal, argues that the problem is primarily traceable to political will:

The income tax department keeps on expanding all the time, but the number of tax payers remains almost the same, i.e., 1.1 million (out of which about 80 per cent pay at source). In spite of all the attractive incentives, neither the business community, nor the feudal lobby are ready to pay the tax due, or have the income tax personnel shown the will to evolve a foolproof, simple, and corruption-free system. All efforts to generate more revenues are bound to fail unless we bring about fundamental changes in the system. Our emphasis should shift from the income tax officer to trade bodies, institutes of chartered and cost accountants, lawyers and professional groups. By involving these groups, the government can create a system of checks and accountability to ensure that corruption, inefficiency, as well as lethargy is brought to a minimum level in the tax collection department.

(Siddiqui, 2001: 20)

In other words, Siddiqui sees the tax collection problem not as a structural constraint that is impossible to overcome, but rather a matter of "will." This means that incumbent leaders do have this as an option to pursue, but they have not pursued it.

Through and after the Musharraf period, the Pakistani central government has continued ostensible efforts to increase domestic extraction. These include recent moves to simplify and improve the tax structure and combat tax fraud. Historically,

168 *Political survival in Pakistan*

evasion and political opposition to such attempts have stymied the central government's ambitious plans. Commercial strikes and urban demonstrations indicate an active opposition to the recent initiatives. Veteran journalist S.M. Fazal, editor of the *Daily News*, has asserted his strong belief that radical efforts to increase direct taxation would produce a political backlash and result in the incumbent being deposed from office (Interview with S.M. Fazal, July 2009). Thus, one reason to avoid tax increases is to prevent challenges to the incumbent. But this view presumes that stated efforts to improve tax collection will actually be implemented and backed by a committed incumbent. An incumbent whose political survival rests on a narrow winning coalition, including functionaries in the tax collection bureaucracy, is not likely to move against a major source for private goods provision, or against favored supporters.

Ironically, even when international financing is designed to improve domestic extraction, it gets siphoned away or diverted to private uses, and the result is further indebtedness without improved tax performance. A recent foreign loan to improve tax collection in Pakistan provides an example. A 150 million dollar World Bank loan given in 2002 sought tax reform by merging sales, excise, and income tax departments. The object was to create a common data warehouse, and improve collection and cut administrative costs through consolidation. In practice, Income Tax and Customs implemented the reforms immediately, "which only benefited their lifestyles like doubling of salaries, purchases of new cars and establishing new buildings with new furniture" (Khan, 2009), and produced no substantive change in the desired direction. Severe opposition from officials in customs (reputed to present especially lucrative rent-seeking opportunities), combined with a political executive reputed for rent-seeking behavior, stymied the needed changes. The World Bank proposal was to reduce high-salary posts to five. A 2009 government decision actually increased high-salary posts to 12.

In effect, the government borrowed millions to improve the tax-GDP ratio, which actually decreased to 9.6 percent from 12 percent. International financing tends to displace the need to generate necessary resources domestically, even when the loan is designed to improve tax collection. This experience suggests that international financial institutions are ineffective agents for improving a dysfunctional fiscal sociology. IFIs, even when their goal appears to be a step toward breaking poor tax collection, appear to present another channel for circumventing the "taxation for representation" bargain on which a broad taxpayer base rests.

Business leader Asad Umar has suggested particular areas that must be taxed to meet spending needs, including "a capital gains tax of real estate and the capital markets, GST [General Sales Tax] on services and a meaningful income tax on large farmers" (Umar, 2008). Landlord exemption from direct taxes on agricultural income has repeatedly aroused controversy. Yet landlord power is such that provincial assemblies recently passed resolutions to the effect that an agricultural income tax would not be imposed, even though there was very little public pressure for this at the time (Interview with former Central Board of Revenue official, March 2009). The measures suggested by Asad Umar imply that a political leader with the

Quasi-states, extraction, and governance   169

right mandate might be able to raise the tax-GDP ratio, although the service sector in particular would require more investment in administrative capacity.

Tax collection is hampered by poor bureaucratic performance:

> The institution responsible for tax collection in the country, i.e. the Central Board of Revenue, suffered from inefficiency, corruption, lack of account-ability, excessive discretionary powers, harassment of honest tax payers and connivance with the unscrupulous.
>
> (Husain, 2003: 134)

Correcting "leakages" due to these problems may add several percentage points to the tax-GDP ratio without changing tax rates. A key problem, however, is that tax evasion reflects a broader problem: the state apparatus is used for private goods rather than the public interest. Tax agents' "connivance with the unscrupulous" extends top-level predatory behavior and replicates the tendency at lower levels. Bureaucratic appointments are too often made to reward a political leader's winning coalition. Furthermore, agents learn that their careers are best furthered not by effective tax collection, but by supporting and not damaging the political leadership and powerful individuals.

Sales taxes in Pakistan tend to be "inflationary and regressive" (Husain, 2000: 143). Pakistan's governments in the 1990s found it difficult to impose general sales tax. VAT has the potential to raise "more revenue with less administrative and economic costs than other broad-based taxes" and is harder to evade than income tax (Husain, 2000: 142–143), but Pakistan's conversion from GST to VAT has been "half-hearted and incoherent" (Husain, 2000: 143). One observer noted that opposition to sales and other indirect taxes is swift civil disobedience and other tactics used by merchants, compared to changes in income tax laws (Interview with civil service official, 2001). This may be because announced changes in sales taxes are more likely to be followed by enforcement efforts compared to changes in income tax laws (which are more easily evaded); it may also be that merchant associations are better organized for mobilization and protest than income tax payers.

An alternative coalition that might counterbalance landlord power has not emerged. Murtaza Khuhro (deputy commissioner of income tax, large taxpayer unit, Karachi) asserts that stagnating provincial revenues from the agricultural sector (based on modest measures such as the "land tax") can be enhanced by "clearing up the ambiguities that characterize our policies on land reforms and empowerment of people" (Khuhro, 2008). This prescription for policy clarity and enforcement is difficult to carry out. Most "big" landlords continue to enjoy disproportionate power and wealth while the impoverished are thoroughly disempowered. Khuhro notes that "economic and non-economic dependence of the poor on the landlords confers social, political, and even spiritual clout on the landholders" (Khuhro, 2008). This perception is widely shared (Interviews, 2008, 2009). A powerful constituency to mobilize for land reform, such as a peasants' movement, has not emerged, as Pakistani leaders have not facilitated representative peasant organizations, and rather acted to crush them (Rehman, 2009a).

170 *Political survival in Pakistan*

An administrator in a government corporation notes that landlords generally control the assemblies so they do not allow an agricultural tax. Beyond this basic problem, there are "horizontal" inequities in the tax system: people at the same earning level are differently taxed. Government servants and salaried workers have their income tax deducted directly from their paychecks. A menial worker who fixes punctured tires can make up to 2000 Rupees a day, or about 60,000 rupees a month, a respectable salary, and more so if one notes that he pays no taxes. Moreover, his electricity connection is probably an illegal *kunda* (a generic method for jerry-rigging a power line to tap electricity), giving him energy for a nominal price. These inequities are demoralizing and prevent a more positive fiscal sociological path from evolving. A public good would be a more effective tax net that broadened the tax base and prevented leakages, evasions, and bribery to avoid taxes (Conversation with a senior government administrator, July 2009).

The horizontal inequity problem was also pointed out by Martinez-Vazquez (2006), whose study found that the tax system according to quintiles is not nearly as regressive as popular perception suggests; in fact, it is mildly progressive for the bottom three quintiles and progressive for the top two quintiles. A bigger problem is "horizontal" inequity in the system: taxpayers with similar income levels are treated unequally due to exemptions and opportunities for tax evasion. Favoritism has been shown to particular sectors: sources and uses of income produce economic ineffi-ciencies and distortions (Martinez-Vazquez, 2006: ii). While the Central Board of Revenue has introduced universal self-assessment for all major taxes, field audits are absent; this reduces the likelihood that citizens will comply with self-reporting requirements (Interview with civil service official, February 2009).

The problems listed above relate to the formal institutional supply of tax laws and their monitoring and enforcement mechanisms. A profound complement is that low political legitimacy makes people unwilling to comply with a regime's initiatives. "Legitimacy" is a notoriously difficult concept to observe and measure. Nevertheless, former government servant Ayesha Siddiqa believes that bad govern-ance and the lack of input into government decision-making reduces potential taxpayers' willingness to comply with laws. Pakistanis are not keen to pay taxes because they have "absolutely no control over the allocation of resources". She traces this to the following: "Any government that fails to demonstrate legitimacy in its actions will find it hard to convince people to agree to pay taxes or declare their assets" (Siddiqa, July 24, 2009). Other analysts have expressed similar views. For example, economist and former finance minister Shahid Javed Burki refers to "no taxation without representation" as the underlying social dictum that must be obeyed if Pakistan's tax/GDP ratio is to be improved (Burki, 2001). This general proposition is in keeping with the fiscal sociology developed by Joseph Schumpeter (see Chapter 1).

There are limits to state action, and effective governance can be understood as an interactive, partnership-based process drawing on dispersed knowledge, as devel-oped in the policy and process literatures. This approach has been developed at length in Subrata Mitra's examination of India (Mitra, 2006). While acknowledging that executive fiat is one step in determining the extraction strategy that is actually

Quasi-states, extraction, and governance   171

implemented, it is nevertheless a critical one. One major leakage between official policy and implementation is corruption in the bureaucratic apparatus and elsewhere. Yet this is reputed to travel all the way up the leadership chain to the leader's favored appointees. Thus, private benefits to a winning coalition help perpetuate bureaucratic weakness. Improving bureaucratic efficiency is a public good that is underprovided when leadership is supported by a narrow winning coalition, and the situation may be exacerbated when high-level bureaucrats belong to that winning coalition.

Corruption and private benefits

Almost every interviewee described corruption as being among Pakistan's biggest problems. Corruption may be described as the use of public office for private benefit. Leaders use such private benefits to enrich themselves and to offer bribes and benefits to their winning coalition members. Agents of the state replicate this at different levels, from high political officeholders to lowly bureaucrats and police. Corruption in Pakistan is notable in

> (a) large scale evasion of taxes and leakages in assessment; (b) kickbacks in government purchases and contracts; (c) contrived losses in public enterprises and public utilities; (d) politically motivated loans by banks and financial institutions; (e) nepotism, favouritism, and sale of posts in government departments particularly in law enforcing agencies; and (f) discretion used in award of licenses, plots, etc.
>
> (Husain, 2003: 158)

Bribery, fraud, embezzlement, tax evasion, rents from import licenses, and selective subsidies are all specific forms that corruption takes (Husain, 2003: 158–159). Tragically, money for social development has mostly not reached target groups, instead going to consultants, contractors, engineers, fraud, or waste (Siddiqui, 2001: 16).

Economist Ishrat Husain describes the 1990s as a decade where economic decision-making was ridden with patronage, cronyism, nepotism, and corruption:

> Unproductive and wasteful public expenditures and schemes, commissions, kickbacks, and favours to party loyalists were the main criteria in the selection of projects.
>
> Almost every single public sector enterprise, bank and institution became dysfunctional, as these were, with some exceptions, manned by people whose hallmark was personal loyalty to the rulers of the day, rather than competence or integrity. The fiscal and quasi-fiscal deficits of WAPDA, KESC, PIA, Railways, Steel Mills, OGDC, and nationalized commercial banks were a major source of hemorrhage of public finances, and were the main contributor to the growing debt burden of the country.
>
> (Husain, 2003: 201)

172 *Political survival in Pakistan*

In other words, people in the winning coalition received lucrative and beneficial posts that they were likely to lose with the regime change. According to Bueno de Mesquita et al. (2003), loyalty to the incumbent tends to be high in small winning coalitions for this reason. Husain (2003) has spelled this out as "personal loyalty to the rulers of the day" as the most important characteristic of these beneficiaries in the winning coalition.

Compared to civilian leaders' winning coalitions, the coalition that delivers military coup leaders to office is smaller. Only as the military leader tries to divert and control challenges to legitimacy are legislatures and electoral mechanisms reintroduced. Interview data from diverse sources suggest that civilian regimes are commonly perceived as more corrupt than military regimes. A political survival interpretation is that because the civilian governments are somewhat broader in their winning coalition, they are somewhat more corrupt. If the winning coalition were sufficiently large and socially encompassing, private goods provision would be reduced and be replaced by public goods provision. In the Pakistani experience the winning coalition for civilian regimes has not reached this level.

A complementary factor in explaining higher corruption among civilian leaders is that military regimes tend to receive larger foreign aid grants. Smaller government revenues from outside sources, combined with the winning coalition's demands for benefits, place pressure on civilian leaders to engage in more predatory behavior. Ayub's close ties to Washington during the Cold War, Zia ul-Haq's collaboration with the US proxy war in Afghanistan against the USSR, and Musharraf's commitment to the "War on Terror" were all accompanied by large aid packages. In contrast, the civilian periods under Z.A. Bhutto and later Benazir Bhutto and Nawaz Sharif saw more restrained donations from abroad (especially from the United States). Under Z.A. Bhutto, Pakistan's "favorite child" treatment was perceived to have ended. Over the Benazir/Nawaz alternating regimes, the Pressler Amendment restricted aid to Pakistan, promised and paid-for fighter planes were not delivered, and sanctions were imposed with nuclear tests. Lowered inflows were accompanied by escalating debt crises. Turning to greater domestic predation may have been a way to finance private goods provision.

Over successive turnovers in officeholders, civilian leaders may have learned that they cannot expect to not last in office as long as military leaders. This likely increases their discount rate, meaning that they are more likely to grab what can be had in the present or near future rather than count on a revenue stream in the more distant future. This may also make civilian leaders more likely to engage in predatory behavior. The perception that the military is less corrupt can be challenged. It is arguable that the only difference with military regimes is simply that resource diversion takes place through more established institutionalized channels associated with special privileges for "Milbus," the military- commercial conglomerate described by Ayesha Siddiqa (see Chapter 3) rather than personal and informal ties. Thus, there is a difference in form, but both military and civilian leaders divert public goods provision into private benefits. Moreover, Milbus privileges continue during civilian regimes as the military is powerful and central to the incumbent's winning coalition.

Policing

Rather than being politically neutral, the Pakistani police "have long been an instrument of political harassment, electoral manipulation, and graft during military *and* civilian regimes" (Cohen, 2004: 157). Unsurprisingly, crime in Pakistan is serious problem. Policing is ineffective and riddled with bribe-taking, rent-seeking behavior (Siddiqui, 2001: 39–49).

> Since 1988, a large number of policemen, sub-inspectors, DPs and even SPs, have been appointed under a system of political patronage. In the Punjab alone, the number of such people totals around 7500. It is not surprising that these policemen have not received proper training and violate all disciplinary rules. In addition, distortions like 'shoulder promotions' have completely destroyed the rank structure and seniority in the police force and resulted in the demoralization of the rank and file.
>
> (Siddiqui, 2001: 43)

Police staffing and promotions are determined by connections rather than merit or seniority. This in turn affects the police's professionalism in discharging its duties.

Political leader and former Air Marshall Asghar Khan reports that in Punjab in the mid-1990s, a police Inspector General stated at a press conference that the unsatisfactory law and order situation was due partly to the fact that 25,000 police recruits had criminal records. Some with criminal records were placed in charge of police stations; the appointments were made directly by the provincial political authority over the police bureaucracy's objections and the Chief Minister overruled a police official by confirming their selection. Similarly, Asghar Khan alleges that 20,000 "similar people" were placed in the Sind police, with "leading dacoits" in charge of police stations (Asghar Khan, 2005: 224). The police force appears to be so politicized that those with criminal pasts can be inducted into law enforcement. This likely reflects the incumbent's preferences, and makes it easier for the incumbent to reward supporters and persecute challengers and rivals, and in general, to pursue private goods rather than the public good.

Extensive police reforms were ordered during Musharraf's regime, seeking major alterations to the system traceable to ordinances from 1863 (Interview with Lt. Gen. Moinuddin Haider, former Interior Minister, 2009). This included an attempt to professionalize the police system in Balochistan, which had historically been dominated by "levies"—forces loyal to particular *sardars* who received government pay for maintaining public order. Twenty-five commissions have examined police reforms since Pakistan's inception. Transparency in induction and insulation from political pressures in personnel decision-making, as well as citizen input through public safety commissions, were major goals. However, Haider noted that these reforms were not properly implemented, and suggested that recent prominent reversals in Balochistan were due to "political" obstacles before administrative ones (Interview with Lt. Gen. Moinuddin Haider, 2009).

174 *Political survival in Pakistan*

A former District Magistrate (the office with general superintendence over policing duties under the 1863 system) admitted that the old system did not work very well, but nevertheless criticized the Musharraf reforms:

> [Under the old system] the prosecution and law and order functions were all centered in police station. Musharraf's law declared that all three will be separate. A person will patrol the crime; if a crime occurs, another office will investigate it, and a third will prosecute it. This makes eminent legal sense, but it totally failed here in Pakistan. Even educated people had to locate the investigation officer; this was difficult to find. Then they would have to find the prosecutor. So although on paper it looks like a very plausible reform [...] people don't know where to go.
>
> (Interview with former District Magistrate, 2009)

In other words, there were information costs that contributed to failures in police reforms, and the problem may have been poor institutional design for the Pakistani context. There are some success stories; well-paid motorway police have a reputation for being corruption-free, compared to the traffic police who earn much less.

Failures in policing have been accompanied by a significant increase in private security services. "By the 1990s Pakistan also had a critical small arms problem, reflected in the growth of private police forces, some of them armed militias, with at least 200 security services commercially operating in the country" (Cohen, 2004: 156). As reported by *Dawn*, July 25, 2009, the All Pakistan Security Agencies Association head asserted that there are 200 security agencies registered with APSAA; these operated with the necessary licenses under formal government requirements. He acknowledged, however, that there were other unregistered, unlicensed security agencies, and this does not count the numerous arrangements made with individuals for bodyguard and watchman services. In Karachi, there are about 80,000 private security guards, compared to 29,000 police personnel in Karachi. A shopping mall's security guards were reported to be wearing uniforms virtually identical to police commando units, with the exception of official belts bearing a police number. This also applies to the Frontier Constabulary force (the force that provides some policing in the Federally Administered Tribal Areas). Although a senior Sindh government official described the practice of imitating police and FC uniforms as illegal, there is little apparent action against violators. The private security forces are seen "in pickup trucks often bearing revolving lights and hooters similar to the ones used on police mobiles, and they are usually seen escorting some large vehicle bearing at best an invalid number plate, if one is present at all" (Hassan, July 25, 2009, 13). Poor data on crime only reinforces the policing problem the country faces.

Insecurity regarding life and property plagues Pakistan. Kidnappings for ransom, extortion, and armed robbery are rife. Criminal violence is compounded by political violence, including drive-by shootings and bombings. Dissatisfaction with the law and order situation is a primary complaint among Karachiites (Various interviews, 2008, 2009). In gruesome incidents, mobs have responded to alleged crimes with

Quasi-states, extraction, and governance   175

swift vigilante justice. Suspected robbers have been burnt alive. Bus drivers usually seek to abscond immediately from a traffic accident, as those who are captured typically suffer a severe beating.

Weakened state authority has produced an "institutional vacuum" which "has been filled by mafias, armed militias, and the informal sector operators" (Siddiqui, 2001: 53–54). Numerous interviewees have echoed this observation, and point to a sizeable governance gap into which quasi-states have stepped. The state is not fulfilling key governance functions and this provides political opportunities and space for quasi-state actors to emerge and consolidate. In my primary fieldwork site, Karachi, gang activity, violent crime, and extortion are widespread. Property rights are insecure and disputed; forged title documents and payments to government registrars often result in multiple claims to the same real estate.

Informal land allocation

Land-grabbing can be described as "self-allocation" that happens when state institutions fail. A "land mafia" developed in Karachi (Siddiqui, 2001: 151):

> The poor people pay for the land, which they purchase from land-grabbers. They pay for the water, which they get from the tankers or through the pipelines—legally or illegally. They pay the electricity man who comes to collect the "*bhatta*" every evening (if they have illegal connections), and they lay some sort of sewerage system themselves. Now they have a neighborhood watch system to secure their life and property. If the communities are doing all this should we denounce it as illegal and refuse to support it with technological advice and social guidance?
>
> (Siddiqui, 2001: 159)

In other words, functional institutions for meeting social needs have developed in the state's absence. An administrator in a government corporation office argued that the land mafia played a role in some ways similar to rural landlords: it made decisions on property rights and allocations, often supplanting or violating official government decisions (Conversation with administrator, July 2009).

*Katchi abadi*s (squatter settlements, literally "raw dwellings") provide a glaring demonstration that social realities have escaped government purview. These are vast, and it is commonly estimated that over half the city's residents live in them. Siddiqui (2001, Chs. 14–16) offers an inspiring alternative that is little applied in Pakistan, but worked in one bold experiment by the Sind Katchi Abadi Authority: offering simplified land tenure to residents first, before other steps. Once they had security of tenure, residents pooled resources and labor to construct housing and develop their property. Eventually, there is potential for communities to organize. In contrast, less successful models first provided the land, infrastructure, and housing, and then brought in people last.

Siddiqui mentions that "provisional certificates" were given but these were often meaningless. The key problem is insecure tenure—if residents face the continual

176 *Political survival in Pakistan*

possibility that they will be evicted, they have little incentive to invest in their dwelling. Fieldwork from settings outside Pakistan has argued that the most successful development in squatter slums happened when residents were given land tenure rights (Neuwirth, 2005). Moreover, housing construction brings multiplier effects to income while it is also possible that housing will produce a sound basis for collaborative civil society associations. "Sanitation has been identified as a key element in catalyzing the community development process. It has been demonstrated in several large community programmes that once the communities are mobilized, and construct the sewerage system, it kicks off development in other sectors" (Siddiqui, 2001: 144). Receiving electricity and water connections is generally done through illegal *kundi* connections. One estimate was that there are 90,000 such illegal connections in Karachi.

Underground and parallel economies

An important corollary to state weakness is the extra-legal or black market economy. An IMF estimate from the 1990s places the "parallel economy" at about 20 percent of the official economy. This underground economy results from "tax evasion, smuggling, corruption and illegal income accruals, drug trade, etc." (Husain, 2000: 2). Husain further asserts that "the recipients of this underground economy income (and here we are not talking about the unorganized informal sector) are largely concentrated in the top quintile income groups, which further exacerbates the already existing income disparities in the country" (Husain, 2000: 3).

Given "the weakness of the state apparatus and lack of performance by the formal sector, it is the black economy and the informal sector which is keeping our economy afloat" (Siddiqui, 2001: 66). The informal sector provides opportunities for exploitation by middlemen and moneylenders:

> The *bhatta* which is collected by government functionaries and other powerful gangs doesn't go into the government exchequer. If this continues unabated, the parallel economy would no doubt expand, but government revenues would never increase.
>
> (Siddiqui, 2001: 66)

According to Siddiqui, a push-cart vendor (*thailay wallah*) may easily pay 15 to 20 rupees a day in *bhatta* protection money to police or municipal officers. Karachi's hawkers' *bhatta* payments are greater than what "big businessmen" pay in income tax (Siddiqui, 2001: 157). In other words, the informal economy competes with the formal economy for resources, and while there is some symbiosis, it ultimately detracts from state power and resources. This impression is borne out by the author's many conversations with *thailay wallah*'s (push-cart vendors) and small business people in 2008 and 2009. One fruit seller described three different entities to whom he regularly paid *bhatta*: the police, the city metropolitan corporation, and a local figure who claimed the fruit seller was operating on his turf. Small business

Quasi-states, extraction, and governance 177

owners described *tanzeems* (self-described political organizations) who come on a monthly basis to collect "donations," often backed by an implicit threat and intimidation. Apparently the *tanzeems* have some skill at identifying people's incomes and asking them to "contribute" accordingly. One anecdote describes someone who won a large "Prize Bond" (a lottery prize). She was told to give a large amount almost immediately (Conversations with various business people and professionals, 2008).

The situation has worsened as state authority has eroded:

> What we see today is an institutional crisis of state authority. Mafias, armed militias and, in some areas, tribal chiefs and feudal lords have created centres of power parallel to that of the state. For any programme of social and economic development to be successfully implemented, it is necessary to restore the writ of the government and make it run throughout the country.
>
> (Siddiqui, 2001: 69)

Effective government requires curbing de facto quasi-states. The capacity for armed violence, however, has been entrenched since the 1980s, when machine guns and other weaponry flooded Karachi, and created the infamous "Kalashnikov culture" in the 1990s. Amnesty International reported in the late 1990s that most political groups in Karachi maintained their own militias (Jones, 2002: 126–127). The government military operation against the MQM in the early 1990s resulted in thousands of casualties, and, according to one analyst writing at the time, was severe enough to threaten the country's survival (Ahmar, 1996: 1047). Removing "Sindhi bias" from job searches (a key grievance felt by the Muhajir community), holding local bodies elections, providing an amnesty for MQM workers, and curtailing and checking police activities have been suggested as ways to defuse the situation (Ayaz Amir, cited in Ahmar, 1996: 1047).

More recently, militant groups have increased their direct attacks on police personnel. This has a tangible impact on the state's ability to enforce law and order. The police uniform also symbolizes the state, and successful attacks show the state to be weak, which emboldens militants further. In 2008, 258 police personnel were killed and 700 injured in terrorist attacks (Mahmood, 2009). It is common to see reports about party activists and workers being assassinated in drive-by shootings and targeted killings. Apparently factional assassinations of activists from the MQM-Haqiqi faction and the MQM numbered over 100 in the first six months of 2009. Other groups, including Jeay Sindh, the PPP, and the ANP have lost personnel to violent attacks. The escalation in violent tactics by quasi-state entities has its most dramatic manifestation in suicide bombings.

Sectarian religious quasi-states

From a political survival perspective, "Islamism" offers frames by which leaders and affinity groups cohere, and is a strategic choice among leaders and some challengers in Pakistan. Adopting ethnic parochialism is another strategic choice

178 Political survival in Pakistan

not necessarily exclusive to "Islamic" appeals. The Jeay Sindh Qaumi Mahaz activists emphasize a different form of Islam—Sufi centered, with a *pir* tradition—and decry the Tablighi Jamaat and Deobandi approach while retaining an alliance with the Barelvi Sunni Tehrik. The MQM has taken a firm public stance against Talibanization; the Taliban's activities are permitted by "no religion" (Interview with MQM member Hamid Abidi, July 2009). Below, I complement Chapter 4 by examining the war-making prowess displayed by selected religious sectarian groups. These suggest a continuing failure in law and order, and point to the possibility that war-making tactics among quasi-state actors will continue to escalate.

Officially, neither the Sipahi Sahaba Pakistan (a Sunni organization) nor the Tahrik-e-Jafriya Pakistan (a Shia group) describe themselves as violent actors. Nevertheless, militants in each have created their own factions, and have earned a reputation as effective specialists in violence. Riaz Basra and others in SSP put together the Lashkar-e-Jhangvi (Jhang's Army, referring to assassinated SSP leader Haq Nawaz of Jhang). Sipah-e-Muhammad Pakistan was created by more militant Shia groups. Those who actually carry out killings in the Lashkar-e-Jhangvi and the SMP are reputed to be about 200 individuals, usually with partial *madrasa* education, and often (particularly in the Lashkar) with combat experience in Afghanistan and Kashmir. Their organization is secretive and hierarchical:

> They work under the direction of "co-ordinators," who obey their respective "commanders." The co-ordinator calls a certain "worker" in his organization on a mobile telephone, which the police cannot trace, and arranges a meeting. He tells this "worker" about the person to be killed, takes him to the neighbourhood where the intended victim lives, and arranges their next meeting. In the meantime, the "worker" studies the neighbourhood and watches the intended victim's movements and routines. On the appointed day, the co-ordinator meets him delivers appropriate weapons to him, and then goes to hide for time in a *madrasah* or a mosque. These "workers" are quite convinced of the righteousness of their own "cause," and they are equally convinced that their victims are the enemies of Islam.
>
> (Syed, 2001: 255)

Those who actually carry out the violence are described as taking action based on religious zeal and dogma, and directed by more literate higher-ups. While this book focuses more on strategic constraints shaping leadership than on the motivations behind those who act as muscle, it is nevertheless worth noting that that there are diverse explanations for "worker" behavior.

Syed suggests that the Lashkar-e-Jhangvi and the SMP raise their money from small business operators:

> When short of funds, they resort to bank robberies, dacoities, kidnapping for ransom, and extortion. They do not think twice about the legality of

Quasi-states, extraction, and governance 179

these activities, because the law is that of a state which they deem to be un-Islamic, and, in their thinking, their acts are calculated to serve the Lord's purposes.

(Syed, 2001: 256)

The law enforcement bureaucracy and police fear a violent response if they crack down on militants. There have been reprisal attacks against bureaucrats:

> In 1996, the commissioner of Sargodha, a Shia, was assassinated. In early 1997, a secretary to the Punjab provincial government, a Sunni, was killed. Ashraf Marath, a senior police officer, was killed by the Lashkar's agents, even though he was a fellow-Sunni, because he insisted upon pursuing the killers of several persons at the Iranian cultural centre in Multan. Newspapers have published reports of police officers sending apologies to the militant sectarian captains for having dared to investigate them, with promises to leave them alone in the future. Riaz Basra, head of the Lashkar, escaped from police custody in 1994, allegedly with the assistance of two members of the provincial assembly who then sheltered him. He is in "hiding," but continues to direct the Lashkar and feels free to communicate with journalists at will. Ghulam Raza Naqvi, head of the Shia "Sipah-e-Muhammad," has been in police custody since December 1996, but apparently the numerous allegations against him are not being investigated with any seriousness or vigour.

(Syed, 2001: 257)

Even in custody, the militant heads are relatively free. The above description refers to the situation from the mid-1990s into the late 1990s. Efforts at sectarian reconciliation are fraught with personal danger for leaders. For example, in the 1980s, Ayatollah Khomeini had suggested that it was no longer useful or pragmatic to denounce those who opposed Ali in Islam's early history. Murid Abbas Yazdani, an SMP commander who took some steps toward rapprochement, was killed by militant associates—a successful challenge to his leadership.

Public education is under-funded and in disrepair. As Cohen (2004) suggests, this has strengthened the Islamist counterculture through the *madaris*, which offer free food, lodging, and education. *Madrasas* continue to provide an important basis for mobilization:

> As a result of the state's official support (or exploitation) of traditional institutions, the number of scholars, Arabic teachers, students, and clerics far exceeds Pakistan's requirements. Moreover, they are ill-adapted to find a job in the modern world. This has created a class of religious lumpen proletariat, unemployable and practically uneducated young men who see religious educations as a vehicle for social mobility, but who find traditional avenues clogged and modern ones blocked.

(Cohen, 2004: 182)

180 *Political survival in Pakistan*

This summarizes one problem the *madrasas* lead to—young men who experience raised expectations and frustration, which amounts to relative deprivation. Efforts to regulate the *madrasa* curricula and to reduce foreign students at *madrasas* may go some way to preventing recruitment from *madrasa* graduates. Nevertheless, the often sectarian affinity groups that emerge from *madrasas* suggest that there will be more recruits for quasi-state autonomist efforts in the future.

There is foreign involvement: Saudi Arabia and Iran have funded Sunni and Shia *madrasas* in Pakistan.

> These madrasahs have spread to smaller towns and they enroll more students than the public elementary and middle schools do. They teach theology, but many of them also teach their students to disapprove of sects other than their own, and give them some military training.
>
> (Syed, 2001: 255)

This suggestion—that Pakistan provides the context for a proxy war between the regional rivals Iran and Saudi Arabia—further demonstrates the blurred internal-external divide in weak state. One distinction between international relations and domestic politics is that international relations are "anarchic" while domestic politics are "hierarchic." In a weak state such as Pakistan, effective hierarchy is low. Conflicts begin to resemble the security dilemmas found in interstate rivalries, a process reflected (and exacerbated) by external actor involvement.

A recent effort has been to empower a less politically strident, contentious Islamic strand. This includes what is termed "Sufi" Islam (Islamabad's supposed patron saint is being celebrated), encouragement to Sunni Tehrik/Barelvis, and such initiatives as a progressive orientation to the International Islamic University in Islamabad as well as the Pak-Turk schools initiative inspired and managed by the Turkish Fethullah Gulen movement. The approach is akin to the religion-building suggested by Cheryl Benard in the RAND study titled *Civil Democratic Islam*. Static assumptions about violent or nonviolent proclivities are usually shallow and often proved wrong. Sunni Tahrik, a group labeled "Sufi" has been associated with sectarian militancy. Its tacit alliance with Jeay Sindh in places might further escalate conflict to destructive contentious tactics.

The Lal Masjid (Red Mosque), an Islamabad complex including a mosque and *madrasa*, developed into something resembling a quasi-state; its leaders had a demonstrated ability to mobilize individuals for war-making, and they sought to enforce the law and public morality as vigilantes. Red Mosque leaders had previously enjoyed military support as they recruited militants to fight in Afghanistan and Kashmir. In 2007, activists (often female *madrasa* students) associated with the Red Mosque apparently tried to enforce their own standards by threatening and harassing individuals and organizations involved in immoral activities, allegedly brothels, and video, and music stores. The activists occupied a library. The police did not intervene. Eventually, however, the military surrounded the compound, and then entered it in a bloody raid. The dramatic confrontation highlighted the apparent threat to the Pakistani state in the capital. The Lal Masjid leaders were

Quasi-states, extraction, and governance 181

the two Ghazi brothers; their location in Islamabad was inherited from the politically favored role their father had played in recruiting for the Afghan war during the 1980s. One brother was killed in the military raid and the other captured. Whether the escalation was intentional by either Lal Masjid leaders or the military is beyond this brief summary. The crisis had consequences for both domestic and foreign publics, signaling both the will to resist by certain Islamists, and the military's willingness to shed blood and crack down on former allies.

Recent violent confrontations in Pakistan have seen suicide bombing tactics. The great number and high death toll have fed insecurity across the country, particularly when attacks have taken place in urban centers such as Lahore, Karachi, Peshawar, and Quetta. Numerous businesspeople from Peshawar have moved elsewhere as insecurity has increased. Newspaper reports describe bomb-making equipment being found with captured alleged terrorists in Karachi. It remains unclear whether suicide bombings will continue to spread. It is not infrequent to see conspicuously armed soldiers guarding thoroughfares, stationed short distances apart. Suicide attacks are destructive and difficult to prevent and have increasingly been adopted by some self-described "Islamic" groups. Maulana Asad Thanvi, the Jamiat Ulema-e-Islam amir for Sind province and the principal of a well-established *madrasa*, rejects the notion that suicide terror is Islamic in nature, because it goes against the Quranic prohibition on suicide. Thanvi argues that the political context provides explanations for suicide terror, demonstrably so because the tactic was popularized in the region by non-Muslim insurgents in Sri Lanka (Interview with Asad Thanvi, July 2009).

Suicide terror analyses have often focused on the actors, their motivations, character, and psyches. Strategic dimensions and political context, as well as learning processes, have been underemphasized. Pape (2005) has argued that the common denominator in suicide terror campaigns is not religious ideology but territorially based self-determination against an occupying force. From a quasi-state perspective, suicide terror can be considered a potent new war-making technology that significantly enhances the ability to resist domination and to retaliate against better supplied and more organized actors. It is a "modular" tactic, comparable to strikes or riots as tactics in contentious politics (Tarrow, 2005: 100).

Devolution

Where the state lacks strong institutions, an effective tax system, and a monopoly on coercion for enforcing the law and property rights, trade tends to fall into the informal economy, with "limited applicability of the rule of law and marginal tax payments, partially regulated by violence," and a "globally organized criminal economy" (Haken, 2006: 2). In such circumstances, governments are forced into "implicitly or explicitly extending concessions to the parainstitutions that *can* regulate the informal and criminal economy through the use of nonstate coercion" (Haken, 2006: 2). "Parainstitutions" can be understood as de facto quasi-state entities. A disturbing implication for a state that cannot monopolize the use of

182 *Political survival in Pakistan*

coercion or effectively collect taxes is that security dilemmas and violent tactics will balkanize the state. Devolution through official channels may forestall this problem.

Authentic devolution has the potential to incorporate quasi-state entities into institutionalized political participation processes. This may help improve governance and reduce the secessionist threat. Democratic participation or civic participation in official processes usually requires a step back from the secessionist position. But it does not mean that the secessionist goal is given up altogether. It may be a tactical decision: civic participation might be a less risky, less costly way to pursue the same goal than violent rebellion. Mujib ur-Rehman's approach is one example—his Awami League contested elections on a platform seeking autonomy for Bangladesh, and for transforming Pakistan into a weak confederation. Mumtaz Ali Bhutto and the Sindh National Front may be pursuing something similar.

In barrister Zamir Ghumro's view, abolishing the Concurrent List (areas in which both the federal and provincial governments can legislate) would be a significant step toward provincial autonomy. Another step would be to create a functional "Council of Common Interests" (CCI) to govern the Federal Legislative List Part II, which includes oil, gas, electricity, railways, Wapda (Water and Power Development Authority), industrial and water development. While parliament can legislate in these areas, "only CCI can formulate and regulate the policies regarding them and supervise and control the departments" (Ghumro, 2008). Despite this constitutional provision, which has significant potential to safeguard provincial interests and offer a voice and possible veto to provincial actors, the CCI has not been implemented. President Farooq Leghari justified dismissing Benazir Bhutto's government in 1996 by citing the non-functioning of the CCI, among other reasons. Yet the CCI has not been addressed at the same level since.

Former State Bank Governor Ishrat Husain argues that even if the CCI has not been functional, there is nevertheless a process in place that includes dispute resolution machinery, with institutions such as the National Finance Commission, Indus System River Authority (Isra), National Economic Council, and Supreme Court, which all have the assigned task of resolving disputes between federation and provinces. In Husain's view, these institutions are sufficient to prevent dispute escalation: "If there are no avenues to ventilate grievances, then extraconstitutional measures are taken. But when these constitutional safeguards are in place, then why should you not go to these bodies and get disputes resolved?" (Interview with Ishrat Husain, 2009).

There have been several initiatives to empower sub-provincial authorities, such as at the district, *tehsil*, or union levels. Former Foreign Minister Sartaj Aziz offers a list, and argues that such efforts were strongest under military regimes, which sought to strengthen the executive against national and provincial legislatures (Aziz, 2009). In 1954, an administrative program called the Village Agricultural and Industrial Development Programme (Village Aid) sought to devolve some authority to the local level. Ayub Khan's Basic Democracies Order of 1959 was the first large-scale legal effort. Local councilors were elected to undertake local development projects, and 120,000 councilors formed the electoral college for

Quasi-states, extraction, and governance 183

the 1964 presidential election. The 1971 PPP government did away with the Basic Democracies system, and introduced the People's Local Government Ordinance of 1972, but no elections were held. An Integrated Rural Development Programme was also introduced in 1972. In 1979, Zia ul-Haq revived local government institutions through the Local Government Ordinance of 1979. In 1979 and 1983, elections were held for union, *tehsil*, and district councils. Civilian governments from 1985 to 1999 continued Zia ul-Haq's system but channeled community development resources through special programs: PM Junejo's Five-Point Program (1986–88); Benazir Bhutto's People's Works Program (1988–90, 1994–96); Nawaz Sharif's Tameer-e-Watan Program (1990–93, 1997–99). Musharraf's martial law regime introduced a more comprehensive, enabled local governance system through the Local Government Ordinance of 2001.

Sartaj Aziz argues that strongest local government ordinances have been issued under military regimes (2009). One interpretation is that local government ordinances are both a way to incorporate Leviathins and to provide a measure of popular support given that the military regime lacks an electoral mandate. There is clearly a political survival element to this. But it could also be argued that local government improves "good governance." Whether good governance emerges from civilian regimes or not is murkier. The local government ordinance processes are heavily politicized, and closely associated with the national regime. The districts tend to be dependent on the distant center for major development financing.

Like Ayub Khan, another military ruler, Musharraf adopted a local democracy system. Establishing local representational units with some jurisdiction circumvents provincial level resistance, gives a democratic semblance without serious national-level threats, and helps divide and rule, by selectively granting and withholding federal funds for *nazims*. Provincial leaders often depict local body leaders as military dictatorship "toadies" or enablers, because they provide a democratic semblance without seriously challenging the central government's power. Provincial leaders also oppose the *nazims'* ability to collect taxes. In comparison, provincial assemblies present a stronger counterweight to the federal center's authority. Furthermore, the largesse to local bodies is viewed jealously by provincial leaders; recent political debate over "provincial autonomy" has been oriented more toward elevating the provincial government over local bodies, rather than empowering the provinces with respect to the federal government (Rehman, 2009b). This is unsurprising from a political survival perspective; each political figure simply tries to maximize the authority and autonomy his or her office enjoys.

The *nazim* (local government) system under Musharraf has arguably helped to support quasi-state authority. This allows challengers to be incorporated into the polity in a somewhat devolutionary scheme. In Karachi, for example, the MQM has come to dominate the local city government. A common perception is that the post-Musharraf regime will displace such local authority. These are lucrative kickback and rent-seeking opportunities, as well as patronage sources. Perhaps the most important non-tax revenue source is land allocations, and some sharp tussles between the

184 *Political survival in Pakistan*

provincial and city governments have already taken place around this issue. The Karachi *nazim* in office in 2009, Syed Mustafa Kamal of the MQM, has become popular and there have been visible public welfare projects under his tenure, such as major road improvements and construction. Furthermore, various residents and merchants reported that *bhatta*-collection had reduced since the *nazim* system was implemented under Musharraf (Interviews, 2008, 2009). One interpretation is that with access to large-scale financing from the central government, the quasi-state entity no longer needs to extract as much from door-to-door collections. Another possibility is that a transition has taken place from "quasi-state" mode to something akin to a political party that functions within officially sanctioned parameters.

Devolution remains incomplete and tenuous. There are unclear and competing jurisdictions at the local level. In Karachi, for example, the right to allocate land for development has seen repeated clashes between the provincial and local governments. The local government system itself appears heavily dependent on the national incumbent's political survival calculations. Consequently, a *nazim* who appears powerful may be soon displaced, with key decisions and commitments questioned and reversed, and the office of *nazim* itself discontinued. Where basic rules are continually rewritten, long-term contracts and commitments are undermined and cannot be enforced. Such uncertainty makes it more difficult to attract and retain domestic and foreign business investment. Hamid Abidi, affiliated with the MQM, has advocated that the local leadership should have the ability to negotiate with foreign partners on investment and trade matters (Interview with Hamid Abidi, July 2009). To be successful in attracting investment, authority would need to clearly delineate where city government jurisdiction ends and other jurisdictions (such as provincial, or military cantonments) begin.

Analysts and observers frequently mention that clearer, autonomous areas for provincial jurisdiction are a necessary piece in Pakistan's political development. Yet Pakistan remains closer to a unitary than a federal state. The central government can and has dismissed provincial governments and replaced with "President's rule," appointing provincial cabinets. One consequence is the continued incentive to pursue quasi-states. Challengers seeking political position do not see meaningful, effective, continuing power within official posts. A provincial minister knows that an executive order from the center can unseat him. Consequently, there is little faith in existing opportunities. Seeking and building a quasi-state can be translated as carving out an enclave on one's own terms. Sectarian religious impulses and the effort to obtain ethnic purity work similarly in the sense that each privileges one affinity group over others.

Conclusion

Citizen survey research examining five South Asian countries (Pakistan, India, Sri Lanka, Bangladesh, and Nepal) showed the Pakistani citizens viewed governance in their country as worse on most dimensions than do citizens of other countries; dimensions include corruption among political leaders and police, government responsiveness to citizens, satisfaction with the civil service, and whether NGOs

Quasi-states, extraction, and governance 185

empower the public (Adeel Malik, 1999). Pakistan was ninth in the world in the 2008 "Failed States Index" based on a ranking compiled by the Fund for Peace; in 2009 Pakistan remained highly vulnerable to failure, with its ranking at tenth (Fund for Peace, 2009).[3] The Hobbes Index of governance (created by the authors of *LOPS*) places Pakistan in the bottom tier of countries. One analyst described severe deprivation captured in Pakistan social indicators from the end of the twentieth century: 67 million people without safe drinking water and without access to health facilities; 89 million deprived of basic sanitation; 740,000 child deaths a year, half due to malnutrition; maternal mortality as high as 600 per 100,000 births (Siddiqui, 2001: 16).

Economist Shahid Javed Burki's assessment is that the GDP would have to grow at 7 percent in order to maintain or decrease poverty incidence in Pakistan (*Dawn*, June 30, 2009, p. 7). To maintain the poverty level, the rate of GDP growth must be twice that of population growth. To reduce the poverty level, the rate of GDP growth needs to exceed this amount, to perhaps three times the level of population growth. It needs to be higher still where income is unequally distributed, as in Pakistan. Burki suggests that for Pakistan, this means a GDP growth rate of 6 or 7 percent per year; but there was very little GDP growth in 2008–09. The poverty incidence has likely increased from 50 million to 55 million; if some estimates are accurate, this will increase by 10 percent per year. Needless to say, the demands on the public sector in such areas as subsidized commodities, relief programs, and law and order will increase. In such a context, greater social upheaval and political violence may emerge, and the need for good governance become more urgent.

To the extent that political survival goals mean that incumbents cannot alter the longer term structural conditions, it is difficult for Pakistan to extricate its fiscal sociology from the quasi-states-poor extraction-poor governance rut. Only Moeen Qureshi, a caretaker prime minister without the need to maintain a longer-term winning coalition, pursued an agricultural tax; he also unveiled massive corruption in lending practices. The fact that someone with different political survival pressures made moves commonly recognized as necessary further bolsters the thesis in Chapter 3. A critical question is what how political survival constraints and incentives might change so that incumbents choose policies more aligned with the public good.

A business executive wryly observed that the easiest law to change in Pakistan is the constitution, which can be changed in hours. In contrast, statutory orders regulating business practices are very difficult to alter, however outdated and absurd. Electricity inspections are still based on direct current, rather than alternating current that has been in use for decades. Factories are required to have water on hand for animals, even though animals are no longer used for transport in many places (Interview with corporate executive, 2009). The basic law, which should be above alteration except in the most exceptional circumstances, has undergone frequent alterations. The mundane rules that affect business operations and bureaucratic red tape are sticky and rigid in contrast. This represents another governance failure. Another corporate executive vehemently asserted that the problem was not

186 *Political survival in Pakistan*

simply poor governance—rather, there was no governance from the top (Interview with senior corporate executive, August 2009).

Like all political actors, Pakistan's leaders and challengers take calculated risks. Yet there is significant uncertainty, and this may have fed what has been suggested as a peculiarly Pakistan style in public presentation: putting a good face on things as a way to hedge bets. One is never quite certain which side will end up outmaneuvering others or simply receiving a lucky hand. As a result, savvy political actors often have to consider future rounds where power relations may have shifted. High profile political prisoners are unlikely to be abused by police because the police themselves fear that their prisoner might one day obtain office, commented one observer (Interview, 2009).

Subrata Mitra's systematic examination of Indian regions provides a valuable contrast to the Pakistani experience, most strikingly in that regions, once perceived as the bane of Indian democracy, are now more often understood as positive contributors (Mitra, 2006). This is publicly felt as letters to the editor of *Dawn* newspaper in 2009 have hotly debated the new provinces issue and drawn comparisons with India, which divided Punjab into three. India created more units early on, and continues to move in this direction; it was able to implement land reforms, and while there are serious problems with corruption, there has been relative regime stability in national government. India is widely perceived as enjoying greater developmental success. These comparisons, while partial and not definitive, suggest routes for further inquiry.

6 Conclusion

The political survival approach focusses on political leaders and challengers and their support coalitions or affinity groups as they manage threats to their incumbency and ascendancy. Theorizing about the logic of political survival has primarily been developed for stable democracies and remains in its infancy in other contexts. This book has offered a political survival-based interpretation of extraction choices by incumbents and quasi-state strategies by challengers in Pakistan. This has implications for fiscal structure and governance in Pakistan, and extends the logic of political survival to weak states with heterogeneous societies and fluid polity rules.

Theoretical works on political survival and state strength inform each other; this helps produce a coherent picture for the Pakistani context and beyond. In weak states with strong, fractured societies, political survival drives mechanisms by which state weakness is perpetuated and quasi-states emerge. An expanded logic of political survival also lays out paths whereby weakness is potentially exacerbated to create state collapse and failure, and conversely, whereby the low extraction/ quasi-state emergence cycle may be stalled or altered. Ideology matters in defining affinity groups, and culture can define a socially learned menu for choice, but the chief explanation for decisions related to extraction and quasi-states rests upon the political survival interests that shape leaders and challengers.

Existing empirical work has touched on bureaucratic failures and on ethnic and religious mobilization, but has not systematically explored where by political survival ambitions have shaped strategic choices by leaders and challengers. In an often opaque context, interview insights into the psychological milieu suggest expectations on which decisions are based. Interviews with bureaucrats and informed government observers offer evidence for mechanisms by which state extraction remains weak; interviews with challengers' affinity group members and observers suggest mechanisms by which quasi-states emerge and are sustained. Secondary accounts and other analyses have provided supplemental evidence.

Bueno de Mesquita et al. (2003) assume that tax rates are a key choice determining incumbent and challenger prospects for political survival and ascendancy; they further suggest that challengers take either "normal" or "revolutionary" paths to office. In Pakistan, rather than the tax rate, it is the tax net, and the general capacity for reallocating resources such as land, that is most consequential. Wars and other

188 *Political survival in Pakistan*

shocks to fiscal requirements have led to more refined international strategies and sometimes to covert money-creation efforts, rather than to dramatic changes in the tax net in Pakistan.

In a weakly institutionalized polity, the "normal" and "revolutionary" can be difficult to distinguish, and challengers in Pakistan have often pursued quasi-state paths. These can take de facto and de jure forms, and may be pursued in tandem with or as an alternative to formally defined, state-supported political offices. Quasi-state strategies produce overlapping and competing jurisdictions and have major implications for governance. A fractured, heterogeneous society, underprovided public goods, and historical learning about negotiable jurisdictions and borders have further fueled quasi-state strategies.

From this perspective, secessionist impulses are one point in a continuum of possible quasi-state behaviors. The "devolution problem" that is frequently referred to in the literature usually does not have a consistent theoretical framework for assessing diverse challengers and their support organizations. Labels such as "ethno-nationalist" carry connotations that can be helpful in some instances but can obfuscate in others. The continuing extractive weakness of the state and emerging quasi-states are mutually reinforcing, contemporaneous processes. This provides coherence and structure to an otherwise chaotic picture.

The Pakistani case contributes hypotheses about how the political survival mechanism operates in weak states with strong, fractured societies. These are listed below in three areas: incumbent leaders' extraction choices, challengers pursuing quasi-state strategies, and how these two relate to governance. Moreover, these extensions to the logic of political survival enter broader conversations about "external" actors in a polity, Islam and ethnicity, institutional fragility, and political capacity. A key challenge for public goods provision in Pakistan is that a broad-based winning coalition is difficult to generate and sustain. Prescriptions and prognoses for improving governance and development must consider the constraints and opportunities presented by such political survival considerations.

Leadership and extraction

Political survival pressures related to winning coalitions shape extraction choices by incumbents, irrespective of stated ideology. In states with a narrow tax base and low tax/GDP ratio, the winning coalition will affect efforts to expand the tax net and to reduce horizontal inequities. In weak states with narrow winning coalitions, non-tax revenues will be preferred to tax revenues where there are intersubstitutable choices. Winning coalitions shape and constrain redistributive policies such as land reform.

Extraction choices go beyond tax rates, into whether the tax net is expanded, and to the pursuit of non-tax revenues, particularly through international transfers and covert financing. Shocks to fiscal requirements, such as wars or price shocks, do not typically produce dramatic increases in direct taxation. International financing, money creation, and indirect taxation policies are preferred. A historical path matters: from their predecessors and their own experiences, incumbents learn

Conclusion   189

about where and how financing can be obtained. Incumbents also learn what compromises and concessions are needed in order to retain their positions. Distributive politics and state-society relations are shaped by similar considerations. These factors affect the fiscal skeleton of the state, and with it, the state's developmental path.

Whatever the stated ideological preferences, incumbent choices about extraction are shaped by their need to maintain a winning coalition and defuse or repel challenges. The key suggestion about taxes in the *Logic of Political Survival*— that autocracies or small-coalition leaders will tax at a higher rate—must be modified. In a weak polity, building extractive capacity is itself a public good. Both coup-based and elected leaders have avoided agricultural taxation, a key area for raising the tax-GDP ratio and reducing horizontal inequities. Extraction often takes place through opaque, sleight of hand techniques; "privatization" in practice provides handouts to favored supporters and the winning coalition, for example.

Military coup-based leaders in Pakistan come to office with support from an initially small coalition. They typically engage in moves that are designed to try to bolster their claims to legitimate leadership without threatening their positions, such as referendums, non-party elections, or local elections. Eventually, coup-based leaders seek to broaden their winning coalition in an effort to retain office. Historically, high foreign aid resources to military regimes have contributed to their stability. Plentiful international support allows incumbents to avoid politically risky expansions in domestic tax extraction. Aid helps support a regime that in turn supports the donor's goals in the region. Irrespective of stated intent, the aid typically does not produce a major enhancement in governance and public goods provision, but is siphoned away into private goods. Under small coalition governments, aid works in the leader's interest rather than the public interest (an argument made by Bueno de Mesquita and Smith, 2009).

Democratically elected leaders come into office on a broader coalition, and prime ministers must retain a majority in the national legislature, comprising what in theory might be a larger winning coalition. The regularity with which elected governments have been removed by coup or dismissal, and their relatively short tenures in office, have meant that elected incumbents have not historically been able to count on a sustained, large winning coalition to retain office. One consequence is that incumbents swiftly seek to ensure that they either eliminate threats or bring potential veto-holders into their winning coalition. At the same time, elected leaders seek to manipulate selection rules and keep the minimal winning coalition that will allow them to retain office. This ensures more loyalty among individual coalition members, who recognize that their special privileges will likely be lost if the incumbent loses office.[1] In the process, public goods provision tends to be compromised. Elected leaders thus have a reputation for higher corruption, and more predatory behavior.

International financing (particularly through debt instruments) as well as money creation policies have been used by most governments, coup-based and elected. Caretaker prime ministers have the shortest time-horizons, and are usually not empowered to do much, but paradoxically have the fewest political survival

190 *Political survival in Pakistan*

constraints. It is noteworthy that the sole agricultural income tax levy took place under a caretaker. Such dramatic shifts suggest that political survival concerns shape fiscal development in decisive ways.

Challengers and quasi-state strategies

In weak states with a strong but fractured society, quasi-state strategies are attractive to challengers irrespective of affinity group. Where a quasi-state strategy has produced demonstrated success for one challenger, other challengers will learn and emulate it. Where the institutional mechanisms for accommodating de jure quasi-state appeals fail, there is greater risk for de facto quasi-states and violent secessionism.

In effect, challengers do not seek existing political office in what might be termed a "normal" process in a stable polity, but by constructing their own political office through quasi-state pursuits. The way "public good" is defined will vary according to how the polity's boundaries are understood. Quasi-states may pursue a public good that is seen as a private good in the national, juridical polity. In a weak polity, there are parallel, overlapping, competing, and conflicting jurisdictions whose boundaries are not formally defined or widely accepted. In the extreme, every challenger who could not secure national office would ideally like a separate state, as an ultimate expression of power and control, preferring to be "the head of a chicken rather than the tail of a phoenix."[2] Short of creating their own state, challengers may accept some de facto or de jure autonomy. That autonomy might be legally recognized and accommodated, or it could be a competing jurisdiction, or it may simply exist side by side with the existing state's apparatus with no formal recognition. These possibilities mean that a challenger might be the head of a chicken and the tail of a phoenix simultaneously.

State repression in Pakistan has been incomplete and selective, and has not eliminated quasi-state strategies. Historical exemplars signal opportunities and provide learning. De jure quasi-state strategies have proliferated. To greater and lesser degrees, de facto quasi-states in Pakistan demonstrate the ability to exert violence, extract resources, and provide services. These can earn respect and concession, cooptation (or compromises with what state managers might see as a nuisance), and in some cases, violent repression (e.g. Akbar Bugti's killing, the detentions of G.M. Syed and Khan Abdul Ghaffar Khan, and the 1990s crackdown on the MQM). A reputation for violence can deter or intimidate rivals as well as boost recruitment by providing empowerment for disenfranchised individuals.

Quasi-states in a weak polity present real alternatives for challengers beyond the normal/revolutionary dichotomy suggested by Bueno de Mesquita et al. (2003). In a weak polity, quasi-states persist, and engage challengers in maneuvers that are strategically responsive to actors inside and outside the polity. Where state-building is not thorough, internal rivals have plausible futures as quasi-state leaders. As state-building proceeds, internal rivals are absorbed or eliminated. They may become the state's clients, be exiled, or be repressed. Low extraction by the state

Conclusion 191

is associated with surveillance and enforcement limitations and ineffective, incomplete policing. Into this void step the quasi-states.

Incumbent extraction choices, quasi-state strategies, and governance

In weak states, inequitable extraction and preferences for non-tax revenues, combined with quasi-state strategies, will exacerbate and be further reinforced by poor governance.

In Pakistan, leader extraction choices have generated a persistently dysfunctional fiscal sociology. Land reforms have been too modest to reduce landlord power. Growing quasi-state strategies have further weakened the rule of law (already an underprovided public good). In combination, these conditions have reinforced poor governance, which in turn makes expanded domestic taxation harder and encourages further quasi-states to emerge. Both Islamists and ethno-nationalists have pursued secessionist/autonomist quasi-state strategies when political survival conditions are right. However, not all Islamists have pursued quasi-states and not all ethno-nationalists have pursued quasi-states.

Political survival incentives around small winning coalitions lead to underprovided public goods. This provides political opportunities for quasi-state challengers, particularly where a polity-wide coalition is difficult to construct or maintain. The result is an ongoing fiscal sociological dysfunction. Outside resources may serve to undermine prospects for change by increasing political survival prospects for small-coalition leaders. This self-reinforcing cycle is not unbreakable. It requires that incumbents locate and retain a broad-based, large coalition for development-oriented change. A fiscal shift toward broad-based, equitable taxation may change things, because it may spark moves down the fiscal sociological path of increased accountability and state effectiveness. But the process is not likely to be smooth, and will generate severe opposition that may undermine the incumbent's political survival and possibly the polity's survival with it. Not taking this path, however, may risk the polity's survival also, as quasi-state challengers become more strident.

An assumption made by some political analysts is that state survival (in its existing form) is the paramount goal of state managers, and that all other objectives will be subverted to this one. Nasr (2001b) describes Pakistan as a "negotiable state" in which secessionist postures are bargaining positions, in an adjustment process termed "right-sizing." The political survival logic applied to weak states with poorly institutionalized borders suggests that border renegotiations are ways that challengers can vie for office and incumbents can consolidate and retain their leadership positions. This is neither "revolutionary" nor "normal," the general distinction used by Bueno de Mesquita et al. (2003) in *The Logic of Political Survival*, and instead reflects ongoing instability and unsettledness in the polity. It may be that state and polity size undergo significant adjustment in the process whereby a challenger obtains office—with both M.A. Jinnah and Z.A. Bhutto's journey to national leadership providing possible manifestations.

192 *Political survival in Pakistan*

Pakistan was created in a process that involved breaking away from a (prospective) federation, and has suffered one national breakup. These experiences have provided historical learning moments for certain challengers. Negotiable borders and prospects for carving out de jure or de facto autonomy or sovereignty influence challengers' political survival calculations. Where states are weak in their monopoly over coercion, in particular, challengers will pursue quasi-state options. The Pakistan case bears this out, and suggests a political survival interpretation. There are strategic reasons for adopting a secessionist/autonomist posture even if one is less than fully committed to this from an ideological position.

Internal and external actors

In Pakistan, one finds organizations that provide protection, extraction, and welfare and warfare services, using violent means to repel internal and external rivals. Such organizations provide some state-like services in a context where the rule of law is weak, and at times anarchic. A traditional subdisciplinary distinction defines international relations as politics *between* countries and comparative politics as politics *within* countries. This distinction is blurred in weak polities. Internal and external challenges can in practice be difficult to separate. In the extreme, a permeable, interpenetrated weak state may be compared to how L. Carl Brown described Middle East politics under the "Eastern Question" system, in which great powers vied for influence and control in territory where Ottoman control was nominal. However, Pakistan's territorial domain since 1971 is not so far flung, and so the analogy is limited.

The divide between "internal" and "external" blurs further when considering the vital role an outside actor like the US plays in providing resources of rule to Pakistani leaders. This can be understood as a patron-client relationship that affects Pakistani decision-makers' perceived constraints and opportunities. Among Pakistani elites and Karachiites generally, and particularly since the 1998 nuclear tests and the "War on Terror," there is high suspicion about American intentions. One manifestation is found in recent concern voiced over plans for expanding the US embassy: they bear an uncomfortably close resemblance to the fortified large-scale structures found in Iraq and Afghanistan.

The *Logic of Political Survival* defines "selectorate" and "winning coalition" in ways that do not exclude those who reside outside a territory. The Pakistani case suggests that this assumption needs to be critically assessed. One interpretation is that the US is a key figure in the Pakistani selectorate, and often the vital player in a winning coalition. There is a tendency for powerful states with large winning coalition leaders to support small winning coalition leaders elsewhere with aid (Bueno de Mesquita et al., 2003). In Pakistan, such support is believed by many actors to be decisive. In an interpenetrated weak state, an external sponsor or outside ally becomes a member of the winning coalition. In other words, the polity is not sealed from the outside world, but is a porous and permeable entity. The US is commonly perceived as a critical winning coalition member in successive Pakistani governments; this has been captured in

Conclusion 193

the saying that "Allah, America, and the Army" are the three As that govern Pakistan's destiny.

In general, the degree to which external actors have a role in domestic politics calls the traditionally understood boundaries into question. Iran and Saudi Arabia have both been associated with material and moral support to different organizations and entities in Pakistan. An Indian hand is often suspected, usually via covert aid by the notorious intelligence agency RAW (Research and Analysis Wing). Political leaders seem to retain their influence quite well even when they are in exile, sometimes self-imposed. Altaf Husain, the MQM head, resides in London and directs his organization through a coordination committee. Both Nawaz Sharif and Benazir Bhutto retained their primacy and returned after years outside Pakistan. It is difficult to draw the line between those who are "foreign" and "domestic," when kingmakers and leaders so routinely reside outside Pakistan.

Islam and ethnicity

Ethnicity and religion provide networks, frames, solidarity, and trust that decrease barriers to collective action. Social capital provides needed glue for productive transactions in society. Yet that social capital can be the basis for exclusive zero-sum activism with outgroups, and produce violent conflict. This is particularly the case in ethnically fragmented contexts. Poor communication, low literacy, and linguistic diversity make it difficult and costly to coordinate and manage long-distance ties in an effective, stable fashion. There is not an encompassing or sufficiently broad affinity group, and the closest possibilities are patriotic attachment to the country or a common denominator Islamic symbol. There have been attempts to identify loyalty to Pakistan with loyalty to Islam; one example is the primary school chant *"Pakistan ka matlab kiya? La ilaha illallah"* (What does Pakistan mean? There is no God but God!). Yet these efforts have not prevented breakaway efforts or secessionist rhetoric, with deep alienation from Pakistan expressed openly in Balochistan, for example. The potential for a genuinely aggregative political party seems low, because parties have not historically been very successful at mass mobilization. They reflect general institutional fragility, and are factionalized along personality lines (such as the PML), ruled by a dynasty (such as the PPP and ANP), or based on an ideological vanguard (such as the Jamaat-e-Islami).

In analyzing Muslim societies, one distorting tendency is to portray "Islamic" actors as driven exclusively or predominantly by ideas rather than interests, and in this sense political exceptional. Another distortion is to treat "Islamic" rationales as a purely instrumental choice by strategic actors pursuing material goals such as class interests. Acknowledging an affinity between ideas and interests does not require assigning causal priority to ideas over interests or vice versa. Complicating this picture, Islamists have an incentive to represent themselves as ideologues, untainted by morally reprehensible political compromise. By appearing to be motivated by principle rather than self-interest, they are more likely to gain religious support and legitimacy. Their task is to convince followers that a particular

194 *Political survival in Pakistan*

policy choice favors "Islam" or the "Islamic way" rather than the individual "Islamists."

Islamic symbols can be deployed in diverse and apparently contradictory ways, partly because there is no widely accepted supreme interpreter and arbiter. Correspondingly, such symbols have not had a monolithic impact. The *ulama* seek to attain and retain this role and to act as gatekeepers, even as the tradition evolves.[3] Public opinion may play a key arbitration role in determining acceptable and unacceptable interpretations, but public opinion, much like the public, is fragmented. Yet appeals to "Islam" still matter; Islam remains what Bobby S. Sayyid has called a "master signifier" (Sayyid, 2004). Although its impact is not uniform, "Islam" retains a critical role in signification and representation before a diverse public. Virtually all political groupings have some reference to Islamic identity and tradition, although it is possible to distinguish between rejectionist secularizers as compared to "opportunistic" and more committed "thoroughgoing" Islamizers (a distinction made by Nasr, 2002). In Pakistan, even secularizers have tended to reference God and religion in pursuing legitimacy.

Incumbent appeals to national loyalty based on Islam remain a double-edged sword because they invite Islamist criticism that the political leadership is inadequately Islamic. Framing as a process is an active and conscious ingredient throughout the political spectrum in Pakistan. The Pakistani experience suggests that leaders and challengers pursue political survival deploy symbols tied to "Islam" selectively and strategically. Z.A. Bhutto moved against the Ahmaddi sect, and made rhetorical and policy gestures that were aimed at obtaining support from Islamic support, particularly as the Nizam-e-Mustafa movement gained strength. Musharraf's "enlightened moderation" message was accompanied by signals that he was willing to crack down on the "bad Muslims" in the Lal Masjid standoff and the Taliban insurgents. Yet these were only some among many competing efforts to frame conflicts with religious symbol.

Aside from sometimes providing a support or a resource for state ideology and challengers, Islam is also the "leitmotif of an otherwise variegated culture" (Jalal, 1990: 278). Commercially, Islam is used to sell and market diverse goods and services. For example, "Islamic honey" is marketed in brightly lit outlets in Karachi, although the merchants are hard-pressed to explain what makes their honey more "Islamic" than other products on the market. "Islamic finance" is supposed to meet Islamic guidelines, although these have been contested. Appearing to adhere to Islamic norms is used to signal a seller's trustworthiness, especially in contracts where there is high information asymmetry and trust is needed—for example, a home-building contractor finds it worthwhile to invest heavily in displays of religious piety. This makes potential clients more likely to retain the contractor's services. To some, betrayed trust and failure to meet expectations has roused a deep disenchantment with "mullahs" or others who self-represent as religious authorities.

Ideas are necessary but not sufficient explanations for ethnic and religious political behavior. Ideas can provide rationales, justifications, and inspiration. However, for these factors to actually translate into political action, opportunities need to be available. To effectively press their demands these groups must have a

Conclusion   195

leadership capable of mobilizing followers. The free-rider problem must be overcome for the mobilization to transform from small groups to mass activities. Resources needed to recruit, organize, and supply participants in a collective effort must be found.

Ethno-nationalists and Islamists have both tried the quasi-state approach. In a weak polity, one way for a challenger to gain high office is to gerrymander vigorously, and through a fait accompli. It is possible to carve out a jurisdiction because the polity is weak. Challengers are rational in that they respond to the environment in which they find themselves and their supporting coalitions. Yet leaders have repeatedly chosen actions that further their political survival rather than what one might deduce from their stated ethnic or religious agenda. This helps explain why an ethno-nationalist group like Jeay Sindh can be broken up into *wafaqi* (federation-friendly) subfactions to compete with hardliners: leaders see rewards in creating a new faction.

From one perspective, "ethnicity" is a category that encompasses religious identity (Horowitz, 1985, cited by Varshney, 2009). From this perspective, religious identity cannot be sufficient to generate different outcomes than linguistic or other social identity-based groupings. But there are some practical differences. Although it is true that in South Asia, suicide bombings were pioneered in the Tamil struggle and not associated with religious inspiration, in Pakistan, suicide bombings are not usually associated with non-religious ethnic groups. At the same time, most groups in Pakistan include some religious references, however vague. The MQM, not usually classified as a religious group, includes a social service arm called "Khidmat-e-Khalq," meaning "service to Creation," a title bearing a religious connotation. MQM members who have been killed are described as "shuhada," the term usually reserved for religious martyrs.

If a challenger can mobilize people once, they are more likely to be ready for collective action again, because they have built up solidarity and a network, and become known and identifiable participants to each other. Hence, it may be strategically wise to mobilize people for a common cause such as responding to an affront to religious sentiments. Once that collective action is successful, the sponsoring organization now retains some capacity to mobilize people further, for more specific goals. The initial mobilization may help regularize and institutionalize participation through organizational ties or recruitment into the organization. An example might be G.M. Syed's career as a Sindhi politician, which was propelled in part by a Hindu-Muslim clash over a disputed religious site.

The Jamaat-e-Islami draws support from the middle class, and a highly disciplined, ideologically committed cadre. It is distinct from other religious political formations. While seeking to appeal to Pakistanis on a non-ethnic, religious ideology basis, the Jamaat-e-Islami allied in provincial government with the regional autonomist Muttahida Majlis-e-Amal coalition in the 2002 election. Jamaat-e-Islami supporters would not view this as a contradiction. Thus, having an Islamist ideology, whether it is the Jamaat-e-Islami form or a different grouping, does not entirely preclude a group from a quasi-state orientation.

196   *Political survival in Pakistan*

The Al-Qaeda approach is reportedly a quasi-state strategy combined with a revolutionary goal. An alleged communiqué from Al-Qaeda leader Ayman Zawahri to Abu Musab al-Zarqawi, the Al-Qaeda in Iraq leader, suggests creating what are in effect quasi-states, starting with a de facto strategy and culminating in a de jure claim: "Establish an Islamic authority or emirate, then develop it and support it until it achieves the level of a caliphate over as much territory as you can to spread its power such as in Iraq" (quoted in Rashid, 2008: 278). The Taliban and loosely allied groups in Pakistan have in some instances followed a similar strategy. Leader Mangal Bagh has recently claimed that his moral police, a vigilante enforcement unit for his edicts, can reach anywhere, while implicitly acknowledging that his immediate domain is much narrower (*Dawn*, July 25, 2008).

The inclusion-moderation debate in recent scholarship has examined questions regarding Islamist participation in coalition governments, elections, and other democratic processes. Schwedler (2006) argues, based on the Yemeni and Jordanian cases, that political inclusion has a moderating influence on Islamist policy stances. The Pakistani experience suggests that in weak states, a critical intervening variable is the degree to which challengers perceive prospects for political office through a quasi-state strategy. Where such prospects are high, and the challenger has poor chances of success at the national electoral level, the challenger may pursue a regional autonomist strategy, without necessarily excluding simultaneous contention for national office. The Jamaat-e-Islami experience in Pakistan suggests this. The quasi-state option's viability mediates how political inclusion might influence the direction taken by Islamist challengers.

Leadership, developmental outcomes, and distributional coalitions

In her 2006 presidential address to the American Political Science Association, Margaret Levi declared that understanding how to establish good government is a major social scientific problem. "Good government" is effective (able to protect the population from violence, ensure property rights, and supply desired public goods) and representative and accountable to the population it is meant to serve (Levi, 2006: 5). Good government is not necessarily democratic. Levi also notes that while there is a vast literature on leadership, what is lacking is a model for how good leadership originates and how it is ensured (Levi, 2006: 11). Dynamic theory is needed to grasp how transformation to good government occurs.

David Hume and James Madison, among others, argued for organizational design that would protect against "knaves"; "our theories must go further to specify what sets of constraints are most likely to motivate and produce able leadership and in what contexts and circumstances" (Levi, 2006: 11). Many Pakistanis would readily describe national and subnational leadership posts as staffed by "knaves" or the equivalent. As a high-level former civil servant asserted, revenue administration and law and order are both critical to good government (Interview with former civil servant, 2009). In both areas, Pakistan has severe deficits. Governance problems are exacerbated by problems in these two, and also defined by them.

Pakistanis often express cynicism about leaders, who are seen as sacrificing morality and principle for power and privilege. According to this widespread view, moral corruption among individual leaders is responsible for the country's failures to provide public goods. Virtually all interviewees mentioned corruption, and many ascribed it to political leaders' individual moral failings. A political survival perspective is agnostic about politicians' moral fiber, and instead focuses on political survival exigencies. According to this view, good leadership decisions regarding development in Pakistan are difficult because political survival considerations shape policy choices. Leaders depend on a narrow winning coalition for political survival; consequently they provide private benefits to a privileged few rather than public goods. Providing public goods does not produce a sustainable winning coalition drawn from beneficiaries; in contrast, not providing private goods means that the existing winning coalition will dwindle and former supporters may defect to rivals.

In the middle of the twentieth century, China and South Korea had arguably suffered invasion, civil war, collapsed administrative machinery, and warlordism. In contrast, Pakistan had an administrative framework, a road and railway network, a canal system, a ship repair shop, and engineering expertise in agricultural and transport (Siddiqui, 2001: 55). Pakistan in the 1950s and 1960s appeared poised for an industrial takeoff in the manner predicted by some development theorists. There was surplus labor coming to the cities, a strong-armed, business-friendly military government, and a well-disciplined bureaucratic leadership. Pakistan imported economic advisors to support national planning. Yet China and South Korea have leapt forward in economic development in comparison to Pakistan.

There are various reasons given, often complementary, as to why a more favorable developmental outcome did not result: military overspending and the resultant investment squeeze, governmental instability making effective planning and policy-making difficult, patronage undermining institutions, civil war, and underprovided public goods. Ayesha Jalal (1995) points to a "political economy of defense," and Ayesha Siddiqua (2007) suggests that the military-business-foundation nexus she terms "Milbus" siphoned resources and investments away from development. In a thoughtful study comparing Pakistan's development with countries in Asia, Omar Noman suggests that underprovided social services reflect an elitist approach to development that fosters inequality and does not choose "inclusive capitalism" (Noman, 1997). This is self-defeating, because investment in human capital, if insufficient, becomes an obstacle to growth.

Business-friendly policies under Ayub did produce growth as well as increasing wealth concentration in what were described as the 22 families. Z.A. Bhutto's nationalizations, although partial and selective, may also have been a failed development policy, turning instead into liabilities and rent-seeking and patronage opportunities rather than growth and development generators. Zia ul-Haq's policies left the landed elites in place and added to the slice of the national pie appropriated by the military. The military, bureaucratic, and landed elites have become increasingly intertwined through intermarriage and social ties. The military increasingly resembles landed and commercial gentry, and landed families usually have highly

198 *Political survival in Pakistan*

placed relatives in military, bureaucratic, and electoral office. Such enhanced ties among winning coalition members have furthered their ability to obtain special privileges and private goods.

Although there have been some changes, narrow, elite-based distributional coalitions retain their hold on the selectorate. They have remained bottlenecks for public goods provision, preventing leaders from enacting significant policy changes that would reduce the private goods these groups benefit from. In Pakistan, the winning coalition has been small, and focused around well-established elite groups. Existing policy paths are difficult to break, because it is difficult to mobilize and maintain an encompassing coalition—a sufficiently large distributional coalition so that its preferences are public goods or majority goods— against the narrow distributional coalitions that often dominate policy choices by incumbents.

Occasional challenges based on popular agitation have succeeded in creating serious problems for incumbents, but have not translated into a sustained large-scale winning coalition that would lead an office-holder to work systematically and consistently for public goods provision. A related problem is that the prominent quasi-state mode of political challenge—oriented as it is to regional and sub-national affinity groups and loci—undermines the possibility that an encompassing coalition would form, emerge, and persist.

Former State Bank Governor Ishrat Husain argues that contract enforcement, reduced corruption, and social service delivery to the poor would have far-ranging implications for growth and development (Husain 2003: 146–147). Pakistan faces severe challenges in each area. Contract enforcement is often ineffective and dispute adjudication is slow, particularly when embroiled in the court system. Numerous anecdotes from interviews testify to problems in contract enforcement. Compared to Singapore, the best performing regional country in costs of doing business, in Pakistan there are more procedures to be followed, it takes longer to reach a settlement, and the costs of reaching a settlement are higher (Burki, 2009b).

Corruption is rife, so much so that Transparency International has rated Pakistan among the world's more corrupt countries on its perceived corruption index (Transparency International, 2002). Virtually all Pakistanis, like other South Asians surveyed, reported paying bribes to police; in Pakistan, however, land administration and tax revenue bureaucracies were ranked as more corrupt compared to four other South Asian countries. Fear that contracting partners will defect makes it necessary to police relationships closely, raising transactions costs. Bodyguards, watchmen, and costly alarm systems are necessary: a small neighborhood pharmacy in a middle-class area in Karachi has at least two armed guards, a closed-circuit television system, and several workers. When combined with the extortion that takes place in protection rackets from "political" militias, businesses face significant hurdles.

In practice, social service delivery meant for the poor is often siphoned away by richer social segments. A civil servant noted that in Sind, a privileged minority estimated to number less than ten percent of the population, routinely expropriated government programs (Siddiqui, 2001: 9). Institutions that are meant to target and serve the poor find their services diverted to other uses, undermining the effort to invest in human capital and provide for development needs.

Institutional fragility

Political survival-oriented behavior in an environment where "normal" politics are difficult to discern have contributed to making rules and institutions fragile and unstable. Politicians pursuing absolute authority have undermined the institutions that may constrain them. An interpretation based on the present study is that political survival as a goal has outweighed political leaders' and challengers' ideological commitment to institutional stability. Rather than risk the possibility that a threat to political survival might develop from institutions, leaders have sought to change basic rules in their favor (often succeeding in this), and thus kept institutions transitory.

An environment rife with political violence and vendetta reflects and contributes to institutional fragility. Insurgencies, counter-insurgency tactics, and covert action by state agencies against opposition groupings have played a role. Assassination, exile, imprisonment, and other punishment on politically motivated, selective charges have been used to eliminate or divert potential rivals. Liaquat Ali Khan was assassinated. Zia ul-Haq was killed in a mysterious plane crash, and conspiracy theories regarding his death continue to abound, finding their way into the popular imagination. Chief of Army Staff Asif Nawaz died suddenly and mysteriously; his brother, the journalist and author Shuja Nawaz described evidence pointing to an assassination (Nawaz, 2008). Zulfiqar, Murtaza, and Benazir Bhutto were all killed, and many also view Shahnawaz Bhutto's death as suspicious. Nawaz Sharif went into exile rather than face possible capital punishment under Musharraf's regime. In Balochistan, Nawab Akbar Bugti was killed in a missile strike as a dispute with Musharraf's government escalated. The MQM's Altaf Hussain runs his organization from London, with phone-in speeches and a media presence; his self-imposed exile reflects concern for his well-being. Targeted killings of political workers in Karachi in 2008 and 2009 numbered in the hundreds. Political loss brings severe consequences, and this encourages a no-holds-barred approach in which vendettas are common, further undermining formal processes.

Institutional development in a Pakistani context requires social forces that work against efforts by incumbents and challengers to manipulate and undermine institutions. If these forces are sufficiently mobilized to retain a check on leader choices, then institutions are more likely to survive attempted subversion. It is not clear whether the lawyers' movement fits this description. Lawyers had a vocal role in advocating for Iftikhar Chaudhury, the chief justice deposed by Musharraf; whether that advocacy translates eventually into a permanent attachment to an independent judiciary, or remains a push for one favored political personality over another, remains to be seen. The optimistic view is that this will signal to future executives that they cannot interfere so high-handedly with the judiciary's independence. If this view is accurate, then it constrains executive power and bolsters the rule of law.

200 *Political survival in Pakistan*

Political survival and political capacity

Pakistan has an economy where large segments are undocumented and the lack of a tax culture make it difficult to extract resources through taxation. Political capacity constraints can limit the policy options available to leaders, but capacity-building is itself a policy choice. The Pakistani experience suggests that political survival considerations have degraded existing capacity in some areas and not promoted additional capacity in others. The fiscal sociology approach emphasizes that political development also rests on where, how, and what extraction took place. In the major area over which the tax net has not been extended (agricultural income), some capacity building is needed (in updating the produce indices used to assess agricultural income, for example).

Such technical hurdles, however, appear minor when compared to the unwillingness to air agricultural tax proposals by incumbents and their winning coalitions. Caretaker Prime Minister Moeen Qureshi's tenure shows that it is not merely political capacity that is the problem. Unconstrained by concerns about retaining his position in the long term, he imposed an agricultural tax for the first time. Critics assailed him as a foreign agent working for policies supported by international financial institutions. Yet the fact remains that when a leader with different political survival constraints came into office, different policies were pursued.

In Pakistan's early days, the bureaucracy enjoyed a nonpartisan reputation. Increasing politicization in the civil service has added to the state's weakness, particularly as political leaders have moved to influence and override appointments, reducing bureaucrats' autonomy. Interview data suggest that the self-image and socialization of bureaucrats has affected their behavior and interactions with incumbent leaders, helping to define from an epistemic and practical perspective what policy options were available to incumbent leaders. This raises questions about the impact morale and esprit de corps may have on strategic calculations. Civil bureaucrats (the early generations in particular) tend to retain an elitist and highly status-conscious mindset, viewing both those from military background and many legislators as intellectually, socially, or morally inferior. The high discretionary powers given to Pakistan's civil service officers brought an aura of authority with them. Retired officers often relate anecdotes that show their insight into social problems and commitment to meaningful changes when compared to incompetent or malintentioned others. While self-serving, such narratives demonstrate a professional pride that appears to have eroded.

Merit-based selection processes in Pakistan's early decades yielded capable and energetic administrators. Over time, incumbents sought to eliminate troublesome figures and replace them with political supporters. Such actions undermined the high integrity that the bureaucratic self-image demanded. One consequence was a comparably high tendency to exploit office for personal gain. Threats to civil servants' tenure, autonomy, job security, and even personal freedom have been accompanied by highly placed bureaucrats' full-fledged entry into winning coalitions and the pursuit of private benefits.

Conclusion   201

High corruption among the police is a common complaint. Where policing reforms have succeeded in reducing corruption, it appears that in addition to higher pay, some significant effort has been made to indoctrinate recruits with an ethical framework. The lesson with the civil service, however, seems to suggest that if political leaders persist in manipulating appointments and punishing independent-minded officers, there may be significant damage to morale in the police force and unabashed further corruption. According to some Pakistanis, and reports describing police appointments awarded to politically favored lawbreakers, this is already a reality.

Fiscal reform and devolution

Economist and former Finance Minister Shahid Javed Burki's prescription for Pakistan's economic development is based on three critical areas: tax reform, land reform, and provincial devolution (Burki, 2008b). Interviews and secondary accounts all testify to these needs; they are commonly acknowledged. The present study argues that political survival pressures on leaders and challengers impede meaningful changes in these areas. Short-term political survival constraints prevent, discourage, or divert incumbents from making needed structural changes for Pakistan's long-term well-being. As public or majority goods remain underprovided or are siphoned into private benefits, poor governance continues to fester, and quasi-state agitation grows. The threat to Pakistan's integrity grows with it. Arriving at a majority view that Burki's prescriptions are needed is not sufficient. For these proposed reforms to be adopted and implemented, political survival constraints and opportunities must be altered.

Devolution, tax reform, and land reform can be risky for an incumbent's political survival. Devolution may provide challengers with additional resources and better position them for further autonomist or secessionist agitation. An effort to broaden the tax net will provoke opposition and defections from the winning coalition. Land reform will likely drive landlords into an opposing coalition. Good governance and public goods provision do not bring sufficient political survival rewards. In contrast, cutting private goods risks defections from an incumbent's winning coalition. Consequently, public goods provision is low in a narrow winning coalition context. Given that devolution, tax reform, and land reform are key public goods, the logic of political survival forces the question: are these accompanied by support coalitions that can provide an incumbent or challenger with a sustainable winning coalition? To date, Pakistan's history suggests otherwise.

In choosing critical policies affecting the country's fiscal skeleton, differing ideological proclivities among Ayub Khan, Z. A. Bhutto, and Zia ul-Haq remained hostage to political survival imperatives. Suboptimal fixes for fiscal problems, such as international financing and covert measures, were preferred because they posed fewer threats to political survival. Efforts to provide more public or majority goods were half-hearted, reversed, or never undertaken. Z. A. Bhutto's nationalizations were a significant move to reallocate some business enterprises to the state. Yet they were selective, became sources for private goods to Z. A. Bhutto's winning

202 *Political survival in Pakistan*

coalition, and acted as a brake on growth. Later leaders' moves toward privatization were less than transparent, and became enrichment opportunities for the well-connected, earning the moniker "piratization." Policies ostensibly in the public interest instead generated private goods for those in the winning coalition.

Irregular and arbitrary political turnover reduce predictability, which make economic contracts more risky and costly. It also gives leaders a high discount rate for the future, making them value present predation over the longer-term rewards that developmental policies might produce. Long-term interests are put on hold for short-term goals. But military rulers with longer-term survival possibilities did not do much better than civilian leaders, suggesting that groups that composed the winning coalitions remained the determining influence in policy choice.

A broad support coalition for a challenger or an incumbent may eventually arise through macrostructural changes in Pakistani society. A bigger middle class would likely have a strong preference for security and clarity in property rights. Collective action hurdles must be overcome to mobilize an encompassing coalition that can sustain an incumbent in office. Such a coalition, if coherent and sustained, can support and push incumbent policies toward public goods provision. Yet the Pakistani experience also shows that civilian leaders seem to work swiftly to narrow their winning coalition, as a way to ensure loyalty and control. (With fewer members in the winning coalition, each individual member feels that her future special privileges are directly tied to the incumbent's tenure in office, and thus will be less likely to defect to a challenger.)

In general, high public goods provision has the potential to undermine and reduce quasi-state challenges. Better infrastructure and law and order and equitable taxes would help integrate the country economically. This in turn has the potential to reduce the relative deprivation on which ethnic mobilization thrives. A rising middle class would reinforce the process. Yet the process would also unleash unpredictable forces. There could be different challenges to the incumbent, such as occupational distributional coalitions. There is the possibility that better infrastructure would facilitate ethnic mobilization, sharpening challengers' ability to rally affinity group members.

An augmented fiscal skeleton can generate social contract expectations and spur a developmental fiscal sociological path. Pakistan's polity is one where smaller winning coalitions routinely succeed. Large-scale mobilizations, such as the Nizam-e-Mustafa movement and the anti-Ayub agitations, have taken place and been potent but short-lived political forces. Challengers and officeholders have not succeeded in retaining a coherent, lasting, and broad-based coalition as a powerful force. For challengers and incumbents to change Pakistan's fiscal sociological path and improve governance, a sustained broad support coalition would be helpful. A very narrow winning coalition will not be likely to support efforts to increase domestic extraction because such a move risks a destabilizing or revolutionary political backlash.

The Pakistani experience suggests that there are extraction choices that differ from simply raising or lowering tax rates, which presuppose an established tax

Conclusion 203

apparatus and system. Expanding domestic direct taxation requires either a broader public mandate that comes with a broad-based and large winning coalition, or a narrow winning coalition regime that has an incumbent willing to resist or repress a roused opposition. It is unclear whether political empowerment for a higher population proportion then brings about higher public goods provision, or whether public goods themselves empower greater numbers in the population. Both may be true, and the answer has implications for political change. The political survival mechanism does not explain the macrostructural processes that may lead to a broader winning coalition and eventually force better public policy. Political survival does help explain why leaders in some contexts persistently make choices that appear to work contrary to the public interest. Macrostructural changes may produce a shift that forces the leader to rely on a broader winning coalition. That broader group would favor policies that are geared toward public goods more than private goods.

Rather than constructing a broad support coalition, challengers often find it easier to pursue quasi-state authority. That a challenger may prefer to be "the head on a chicken rather than the tail on a phoenix" adds further impetus to the quasi-state strategy. The consequence is an increasingly fragmented polity, with heightened risk of violent internal conflict. Provincial and local autonomy issues are potential challenges to the state and the incumbent's authority, and may take secessionist forms. Seeking complete de jure sovereignty rather than simply de facto autonomy within the Pakistani polity may well be the eventual path that some quasi-state leaders follow. If, however, power can be devolved effectively to the provinces, then some challengers may be satisfied and more stable governance and higher public goods provision may result. For that to happen, the rules of the game have to become established and accepted. This is not easy in a crisis-ridden context where the controversial One Unit Scheme integrating West Pakistan into a single province and engineering East Pakistan's secession are not-too-distant memories. Local and provincial authorities have oscillated in jurisdiction and strength, depending on the political machinations at the center.

In Pakistan, what is apparently "national" political activism remains largely rooted in quasi-states. Regarding the new "internationalism" among activists, Sidney Tarrow finds that apparent transnational activism remains rooted in sovereign states (Tarrow, 2005). This observation may be mirrored in a weak state like Pakistan. The sovereign state has a competitor, the quasi-state. In an apparently broad social movement where "quasi-states" are the key organizational bases, movement participation will be contingent on compatibility with quasi-state priorities. In other words, activists will first consider how the movement benefits or costs their quasi-state project before deciding on participation. Overlooking the quasi-state dimension may produce misleading assessments. Political activism that appears to reach around the country may instead represent parochial quasi-state efforts. Whether such activism can indeed produce an inter-ethnic, inter-sect, and internally diverse coalition on a Pakistan-wide basis remains to be seen.

A critical question is whether quasi-states will disappear, persist as alternative governance entities, eventually becoming recognized as sovereign entities, or be

204 *Political survival in Pakistan*

incorporated as fully recognized subunits within the national polity. Decentralization could strengthen Pakistan's integrity as a state by providing better governance, or weaken it, by allowing subunits a greater prospect for defection and secession. This is a dilemma faced by state managers. That Pakistan might break up was an early fear, and it was realized with Bangladesh's creation. One question is whether decentralization and devolution might incorporate and retain subunits within the polity. Early leaders, such as Chaudhry Khaliquzzaman, felt that the provinces would hold Pakistan hostage to blackmail, and true democracy could not be allowed because they would push to secede; therefore, a strong centralized government was needed. *Daily News* editor S. M. Fazal asserted that during referendums on accession to Pakistan there was substantial opposition, and this meant that free elections would always yield a result empowering those opposed to the Pakistan state project (Interview with S.M. Fazal, 2009). Such fears seem to preclude authentic devolution. One worry is that outside forces will exploit local dissatisfactions and support destabilizing secessionism or active rebellions. India is the usual threat voiced by Pakistan's elites.

The struggle for genuine federalism against a unitary state remains an unfolding battle in many developing countries. Pakistan's challengers reveal that that there is an active dual possibility that entrepreneurial political challengers pursue. They negotiate an environment where they might face repression or inclusion. Their secessionist or autonomist postures might be a bargaining chip, an extreme position from which they can compromise in return for a valuable appointment within the polity framework. At the same time, the de facto quasi-state status allows them to exert informal or extra-legal authority, and to have a survival apparatus in place against attempted repression by the state. This typically comes with firepower and the organizational means to deploy violent tactics.

Effectively incorporating quasi-states involves some trust, and can be modeled as a Prisoner's Dilemma game. Incumbents who devolve authority hope that a challenger will not turn newfound jurisdiction into the basis for a revolutionary or secessionist challenge. A challenger who accepts the offered official jurisdiction by an incumbent hopes that this is not a symbolic move purely, but one that devolves true authority and control. If one side defects while the other cooperates, the defector gains an advantage. If both defect, the outcome is likely to be a bloody confrontation, one that is at least in the medium term a significant negative for both sides.

In a way, the lesson of the 1970 elections is that cooperation by one side (electoral participation) did achieve the expected outcome, as there was a defection from the other side. Mujib ur-Rehman's party pursued a heavily autonomist platform through Pakistan's first universal election, an official selection institution. But when his party won and obtained a clear majority, the central state apparatus, concentrated as it was around the West Pakistani political establishment, did not allow him to form a government. This defection was accompanied by a bloody showdown, eventually a humiliating loss for Pakistani self-image, and what may have been a Pyrrhic victory for Mujib ur-Rehman. This offered a lesson for future

Conclusion 205

challengers: trusting powerful central state agents or winning coalition members is a risky gamble.

Given that a similar Prisoner's Dilemma game is played by other challenger-incumbent dyads in different iterations, the lesson from Mujib's experience is that the Pakistani state's leadership is likely to defect. The 1970 elections and subsequent civil war provided a dramatic historical juncture that sparked learning among other actors. G.M. Syed's career suggests this interpretation, as well as the early positions held by the MQM, and comments made in interviews regarding Balochi secessionism.

Provincial autonomy, devolution, confederalism and federalism are labels that interviewees used to describe strategies to preserve the Pakistani state's integrity. The common theme is recognizing the polity's composite nature and bringing actual or nascent quasi-states into a common framework that includes a central government, albeit with a more restricted jurisdiction. Interviewees from different backgrounds expressed their conviction that the present course was unsustainable and that major changes were needed. Devolving authority would likely improve policy effectiveness because policy-makers would be closer to the social contexts that they are seeking to affect. Offering such authority would also provide challengers with prospects for more powerful local office and incorporate them into the national polity's fold.

Class-based affinity groups

Social class provides one potentially far-reaching affinity group on which challengers can draw. However, prospects for revolutionary change remain uncertain. There have been broad-based agitations that have threatened incumbents, such as the anti-Ayub demonstrations, and the activism that produced the Pakistan National Alliance against Z.A. Bhutto. Yet these have failed to transform into a sustained basis for a challenger to remove the incumbent, remake the system, and retain office. The prospects for a class-based radical shift in Pakistan are low because there are too many ethnic and social divides that cross-cut and fragment a revolutionary coalition.

Writing in 2001, civil servant Tasneem Siddiqui did not believe a Pakistan breakup, civil war, or revolution was imminent, because the "economic fundamentals are very strong" with "no shortage of essential goods like food grains, edible oil, milk, or petrol" and the poor are not organized on a class basis (Siddiqui, 2001: 61). Things may be changing because essential goods, especially food staples, have seen sharp price hikes or shortages in 2008. Sharp increases in cooking oil prices and rising milk prices were accompanied by accusations that the milk supply is contaminated (see *Dawn* from the week of April 1, 2008). It was common to see long lines for subsidized wheat, often attended by day laborers or maids who were sacrificing a day's wages while seeking to obtain cheaper food. While mass activism based on broad economic class may be difficult to sustain, narrower occupational ties may provide another avenue for activism. The lawyers' protest mobilizations in 2007 and 2008 provide one example.

206 *Political survival in Pakistan*

A different shift may simply follow the middle class's growth. Increased numbers from the middle class of non-feudal background contested and won seats in the 2008 elections (Dalrymple, 2008):

> The rise of the middle class was most clear in the number of winning candidates who, for the first time, came from such a background. In Jhang district of the rural Punjab, for example, as many as ten out of eleven of those elected are the sons of revenue officers, senior policemen, functionaries in the civil bureaucracy, and so on, rather than usual feudal zamindars. This would have been unthinkable ten years ago.
>
> Even the most benign feudal lords suffered astonishing electoral reverses. Mian Najibuddin Owaisi was not just the popular feudal lord of the village of Khanqah Sharif in the southern Punjab, he was also the sajjada nasheen, the descendant of the local Sufi saint, and so, like Sadruddin Shah, regarded as something of a holy man as well as the local landowner. But recently Najibuddin made the ill-timed switch from supporting Nawaz Sharif's PML-N to the pro-Musharraf Q-League.
>
> (Dalrymple, 2008)

Najibuddin lost his constituency to a middle-class candidate, the first loss of his family since their entry into politics in 1975. This indicates a possible shift away from landlord power.

That assessment, however, is premature. Dalrymple's optimism can be contrasted with different views. Electoral turnout remains low by South Asian standards. Even when not in a position to legislate, landlords often carry quasi-state power. Focusing on elected "middle class" representatives ignores the fact that to govern effectively and make meaningful changes, one must consider the fact that the state apparatus for policy implementation is intimately tied to landlords and figures tainted by corruption scandals. A business professional stated another common view: Pakistan is not ready for democracy because the masses do not know how to proceed; they do what a *wadera* tells them to, or are manipulated by propaganda, or have poor information, or have limited critical thinking skills (Conversation with businessperson, April 2008).

Moreover, in order to create meaningful governance reforms, a growing middle class must bring with it a new set of political survival constraints and pressures on the incumbent. A growing middle class alone is not sufficient; its weight in numbers must be translated to political survival mechanisms. An obvious mode is through legislative elections, but the victors must not be constrained by heavy-handed vetoes such as the contentious Article 58 2 (b), the president's power to dismiss the government, or by a lack of oversight over budgetary items such as defense. These empower narrow groups over a broader social class in the selectorate. Rather than having a situation where any winning coalition can be broken if support from a particular coalition member is withdrawn, political survival mechanisms need to be altered so that any winning coalition would require significant middle and

Conclusion 207

lower-middle class support. Various political groupings have sought to appropriate the middle class mantle. Benazir's declared focus was to build the middle class. The MQM also portrays itself as a middle class party. The Jamaat-e-Islami's cadres are also largely drawn from the middle class. In other words, there are political leaders and formations that have or claim to have or seek to have a middle class constituency. Yet this in itself is likely to be insufficient, unless it can translate into a sustained winning coalition that does not fragment and is not easily supplanted by narrow, elite distributional coalitions.

Altering the fiscal path

A leader seeking political survival and serious tax reform must work to forge a countervailing economic lobby that outweighs narrow distributional coalitions. A broad-based tax net will, in the fiscal sociology envisaged by Schumpeter, be associated with a government that is responsible to a broader segment in the polity on which it depends for resources. That broader grouping may be the "encompassing coalition" that is needed. The causal sequence to achieve this is not entirely clear: it may be that the broad coalition develops after a heightened tax effort, or that an expanded tax effort comes once a broader coalition is in place. Whichever takes place, the political survival approach suggests that at critical decision junctures, such as external shocks that produce heightened fiscal requirements, the political survival calculations made by incumbents are intervening factors.

Someone who seeks governance or economic reform without carefully considering the weak polity context is likely to encounter unintended consequences and perverse results. Quasi-state entities can foul up policy goals, because they are alternative and rival mechanisms by which resources are allocated. Generating a better fiscal sociology through executive decision is not easy, to say the least. First, fiscal sociology is unpredictable. Second, the political backlash may remove the incumbent from office and undo needed reforms. Third, the changes needed might have to do with structural factors beyond the executive's control. If the overriding concern leaders have is ensuring their tenure in office, then generating an alternative, sustainable winning coalition is key to policy changes. This is difficult. The incumbent must be creative and engineer the appropriate affinity group; this may require molding or locating a distributional coalition that outweighs the smaller ones.

State centralization is sometimes considered a dimension of state strength. By this definition, a confederation is a weak state while a unitary state is strong. Pakistan's central governments have not devolved significant power to the provincial levels, despite the 1973 Constitution's pledge to eliminate the "Concurrent List" (legislative subjects over which both the central and the provincial governments have jurisdiction). The irony is that some significant and lasting devolution—in other words, weakening the state along the political centralization dimension—may improve governance, reduce law and order problems, and eventually allow the central state to become stronger on other dimensions.

208 *Political survival in Pakistan*

Pakistan has had a perverse fiscal sociology, and a quasi-state tradition. A key problem in Pakistan's intergovernmental fiscal system is the "low level of own-source revenues generated by local governments, and the failure to tie together the quality and quantity of services delivered, on the one hand, with the cost of those services, on the other" (Peterson, 2002). Making this link clearly would allow citizens to compare the costs they incur with respect to the service quality that they receive, and offer feedback accordingly. Adjustments to increase fiscal federalism may be a way to devolve authority, help absorb quasi-states formally into the polity, and improve governance.

Thus, the seeds of future success may lie in appropriate federalism and fiscal decentralization, so that there is more local responsiveness. A key difficulty is that de facto quasi-state authority does not usually occupy a formally delineated institutional position, but performs extra-legal activity in a near-vacuum. In that near-anarchy, organizations that survive must be able to purvey physical security and violence. Where security dilemmas arise, a logic of consequences prevails that is closer to real-politik and further from institutionalized dispute resolution norms. Without careful management, warlordism may result.

Equitable, broad-based taxation is one feature in a fiscal sociological path wherein a social contract between rulers and ruled produces a powerful impulse for good governance. In Pakistan, a polity where winning coalitions are usually narrow, the tax net small, transactions often undocumented, and tax culture weak, the social contract of broadly extracted resources for desired public goods has been sidestepped. Prescriptions for policy change and reform must take political survival constraints into account. International borrowing and inflationary money creation remain "soft options" in comparison to broad-based direct taxation. Challengers struggle to develop broad-based and lasting support coalitions. Quasi-state strategies remain appealing. A reinforcing three-way relationship between narrow winning coalitions for incumbents, quasi-state entities, and poor governance makes it difficult to obtain improved development outcomes. Unless these conditions shift and political opportunities change, reform-minded individuals are unlikely to succeed.

Notes

1 Political survival in a weak state

1 Gilpin (1981) uses this logic in his "hegemonic stability" argument. A preponderant country in the world provides public goods such as trade and financial order because it suits that country's private interests.

2 Rasler and Thompson question "the value of maintaining the internal-external distinction when pursuing questions related to the state-making consequences of war" (Rasler and Thompson, 1989: 12). Internal warfare may frequently involve the foreign allies of various warring parties. For this reason, it is reasonable to not focus exclusively on those events defined as "international" wars, but to include those events defined as "civil" wars as relevant shocks as well.

3 Varshney (2002) lists four approaches to understanding how ethnicity and politics interact: the essentialist, instrumentalism, constructivist, and institutionalist. Essentialists presume a pre-existing, primordial ethnic identity and attachment that is relatively state. Instrumentalists emphasize that ethnicity is a concept deployed and manipulated strategically by elites for political and economic power. Post-modernists claim that a knowledge elite constructs group categories, power centers promote particular constructions, and these affect "the people"; elites use social categories in post-colonial societies selectively based on preconceptions about society's building blocks and by calculating what divisions would maintain their power (Varshney, 2002: 32). "Unpostmodern" constructivists see mutually influencing relationships, in that elites must construct identities that are close to ground realities, and alternative identities and ethnicities can be used to undermine the old order, as nationalism arguably does (Varshney, 2002: 32).

2 Weak state, strong society, negotiable polity

1 Other forms of appropriation were also used. In the course of World War II, a major portion of the industrial and commercial product of British India was directed toward military requirements (Tomlinson, 1992: 277).

2 In contrast, modern India consists of 25 states which vary in size and population. The 1961 census placed India's population at 439 million (Chandrasekhar, 1965: 11). The 1981 census put the population of India at 702 million (Joshi and Little, 1984: 13); two decades later, India reached the 1 billion mark (Dawn, May 11, 2000: www.dawn.com/2000/05/11).

3 Anwar Syed describes the "astounding plan of Qazi Husain Ahmad, head of the Jamaat-e-Islami, to raise an army of five million to surround the National Assembly in Islamabad, make its members prisoners in the building, and thus force the government to surrender authority to the invaders" (Syed, 2001: 260). There is a sense of siege palpable in some observations regarding the Jamaat-e-Islami, based on fear that a coercive takeover is apparently an option the Jamaat-e-Islami would consider.

210 *Notes*

4 This distinction is based partly on oral comments by Quinn Mecham in his analysis of Turkey at the American Political Science Association Annual Meeting, September 6, 2009, in Toronto.

5 For example, the National Highway Authority advertised job openings (*Dawn*, August 6, 2009, p. 17). A chart had subheadings for salary, available posts, qualifications, experience, age limit, and "Quota." For example (Director) had 26 vacancies. The listed quotas were: Punjab, 11; Punjab-Woman, 1; Punjab-NonMuslim, 1; Sindh (Urban), 2; Sindh (Rural), 3; NWFP, 3; Balochistan, 1; FATA/NA, 1; AJK, 1; and Merit, 2. These are apportioned based on a formula. One can see the Sindh divide between Mohajir (who tend to be in the urban areas) and Sindhi (who tend to be rural); some Mohajirs express resentment at the arrangement and believe that they would gain more positions if they were given on merit. Moreover, out of 26 positions, only 2 are being given on "Merit" alone. There is competition within each area category.

3 Leadership and extraction

1 The literature on public finance policy in developing countries is generally concerned with government taxation, borrowing, and spending policies that are designed to promote economic development while maintaining monetary stability (see, for example, Sreekantaradhya, 1972: 14). The obvious function of taxes is to raise revenue, but they may also be imposed to redistribute wealth, correct market distortions, and guide consumer decisions (Joshi and Little, 1996: 63). Classics in the public finance literature have examined the role of taxation and other forms of government finance in mobilizing resources for economic development. These consequences, often the traditional concern of analysts of fiscal policy, are not explored extensively here. The focus here is on how political survival constraints shape revenue-raising strategies; it is assumed that chosen strategies have sociological and developmental implications.

2 In India in 1980/81, for example, the central government's revenue collection amounted to 10.3 percent of GDP, while that of the states was 5.4 percent (Joshi and Little, 1994: 22). Furthermore, part of the revenues of the states in India reflects the extractive efforts of the central government because the states are constitutionally entitled to a portion of the income and excise taxes levied by the central government (Joshi and Little, 1994: 22).

3 Anecdotes describe ministers using wooden boxes in place of tables (Talbot, 1998: 100).

4 The term "fiscal deficit" (interchangeable with the term "budget deficit") has been used by the IMF and in the US and other industrialized countries and refers to the difference between total government expenditure and current revenues (Chelliah, 1996: 50). Chelliah equates the fiscal deficit to net borrowing by the government, or the net addition to the public debt (Chelliah, 1996: 50–51).

5 See Modelski's discussion of Kautilya and the ancient Hindu international system (Modelski, 1964).

6 Brines also asserts that efforts by Ayub to invoke the CENTO and SEATO pacts in Pakistan's defense were futile (Brines, 1968: 353).

7 SDR stands for Special Drawing Rights and is a form of loan from the IMF. Formally, IMF credits are "purchases of foreign currency with a repurchase obligation" (Datta, 1992: 164). Thus, IMF credits simply allow a country to increase the hard currency available to it when needed, and are a form of indebtedness to international sources.

8 It appears that actions that consolidated the state as a tax-extractor happened at the same time as the increased receipts of foreign aid—echoing the finding that better extractors domestically also tend to receive more resources from the international realm (Malik, 2000). However, the substantive long-term consequences of Ayub's efforts at increasing domestic extraction are not clear. Furthermore, it is not apparent that the increase in foreign receipts was the result of perceptions of the Pakistani state's greater creditworthiness.

Notes 211

9 Maulana Asad Thanvi of the Jamiat Ulema-e-Islam offers a dissenting opinion, suggesting that because the lands were unjustly allocated under foreign influence in the first place, they could be redistributed (Interview with Asad Thanvi, 2009).

4 Challengers in a weak polity

1 There were contrary narratives on Muslim identity. The religious leader and public intellectual Abul Kalam Azad, in contrast, considered Muslims to belong to a World Muslim Brotherhood (Stepaniants, 2001). Azad transitioned from religious to secular nationalism. His views evolved such that he eventually described Hindus and Muslims as a united nation, when he addressed the 1940 Ramgarh Indian National Congress as president:

> Our language, our poetry, literature, society, our tastes, our dresses, our traditions and the innumerable realities of our daily life bear the zeal of a common life and a unified society [...] Our social intercourse for over one thousand years has blended into a united nationalism.
>
> (cited in Stepaniants, 2001)

What constituted "nation" in British India varied dramatically depending on who was asked.
2 The early struggle for Kashmir can be described as a state-supported de facto effort in which tribal irregular fighters entered Kashmir, seeking to thwart the maharajah's inclination to accede to India. The Pakistani government became officially involved later on, and war between Pakistan and India broke out.
3 Ziring reports the following sequence of events:

> J.A. Rahim, the PPP Secretary-General, and the single most important individual behind the formation of the PPP, accompanied Bhutto to Dhaka and returned with him on that fateful trip. Rahim later said that the separate PPP negotiating team which he led had gone to Dhaka with a compromise formula in hand. Unlike Bhutto, they knew nothing of the army plan to violently strike at the heart of the Awami League. He asserted that he and other members of his delegation had met with members of the Awami League, and that together they had come to an agreement on the matter of forming a government and drafting a new constitution for Pakistan [...] In fact, the negotiators had agreed on the need to draft three separate constitutions, i.e., one for East Pakistan, one for the provinces of West Pakistan, and another that would follow the federal principle and sustain Pakistan's territorial integrity. To put the plan into operation the conferees insisted on the termination of martial law, an end to junta rule, and the establishment of a caretaker civilian government. Only Bhutto's approval was required, Mujib having given his assent. But when approached by Rahim, Bhutto vetoed their efforts. The PPP leader was on the one hand too committed to the junta, while on the other, he believed that this political future would be enhanced by the elimination of the Awami League.
>
> (Ziring, 1997: 353)

4 Maulana Asad Thanvi argues that this division is overblown, asserting that Barelvi and Deobandi sects emerge from the same Hanafi background (Author interview with Maulana Asad Thanvi, 2009). Elsewhere, a Barelvi preacher made clear that he would be open to marriage proposals for his daughter from a Deobandi-background Muslim. Thus, there are countervailing tendencies to sectarianism across the Deobandi-Barelvi divide, although they may be more prominent among the elites who propagate a "high" Islam.

212 *Notes*

5 The interviewee also asserted that 60 percent of Sind's population was originally Balochi.
6 Recently, the MQM leadership in Karachi has suggested that the city has large Pushtun-dominated no-go areas in which the writ of formal government cannot prevail. The MQM rhetoric against "Talibanization" suggests that these neighborhoods have become de facto quasi-state territories. Ironically, a similar charge was leveled against the MQM in the 1992 military operation in Karachi.
7 Others estimate a lower death toll; according to Stewart and Hyat (2002: 111), the Mohajir movement cost between 2000 and 5000 lives between 1984 and 2000.

5 Quasi-states, extraction, and governance

1 A parallel in the Turkish experience may be the so-called "deep state," in which actors loosely affiliated with the security apparatus are associated with manipulative, sometimes violent, political intervention.
2 The first caretaker prime minister, Ghulam Mustafa Jatoi, and the second, Balkh Sher Mazari, held office for short periods. In 1993, Moeen Qureshi became the third caretaker prime minister in Pakistan, and had just over three months in office. Meraj Khalid was the fourth caretaker prime minister.
3 The Fund for Peace puts out a yearly Failed States Index that scores and ranks states along economic, social, and political/military indicators for their weakness (Fund for Peace, 2009).

6 Conclusion

1 In contrast, members of a larger winning coalition have smaller individual shares of goods provided by the incumbent, may become members of a future winning coalition under a different leader, and have less to lose if the incumbent loses office.
2 This is a Chinese saying (Wang, 2009). It implies that having an autonomous jurisdiction under one's control is preferable to being a secondary functionary in a larger entity.
3 M. Qasim Zaman's term "custodians of change" is an apt label (Zaman, 2002).

Bibliography

Afzal, M. Rafique (2001). *Pakistan: History and Politics, 1947–1971*. Oxford: Oxford University Press.

Ahmad, M. (1970). *Government and Politics in Pakistan*. Karachi.

Ahmar, Moonis (1996), "Ethnicity and State Power in Pakistan: The Karachi Crisis." *Asian Survey*, Vol. 36, No. 10, pp. 1031–1048.

Ahmed, Farooq (2009). "People of Gilgit-Baltistan Seek Role in Framing of Package." *Dawn*, July 29, 2009, p. 9.

Ahmed, Feroz (2002). "Ethnicity, State, and National Integration", in Naseem, S.M. and Khalid Nadvi, eds., *The Post-Colonial State and Social Transformation in India and Pakistan*. Oxford: Oxford University Press.

Ahmed, Viqar and Rashid Amjad (1984). *The Management of Pakistan's Economy 1947–82*. Karachi: Oxford University Press.

Akhtar, Rafique (1992). *Pakistan Year Book (1992–1993)*. Twentieth Edition. Karachi: East and West Publishing Company.

Alam, Shahid (2002). "How Different Are Islamic Societies?" Published on February 4, 2002, in *Counterpunch* (online edition). Downloaded on October 20, 2002 from http://www.counterpunch.com/alamsocieties.html

Alavi, Hamza (1976). "Rural Elite and Agricultural Development in Pakistan", in R.D. Stevens, Hamza Alavi, and Peter Bertocci, eds., *Rural Development in Pakistan and Bangladesh*. Hawaii: University of Hawaii Press.

Ali, Abbas (2009). "Political Unrest in Gilgit-Baltistan." *Dawn*, July 26, 2009, p. 19.

Ali, Imran Anwar (2001). "Business and Power in Pakistan," in Anita Weiss and S. Zulfiqar Gilani, eds., *Power and Civil Society in Pakistan*. Karachi: Oxford University Press.

Ali, Kamran Asdar (2005). "The Strength of the Street Meets the Strength of the State: The 1972 Labor Uprising in Karachi." *International Journal of Middle East Studies*, Vol. 37, pp. 83–107.

Ali, Syed Mubashir and Faisal Bari (2000). "At the Millenium: Macro Economic Performance and Prospects," in Craig Baxter and Charles Kennedy, eds., *Pakistan 2000*. Oxford: Oxford University Press.

Almeida, Cyril (2008). "The Supremacy Myth." *Dawn*, April 8, 2008, p. 7.

Almeida, Cyril (2009). "Rich government, poor people." *Dawn*, July 3, 2009, p. 7.

Almond, Gabriel A., R. Scott Appleby, and Emmanuel Sivan (2003). *Strong Religion: The Rise of Fundamentalisms Around the World*. Chicago: University of Chicago Press.

Ames, Barry (1987). *Political Survival: Politicians and Public Policy in Latin America*. Berkeley: University of California Press.

214 *Bibliography*

Anderson, Lisa (1990). "Policy-Making and Theory-Building: American Political Science and the Islamic Middle East," in Hisham Sharabi, ed., *Theory, Politics, and the Arab World: Critical Responses*. New York: Routledge.

Ansari, Javed Akbar (1999). "Macroeconomic Management: An Alternative Perspective," in Shahrukh Rafi Khan, ed., *50 Years of Pakistan's Economy: Traditional Topics and Contemporary Concerns*. Karachi: Oxford University Press.

Axmann, Martin (2009). *Back to the Future: the Khanate of Kalat and the Genesis of Baloch nationalism, 1915–1955*. Karachi; New York: Oxford University Press.

Ayub, Imran (2008). "Secretariat fire caused by arson, says report". *Dawn* April 15, 2008, p. 17.

Aziz, Mazhar (2006). *Military Control in Pakistan: The Parallel State*. London, New York: Routledge.

Aziz, Sartaj. (2009). "Future of Devolution." *Dawn*, May 27, 2009, p. 7.

Bahadur, Kalim (1975). "The Jama'at-i-Islami of Pakistan: Ideology and Political Action." *International Studies*, January 1975, Vol. 14 Issue 1, pp. 69–84.

Balbus, Isaac (1973). "The Concept of Interest in Pluralist and Marxist Analysis," in I. Katznelson, G. Adams, P. Brenner, and A. Wolfe, eds., *The Politics and Society Reader*. New York: David McKay.

Baldev, Raj Nayar (2000). "India's Quest for a Major Power Role after the Nehru Era: The Long Road to Building Capabilities and Attenuating Constraints". Manuscript presented at International Studies Association Annual Conference, Los Angeles, 2000.

Baloch, Latif. (2008). "Baloch Leader Urges Halt to 'Vindictive' Activities." *Dawn*, April 28, 2008, p. 13.

Barnett, Michael (1992). *Confronting the Costs of War: Military Power, State, and Society in Egypt and Israel*. Princeton: Princeton University Press.

Barnett, Michael (1998). *Dialogues in Arab Politics: Negotiations in Regional Order*. New York: Columbia University Press.

Bashir, Javed (2008). "A tidal wave (Book Review of) Osama Siddique's The Jurisprudence of Dissolutions: Presidential Power to Dissolve Assemblies under the Pakistani Constitution and Its Discontent." *Dawn Books and Authors*, June 22, 2008, pp. 6–7.

Bates, Robert H. (1997). "Area Studies and Political Science: Rupture and Possible Synthesis." *Africa Today*, Vol. 44, No. 2, April–June.

Bates, Robert H., Avner Greif, Margaret Levi, Jean-Laurent Rosenthal, and Barry Weingast (1998). *Analytic Narratives*. Princeton: Princeton University Press.

Baxter, Craig (2001). "Political Development in Pakistan," in Hafeez Malik, ed., *Pakistan: Founders' Aspirations and Today's Realities*. Oxford: Oxford University Press.

Bayat, Asef (2005). "Islamism and Social Movement Theory." *Third World Quarterly*, Vol. 26, No. 6, pp. 891–908.

Beblawi, Hazem and Giacomo Luciani (1987). "Introduction," in *The Rentier State*. London: Croom Helm.

Bill, James A. and Carl Leiden (1984). *Politics in the Middle East*. Boston: Little Brown.

Book Review and Press (2007). Interview with Ayesha Siddiqua-Agha, June 3, 2007.

Brand, Laurie (1994). *Jordan's Inter-Arab Relations: The Political Economy of Alliance Making*. New York: Columbia University Press.

Brines, Russell (1968). *The Indo-Pakistani Conflict*. London: Pall Mall Press.

Brown, W. Norman (1963). *The United States and India and Pakistan*. Cambridge: Harvard University Press.

Brumberg, Daniel (2004). "Book Review, *Jihad by Gilles Keppel*". *International Journal of Middle East Studies*, Vol. 36, pp. 512–514.

Bibliography 215

Brynen, Rex (1992). "Economic Crisis and Post-Rentier Democratization in the Arab World: The Case of Jordan." *Canadian Journal of Political Science*, Vol. 25, No. 1, March.

Bueno de Mesquita, Bruce, and Alastair Smith (2009). "Political Survival and Endogenous Institutional Change" *Comparative Political Studies*, Vol. 42, No. 2, February, pp. 167–197

Bueno de Mesquita, Bruce, and Alastair Smith (2009b). "The Political Economy of Aid." *International Organization*, Vol. 63, Spring, pp. 309–340.

Bueno de Mesquita, Bruce, Alastair Smith, Randolph M. Siverson, and James D. Morrow (2003). *The Logic of Political Survival*. Cambridge, Mass: MIT Press.

Bulliet, Richard (2004). *The Case for Islamo-Christian Civilization*. New York: Columbia University Press.

Burki, Shahid Javed (2001). "Politics of Power and Its Economic Imperatives: Pakistan, 1947–99" in in Anita Weiss and S.Zulfiqar Gilani, eds. *Power and Civil Society in Pakistan*. Karachi: Oxford University Press.

Burki, Shahid Javed (2008a). "Resolving Old Disputes." *Dawn*, April 29, 2008, p. 6.

Burki, Shahid Javed (2008b). "Op-Ed Column." *Dawn*, March 19, 2008, p. 7.

Burki, Shahid Javed (2008c). *Changing Perceptions, Altered Reality: Pakistan's Economy under Musharraf, 1999–2006*. New York: Oxford University Press.

Burgat, Francois and William Dowell (1993). *The Islamic Movements in North Africa*. Austin: University of Texas Press.

Burki, Shahid Javed (2009a) (*Dawn* June 30 09 p. 7).

Burki, Shahid Javed (2009b). "The Cost of Doing Business." *Dawn*, February 23, 2009. Accessed on September 27, 2009 from http://www.dawn.com/2009/02/23/ebr20.htm.

Callard, Keith (1957). *Pakistan: A Political Study*. London: Allen and Unwin.

Candler, George (2000). Personal communication.

Castells, Manuel (1997). *The Power of Identity*. Oxford: Blackwell.

Chandrasekhar, S. (1965). *American Aid and India's Economic Development*. New York: Praeger.

Cheema, Ali (2003). "State and Capital in Pakistan: The Changing Politics of Accumulation," in A.M. Reed, ed., *Corporate Capitalism in Contemporary South Asia: Conventional Wisdoms and South Asian Realities*. Palgrave, London.

Chelliah, Raja J. (1996). *Towards Sustainable Growth: Essays in Fiscal and Financial Sector Reforms in India*. Delhi: Oxford University Press.

Chowdhry, G.W. (1968). *Pakistan's Relations with India, 1947–1966*. London: Pall Mall Press.

Choudhury, G.W. (1975). *The Last Days of United Pakistan*. Bloomington: Indiana University Press.

Clark, Grace (2000). "Pakistan's Zakat and Ushr System from 1979 to 1999," in Craig Baxter and Charles Kennedy, eds., *Pakistan 2000*. Oxford: Oxford University Press.

Coase, Ronald H. (1937). "The Nature of the Firm." *Economica*, Vol. 4, No. 16, pp. 386–405.

Cohen, Stephen P. (1999). "The United States, India, and Pakistan: Retrospect and Prospect" in Harrison, Selig S., Paul H. Kreisberg, and Dennis Kux, eds., *India and Pakistan: The First Fifty Years*. Cambridge (U.K.): Cambridge University Press.

Cohen, Stephen P. (2004). *The Idea of Pakistan*. Washington, DC: Brookings Institution Press.

Dahrendorf, Ralf (1959). *Class and Class Conflict in Industrial Society*. Stanford, CA: Stanford University Press.

Dalrymple, William (2009). "A New Deal in Pakistan." *The New York Review of Books*, Vol. 55, No. 5, April 3, 2008. Accessed on July 16, 2009 from http://www.nybooks.com/articles/21194

216 *Bibliography*

Datta, Bhabatosh (1992). *Indian Planning at the Crossroads*. Delhi: Oxford University Press.

Dawn (Staff Reporter). (2008). "No positive change in Balochistan situation in sight". April 3, 2008, p. 18.

Dawn (unnamed author) (2009). "Killing of JSQM Man Sparks Protests." *Dawn*, July 25, 2009, p. 1.

Delacroix, Jacques (1980). "The Distributive State in the World System". *Studies in Comparative International Development* 15, 3.

Dewey, Clive (1991). *The Settlement Literature of the Greater Punjab* Delhi: Manohar.

Durrani, Tehmina (1991). *My Feudal Lord*. New Delhi: Sterling Publishers.

Durrani, Tehmina with William and Marilyn Hoffer (1996). *My Feudal Lord: A Devastating Indictment of Women's Role in Muslim Society*. London: Corgi Books.

Eijffinger, Sylvester C.W. and Jakob de Haan (1996). *The Political Economy of Central-Bank Independence*. Princeton, NJ: Princeton University.

Evans, Jocelyn (2004). "Fitting Extremism into the Rational Choice Paradigm". *Government and Opposition*, Vol. 39, 1, pp. 110–118.

Evans, Peter B. (1985). Dietrich Rueschemeyer, Theda Skocpol, eds. *Bringing the State Back In*. Cambridge; New York: Cambridge University Press.

Evans, Peter B. (1989). "Predatory, Developmental, and Other Apparatuses: A Comparative Political Economy Perspective on the Third World State." *Sociological Forum* 4 (4): 561–587.

Fearon, James (2004). "Ethnic Mobilization and Ethnic Violence". Accessed June 20, 2010 from www.stanford.edu/~jfearon/papers/ethreview.pdf

Foust, Joshua, and Jeb Koogler. "Myth in Al-Qaeda's Home," *The Christian Science Monitor*, July 10, 2008. Downloaded on August 4, 2008 from http://news.yahoo.com/s/csm/20080710/cm_csm/ykoogler

Fund for Peace (2009). "Failed States Index". Accessed on September 15, 2009 from www.fundforpeace.org.

Gall, Carlotta (2008). "Old-Line Taliban Commander Is Face of Rising Afghan Threat." *The New York Times*, June 17, 2008. Accessed on 2008 from http://www.nytimes.com/2008/06/17/world/asia/17warlord.html?sq=haqqani&st=nyt&scp=1&pagewanted=all

Ganguly, Sumit (1994). *The Origins of War in South Asia: The Indo-Pakistani Conflicts since 1947*. 2nd ed. Boulder: Westview Press.

Gazdar, Haris (2008). "Health of the Federation". *Dawn* February 13, 2008.

Ghumro, Zamir (2008). "Promising Autonomy to Provinces." *Dawn*, April 26, 2008, p. 13.

Gilpin, Robert (1981). *War and Change in World Politics*. Cambridge: Cambridge University Press.

Goode, Richard (1984). *Government Finance in Developing Countries*. Washington, DC: Brookings Institution Press.

Grare, Frederic (2006). *"Islam, Militarism, and the 2007–2008 Elections in Pakistan"*. Carnegie Papers, South Asia Project Number 70, August 2006. Carnegie Endowment for International Peace.

Gurr, Ted Robert (1970). *Why Men Rebel*. Princeton: Princeton University Press.

Haken, Nate (2006). "Economic Reform in Weak States: When Good Governance Goes Bad" *Fund for Peace Globalization and Human Rights Series*. Accessed June 19 2010 from http://www.fundforpeace.org/web/images/stories/programs/haken_governance_reform.pdf

Hanif, Mohammed (2008). *A Case of Exploding Mangoes*. New York: Alfred Knopf.

Haq, Farhat (1995). "Rise of the MQM in Pakistan: Politics of Ethnic Mobilization." *Asian Survey*, Vol. 35, No. 11, November, pp. 990–1004.

Bibliography 217

Haqqani, Husain (2005). *Pakistan Between Mosque and Military*. Lahore: Vanguard Books (Pvt) Ltd.

Harrison, Selig S., Paul H. Kreisberg, and Dennis Kux, (1999). "Introduction" in Harrison, Selig S., Paul H. Kreisberg, and Dennis Kux, eds., *India and Pakistan: The First Fifty Years*. Cambridge (U.K.): Cambridge University Press.

Hashem, Mazen (2006). "Contemporary Islamic Activism: The Shades of Praxis". *Sociology of Religion* 2006 67, 1: 23–41.

Haydar, Afak (2001). The Sipah-e-Sahaba Pakistan, in Hafeez Malik, ed., *Pakistan: Founders' Aspirations and Today's Realities*. Oxford: Oxford University Press.

Hoffmann, Philip (2006). "Opening Our Eyes: History and the Social Sciences." *Journal of the Historical Society*, Vol. VI, No. 1, March.

Hoff, Samuel (2006). "Book Review, The Logic of Political Survival." *International Social Science Review*, Vol. 82, Nos. 3, 4, pp. 175–176.

Holcombe, Randall G. (2005). "Book Review, The Logic of Political Survival." *The Independent Review*, Vol. IX, No. 3, Winter, pp. 456–459.

Horowitz, Donald (1985). *Ethnic Groups in Conflict*. Berkeley: University of California Press.

Hourani, Hani and Hussein Abu-Rumman, eds. (1996). *The Democratic Process in Jordan … Where to? Deliberations of the Conference* on "Democratic Process in Jordan: Realities and Prospects" held in Amman from 31 May until 2 June 1994. Amman: Al-Urdun Al-Jadid Research Center.

Husain, Irfan. (2008). "Appeasement and Apathy." *Dawn*, June 28, 2008, p. 7.

Husain, Ishrat (2003). *Economic Management in Pakistan, 1999–2002*. Oxford: Oxford University Press.

Husain, Ishrat (2000). *Pakistan: The Economy of an Elitist State*. Oxford: Oxford University Press.

Husain, Mir Zuhair (2003). *Global Islamic Politics*. New York: Longman.

Hussain, Akmal (1989). "Behind the Veil of Growth: The State of Pakistan's Economy" in Ponna Wignaraja and Akmal Hussain, eds., *The Challenge in South Asia: Development, Democracy and Regional Cooperation*. Tokyo and London: United Nations University and Sage Publications.

Idris, Kunwar (2009). "Corruption in democracy" *Dawn*, July 26, 2009, p. 7.

Ikenberry, G. John (1988). "Conclusion: An Institutional Approach to American Foreign Economic Policy." *International Organization, Vol.* 42 Winter: 219–243.

Inayatullah, 2002. "Ethnonationalism and Democracy: Is Coexistence Possible?" in Naseem, S. M. and Khalid Nadvi, eds., *The Post-Colonial State and Social Transformation in India and Pakistan*. Oxford: Oxford University Press.

Iqbal, Ali Iqbal *"Feudals and Pirs, Book Review of Pakistan Kay Siyasi Waderay by Aqeel Abbas Jafri."* Dawn Books and Authors, June 15, 2008, p. 11.

Jackson, Robert (1987). "Quasi-states, Dual regimes, and Neoclassical theory: International Jurisprudence and the Third World". *International Organization*, Vol. 41, No. 4, pp. 519–547.

Jafri, Aqeel Abbas (1993). *Pakistan Kay Siyasi Waderay*. Lahore: Jehangir Books.

Jalal, Ayesha (1990). *The State of Martial Rule: The Origins of Pakistan's Political Economy of Defense*. Cambridge: Cambridge University Press.

Jalal, Ayesha (1995). "Conjuring Pakistan: History as Official Imagining" *International Journal of Middle East Studies*, Vol. 27, No. 1, February, pp. 73–89.

Jalal, Ayesha (2000). *Self and Sovereignty: Individual and Community in South Asian Islam since 1850*. London, New York: Routledge.

Jehangir, Asma (2008). "Enter the PM." *Dawn News*, February 15, 2008.

218   Bibliography

Jones, Garth N. (1997). "Pakistan: A Civil Service in an Obsolescing Imperial Tradition". *Asian Journal of Public Administration* Vol. 19, No. 2 December, pp. 321–364.

Jones, Owen Bennett (2002) *Pakistan : Eye of the Storm*. New Haven: Yale.

Joshi, Vijay, and I.M.D. Little (1994). *India: Macroeconomics and Political Economy 1964–1991*. Delhi: Oxford University Press.

Joshi, Vijay, and I.M.D. Little (1996). *India's Economic Reforms 1991–2001*. Oxford: Clarendon Press.

Kasfir, Nelson (2004) "Domestic Anarchy, Security Dilemmas, and Violent Predation: Causes of Failure". in Rotberg, Robert I., ed. *When States Fail: Causes and Consequences*. Princeton: Princeton University Press.

Kasi, Amanullah (2009). "Call for Creation of Pashtoon Province." *Dawn*, July 1, 2009, p. 5.

Katzenstein, Peter (1977). "Conclusion: Domestic Structures and Strategies of Foreign Economic Policy." *International Organization*, Vol. 31, Autumn, p. 892.

Kavic, Lorne J. (1967). *India's Quest for Security: Defence Policies, 1947–1965*. Berkeley: University of California Press.

Keppel, Gilles (2003). *Jihad: The Trail of Political Islam*. Cambridge, Mass: Belknap Press of Harvard University Press.

Khan, Aftab Ahmad (1997). "Economic Development" in Rafi Raza, ed. *Pakistan in Perspective 1947–1997*. Karachi: Oxford University Press.

Khan, Bashir Ahmed (1999). "Financial Markets and Economic Development in Pakistan: 1947–1995," in Shahrukh Rafi Khan, ed., *50 Years of Pakistan's Economy: Traditional Topics and Contemporary Concerns*. Karachi: Oxford University Press.

Khan, Irum (2008). "New Agenda for New Beginning." *Dawn*, April 1, 2008, p. 7.

Khan, Mahmood Hasan (1999). "Agricultural Development and Changes in the Land Tenure and Land Revenue Systems in Pakistan," in Shahrukh Rafi Khan, ed., *50 Years of Pakistan's Economy: Traditional Topics and Contemporary Concerns*. Karachi: Oxford University Press.

Khan, Mahmood Hasan (2002). "Changes in the Agrarian Structure of Pakistan," in S.M. Naseem and Khalid Nadvi, eds., *The Post-Colonial State and Social Transformation in India and Pakistan*. Oxford: Oxford University Press.

Khan, M. Ilyas (2008). "Will Pakistan's militants lay down arms?" *BBC News* April 25, 2008. Downloaded from http://news.bbc.co.uk/2/hi/south asia/7366305.stm.

Khan, Mubarak Zeb (2009). "Govt Reverses World Bank Tax Reforms Project." *Dawn*, July 1, 2009, p. 17.

Khan, Sayeed Hasan (2005). "Critical Reflections of a Mohajir," *Logos*, Vol. 4, No. 1, Winter. Accessed on July 23, 2009 from http://www.logosjournal.com/issue_4.1/khan.htm

Khan, Sayeed Hasan and Kurt Jacobsen (2008). "A New Political Party Needed." *Dawn*, September 17, 2008. Accessed on July 2009 from http://www.dawn.com/2008/09/17/op.htm

Khan, Sayeed Hasan and Kurt Jacobsen (2009). "Political culture of Pakistan". *Dawn* August 11, p. 7.

Khan, Shahrukh Rafi, ed. (1999). *50 Years of Pakistan's Economy: Traditional Topics and Contemporary Concerns*. Karachi: Oxford University Press.

Khuhro, Murtaza "Enigma of agricultural income tax" *Dawn*, March 17, 2008.

King, Gary and Langche Zeng (2001). "Research Note: Improving Forecasts of State Failure." *World Politics*, Vol. 53, July, pp. 623–658.

Kinne, Brandon (2005). "Decision Making in Autocratic Regimes: A Poliheuristic Perspective." *International Studies Perspectives*, Vol. 6, pp. 114–128.

Kolsto, Pal (2006). "The Sustainability and Future of Unrecognized Quasi-States." *Journal of Peace Research*, Vol. 43, No. 6, pp. 723–740.

Bibliography 219

Krasner, Stephen (1978). *Defending the National Interest*. Princeton: Princeton University Press.

Kukreja, Veena (2005). "Misplaced Priorities and Economic Uncertainties," in Veena Kukreja and M.P. Singh, eds., *Pakistan: Democracy, Development, and Security Issues*. New Delhi: Sage Publications India.

Kukreja, Veena, and M.P. Singh, eds. (2005). *Pakistan: Democracy, Development, and Security Issues* New Delhi: Sage Publications India.

Kumar, Satish (2005). "Reassessing Pakistan as a Longterm Security Threat," in Veena Kukreja and M.P. Singh, eds., *Pakistan: Democracy, Development, and Security Issues*. New Delhi: Sage Publications India.

Kuru, Ahmet T (2009) *Secularism and State Policies toward Religion: the United States, France, and Turkey*. Cambridge; New York: Cambridge University Press.

Lasswell, Harold (1950 {1936}). *Politics· Who Gets What, When, and How*. New York: Peter Smith.

Levi, Margaret (1981). "The Predatory Theory of Rule". *Politics and Society* 10, 4: 431–465.

Levi, Margaret (1988). *Of Rule and Revenue*. Berkeley: University of California Press.

Levi, Margaret (2006). "*Perspectives on Politics* Presidential Address: Why We Need a New Theory of Government." *APSR*, Vol. 4, No., March, pp. 5–19.

Lichbach, Mark Irving (1995). *The Rebel's Dilemma*. Ann Arbor: University of Michigan Press.

MacFarquhar, Neil (2002). "Egyptian Group Patiently Pursues Dream of Islamic State." Article in the *New York Times*, January 20, 2002. New York: The New York Times Company. Accessed On June 20, 2010. from http://www.nytimes.com/2002/01/20/international/middleeast/20EGYP.html?ex=1012194000&en=84a2e34e80ed82c9&ei=5040&partner=MOREOVER

Mahdavy, Hussein (1970). "The Patterns and Problems of Economic Development in Rentier States: The Case of Iran," in M.A. Cook, ed., *Studies in the Economic History of the Middle East: From the Rise of Islam to the Present Day*, pp. 37–61. London: Oxford University Press.

Mahmood, Abid (2009). "Creating a people-friendly police". *Dawn* Aug 9, 2009. Accessed June 19, 2010 from http://www.dawn.com/wps/wcm/connect/dawn-content-library/dawn/in-paper-magazine/encounter/creating-a-peoplefriendly-police-989

Mahmud, S.F (1988). *A Concise History of Indo-Pakistan*. Oxford: Oxford University Press.

Malik, Adeel (2000). "Citizens' Perceptions of Governance: An Overview," *Technical Annex to Mahbub ul Haq, Human Development in South Asia 1999*, Oxford University Press.

Malik, Anas (1999). "Understanding the Political Behavior of Islamists: The Implications of Modernization, Socialization, and Rational-Choice Based Approaches." *Studies in Contemporary Islam*, Vol. 1, No. 1.

Malik, Anas (2000). "War Shocks, Political Capacity, and Regime Extraction Policy: an empirical evaluation." Paper presented at International Studies Association Annual Conference, Los Angeles, California, March 2000.

Malik, I. (1995). "Ethno-Nationalism in Pakistan: A commentary on Muhajir Qaumi Mahaz (MQM) in Sindhi." *South Asia*, Vol. 18, No. 2, pp. 60–61.

Malik, Iftikhar H. (1997). *State and Civil Society in Pakistan: Politics of Authority, Ideology, and Ethnicity*. New York: St. Martin's Press.

Martinez-Vazquez, Jorge (2006). "Pakistan: A Preliminary Assessment of the Federal Tax System." International Studies Program Working Paper 06–24. Georgia State University Andrew Young School of Policy Studies. Accessed on July 8 2009 from http://aysps.gsu.edu/isp/files/ispwp0624.pdf

220 Bibliography

McAdam, D., J. McCarthy, and M. Zald (1996). *Comparative Perspectives on Social Movements: Political Opportunities, Mobilizing Structures, and Cultural Framings.* Cambridge: Cambridge University Press.

McFaul, Michael (2002). "The Fourth Wave of Democracy and Dictatorship: Noncooperative Transitions in the Postcommunist World." *World Politics*, Vol. 54, No. 2, pp. 212–244. Downloaded on September 2, 2002, from http://muse.jhu.edu/journals/world_politics/v054/54.2mcfaul.pdf

Migdal, Joel (1988). *Strong Societies and Weak States: State-Society Relations and State Capabilities in the Third World.* Princeton, NJ: Princeton University Press.

Mir, Hamid (2009). "Do We Know Anything about Lahore Resolution?" *The News*, March 23, 2009. Accessed on July 17, 2009 from http://www.thenews.com.pk/daily_detail.asp?id=168680

Mitra, Subrata (2006). *The Puzzle of India's Governance: Culture, Context, and Comparative Theory.* London, New York: Routledge.

Modelski, G. (1964), "Kautilya: foreign policy and international system in the ancient Hindu world", *The American Political Science Review*, Vol. 58 No.3, pp. 549–560.

Moore, Mick (2004). "Revenues, State Formation, and the Quality of Governance in Developing Countries." *International Political Science Review*, Vol. 25, No. 3, July, pp. 297–319.

Morrison, Kevin M. (2009). "Oil, Nontax Revenue, and the Redistributional Foundations of Regime Stability." *International Organization*, Vol. 63, No. 1, Winte, pp. 107–138.

Mortensen, Greg and David Oliver Relin (2007). *Three Cups of Tea One Man's Mission to Promote Peace … One School at a Time.* New York: Penguin Books.

Mottahadeh, Roy (2007). *Oral comments.* Islamic Studies Conference. Prince Waleed bin Talal Center, Harvard University, Fall 2007.

Mufti, Malik (1999). "Elite Bargains and the Onset of Political Liberalization in Jordan." *Comparative Political Studies*, Vol. 32, No. 1, February, pp. 100–129.

Mufti, Malik (1996). *Sovereign Creations: Pan-Arabism and Political Order in Syria and Iraq.* Ithaca, NY: Cornell University Press.

Munson, Henry (1996). "Book Review of *The Vanguard of the Islamic Revolution: The Jamaat-i-Islami of Pakistan* by Seyyed Vali Reza Nasr." *International Journal of Middle East Studies*, Vol. 28, No. 4, pp. 633–634.

Naseem, S.M. and Khalid Nadvi, eds., *The Post-Colonial State and Social Transformation in India and Pakistan.* Oxford: Oxford University Press.

Nasr, Seyyed Vali Reza (1994). *The Vanguard of the Islamic Revolution: The Jama'at-i-Islami of Pakistan.* London, New York: I.B. Tauris.

Nasr, Seyyed Vali Reza (1996). *Mawdudi and the Making of Islamic Revivalism.* New York: Oxford University Press.

Nasr, Seyyed Vali Reza (2001a). *Islamic Leviathan: Islam and the Making of State Power.* New York: Oxford University Press.

Nasr, Seyyed Vali Reza (2001b). "Negotiating the State: Borders and Power Struggles in Pakistan," in Brendan O'Leary, Ian Lustick, and Thomas Callaghy, eds., *Right-sizing the State: The Politics of Moving Borders.* Oxford: Oxford University Press.

Nawaz, Shuja (2008). *Crossed Swords: Pakistan, Its Army, and the Wars Within.* Oxford: Oxford University Press.

Neuwirth, Robert (2005). *Shadow Cities: A Billion Squatters, A New Urban World.* New York: Routledge.

Nizamani, Haider (2008) "Is there feudalism in Pakistan?." *Dawn*, April 30, 2008, p. 7.

Noman, Omar (1990). *Pakistan: Political and Economic History Since 1947.* Revised Edition. London: Kegan Paul International.

Bibliography 221

Noman, Omar (1997). *Economic and Social Progress in Asia: Why Pakistan Did Not Become a Tiger*. Karachi: Oxford University Press.

Noorani, A.G. (2009). "Checks on corruption". *Dawn*, July 25, 2009, p. 7.

North, Douglass (1981) *Structure and Change in Economic History* New York: W.W. Norton & Co.

Olson, Mancur (1982). *The Rise and Decline of Nations: Economic Growth, Stagflation, and Social Rigidities*. New Haven: Yale University Press.

Olson, Mancur (1993). "Dictatorship, Democracy, and Development". *American Political Science Review* 87, 3: 567–576.

Organski, A.F.K. (1997). "Theoretical Link of Political Capacity to Development" in Arbetman, Marina and Jacek Kugler, eds., *Political Capacity and Economic Behavior*. Boulder: Westview Press.

Organski, A.F.K., Jacek Kugler, Timothy Johnson, and Youssef Cohen (1984). *Birth, Death, and Taxes*. Chicago: University of Chicago Press.

Owen, John M. (1994). "How Liberalism Produces Democratic Peace." *International Security*, Vol. 19, No. 2, Autumn, pp. 87–125.

Pape, Robert (2005). *Dying to Win: The Strategic Logic of Suicide Terrorism*. New York: Random House.

Pasha, Hafiz and Mahnaz Fatima (1999). "Fifty Years of Public Finance in Pakistan: A Trend Analysis," in Shahrukh Rafi Khan, ed., *50 Years of Pakistan's Economy: Traditional Topics and Contemporary Concerns*. Karachi: Oxford University Press.

Pegg, Scott (1998). *International Society and the De Facto State*. Aldershot, UK: Ashgate Publishing.

Peterson, George (2002). "Pakistan's Fiscal Decentralization: Issues and Opportunities." *Draft prepared for World Bank*. Accessed August 12 2009 from http://siteresources.worldbank.org/PAKISTANEXTN/Resources/pdf-Files-in-Events/IRISD/FiscalDecentral.pdf

Qureshi, Saleem M.M. (2005). "Pakistan: Islamic Ideology and the Failed State?" in Veena Kukreja and M.P. Singh, eds., *Pakistan: Democracy, Development, and Security Issues*. New Delhi: Sage Publications India.

Rahman, Shamim-ur (2008). "The Issues at Stake on Feb 18." *Dawn*, February 15, 2008, pp. 17–18.

Rashid, Ahmed (1988) *Descent into Chaos : the United States and the Failure of Nation Building in Pakistan, Afghanistan, and Central Asia*. New York: Viking.

Rasler, Karen, and William Thompson (1989). *War and Statemaking*. Boston: Unwin Hyman.

Raza, Rafi (1997a). "Introduction: The Genesis of Pakistan" in Rafi Raza, ed. *Pakistan in Perspective 1947–1997*. Karachi: Oxford University Press.

Raza, Rafi (1997b). "Constitutional Developments and Political Consequences". in Rafi Raza, ed. *Pakistan in Perspective 1947–1997*. Karachi: Oxford University Press.

Rehman, I.A. (2008a). "The Trichotomy Myth." *Dawn*, March 20, 2008, p. 7.

Rehman, I.A. (2008b). "Call for 'Recreating the Country with Cultural Revolution.'" *Dawn*, April 28, 2008, p. 17.

Rehman, I.A. (2009a). "The Quaid Won't Have It." *Dawn*, August 13, 2009, p. 7.

Rehman, I.A. (2009b). "Local Government Blues." *Dawn*, July 16, 2009, p. 7.

Rizvi, Hasan Askari (2000). *The Military & Politics in Pakistan, 1947–1997* Lahore: Sang-e-Meel Publications.

Riaz, Mohammed, "Merger of Fata with NWFP Not Easy." *Dawn*, March 25, 2008.

Rotbert, Robert I., ed. (2004). *When States Fail: Causes and Consequences*. Princeton: Princeton University Press.

222 *Bibliography*

Russett, Bruce, Christopher Layne, David E. Spiro, Michael W. Doyle (1995). "The Democratic Peace (in Correspondence." *International Security*, Vol. 19, No. 4, Spring, pp. 164–184.

Rizvi, Hasan-Askari (2001). "The Military," in Anita Weiss and S. Zulfiqar Gilani, eds., *Power and Civil Society in Pakistan*. Karachi: Oxford University Press.

Ross, Michael (2001). "Does Oil Hinder Democracy?" *World Politics*, Vol. 53, No. 3, pp. 325–361.

Rothermund, Dietmar (1988). *An Economic History of India: From Pre-Colonial Times to 1986*. New York: Croom Helm.

Roubini, Nouriel (1991). "Economic and Political Determinants of Budget Deficits in Developing Countries." *Journal of International Money and Finance*, Vol. 10, pp. S49–S72.

Sabl, Andrew (2002). "Community Organizing as Tocquevillian Politics: The Art, Practices, and Ethos of Association." *American Journal of Political Science*, Vol. 46, No. 1, pp. 1–19.

Said, Edward (1979). *Orientalism*. USA: Random House.

Sayyid, Bobby S. (2004). *A Fundamental Fear: Eurocentrism and the Emergence of Islamism*. London: Zed Books.

Schwedler, Jillian (1995). "Introduction," in Jillian Schwedler, ed., *Toward Civil Society in the Middle East? A Primer*. Boulder: Lynne Rienner Publishers.

Schwedler, Jillian (2006). *Faith in Moderation: Islamist parties in Jordan and Yemen*. Cambridge, NY: Cambridge University Press.

Shafik, Nemat (1999). "Labor Migration and Economic Integration in the Middle East," in Michael C. Hudson, ed., *Middle East Dilemma: The Politics and Economics of Arab Integration*. New York: Columbia University Press.

Shah, Anwar (1997). "Federalism Reform Imperatives, Restructuring Principles and Lessons for Pakistan," *The Pakistan Development Review*, Vol. 36, No. 4, Part II, Winter, pp. 499–537.

Shah, Aqil (2008). "Demilitarising the Bureaucracy." *Dawn*, May 4, 2008, p. 6.

Sharabi, Hisham (1990). "Editor's Preface," in Hisham Sharabi, ed., *Theory, Politics, and the Arab World: Critical Responses*. New York: Routledge.

Siddiqa, Ayesha (2007). *Military, Inc.: Inside Pakistan's Military Economy*. London: Pluto Press.

Siddiqa, Ayesha (2008). "The Debate on Feudalism". Op-ed in *Dawn*. Accessed on October 15, 2009 from http://www.naitazi.com/2008/02/02/the-debate-on-feudalism/

Siddiqa, Ayesha (2009). "No capacity to govern". *Dawn*, July 24 2009. Accessed on June 18, 2010 from http://www.dawn.com/wps/wcm/connect/dawn-content-library/dawn/the-newspaper/columnists/ayesha-siddiqa-no-capacity-to-govern-479

Siddique, Osama (2008). *The Jurisprudence of Dissolutions: Presidential Power to Dissolve Assemblies under the Pakistani Constitution and Its Discontents*. Karachi: Zaki Sons.

Siddiqui, Kalim (1972). *Conflict, Crisis, and War in Pakistan*. New York: Praeger.

Siddiqui, Tasneem Ahmad (2001). *Towards Good Governance*. Oxford: Oxford University Press.

Sikand, Yoginder (2002). "The Emergence and Development of the Jama'at-i-Islami of Jammu and Kashmir (1940s–1990)," *Modern Asian Studies*, Vol. 36, No. 3, pp. 705–751.

Sisson, Richard and Leo E. Rose (1991). *War and Secession: Pakistan, India, and the Creation of Bangladesh*. Berkeley: University of California Press.

Snider, Lewis W. (1990). "The Political Performance of Governments, External Debt Service, and Domestic Political Violence." *International Political Science Review*, Vol. 11, No. 4, pp. 403–422.

Bibliography 223

Snider, Lewis (2005). "Political Risk: The Institutional Dimension." *International Interactions*, Vol. 31, No. 3, July, pp. 203–222.

Snider, Lewis W. (1996). *Growth, Debt, and Politics: Economic Adjustment and the Political Performance of Developing Countries*. Boulder: Westview Press.

Snow, D., E.B. Rochford, S.K. Worden, and R.D. Benford (1986). "Frame Alignment Processes, Micromobilization, and Movement Participation." *American Sociological Review*, Vol. 51, pp. 464–481.

Sobhan, Rehman (2002). "South Asia's Crisis of Governance: Avoiding False Solutions," in Khadija Haq, ed., *The South Asian Challenge*. Oxford: Oxford University Press.

Sodaro, Michael (2008). *Comparative Politics: A Global Introduction*. Boston: McGraw-Hill.

Solingen, Etel (2007) "Pax Asiatica versus Bella Levantina: The Foundations of War and Peace in East Asia and the Middle East." *American Political Science Review* 101, No. 4 (November): 757–780.

Soomro, Rahmatullah (2008), "Slain JSQM Worker Laid to Rest," *Dawn*, March 29, 2008, p. 4.

Spruyt, Hendrik (1994). *The Sovereign State and Its Competitors: An Analysis of Systems Change*. Princeton, NJ: Princeton University Press.

Sreekantaradhya, B.S. (1972). *Public Debt and Economic Development in India*. New Delhi: Sterling Publishers.

Stepaniants, Marietta (2001). "Ethnicity and Religion." Paper archived at CRN Working Paper Archive. Accessed on August 2009 from www.dartmouth.edu/~crn/crn_papers/Stepaniants2.pdf

Stewart, Francis and Taimur Hyat (2002). "Conflict in South Asia: Prevalence, Costs, and Politics". in Khadija Haq, ed., *The South Asian Challenge* Oxford: Oxford University Press.

Stewart, Peter and Jenny Sturgis (1995). *Pakistan: Meeting the Challenge*. London: Euromoney Publications PLC.

Subohi, Afshan (2008). "Government Told to Restrict Borrowing." *Dawn*, April 1, 2008, p. 9.

Subrahamanyam, K. (1982). *Indian Security Perspectives*. New Delhi: ABC Publishing House.

Syed, Anwar H. (2001). "The Sunni-Shia Conflict in Pakistan," in Hafeez Malik, ed., *Pakistan: Founders' Aspirations and Today's Realities*. Oxford: Oxford University Press.

Syed, Ghulam Murtaza (2009 {1974}). *A Nation in Chains*. Accessed on July 16, 2009 from http://www.sindhudesh.com/gmsyed/nation/saeen-book5.htm

Talbot, Ian (1998). *Pakistan: A Modern History*. New York: St. Martin's Press.

Talbot, Ian (2005). *Pakistan: A Modern History*. Expanded and Updated Edition. New York: Palgrave Macmillan.

Tariq, Rana (2009). "More Provinces Plot of Enemy Forces: Pirzada." *Weekly Pulse*, July 2, 2009. Accessed on July 2009 from http://www.weeklypulse.org/pulse/article/3817.html

Tarrow, Sidney (2005). *The New Transnational Activism*. Cambridge: Cambridge University Press.

Taylor, David (2005). "Religion and Politics," in Devin T. Hagerty ed., *South Asia in World Politics*. Oxford University Press (2006) USA: Rowman and Littlefield.

Tellis, Ashley J. (1997). *Stability in South Asia*. Santa Monica: Rand.

Thomas, Raju G.C. (1986). *Indian Security Policy*. Princeton: Princeton University Press.

Thompson, William R. and Richard Tucker (1997). "A Tale of Two Democratic Peace Critiques." *The Journal of Conflict Resolution*, Vol. 41, No. 3, June, pp. 428–454.

Thornton, Thomas Perry (1999). "Pakistan: Fifty years of insecurity" in Harrison, Selig S., Paul H. Kreisberg, and Dennis Kux, eds., *India and Pakistan: The First Fifty Years*. Cambridge (U.K.): Cambridge University Press.

Tilly, Charles (1978). *From Mobilization to Revolution*. USA: McGraw-Hill.

224 *Bibliography*

Tilly, Charles (1985). "War Making and State Making as Organized Crime," in Peter Evans, Dietrich Rueschemeyer, and Theda Skocpol, eds., *Bringing the State Back In*. Cambridge: Cambridge University Press.

Tilly, Charles (1990). *Coercion, Capital, and European States, AD 990–1990*. Cambridge, MA, USA: B. Blackwell.

Tocqueville, Alexis de (1838). *Democracy in America*. Tr. by Henry Reeve. London, Saunders, and Autley.

Tomlinson, B.R. (1992). "Historical Roots of Economic Policy" in Roy, Subroto and William E. James, eds., *Foundations of India's Political Economy: Towards an Agenda for the 1990's*. New Delhi: Sage Publications.

Transparency International (2002). "Police, Then Judiciary Most Corrupt Public Institutions in South Asia, Reveals TI Survey." *Press Release: South Asia Survey*, December 17, 2002. Accessed on September 27, 2009 from http://www.transparency.org/news_room/latest_news/press_releases/2002/2002_12_17_south_asia_survey

Umar, Asad (2008). "Outlining Economic Priorities." *Dawn*, April 4, 2008, p. 7.

Varshney, Ashutosh (2002). *Ethnic Conflict and Civic Life: Hindus and Muslims in India*. New Haven, CT: Yale University Press.

Varshney, Ashutosh (2009). Oral comments as Discussant. Panel on "Disaggregating Civil Wars." *American Political Science Association Annual Conference*, September 2009, Toronto, Canada.

Walker, Stephen G. (2004). "Leaders and the Logic of Political Survival." *International Studies Review*, Vol. 6, pp. 486–488.

Walsh, Declan (2008), "Taliban Commander Calls for Ceasefire in Pakistan Border Area," *The Guardian*, April 25, 2008. Accessed on April 2008 from http://www.guardian.co.uk/world/2008/apr/25/pakistan.afghanistan?gusrc=rss&feed=networkfront

Wang, Juan (2009). *Personal conversation with the author*.

Wickham, Carrie Rosefsky (2002). *Mobilizing Islam: Religion, Activism, and Political Change in Egypt*. New York: Columbia University Press.

Wiktorowicz, Quintan, ed. (2004). *Islamic activism: a Social Movement Theory Approach*. Bloomington, Ind.: Indiana University Press.

Weinbaum, Marvin G. (1999). "Pakistan: Misplaced priorities, missed opportunities" in Harrison, Selig S., Paul H. Kreisberg, and Dennis Kux, eds., *India and Pakistan: The First Fifty Years*. Cambridge (U.K.): Cambridge University Press.

Weiss, Anita and S.Zulfiqar Gilani, eds. (2001). *Power and Civil Society in Pakistan*. Karachi: Oxford University Press.

Wolpert, Stanley (2006). *Shameful Flight: the Last Years of the British Empire in India* New York: Oxford University Press.

Yousaf, Nasser (2009). "State of Pukhtun Nationalism." *Dawn*, July 22, 2009, p. 6.

Zafar, S.M. (2000). "Constitutional Developments in Pakistan, 1997–99," in Craig Baxter and Charles Kennedy, eds., *Pakistan 2000*. Oxford: Oxford University Press.

Zaidi, S.Akbar (1999). *Issues in Pakistan's Economy*. Karachi: Oxford University Press.

Zaidi, S.Akbar (2008). "Op-Ed column." *Dawn*, May 3, 2008, p. 7.

Zakaria, Fareed (2001). "The Origins of Islamic Fundamentalism." *Published on October 15, 2001 as in a series of articles for Newsweek magazine*. Downloaded on October 22, 2002 from http://www.msnbc.com/news/639273.asp?0sp=w17b4

Zaman, Muhammad Qasim (2002). *The Ulama in Contemporary Islam: Custodians of Change*. Princeton: Princeton University Press.

Ziring, L (1988). 'Public Policy Dilemmas and Pakistan's Nationality Problem: The Legacy of Zia ul-Haq.' *Asian Survey*, Vol. 28, No. 8, August.

Ziring, Lawrence (1997). *Pakistan: A Political History.* Oxford: Oxford University Press.

Ziring, Lawrence (2005). "Pakistan: Terrorism in Historical Perspective," in Veena Kukreja and M.P. Singh, eds., *Pakistan: Democracy, Development, and Security Issues.* New Delhi: Sage Publications India.

Zubaida, Sami (1992). "Islam, the State, and Democracy: Contrasting Conceptions of Society in Egypt." *Middle East Report*, November–December 1992, pp. 2–10.

Index

A

"Aabiyaana" water tax 95

Abu Musab al-Zarqawi (Al-Qaeda leader in Iraq) 196

accommodational policy 14

actors, internal and external 192–3

administrative capacity 163–71; domestic debt 165; foreign loan to improve tax collection 168; horizontal inequity problem 168–70; ineffective record keeping 166; institutional strengthening 166; narrow tax base 165; positions as patronage 164; sales taxes 169; taxation for representation bargain 168; taxation, problem of 165

affinity(ies) 21–2; class-based groups 205–7; group 2, 13, 24, 26–7, 38, 48, 95, 108, 111, 113, 116, 128, 135, 139, 146, 149, 177, 180, 184, 187, 190, 193, 198, 202, 205, 207; motives 22

Afzal, M. Rafique 41–2, 49, 76, 79–80, 97

Agartala conspiracy in 1968 83, 120

agencies 47, 112; "agency-wallay" 151; All Pakistan Security Agencies Association 174; American 98; intelligence 112, 151, 156; state 199; tribal 48; unlicensed security 174; Washington 154; wealthy patrons 112

agitational politics 109, 124

Agrarian Reform Committee 79

agrarian unrest 75

Ahmad, M., 79

Ahmaddis 37, 42

Ahmar, Moonis, 56, 136, 141–2, 177

Ahmed, Farooq, 147–8

Ahmed, Feroz 136, 145

Ahmed, Viqar 74, 84–5, 93

Ahrar's activism (1950s) *vs.* Ahmadi community 36–7; 1953 anti-Ahmad

agitation 37; Ahmaddis 37; Daultana, Mumtaz (Chief Minister in Punjab province) 37; Sunni militants (Shias) 37

Aid-to-Pakistan Consortium 86

Akhtar, Rafique 39

Alavi, Hamza 54, 63–4

Ali, Abbas 147–8

Ali, Imran Anwar 62

Ali, Kamran Asdar 95

All Pakistan Muhajir Student Organization (APMSO) 136–7

All Pakistan Security Agencies Association 174

Almeida, Cyril 38, 73

Al-Qaeda 44, 196

"altruistic" leadership 5

American Political Science Association 196

Ames, Barry 3, 5

Amjad, Rashid 74, 84–5, 93

Anglo-American embargo 85

1953 anti-Ahmadi agitation 37

1974 anti-Ahmadiya movement 123

anti-Ayub agitation 120–1, 202

Anwar Ali, Imran (historian) 63–4

APMSO *see* All Pakistan Muhajir Student Organization (APMSO)

Article 58 2 (b) 68

austerity program 86

Awami National Party (Khan, Asfandyar Wali) 52, 91, 141

Axmann, Martin 133

Ayub, Imran 166

Aziz, Mazhar 61

Aziz, Sartaj 155, 182–3

B

Bagh, Mangal 196

Bahadur, Kalim 116

Index 227

Bahawalpur, autonomy for 146–7
Baig, General Aslam 39, 156
Balawaristan National Party 148
Balbus, Isaac 25
Baldev, Raj Nayar 85, 92
Baloch, Latif 132, 134
Balochistan, challengers in 132–5; armed
    conflicts (1948–1958/1962–1968)
    132–3; Baloch, Mohyuddin 134;
    Bizenjo, Baba-e-Balochistan (father of
    Balochistan) 133; Bugti, Akbar 134;
    cross-border Balochi movement 132;
    "Great Game" and Baloch, Prince
    Mohyuddin 134; Gwadar port
    development 135; Kalat revolt (Ahmed
    Yar Khan) 132; "Khan of Kalat"/armed
    defiance 132; Mengal, Sardar Attaullah
    133–4; military engagement,
    1962–1968/1974–1978 133; NAP and
    JUI government dismissal 133; official
    transcript 134; Pakistan Oppressed
    Nations Movement 133; secular 132;
    subunits 132
Bangladesh: 1971 war 129; creation 115,
    136, 204; crisis 92; Government of
    Bangladesh in Calcutta 50; nationalist
    guerrillas 50; SAARC summit 50, 99;
    secession 51, 67, 108, 122
Barelvi-oriented Sunni Tahrik 27
Bari, Faisal 166
Barnett, Michael 1, 5, 10, 12–15, 72–3
Bashir, Javed 38–9, 161
1959 Basic Democracies Order 52, 82–3,
    182–3; *see also* Khan, Ayub regime
    (1958–1969)
Bates, Robert H 73
Bayat, Asef 22–3, 25, 27
Beblawi, Hazem 2
Bengali nationalism 120
bhatta (bonus)/*tanzeems* (social
    organizations) 112
Bhutto, Benazir 42, 44, 51–2, 54, 58, 62,
    66–9, 128, 130, 132, 134, 138, 149,
    152, 155–9, 162–3, 172, 182–3, 193,
    199, 207; assassination 67; charged
    with crimes/faced detention or exile 67;
    second tenure as prime minister 159;
    support and split of army 156–7
Bhutto, Mumtaz Ali 46, 106–7, 130–2, 182;
    de jure quasi-state 131; provincial
    autonomy 131; Sindh National Front
    130; Sindh-Balochistan-Pushtun
    Front 130

Bhutto, Zulfikar Ali regime (1971–1977)
    42, 62, 67, 88–97, 106, 122, 125,
    130, 147, 157; 1973 Constitution 90;
    1973 parliamentary law 90; "anti-state
    activities" 91; as challenger 122–4
    (1974 anti-Ahmadiya movement 123;
    Non- Recognition of Bangladesh
    movement of 1972–74 124; Operation
    Searchlight 122; Pakistan People's
    Party 122); challenges 91
    (Nizam-e-Mustafa 122; PNA agitation
    for Nizam-e-Mustafa in 1977 123);
    detained and executed 67;
    Hamood-ur-Rehman Commission 89;
    international financing (Bangladesh
    crisis 92; Chinese aid reduction 92;
    debt burden, increase in 92; foreign
    loans 93; negative economic
    consequences 92–3); land reform 95–7
    (1977 Finance Act 96; 1977 land
    reform legislation 96; affinity group 95;
    "Canal tax" or "Aabiyaana" water tax
    95; Land Reform Act of 1972 95);
    mukhtar nama (power of attorney),
    retaining 96; Nizam-e-Mustafa
    movement 96; urban worker threats
    95); "mass protest movement" 91;
    Nizam-e-Mustafa (religious political
    order) 88; "People's Army" model 89;
    PNA 91, 123–4, 205; post-1971 period
    89; PPP organizational machine 90;
    taxation 93–5 ("entrepreneurial strike"
    94; factors, potential linkage 94;
    "Nationalizations" 94–5)
Bizenjo, Baba-e-Balochistan (father of
    Balochistan) 133
blasphemy laws (Zia ul-Haq) 38
Brines, Russell 33, 49, 84–6, 210
British colonial legacy 34, 63; British
    revenue collection 33; British rule 34;
    Indian Administrative Service and
    Civil Service of Pakistan 34; Indian
    Civil Service 34; National policies 34;
    pre-Partition army in India 34; Russian
    threat to North-West India 34
British revenue collection 33
Brown, L. Carl 192
Brown, W. Norman 33, 74–8, 84
Bueno de Mesquita, Bruce 1, 3–4, 8,
    17–18, 21, 28, 60, 62, 107, 172,
    187, 189–92
Bugti, Akbar 68, 134, 190, 199
Bulliet, Richard 41

228 *Index*

bureaucracy, military and civil 54–62;
Ayesha Siddiqua (Director of Naval
Research) 57–8; cardinal rule for
business 58; civil service examinations
56; elections in Pakistan 62; Fauji/
Shaheen/Bahria Foundations 58;
Federal Security Force 60; Ghulam
Mohammad, Civil servant 55; "good
governance" (Mazhar Aziz) 61;
Government of India Act 1935 57;
Husain, Ishrat (economist) 62; Kakul,
Pakistan Military Academy at 61;
Khan, Maulvi Tamizuddin (speaker)
55; Khwaja Nazimuddin
(governor-general) 55; landlords in
South Punjab 58–9; legislative
institutions 54; military elite 59; under
Mirza, Iskander 57; Musharraf
declaration 59–60; Pakistan Army's
history 59; Pakistani military 56;
political affairs, military's role in 57;
quasi-states 61; quota system 56;
second Constituent Assembly,
creation of 56; selectorate in Pakistan
61–2; Shuja and Asif Nawaz 60;
universal franchise national legislature
elections 57; "vice-regalism" 55; Zia
ul-Haq's regime 60
Burki, Shahid Javed 71, 87, 106, 120,
135–6, 163, 170, 185, 198, 201
business 65–7; agricultural income 66;
among Nawaz Sharif's family 65;
Habibs and Ispahanis (business
families) 65; Iftikhar Chaudhry (Chief
Justice) 66; international financing 67;
national interest 67; Pakistani winning
coalition 66; political survival *vs.*
ideology dilemma 67; under Zulfiqar
Ali Bhutto's nationalizations 65

C

Canal tax (Aabiyaana water tax) 95
caretaker governments 162–3; Khalid,
Meraj 163; "Washington Consensus"
policies 162–3; Qureshi, Moeen 106,
162, 200
Carter (US President) 99
central bank autonomy 104
Central Selection Board (CSB) 60
Central Treaty Organization in 1959 77
challengers: definition 3; interests of (moral
interests 25; objective and subjective
interests 25; official transcripts 25); and

quasi-state strategies 190–1 (low
extraction 190; normal process in
stable polity 190; normal/revolutionary
dichotomy 190; state repression 190);
in strong society 17–25, 19 (actors'
strategic choices 21; affinities 21–2;
anarchy 18; assessing interests 25;
contest based on revolutionary or
normal politics 20; de facto quasi-states
20; elective affinity approach 22;
groups and groupness 22–4; internal
and external threats 18; Leviathins 19;
normal/revolutionary challenge 18;
quasi-state, key elements 18–19;
selectorate/winning coalition 19;
strategies 18; strong society/strongmen
17; war-making/state-making activities
20); types 110; in weak polity *see* weak
polity, challengers in
Chandrasekhar, S., 209
Chaudhry Khaliquzzaman 204
Cheema, Ali 146
Chelliah, Raja J 210
China 33, 76, 84–6, 92, 197
Choudhury, G. W., 55, 74
civil bureaucracy 31, 54, 57, 62, 82, 162, 206
Civil Intelligence Bureau 157
Civil Services Academy (CSA) 60
Clark, G., 101
Class-based affinity groups 205–7
Coase, Ronald H 7
coercion 1, 63, 65, 115, 181–2, 192
Cohen, Stephen P 2, 31, 45, 48, 50,
84, 99, 116, 124–5, 129, 133,
136, 140, 143, 147, 158–9, 162,
173–4, 179
Concurrent List 36, 39, 52, 182, 207
conflict groups 23, 109
1973 Constitution 39, 59, 90, 96, 207
constitutional instability 38–40, 68, 70;
1997 Sharif, Nawaz government 40;
Article 58 Clause 2 (b) 39; Baig, Aslam
(Former Chief of Army Staff General)
39; Chief Justice Sajjad Ali Shah 40;
constitution-making and marital laws
38; federal republic, Pakistan as 38;
Government of India Act 1935 38;
Independence Act 1947 38; Judges of
superior judiciary (by Musharraf) 40;
Junejo government 39; Khan, Ayub
(president-centric) 1962 constitution
(Article 23 (3)/24) 39; Legal
Framework Order (2002) by General

Index   229

Musharraf 40; Nawaz Sharif's appeal
39; Presidency by Khan, Yahya (chief
of Army Staff) 39; President Khan,
Ghulam Ishaq (1993) 39; Section 92A
into Independence Act (Jinnah) 38;
successful lawyer's movement (Chief
Justice Chaudhry, Iftikhar) 40; Zia
ul-Haq's martial law regime 39; Zulfiqar
Ali Bhutto's 1973 constitution 39
corruption and private benefits 171–2;
foreign aid grants, military regimes
172; forms of corruption 171;
privileges for "Milbus" 172
1958 coup 81
cross-border Balochi movement 132
CSP recruitment system 120
cultural nationalism 141

D

Dahrendorf, Ralf 23
Dalrymple, William 206
Datta, Bhabatosh 210
Daultana, Mumtaz (Chief Minister in Punjab
province) 37, 44, 80, 158
de facto quasi-state phenomenon 141–2
de Haan, Jakob 10
Decade of Development 81
Decentralization 73, 131, 204, 208
democracies: "Basic Democracies" system
(Khan, Ayub) 4, 82–3, 182–3; resource
distribution in 4
Deobandi schools 129
Deobandi-influenced Tablighi Jamaat 27
developmentalist 70, 88; secularist 81
developmental/predatory or rent-seeking
state 6
devolution 20, 139, 149, 161, 181–4,
188, 207; fiscal reform and 201–5
(1970 elections 201; internationalism
203; One Unit Scheme 203;
piratization 202; quasi-state authority,
preference of 203; short-term political
survival constraints 201); Musharraf's
139, 161; Parainstitutions 181;
potential to incorporate quasi-state
entities 182
Dewey, Clive 50
disenfranchised, definition 4
disputed borders 45–6; British India and
Afghanistan, treaty between 46;
Durand Line 46; Kashmir, Indian
military occupation in 45
Distributive politics 188–9

Dogra Raj 147
Durrani, Tehmina 95

E

East Pakistan: regional elections 49 (Awami
League 49; East Pakistan Assembly
(March 1957) 49; Pakistan People's
Party 49); and Rehman, Mujib-ur
119–22 (Agartala conspiracy in 1968
120; anti-Ayub agitation 119–21;
Bengali nationalism 120; CSP
recruitment system 120; Khan, Yahya
regime 121; *Mujahid* 122; Mukti
Bahini 121–2; Six-Point Program
(Awami League's demands) 120–1;
United Front 119)
East Pakistan Smuggling of Food Grains Act
(1950) 79
"Eastern Question" system 192
EBDO (Elective Bodies (Disqualification)
Order) 81
Eijffinger, Sylvester C. W 10
elective affinity approach 22
elitist state (by economist Husain) 31
enlightened moderation message
(Musharraf) 149, 194
entrepreneurial strike 94
ethnicity 21, 24, 48, 110–11, 137, 188,
193, 195; and Islam 193–6 (Al-Qaeda
approach 196; "bad Muslims" in Lal
Masjid standoff 194; enlightened
moderation message (Musharraf) 194;
Islamic finance 194; Islamic honey
194; Islamic symbols 194; Jamaat-e-
Islami 195–6; Muttahida Majlis-e-
Amal coalition 195; Nizam-e-Mustafa
movement 194; public opinion 194;
social capital 193; suicide bombings
195; thoroughgoing Islamizers 194;
wafaqi (federation-friendly) 195;
Yemeni and Jordanian cases 196); and
religion 24
ethno-nationalism 111
ethno-nationalist labels 106, 113, 188,
191, 195
Evans, Peter. B., 6–7, 12
exemplary predatory state (Zaire) 7
external financing 151
extraction: cash balances of undivided India
74; defense establishment 74; indirect
taxation 75; installation of basic
industries 74; international financing
76–7 (capital budget 76; US anti-Soviet

230 *Index*

strategy 76; US assistance to Pakistan 77; war footing 76); land reform 79–80 (*jagirs* and *inams* (awards) 79; Land ownership reform 79; Land Reform Bills 80; PML Agrarian Reform Committee 79; zamindari (landholding) system 80); and leadership *see* leadership and extraction; minor international economic shock 75; Muslim League 75; refugees resettlement 74; resources for war-making 75; shocks and 12–13, 13 (external shocks 12; international shocks 12; sub classification of shocks 12); state apparatus 75; strategy 2; taxation 77–9 (1886 Income Tax Act 77; 1922 Income Tax Act 77; budget proposal in 1958 78; East Pakistan Smuggling of Food Grains Act (1950) 79; Harvard Advisory Group on five-year development plan 78)

F

Fata (Federally Administered Tribal Areas) 48, 141–3
Fazal, S. M. (journalist) 167–8
Fearon, James 24
Federal Public Service Commission (FPSC) 60
feudalism 65, 79; debate on (Ayesha Siddiqua's (Defence Secretary) 65; Haider Nizamani 65; Ishrat Husain 65; Zaidi, S. Akbar (Economist) 65)
"feudals" 31, 54, 59, 64–5, 67, 79, 88, 95–8, 110, 158, 163, 167, 177, 206
1977 Finance Act 96
financing government expenditures: borrowing/financing abroad 11 (domestic borrowing 11); money creation/accommodational policies 10–11 (inflation 11; seignorage 10; taxation/domestic extraction 10; non-tax sources of finance 10; tax, definition 10; taxable capacity and tax effort 10)
fiscal path 207–8; "Concurrent List" elimination of 207; encompassing coalition 207; equitable, broad-based taxation 207–8; state centralization 207
fiscal reform and devolution 201–5; 1970 elections 201; internationalism 203; One Unit Scheme 203; piratization 202; quasi-state authority, preference

of 203; short-term political survival constraints 201
fiscal sociology 2, 6, 8, 71, 105, 115, 149, 152, 168, 170, 185, 191, 200, 207–8
foreign aid 1–2, 8, 16, 77–8, 81, 84–5, 88, 91–2, 151, 172, 189
Fourteenth Amendment, Article 63A 159–60
Foust, Joshua 47, 143
Frontier Crimes Regulations 49, 140–1
"Frontier Gandhi" (Khan, Abdul Ghaffar) 115, 139–41

G

Gall, Carlotta 142
Ganguly, Sumit 32–3, 50
Gazdar, Haris 44, 52
Ghumro, Zamir 182
Gilgit-Baltistan 27, 147–8
Gilpin, Robert 209
global war on terror 67, 149
Goode, Richard 10–11, 14, 103
Government of Bangladesh 50
Grare, Frederic 142
"Great Game" and Baloch 134
Green Revolution 71
Groups and groupness: charisma, Weber's concept of 23; collective action problems 23; conflict groups 23; distributional coalitions 23; ethnicity and religion 24; ethnonationalism 24; ideas and symbols 23; relative deprivation 23; social movement (definition 23; organizations 23–4)
Gul, Hamid (ISI head) 156
Gurr, Ted Robert 23, 135
Gwadar port development 135

H

Haken, Nate 181
Hamood ur-Rehman Commission 89–90, 114
Hanif, Mohammed 67, 98
Haq, Farhat 136–7
Harrison, Selig S 32, 35
Harvard Advisory Group: on five-year development plan 78; for national planning advice 81
Haydar, Afak 37
Hindus: as British allies 129; influence on East Pakistani Bengalis 129; in Pakistan 36
"Hobbes Index" 28, 185
Holcombe, Randall G 4

Holders of Representative Offices (Prevention of Misconduct) Act 157
Horowitz, Donald 195
Hudood Ordinances (Zia ul-Haq) 42, 149
Human Rights Commission 64, 156
Husain, Altaf 193
Husain, Irfan 11, 31, 35, 42, 62, 64–5, 72–3, 104, 143, 152, 154, 163–7, 169, 171–2, 176, 182, 198
Husain, Ishrat (former State Bank Governor) 11, 31, 72–3, 104, 165, 182, 198
Husain, Mir Zuhair 75
Hussain, Akmal 135–8, 199
Hussain, Altaf and MQM 135–9, 199; APMSO 136–7; Bangladesh's creation 136; "independent Sindh" slogan 137; MQM 137–8 (welfare/social service 138); "Muhajir" label 135–6; Muhajir mobilization 137; Muhajir Qaumi Mahaz's emergence 136; Quaid-e-Tehrik (Leader of the Movement) 137; "stationary bandit" problem 139
Hyat, Taimur 109, 122, 133, 212
hyper-patriotism 47, 112

I

Idris, Kunwar 156
Ikenberry, G. John 12
1886 Income Tax Act 77
1922 Income Tax Act 77
incumbent extraction choices, quasi-state strategies/governance 191–2; land reforms 191; negotiable state 191; right-sizing 191
"independent Sindh" slogan 137
India with Pakistan, contrast 32; 1857 "Indian Mutiny" 32; agriculture and export earnings 35; attacks and counter-attacks 33; British taxation in India (Nasr) 33; destructive tank battles 33; income inequality measures 35; India's security thinking 33; Kuznets curve hypothesis 35; low-income countries 35; Martial law regimes *see* Martial law regimes; mid-1700s Mughal rule 32; military rule in Pakistan 35; Pakistan's security thinking 33; poverty and low living standards 35; UN Security Council ceasefire resolution 33; War of Independence 32
indirect taxation policies 188

inflation 11, 71, 81, 93, 103–4, 153, 155, 165, 169, 208
informal land allocation 175–6; *Katchi abadis* (squatter settlements) 175; land-grabbing (self-allocation) 175
institutional fragility 188, 193, 199
institutions and winning coalitions: business 65–7; feudalism debate 65; landlords 62–4; military and civil bureaucracy 54–62; state institutions *vs.* government institutions 53–4; *see also individual entries*
insurgency 91, 143; American- Pakistani attempts to root out Taliban 141; counter-insurgency tactics 199; in East Pakistan 116; Khidmat-e-Khalq division 138; Taliban 48; in tribal areas 142–4
Intelligence Bureau (IB) civilian 47, 112, 137, 157
internal jurisdictions 46–53; 2008 National Assembly elections 52; Awami National Party 52; Balochistan grievances 46–7; Bangladesh's secession 51; Bhutto, Mumtaz Ali (Sindhi nationalist) 46; British in administrative decision-making 49; "Concurrent List" policy 52; December 1970 elections 49 (Awami League 50; Pakistan People's Party 50); East Pakistan's regional elections 49; ethnic segments and groups 52; free elections 46; Frontier Crimes Regulations 49; FRs (Frontier Regions) 48; Government of Bangladesh 50; hyper-patriotism 47; Indian counter-attack 50; inter-provincial accommodation 52; Jalal, Ayesha (1990) 47 (non-elected institutions *vs.* elected institutions 47); *jirga* 48; Khan, Wali (Pukhtun nationalist) 47–8; Muslim League victory electoral waves 52; National Finance Council 46; nationalist movements 51; NWFP joining Afghanistan 47; One Unit Scheme of West Pakistan 47; Pakistani air raid 50; Policy-makers in Pakistan's 49; Provincial autonomy 46; reciprocal ceasefire announcements (by Indira Gandhi and Yahya Khan) 50; regionalist and ethnic tensions 51–2; seven tribal agencies, in independent Pakistan 48; Sind-based Punjabis 53;

232 Index

Sindhi landlords 51; Taliban insurgency 48; tribal Pukhtuns 48; West Pakistan Province 49; Zia-ul-Islam Zuberi 50

international financing: Bhutto, Zulfikar Ali regime (1971–1977) (Bangladesh crisis 92; Chinese aid reduction 92; debt burden, increase in 92; foreign loans 93; negative economic consequences 92–3); early years of extraction 76–7 (capital budget 76; US anti-Soviet strategy 76); US assistance to Pakistan 77; "war footing" 76); Khan, Ayub regime (1958–1969) 84–6 (1965 war with India 84–5; Aid-to-Pakistan Consortium 86; Anglo-American embargo 85; deterioration in US-Pakistan relationship 84; military aid 84; military mission sent to Moscow 85; relationship with China 84; Soviet-Pakistani military aid agreement 86; US economic aid 84); Zia ul-Haq regime (1977–1988) 99–100 (labor remittances from Middle East 100; "second Cold War" between US and USSR 99; structural imbalances after 1979 oil shock 100; U.S. law violations 99)

International Monetary Fund (IMF) 16, 86, 92–3, 100, 154, 159, 162–3, 176

international society, definition 5–6

Inter-Services Intelligence (ISI, military) 47, 112, 137, 156

"investment squeeze" (trade-offs) 31, 197

IPE shocks: based revenue crisis 16; and consequences for state power 15–16; and war shocks, distinctions 15

Iqbal, Ali Iqbal 54, 64

Islam and ethnicity 193–6; Al-Qaeda approach 196; "bad Muslims" in Lal Masjid standoff 194; "enlightened moderation" message (Musharraf) 194; Islamic finance 194; Islamic honey 194; Islamic symbols 194; Jamaat-e-Islami 195–6; Muttahida Majlis-e-Amal coalition 195; Nizam-e-Mustafa movement 194; public opinion 194; social capital 193; suicide bombings 195; "thoroughgoing" Islamizers 194; *wafaqi* (federation-friendly) 195; Yemeni and Jordanian cases 196

Islam and Pakistan 40–3; guerrilla resistance movements, *pirs* in 40; Hudood Ordinances of February 10, 1979 (Offence of Zina (fornication and adultery) Ordinance 42; qazf (slander or false accusation) 42); Islam in danger, Muslim League slogan 40; Islamic consciousness 40; Islamic order 41; Islamic postures 43; Islamistan (Khaliquzzaman) 42; Jamaat-e-Islami 41; Jamiat Ulema-e-Islam 41; Jamiat Ulema-e-Pakistan 41; Munir Report, 1954 Commission of Enquiry publication 41; Muslims in post-Partition India 42; Objectives Resolution 41 (Khan, Liaquat Ali compromise with religious leaders 41; Nizam-e-Mustafa agitation *vs.* Z.A. Bhutto regime 41); Official Islamization 43; Roman Catholicism (Muslim pope 41; Pakistan's television program "Aalim Online" 41; Sunna (teaching of Prophet Muhammad) 40; *ulama* (religious scholars) 40); rulers 42 (Bhutto, Zulfikar Ali 42; Jinnah, Fatima (JI support) 42; Khan, Ayub (Military ruler) 42; Khan, Yahya 42; Zia ul-Haq 42); *Sajjada nasheens* (authority in religious shrines) 40; Sind Provincial League 42; State Islamization 42; Sufi saints *(pirs)* and followers *(mureeds)* 40; Thanvi, Maulana Asad (Jamiat Ulema-e-Islam) 43; Zia ul-Haq (successors) 42 (Benazir Bhutto 42; Nawaz Sharif (Zia ul-Haq's protégé) 42; penal code, added sections to 42)

Islam in danger (pre-Partition slogan) 40, 112, 149

Islami Jamiat-e-Talaba (IJT) 116–17, 124, 136–7

Islamic finance 194

Islamic fundamentalism 105

Islamic honey 194

Islamic socialism 42, 64, 105, 126

Islamic symbols 40, 123, 194

J

Jacobsen, Kurt 48, 68

jagirs and *inams* (awards) 79–80; abolision of *jagirs* 87

Jalal, Ayesha 2, 31, 41–2, 44, 47–8, 51, 53, 71, 74–9, 84, 89, 103, 114–16, 120, 132–3, 136, 140, 194, 197

Index 233

Jamaat-e-Islami (JI) 27, 41–2, 44–5, 116, 137, 139, 157–9, 193, 195–6, 207; leaders 45 (Maulana Maududi (1941 to 1972) 45; Mian Tufail (1987) 45; Qazi Hussain Ahmed (1987) 45; tactical flexibility 45)

Jeay Sindh: activists 29, 126, 128 (history of 129); Syed, G. M. and 124–30 (armed uprising in Sind in 1983 128; Bazm-e-Soofia-e Sindh 124; "Jiyai Sindh"(Long Live Sind) 124; "mini-insurgency" (1989) 126–8; Mohajirs 124; Muslim League-oriented communal agitation 127; Sindhi independence movement 129–30; Sindhi nationalism 124; support for Jinnah in favor of Pakistan movement 126–7; violence 130)

jihad 98, 116, 141–2

Jinnah, Fatima 42, 45, 116, 157

Jinnah, Mohammed Ali 38; as challenger/ leader 117–19 (agreement between Muslim League and Congress 118; federation plan (Scheme A) 118; political survival perspective 119; Quaid-e-Azam 117; Simla summit 117; support from Pir of Manki Sharif 114; two-nation theory 117); constitutional instability (Section 92A into Independence Act 38); Muslim League 44; nation, definition 113; support of Jeay Sindh in favor of Pakistan movement 126–7

"Jiyai Sindh" (Long Live Sind), party 124; *see also* Jeay Sindh

Jones, Garth. N., 56

Jones, Owen Bennett 137–9, 177

Jordanian case 196

Joshi, Vijay 34, 209–10

judicial assassination 97, 156

Judicial judgment 68

Junejo, Mohammad Khan 98, 146

K

Kalat revolt (Khan, Ahmed Yar) 132, 134

Kasfir, Nelson 18

Kashmir 32–3, 45–6, 50, 74, 76, 84–5, 98, 108, 116, 120, 122, 141, 147, 178, 180; 1965 conflict (Rann of Kutch) 33; clashes of March 1948 76; conflict 74; incorporated fully into Indian state 33; over joining Pakistan 32; UN-brokered mediation 32; UN-resolved plebiscite in Kashmir 33

Kasi, Amanullah 144

Katchi abadis (squatter settlements) 175

Katzenstein, Peter 9

Kavic, Lorne J 34, 75

Khalid, Meraj 163

Khaliquzzaman 42, 115, 204

Khalistan 108, 118

Khan, Sardar Attaullah 134

Khan, Abdul Ghaffar 115, 139–41

Khan, Aftab Ahmad 78, 99–100

Khan, Ahmad Yar 132, 134

Khan, Asfandyar Wali 141

Khan, Asghar 173

Khan, Ayub regime (1958–1969): 1958 coup 81; abdication 67; anti-Ayub sentiments, Tashkent Declaration 82; "Basic Democracies" system 82; "Decade of Development" 81; Harvard Advisory Group for national planning advice 81; International financing 84–6 (1965 war with India 84–5; Aid-to-Pakistan Consortium 86; Anglo-American embargo 85; "deterioration" in US-Pakistan relationship 84; military aid 84; military mission sent to Moscow 85; relationship with China 84; Soviet-Pakistani military aid agreement 86; US economic aid 84); land reform 87–8 (Land Reform Act of February 1959 87); One Unit Scheme 83; open corruption 81; resignation under pressure 82; secularist developmentalist 81; taxation (1964 Taxation and Tariffs Commission 87; austerity program 86; Income and corporate taxes 87; Produce Index Unit 86; Taxation Enquiry Committee of 1959 86); Yahya Khan's leadership 82–3

Khan, Bashir 130

Khan, Dera Ghazi 145

Khan, Dera Ismail 145

Khan, Ghulam Ishaq 39, 68, 157

Khan, Haji Mira Ali 48

Khan, Hashim 47

Khan, Irum 68

Khan, Liaquat Ali 38, 42, 115, 158–9, 199; assassination 67, 199; compromise with religious leaders 41

Khan, M. Ilyas 141

Khan, Mahmood Hasan 77, 80, 86–7, 95, 106

234 *Index*

Khan, Mairaj M 95
Khan, Marshal Asghar 82–3, 120
Khan, Marshall Ayub 120
Khan, Maulvi Tamizuddin 55
Khan, Mubarak Zeb 48
Khan, Nematullah 139
Khan of Kalat 115, 132
Khan, Sadiq Mohammad 146
Khan, Sayeed Hasan 117
Khan, Shahrukh 86
Khan, Wali 47
Khan, Yahya 26, 30, 39, 42, 49–50, 57, 59, 67, 83, 110, 120–2, 144
Khidmat-e-Khalq (service to Creation) 138, 195
Khudai Khidmatgar (servants of God) movement 140; "Red Shirts" (members) 139
Khuhro, Murtaza 169
Kissinger 86
"knaves" 196
Koogler, Jeb 47, 143
Korean War 75
Krasner, Stephen 9
Kukreja, Veena 33, 94
Kuru, Ahmet. T., 9
Kuznets curve hypothesis 35

L
Lahore Resolution 113, 125
Lal Masjid standoff: "bad Muslims" in 194
land distribution efforts 106–7
Land ownership reform 79
land reform: Bhutto, Zulfikar Ali regime (1971–1977) 95–7 (1977 Finance Act 96; 1977 land reformlegislation 96; affinity group 95; "Canal tax" or "Aabiyaana" water tax 95; Land Reform Act of 1972 95; mukhtar nama (power of attorney), retaining 96; Nizam-e-Mustafa movement 96; urban worker threats 95); early years of extraction 79–80 (*jagirs* and *inams* (awards) 79; Land ownership reform 79; Land Reform Bills 80; PML Agrarian Reform Committee 79; zamindari (landholding) system 80); Khan, Ayub regime (1958–1969) 87–8 (Land Reform Act of February 1959 87); Zia ul-Haq regime (1977–1988) 102 (Qazal Bash case 102)
Land Reform Act in 1959 71, 87

Land Reform Act of 1972 95
Land Reform Bills 80
1977 land reform legislation 96
landlords 62–4; *batai* system 64; British colonial legacy 64; *haris*, landless peasants 64; Human Rights Commission 64; hydraulic political economy 63; in Jhang District 37 (rural and urban population (non-Syed and Sunni) 37; Shia to Syed 37); land ownership concentration in Pakistan 64; *Mai Bap* culture 63; mercantile era, British economy 63; political 64 (Convention Muslim League 64; feudal families 64; Islamic socialism 64; Majlis-i-Shoora 64; republicanism 64); political landlords 64; power in Pakistan 62; powerful 110; 1901 Punjab Alienation of Lands Act 63; "*Saieen*" (Sindhi landholder) 63; Sindhi 51; in South Punjab 58–9; *tabarrabazi* (slander), by Shia 37
language, issues 36
Lashkar-e-Jhangvi (Jhang's Army) 178
Lasswell, Harold 1, 61
Latin American politics 5
lawyers' protest mobilizations 205
leaders, autocratic/democratic 4
leadership: definition 3; developmental outcomes/distributional coalitions 196–9 (Business-friendly policies under Ayub 197–8; China and South Korea, invasions in 197; contract enforcement 198; cynicism about leaders 197; inclusive capitalism 197; knaves 197; Milbus 197; organizational design 197); and extraction *see* leadership and extraction
leadership and extraction 188–90; Bhutto, Zulfikar Ali regime (1971–1977) 88–97; caretaker prime ministers 189; choice of public finance strategy 72–3; compared to Israel 73; deficit spending 72; democratically elected leaders 189; extraction in Pakistan, early years 74–80; fiscal decentralization 73; high military spending and debt servicing 71; horizontal inequities, tax 73–4; financing 189; interprovincial tension 73; Khan, Ayub regime (1958–1969) 80–8; military coup-based leaders 189 (international support 189); money creation 102–4

(bank autonomy 104; currency issue and central banking 103); inflationary effects 103; public goods provision 189; regression analysis of developing countries 74; relationships 72; restructural strategies 73; vertical imbalance issue 73; Zia ul-Haq regime (1977–1988) 97–102

Levi, Margaret 2–3, 5, 16, 24, 28, 73, 196

Lichbach, Mark Irving 23

liquidity crises: solutions to 15

Little, I. M. D., 34, 209–10

The Logic of Political Survival (LOPS) 1, 3, 18, 54, 86, 163, 189, 191–2

"loyalty norm" 5, 62

Luciani, Giacomo 2

M

madrasa training (Maulana Haq Nawaz Jhangvi) 37

Mahdavy, Hussein 2

Mahmood, Abid 177

Mahmud, S. F., 112

Malaysia with Pakistan, contrast 35; lacked effective machinery of government 35; Pakistan's new administration 36; weak states 35

Malik, Adeel 185, 210

Malik, Iftikhar. H., 156

manazra 37

Mandal, J. N. 36, 115

mantra from *LOPS* 4

Martial law regimes 35; General Pervez Musharraf's regime (1999) 35; Khan, Ayub's rule (1958) 35; Zia Ul-Haq's regime (1977) 35

Martinez-Vazquez, Jorge 74, 170

mass activism 205

mass protest movement 91

Material aid 72

Mengal, Sardar Attaullah Khan 133–4

micro-nations 147

Migdal, Joel 5, 9, 13, 15, 17, 30, 34

Milbus 31, 101, 162, 172, 197; methods 101–2

military aid 77, 84–6, 104

military bureaucracy 54–62; *see also* bureaucracy, military and civil

military coup-based leaders 189

military engagement (1962–1968/ 1974–1978) 133

Mirza, Iskander 87

Mitra, Subrata 170, 186

Modelski, G., 210

Mohajir Qaumi Mahaz (Mohajir National Movement) 139

money creation 2, 10–11, 14, 71–2, 93, 102–5, 151, 188–9, 208

monopoly power 7

Moore, Mick 2, 6, 8

Morrison, Kevin. M., 2, 71

Movement for the Restoration of Democracy (MRD) 97–8, 100, 137

MRD and survival instinct 100, 153

Mufti 101, 123, 142

Muhajir mobilization 137

Muhajir Qaumi Mahaz's emergence 136

Muhammad, Mian Tufail 117

"Mujahid" 122

mukhtar nama (power of attorney), retaining 96

Mukti Bahini 121–2

mullahs 132, 142, 194

Musharraf, Pervez: assassination attempts 67; declaration 59–60; devolution 139, 161; "enlightened moderation" message 149, 194; Judges of superior judiciary 40; Legal Framework Order (2002) 40; national reconstruction 153–4; regime (1999) 35; rulership strategies 160–2 (anti-Musharraf agitation 162; Article 58 2 (b) restoration 161; lawyers' movement 161–2; Legal Framework Ordinance 161; "long march" 161; military's patriotic image 162; Referendum 161; role for military in decision-making 161; War on Terror 161)

Muslim League 37, 40–2, 44, 52, 55, 64, 75, 79–80, 112, 115–20, 125–8, 137, 140, 149; "Al-Faida Group" ("Al-Qaeda") 44; Deoband ulama 44–5; dominated by Jinnah 44; Jamaat-e-Islami (JI) 44–5 (leaders 45; Muttahida Majlis-e-Amal (MMA, Allied Action Congregation) 45); mass party in 1939 44; Nawaz Sharif's faction 44; Pakistan Muslim League (PML) 44; Pakistan People's Party 44 (Pir Pagaro group 44); Qaiyum Muslim League 44; religious parties 44; Shariat lobby 44

Muslim League victory electoral waves 52

Muslims in Uttar Pradesh 36

236 Index

Muttahida Majlis-e-Amal (MMA)
45, 140–1; alliance of religious parties
141; coalition 195; NWFP religious
coalition 42
Muttahida Qaumi Movement (MQM) 27,
52, 135–9, 157–9, 177–8, 184, 190,
193, 195, 205, 207
"*muttarwala*" 138
Mutual Defense Assistance Agreement 77
My Feudal Lord (Durrani) 95

N

Naji, Nawaz Khan 148
NAP and JUI government dismissal 133
Nasr, Seyyed Vali Reza 2, 34–6, 42–3,
71, 87, 101, 116–17, 124, 129,
191, 194
nation, definition (Jinnah) 113
National Finance Commission 73, 182
National Institutes of Public Administration
(NIPAs) 60
national leadership after Zia ul-Haq 152–5;
American aid reduction 154; bank
privatizations 155; Benazir Bhutto
privatization 155; commercial loans
153; electricity distribution 155; "era of
structural adjustment", 1988 onwards
154; 1991 Gulf War 154; international
borrowing 153; national reconstruction
(Musharraf) 153–4; privatization and
nationalizations 154–5; sale of Zeelpak
Cement Factory 155
national political activism 203
National Security Council (NSC) 57
National Student Federation (NSF) 136–7
Nationalizations 65, 72, 81, 93–5, 154,
197, 201
Nawaz Sharif: bill to enshrine Sharia 159;
bill to prevent floor-crossing 159;
constitutional instability (1997
government 40; appeal 39);
"counter-coup" 160; exile 199; faction,
Muslim League 44; homegrown fiscal
reforms 159; identity-based political
confrontation in Punjab 158; Ittefaq
Foundry 157; quasi-states 155–60;
Sharia bill 159
Nawaz, Shuja 59–60, 122, 199
Neuwirth, Robert 176
Nixon 86
Nizamani, Haider 65
Nizam-e-Adl: religious law 42; System of
Justice program 140

Nizam-e-Mustafa: agitation in 1977 123;
movement 96, 194, 202; Order of
the Prophet 122; religious political
order 88
Noman, Omar 92–6, 153, 197
Non-Recognition of Bangladesh movement
(1972–74) 124
non-tax revenues 2, 70–1, 183, 188, 191
nonwar IPE shocks and consequences for
state power 15–16; IPE and war
shocks, distinctions 15; IPE
shock-based revenue crisis 15; options
for regimes 16; problem with short-
term "quick-fix" package 15; revenue
crises, liquidity and solvency 15;
revenue shocks 15; solutions to
liquidity crises 15; solutions to
solvency crisis 15
Noorani, A. G., 57
normal path 187
North, Douglass 3, 6–7, 12, 17
North's model of state 7
1998 nuclear tests 192
NWFP plebiscite 140

O

Objectives Resolution 36, 41, 115
official Islam 25, 43, 113, 116
Olson, Mancur 16, 23
One Unit Scheme 47, 49, 83, 87, 146, 203
opportunity cost 7
optimism (Dalrymple's) 206
Organski, A. F. K., 2, 6, 9, 17

P

Pakhtoonkhwa (Pakhtun Brotherhood) 141
Pakhtunistan 47, 140
Pakistan Administrative Staff College
(PASC) 60
*Pakistan in the Twentieth Century: A
Political History* 107
Pakistan Muslim League (PML) 41–2, 44,
51, 68, 79–80, 98, 152, 193, 206;
Agrarian Reform Committee 79
Pakistan National Alliance (PNA) 91,
123–4, 205; agitation for
Nizam-e-Mustafa in 1977 123
Pakistan Oppressed Nations Movement 133
Pakistan People's Party 44, 49–50,
66, 122
Palejo, Rasul Bux 128
Pape, Robert 181
1973 parliamentary law 90

Index 237

partition in 1947 32–6, 40–2, 56, 64, 75–6, 80, 112, 125, 135, 146; ethnic cleansing 32; refugees 32; West and East Pakistan 32

Pasha, Hafiz 63

Pashtoon, Rafiq 144

Pata (Provincially Administered Tribal Areas) 48

"People's Army" model 89

Peterson, George 208

piratization 202

PODO (Public Offices (Disqualification) Order) 81

policing 173–5; extensive police reforms in Musharraf's regime 173; insecurity of life and property 174–5; institutional vacuum 175; staffing and promotions 173; transparency in induction and insulation 173

political landlords 64; Convention Muslim League 64; feudal families 64; Islamic socialism 64; Majlis-i-Shoora 64; republicanism 64; *see also* landlords

political parties 43–5; elections to National Assembly 44; Muslim League 44; in Pakistan 43; Pakistan People's Party 44; religious parties 44; responsible party government 43; *Shaheed* (martyr) group 44

political survival in weak state 200–1; administration of regime 5; "altruistic" leadership 5; Caretaker Prime Minister Moeen Qureshi's tenure 200; challengers in strong society *see* challengers; corruption among police 200–1; disenfranchised, definition 4; extraction strategy 2; ideal-type of state, definition 5; international society, definition 5–6; leaders, autocratic/democratic 4; leadership, definition 3; loyalty norm 5; mantra from *LOPS* 4; merit-based selection processes 200; method and data 25–8 (bureaucratic machine context 26; interviews, secondary accounts, and official statements 26–7; Jeay Sindh activists 27; Muttahida Qaumi Movement 27; poetry 25; "vice-regalism" 26; narrow tax base and low tax effort 2); nonwar IPE shocks and consequences for state power 15–16; perspectives on state strength 8–9; *see also* state; real states 5; regime type and fiscal policy 16–17;

resource distribution in democracies 4; role of institution 1, 10–11; selectorate, definition 4; shocks and extraction 12–13; state 6–8; strategic and tactical decision-making 2; war making and state making 13–15; winning coalition, definition 4

Politics, definition (Lasswell, Harold) 1

Post-colonial South Asia 108; secessionist and "autonomist" movements 108

PPP's power base in Sind 68; Akbar Bugti (Balochi nationalist leader) 68; Balochistan and NWFP 68

Pressler Amendment 172

privatization 154–5, 189, 202

Produce Index Unit 86, 96

property rights 7, 9, 17, 28, 70, 166, 175, 181, 196, 202

provincial autonomy 39, 46, 52, 77, 91, 131, 134, 152, 182–3, 205

Pukhtun nationalist Wali Khan 47–8; Gohar Ayub (son of national leader Ayub Khan) 48; National Awami Party from Red Shirt organization 48

Punjab Muslim League 80

Pushtun nationalism//ethnonationalism 139–40, 142; Khudai Khidmatgar organization (Red Shirts) 139; Khudai Khidmatgar (servants of God) movement 140; NWFP plebiscite 140; Pakhtunistan 140

Q

Qari 142

Qazal Bash case 102

Quaid-e-Tehrik (Leader of the Movement) 137

quasi-states: administrative capacity and political will 163–71 (deficit financing strategy 166; domestic debt 165; foreign loan to improve tax collection 168; horizontal inequity problem 168–70; ineffective record keeping 166; institutional strengthening 166; narrow tax base 165; positions as patronage 164; sales taxes 169; taxation for representation bargain 168; taxation, problem of 165); Benazir and Nawaz Sharif 155–60; caretaker governments 162–3; corruption and private benefits 171–2; devolution 181–4; external financing 151; financing a quasi-state actor 151;

238 Index

incumbents and challengers 152; informal land allocation 175–6; Musharraf's rulership strategies 160–2; national leadership after Zia ul-Haq 152–5; policing 173–5; reason for existence 150–1; resources 151; sectarian religious quasi-states 177–81; state weakness 151; underground and parallel economies 176–7
Qureshi, Moeen 106, 162
Qureshi, Saleem M. M 2

R

Rahman, Shamim-ur 52
Rasler, Karen 6, 12, 209
RAW (Research and Analysis Wing) 193
Raza, Rafi 35, 179
real states 5
Realists 15
refugees 32, 50, 74, 136, 138
regime: administration of 5; types and fiscal policy 16–17 (autocracies and democracies, taxation in 16; efficient property rights 16–17; large-coalition systems 16; linkages between regime type and extraction strategy 17)
Rehman, I. A., 35, 169, 183
Rehman, Mujib-ur: East Pakistan and 119–22 (Agartala conspiracy in 1968 120; anti-Ayub agitation 119–21; Bengali nationalism 120; CSP recruitment system 120; *Mujahid* 122; Mukti Bahini 121–2; Six-Point Program (Awami League's demands) 120–1; United Front 119; Yahya Khan regime 121)
religio-nationalism 111
religious parties 44; Jamiat Ulema-e-Islam's powerful faction (JUI-F) 44; political (Jamaat-e-Islami 44; Jamiat Ulema-e-Islam 44; Jamiat Ulema-e-Pakistan 44)
restructural strategy 14, 73
revenue shocks 12, 15
Revival of the Constitutions Order (RCO) 98
revolutionary paths 187
Riaz, Mohammed 48
right-sizing 191
Rizvi, Hasan Askari 33, 39, 42, 44–7, 49, 57, 79–83, 87, 89–91, 95, 98
Rose, Leo. E., 49–50, 76, 86, 92
Rothermund, Dietmar 102

Roubini, Nouriel 10, 12, 15, 99–100
ruler and constituents, terms of exchange 7

S

SAARC (South Asian Association for Regional Cooperation) summit in Dhaka in 1985 99
Saraiki ethno-nationalism 145–7; autonomy for Bahawalpur 146–7; Saraiki Qaumi Movement (Saraiki National Movement) 145; tanzeem in 1990s 145
Saraiki Qaumi Movement (Saraiki National Movement) 145
Sayyid, Bobby S. 194
Schwedler, Jillian 196
"second Cold War" (between US/USSR) 99
sectarian religious quasi-states 177–81
secular developmentalism 105
secularist developmentalist 81
seignorage 10, 72–3, 93, 103–4
selection institutions and winning coalitions: state institutions *vs.* government institutions 53–4 (democracy in Pakistan (five groups) 54; elected governments in Pakistan 54; electoral measures and innovations 53–4; LOPS 54; principal agent problems 53); *see also individual entries*
selectorate 4, 18, 21, 31, 56, 61–2, 64, 67, 109, 111, 121–2, 162, 192, 198, 206; and winning coalition 3, 19
separatist ethnic minority groups 113
"service solidarity" 102
Shadin Bangla Kendriya Chattra Parishad (Independent Bangladesh Central Student's Union) 120
Shah, Aqil 51, 60–1
shocks and extraction 12–13; external shocks 12; international shocks 12; sub classification of shocks 12; *see also* extraction
short-term "quick-fix" package 15
"*shuhada*" 138, 195
Siddiqa, Ayesha 170, 172
Siddiqui, Kalim 32, 84, 86, 91
Siddiqui, Tasneem Ahmad (highest civilian medal) 116, 120, 167, 171, 173, 175–7, 185, 197–8, 205
Simla conference (1946) 119
Sind Katchi Abadi Authority 175
Sindh National Front 130, 182
Sindh-Balochistan-Pushtun Front 130

Singh, M. P., 33
Sino-Pakistan border agreement (1963) 33
Sipah-e-Sahaba Pakistan (SSP) program 37, 178; Pakistan (Sunni state) 37; rally, slogan of 37
Sisson, Richard 49–50, 76, 86, 92
Six-Point Program (Awami League's demands) 120–1
Smith, Alastair 1, 8, 189
smuggling (profitable criminal activities) 79, 81, 112, 129, 142, 176
Snider, Lewis. W., 9, 11–12, 15
Sobhan, Rehman 43, 60, 155, 159–60
social capital 111, 193
social movement 23–4, 27–8, 203; definition 23; organizations 23–5
Sodaro, Michael 43
Solingen, Etel 1
solvency crisis 15, 105
Soomro, Rahmatullah 130
South East Asia Treaty Organization (SEATO) 77, 210
"southern Pashtoonkhwa" 144
Soviet-Afghan conflict 99
Soviet-Pakistani military aid agreement 86
Spruyt, Hendrik 22
Sreekantaradhya, B. S., 210
state: basic activities (extraction 6; protection 6; state-making 6; war-making 6); ideal-type of, definition 5; power 13; rulership/extraction and fiscal sociology 6–8; -society relations 12, 19, 70, 72, 88, 154, 189; strength, perspectives on 8–9 (political will and capacity 9; "public bad" than "public good" consequences 9; strength in different realms 8–9; tax rate 9); survival 31–2; weakness 151; *see also* weak state and negotiable polity
State and Civil Society in Pakistan (Malik, Ifitkhar) 156
state failure 32, 108, 121
state institutions *vs.* government institutions 53–4; democracy in Pakistan (five groups) 54; elected governments in Pakistan 54; electoral measures and innovations 53–4; LOPS 54; principal agent problems 53; *The State of Martial Rule* 31, 71
state power, non war IPE shocks and consequences 15–16; IPE and war shocks, distinctions 15; IPE

shock-based revenue crisis 15; options for regimes 16; problem with short-term "quick-fix" package 15; revenue crises, liquidity and solvency 15; revenue shocks 15; solutions to liquidity crises 15; solutions to solvency crisis 15
"stationary bandit" problem 139
Stepaniants, Marietta 113, 211
Stewart, Francis 109, 122, 133, 212
Stewart, Peter 94, 100, 103–4, 154
Sturgis, Jenny 94, 100, 103–4, 154
Subohi, Afshan 165
Subrahamanyam, K., 33
suicide bombings 177, 181, 195
Sunni and Shia, conflict between 117
Sunni militants 37
Syed, Anwar. H., 45, 178–80, 209
Syed, Ghulam Murtaza 122, 124–30, 158, 190
Syed, G. M. and Jeay Sindh 124–30; armed uprising in Sind in 1983 128; Bazm-e-Soofia-e Sindh 124; Jeay Sind activists (narration of history 129; Sunni Tahrik (Barelvi-affiliated militant religious organization) 129); "Jiyai Sindh" (Long Live Sind) 124; "mini-insurgency" (1989) 126–8; Mohajirs 124; Muslim League-oriented communal agitation 127; Sindhi independence movement 129–30; Sindhi nationalism 124; Sindhi political leader 122; support for Jinnah in favor of Pakistan movement 126–7; violence 130

T

tabarrabazi (slander), by Shia landlords 37
Tablighi Jamaat 27, 129, 178
Tahrik-e-Jafriya Pakistan (a Shia group) 178
Talbot, Ian 2, 34, 40, 44, 50, 54–5, 60, 64, 67, 74–6, 82, 85, 87, 89, 92–3, 99, 103, 116, 120, 125, 128, 130, 132–4, 137–8, 145, 156, 158, 161–3, 165, 210
Taliban 142–3
Tariq, Rana 146
Tarrow, Sidney 23, 181, 203
Tashkent Declaration 82
tax: definition 10; effort 2, 10, 207; horizontal inequities 73–4, 170, 188–9; revenues 7–8, 11, 16, 72, 188
taxable capacity 9–10
taxation: Bhutto, Zulfikar Ali regime (1971–1977) 93–5 (entrepreneurial

240 *Index*

strike 94; factors, potential linkage 94;
Nationalizations 94–5); early years of
extraction 77–9 (1886 Income Tax Act
77; 1922 Income Tax Act 77; budget
proposal in 1958 78; East Pakistan
Smuggling of Food Grains Act (1950)
79; Harvard Advisory Group on
five-year development plan 78; indirect
taxation 75); equitable, broad-based
207; Khan, Ayub regime (1958–1969)
(1964 Taxation and Tariffs Commission
87; austerity program 86; income and
corporate taxes 87; Produce Index Unit
86); Taxation Enquiry Committee of
1959 86); Zia ul-Haq regime
(1977–1988) 100–2 (increase in
domestic debt 100; Milbus methods
101–2; MRD and survival instinct 100;
service solidarity 102; "Zakat and Ushr"
Ordinance, Islamization effort 101)
1964 Taxation and Tariffs Commission 87
Taxation Enquiry Committee of
1959 86
Taylor, David 141, 152
Tehrik-e-Taliban Pakistan 142
Tellis, Ashley. J., 33
"The Crisis of the Tax State" (Joseph
Schumpeter's essay) 6, 8
Thomas, Raju G. C 33
Thompson, William R 6, 12, 209
Thornton, Thomas Perry 71
"thoroughgoing" Islamizers 42, 194
Tilly, Charles 2, 6, 19–20, 23, 138,
144, 147
Tomlinson, B. R., 33, 209
Tract on Monetary Reform (1971) 11
Transparency International 165, 198

U
ulama 40–1, 44–5, 101, 194
Umar, Asad 224
underground economies 176–7; bhatta
payments 176; "Kalashnikov culture"
177; parallel economy 176
unearned revenues 8
United Front 119
US anti-Soviet strategy 77
US economic aid 84
Uttar Pradesh, Muslims in 36

V
Varshney, Ashutosh 24, 111, 195, 209
vertical imbalance issue 73

vice-regal tradition 31, 55
Vice-regalism 26

W
wafaqi (federation-friendly) 195
Walker, Stephen. G., 3, 5
Walsh, Declan 142
Wang, Juan 212
war economy 141
War of Independence 32
War on Terror 154, 161, 172, 192
war shocks: and IPE, distinctions 15
war with Baloch in 1974–8 133
war with India: 1965 49, 84–5; 1971 122
Warmaking and statemaking 13–15;
challengers, role of 14; domestic
extraction 15; leader's extraction, war
preparation/political stability 14;
restructural strategy
"Washington Consensus" policies 163
weak polity, challengers in: appeals to
national unity 115; appeals to unity
based on religious affiliation 115;
Awami National Party (Khan,
Asfandyar Wali) 141; Bhutto, Zulfikar
Ali 122–4; challenger types 110;
challengers in Balochistan *see*
Balochistan, challengers in; coercion
115; East Pakistan and Rehman,
Mujib-ur *see* Rehman, Mujib-ur;
ethnicity and Islamism 110–11;
G.M. Syed and Jeay Sindh 124–30;
Hussain, Altaf and MQM 135–9;
insurgency in tribal areas 142–4;
Islami Jamiat Talaba 116; Jinnah as
challenger/leader 117–19; joining
winning coalition 111–12; Lahore
Resolution 113; links to previous
ruling coalition 110; Mumtaz Ali
Bhutto 130–2; new provinces, search
for 144–8 (Gilgit-Baltistan
autonomists 147; micro-nations 147;
Northern areas 147–8; Saraiki
ethno-nationalism 145–7; "southern
Pashtoonkhwa" 144); official
Islamism 116; paths under particular
incumbents, themes 111; pir or sajjada
nasheen 110; powerful landlords 110;
Pushtun ethnonationalism 139–40;
quasi-state/national office and
additional possibilities 109–10; quasi-
states, resources for 112 (agencies 112;
bhatta (bonus)/*tanzeems* (social

Index 241

organizations) 112); hyperpatriotism 112; smuggling (Profitable criminal activities) 112; religio-autonomism (Awami National Party (Khan, Asfandyar Wali) 140; Federally Administered Tribal Areas region 141; Muttahida Majlis-e-Amal, alliance of religious parties 141; Nizame-Adl (System of Justice) program 140; "Pakhtoonkhwa" (Pakhtun Brotherhood) 141; Taliban leaders 142; war economy 141); religio-nationalism and ethno-nationalism 111; religious political parties (Islami Jamiat Talaba 116; Jamaate-Islami (Maulana Maududi) 116); Saraiki ethno-nationalism 145–7; separatist ethnic minority groups 113

weak state and negotiable polity 30–69; constitutional instability 38–40; current context 67–9; disputed borders 45–6; internal jurisdictions 46–53; Pakistan and Islam 40–3; *see also* Islam and Pakistan; political parties 43–5; selection institutions and winning coalitions in Pakistan (business 65–7); *see also individual entries*

Weinbaum, Marvin G 73

West Pakistan Province 49; One Unit Scheme of West Pakistan 47; West Pakistan Assembly (July 1957) 49

Wickham, Carrie Rosefsky 23, 42

Wiktorowicz, Quintan 23, 25

winning coalitions 1, 4, 34, 53–4, 106, 115, 162, 172, 188, 191–2, 200, 202, 208; business 65–7 (agricultural income 66; among Nawaz Sharif's family 65; Habibs and Ispahanis (business families) 65; Iftikhar Chaudhry (Chief Justice) 66; international financing 67; National interest 67; Pakistani winning coalition 66; political survival *vs.* ideology dilemma 67; under Zulfiqar Ali Bhutto's nationalizations 65); feudalism debate 65 (Haider Nizamani 65; Husain, Ishrat 65); S. Akbar Zaidi (Economist) 65; Siddiqua, Ayesha (Defence Secretary) 65); landlords 62–4 (Anwar Ali, Imran (historian) 63–4; *batai* system 64; British colonial legacy 64; *haris,* landless peasants 64; Human Rights Commission 64;

hydraulic political economy 63; land ownership concentration 64; *Mai Bap* culture 63; mercantile era, British economy 63; political landlords 64; power in Pakistan 62; 1901 Punjab Alienation of Lands Act 63; "*Saieen*" (Sindhi landholder) 63); military and civil bureaucracy 54–62 (cardinal rule for business 58; civil service examinations 56; elections in Pakistan 62; Fauji/Shaheen/Bahria Foundations 58; Federal Security Force 60; Ghulam Mohammad, Civil servant 55; good governance (Mazhar Aziz) 61; Government of India Act 1935 57; Husain, Ishrat (economist) 62; under Iskander Mirza 57; Kakul, Pakistan Military Academy at 61; Khwaja Nazimuddin (governor-general) 55; landlords in South Punjab 58–9; Legislative institutions 54; Maulvi Tamizuddin Khan (speaker) 55; military elite 59; Musharraf declaration 59–60; Pakistan Army's history 59; Pakistani military 56; political affairs, military's role in 57; quasi-states 61; quota system 56; second Constituent Assembly, creation of 56; selectorate in Pakistan 61–2; Shuja and Asif Nawaz 60; Siddiqua, Ayesha (Director of Naval Research) 57–8; universal franchise national legislature elections 57; vice-regalism 55; Zia ul-Haq's regime 60); state institutions *vs.* government institutions 53–4 (democracy in Pakistan (five groups) 54; elected governments in Pakistan 54; electoral measures and innovations 53–4; LOPS 54; principal agent problems 53); *see also* selection institutions and winning coalitions

Wolpert, Stanley 32, 118

World Trade Organization 165

Y

Yemeni case 196

Yousaf, Nasser 142

Z

Zafar, S. M., 39–40, 160

Zaidi, S. Akbar 26, 65, 84, 86–7, 89, 92–4, 96, 100, 104, 154

242 *Index*

"Zakat and Ushr" Ordinance, Islamization effort 101
Zaman, Muhammad Qasim, 40, 44–5, 212
zamindari (landholding) system 79–80
Zardari, Asif Ali 44, 52, 155, 157
Zawahri, Ayman (Al-Qaeda leader) 196
Zia ul-Haq regime (1977–1988):
assassination 67; international financing 99–100 (labor remittances from Middle East 100; "second Cold War" between US and USSR 99; structural imbalances after 1979 oil shock 100; U.S. law violations 99); judicial assassination 97; land reform 102 (Qazal Bash case 102); Movement for the Restoration of Democracy 97; mysterious plane crash 199; national leadership after *see* national leadership after Zia ul-Haq; Revival of the Constitutions Order (RCO) 98; SAARC summit in Dhaka in 1985 99; Soviet-Afghan conflict 99; taxation 100–2 (increase in domestic debt 100; Milbus methods 101–2; MRD and survival instinct 100; service solidarity 102; "Zakat and Ushr" Ordinance, Islamization effort 101)
Ziring, Lawrence 2, 31, 37, 39, 48, 53, 55–6, 87–8, 107, 115, 120–3, 128–30, 133, 137, 140, 156–9, 211

eBooks – at www.eBookstore.tandf.co.uk

A library at your fingertips!

eBooks are electronic versions of printed books. You can store them on your PC/laptop or browse them online.

They have advantages for anyone needing rapid access to a wide variety of published, copyright information.

eBooks can help your research by enabling you to bookmark chapters, annotate text and use instant searches to find specific words or phrases. Several eBook files would fit on even a small laptop or PDA.

NEW: Save money by eSubscribing: cheap, online access to any eBook for as long as you need it.

Annual subscription packages

We now offer special low-cost bulk subscriptions to packages of eBooks in certain subject areas. These are available to libraries or to individuals.

For more information please contact webmaster.ebooks@tandf.co.uk

We're continually developing the eBook concept, so keep up to date by visiting the website.

www.eBookstore.tandf.co.uk